Social Issues, Justice and Status

nova
science publishers
www.novapublishers.com

Social Issues, Justice and Status

Sustaining Communities: Prospects and Challenges
Georgios O. Tsobanoglou, PhD, Aikaterini T. Kokkinou, PhD (Editors)
2022. ISBN: 978-1-68507-893-5 (Hardcover)
2022. ISBN: 979-8-88697-092-0 (eBook)

Reduction and Prevention of Youth Violence
Susan T. Sanders (Editor)
2022. ISBN: 979-8-88697-133-0 (Hardcover)
2022. ISBN: 979-8-88697-187-3 (eBook)

School Violence: Causes, Prevention and Safety Measures
Wesley R. Brown (Editor)
2022. ISBN: 979-8-88697-103-3 (Hardcover)
2022. ISBN: 979-8-88697-174-3 (eBook)

Slavery Throughout the Ages
James Biser Whisker (Author), Kevin R Spiker, PhD (Author)
2021. ISBN: 978-1-53619-913-0 (Hardcover)
2021. ISBN: 978-1-68507-142-4 (eBook)

An Interdisciplinary Study of Issues Surrounding Social Justice: From Frederick Douglass to Martin Luther King Jr. and Malcolm X
Robert F. Kronick, PhD (Editor)
2021. ISBN: 978-1-53619-662-7 (Softcover)
2021. ISBN: 978-1-53619-972-7 (eBook)

More information about this series can be found at
https://novapublishers.com/product-category/series/social-issues-justice-and-status/

Gary I. Lilienthal, PhD and
Muhamad Hassan bin Ahmad, PhD
Editors

Regulation of the Professions in East Asia

nova
science publishers
www.novapublishers.com

DOI: https://doi.org/10.52305/KNYO9191

Library of Congress Cataloging-in-Publication Data

ISBN: 979-8-88697-409-6

Published by Nova Science Publishers, Inc. † New York

Contents

Foreword	.... vii Amardeep Bhardwaj
Preface	 ix
Chapter 1	**The Fit and Proper Person Test: The Theory** .... 1 Gary I. Lilienthal, Nehaluddin Ahmad and Muhamad Hassan bin Ahmad
Chapter 2	**The 'Fit and Proper Person' in Malaysia and Singapore** .... 41 Ashgar Ali Ali Mohamed, Muhamad Hassan bin Ahmad and Gary I. Lilienthal
Chapter 3	**The Origin of the Professions** .... 63 Gary I. Lilienthal and Nehaluddin Ahmad
Chapter 4	**The Fitness and Propriety of Subaltern Groups** .... 123 Gary I. Lilienthal and Muhamad Hassan bin Ahmad
Chapter 5	**Délation of Character** .... 165 Gary I. Lilienthal and Muhamad Hassan bin Ahmad
Chapter 6	**The Stasis of Disrepute** .... 217 Gary I. Lilienthal and Muhamad Hassan bin Ahmad
Chapter 7	**Child Labor and the Subaltern Working Class** .... 245 Salim Ibrahim Ali and Gary I. Lilienthal

Chapter 8 **Coercive Moral Hazard**......277
Gary I. Lilienthal
and Muhamad Hassan bin Ahmad

About the Editors......311

Index 313

Foreword

I am delighted to write this foreword, as an exponent of large-scale regulation of professional groups. My last military assignment was as Chief Instructor and Head of Faculty at the Indian Defence Services Staff College, a globally recognised institute of military excellence and one of the world's premier defence training establishments. Prior to that, I had held portfolios at successively higher levels, including that of Assistant Chief of Integrated Defence Staff and Additional Director General at the Indian Ministry of Defence, Chief Planning Officer of the United Nations Mission in Angola, Director Operational Logistics at Army HQ, Senior Faculty and Directing Staff at the Army War College and Colonel General Staff at the Army Training Command.

Having received two distinguished service awards, I have had extensive military operations command and staff experience. I am a graduate of the Indian Defence Services Staff College and of the Higher Command courses, having served on the Board of Management of the Centre for Strategic Studies and Simulation at the United Services Institution of India, which is India's pre-eminent strategic think-tank. Memberships have included The International Emergency Management Society, the All India Management Association, the Board of Examiners for PhDs of the University of Madras, and the Experts Committee of the Indira Gandhi National Open University – INMAS – HQ IDS (Joint Initiative).

I hold academic credentials including, a Doctor of Philosophy degree in Defence Studies, a Masters of Philosophy degree, a Masters of Science degree and a Senior Level Diploma in Management. As an experienced public speaker, and having lectured extensively at prestigious institutions both in India and abroad, I have a number of published scholarly articles to my credit and have served on the editorial boards of two leading defence journals, the *War College Journal* and *Pinnacle*, and have now written the published work *Disaster Management: Optimising the Global Military Response*.

The book, entitled "Regulation of the Professions in East Asia," is a work rarely seen in the field of human resources. It covers the "fit and proper" rules, and an appendant body of arcane procedures, that apparently come down to us from the times of ancient Rome and Greece. As such, they constitute a kind of international legislation, working in Commonwealth countries throughout the world. So little is commonly understood about these rules, that I believe we must set out to familiarise ourselves with them, in order to see exactly what underlying norms we are accepting from European cultures. The book's editors, Professor Dr. G. I. Lilienthal and Dr. Muhamad Hassan Ahmad, have worked with expert co-authors to produce an extraordinary exegesis of these norms, how they operate, and how they relate to our current system of professional regulation. This book has also been well-informed by Professor Lilienthal's 2021 prior book publication, SCOPUS-indexed, on "Human Capital and Development", published in New York by the same publishers as this new book.

This book, "Regulation of the Professions in East Asia", explains the operating professional regulation schema in the following themes: The Fit and Proper Person Test - The Theory; The 'Fit and Proper Person' in Malaysia and Singapore; The Origin of the Professions; The Fitness and Propriety of Subaltern Groups; Délation of Character; The Stasis of Disrepute; Child Labor and the Subaltern Working Class; and, Coercive Moral Hazard. These chapters are highly unusual intellectual voyages into the depths of a misunderstood foreign-developed system of regulation.

Thus, I agreed to write this foreword so that our officials and corporate colleagues can now consider what this book advises us about how we regulate our professionals, and therefore, how we protect our national systems of governance. The book's final chapter, on Moral Coercion, shows us exactly why this book matters to our entire system of corporate governance.

Major-General Amardeep Bhardwaj, PhD (Retd.)
India
09 Aug 2022

Preface

This book delves into the "mechanics" of the "fit and proper test", as it functions around the world as *de facto* Imperial legislation, emanating from Western Europe, and followed without further analysis by systems of governance in East Asia. The meaning of the term "fit and proper", for assessing people as professionals, in contrast to a well structured good character test, is insufficiently specific to be used as a set of criteria for admission to a profession. The parties to a "fit and proper" assessment are actually the court and members of the public, with the court making a judgment in its own cause, and without the public ever participating in the assessment. A "fit and proper" assessment suggests a systemic inquiry against the applicant, inferring both bias and inherent public denunciation.

In today's western capitalist states, which use the Imperial "fit and proper" test for assessing the propriety of professionals, the rule of kings is gone, so that the bourgeoisie now rules by both domination and by hegemony, free of royal humunculus, where domination is rule by force and hegemony is rule by consent of the working class. This is coordinated by professional advice to subaltern masses, as a *de facto* transmission of bourgeois ideology, where the advice is set up to have essential value to them. The 'historical bloc' is a structural conception that coordinates society just as a king used to do, by use of references to bundles of myths as historical forces. Now, the dominant bourgeoisie must form a unifed ideology to articulate this unified ideology to the masses, as a deliberately formed subaltern group, and project onto them what they have learned in their years of higher education. When the masses nevertheless fail to consent, either actively or passively, the state resorts to the exercise of coercive power over them by legally enforcing discipline onto such recalcitrant groups. Similarly, in former times, the king had power to create and dismantle professions, by means of proceedings in *quo warranto*. The so-called freedom of the city was the device by which the right to make a professional level of living was enforced, now turned into professional regulation. Through this process and structure, the mercantile gilds became today's hegemonic professions. The historical bloc forming a superstructure to keep these professional groups in this hierarchy amounted to the public fear of deceit in the trades.

These hegemonic groups are created and formed deliberately, as subaltern groups, by the constituents of Civil Society, which included the churches, the schools and the NGOs. They deploy the priestly precept of the *mysterium tremendum*, as a great or profound protean mystery, so that it provides an opportunity for public manipulation of reality. There is therefore an inferred non-priestly subaltern mass of assumed religious adherents, whose reality is controlled by public practices of forced remembrance, but with operative alterity really having existed prior to the commanding group's cognising its own apparent moral superiority. If emerging language placed alterity into a structure of existence, then there must have been a second level of alterity, where the one level forever corrected the other, with the first other imagining it had a right from birth to correct the second "fallen" other by altering the canonisation of the meaning of words. This is the professions in their formative phase. In this way, Luther had used gospels to replace, and alter at will, the deity itself, rendering the deity protean, suggesting the construction of a descending chain of meanings between the deity and the gospels. This implies a subaltern group is somehow morally obliged to the commanding social group through the commanders' moral altitude. To stabilise this social paradigm, women are structured as unifying signifiers, subject at any time to command alteration of the doxa within their significations, to bind together both alterity and the confected religious institution version of the ancient custom of matrimony, in order to command the entire human project of propriety.

When propriety is apparently violated, in the view of the commanding elements of society, they use commonplace to attack the target person's past life events. It sets out to amplify only what the public mind has already acknowledged and hated. It allows the assumption of a mere indicium of hypothesis of guilt, regardless of overwhelming evidence to the contrary. This had allowed délation to rise to the rank of high sacred duty, filling the land with spies, rendering every man an object of suspicion by hegemonic groups. Consequent denunciation, in outline, was to reveal the hidden, to collate small pieces of knowledge gleaned from individuals into a general corpus of understanding, and last, therefore, to protect the state from its opponents. This was a mass exercise in weak inductive reasoning, but persuasive to public opinion. It allowed public debate to convert a paramount duty to save the state into an individual duty and derived right of denunciation. The Jacobins tried to resolve the contradictory locus of the "sovereign people", as it validated all folk maxims, by grounding the Terror in the expulsion of its opposition. Now, they could peer into the darkness of a newly voiceless imagined opposition personality or character, to make this imaginary secret public. This suggested the genesis in removal of political opposition of declaring a person not "fit and proper".

Such "fit and proper" administrative determinations were in the nature of an asystatic question, specifically the *asystatic* question of "disreputable", incapable of *stasis* because it did not have any issue. Without stasis, it could never, in logic, be judged. Thus, the subaltern groups, such as professionals have been constructed to receive less justice from their superior professional associations, while those inside the professional associations are protected as reputable merely by their own definition. To satisfy the axiom of modern stasis, accusing someone of violating either a legal or a moral norm must specify the violated norm, which must be neither unstable nor overly strict or absolute in liability, or else everyone breaches it. With everyone breaching confected moral norms, by dint of the way they are defined, those who command society through bourgeois hegemony may choose at will who to denounce with commonplace.

This capriciousness is made easier by deliberate creation of a long term working class, as followers, clients of the bourgoisie, and who are unable to escape their subaltern status. Thus, since children are most easily managed and are not as aware of their rights, the use of child labor significantly prevents the development of children. In Iraq, for example, children's economic exploitation has now become the norm, preventing them from going to the schools and enjoying any opportunities for social integration. This suggests that the natural hegemonic consequences of the US invasion of Iraq created a long-term working class, unaware of its potential, through the restrictions on it to access to education and to achieve social integration.

But what of "fit and proper" people, when they take a job as an employee? These are very highly trained people, at a level of substantive knowledge much higher than that of line managers. When managerial principals misrepresent the terms of the employment contract, they will likely exploit their agents towards the end of the agent's employment, as employers typically had feared agent resignation in the early stages of the agreement. A "fit and proper" employee could be forced to remain in a state of moral hazard until the unfair employer released him or her from the contract of employment, this force based in duties arising from judicial policies of employee subordination. These are exemplified in coercive duties to endure employer disciplinary powers. An employed "fit and proper" person can, in theory, be in an ever-increasing state of moral hazard, which automatically implies the operation on them of commonplace denunciation.

Chapter 1

The Fit and Proper Person Test: The Theory

Gary I. Lilienthal[1,*], PhD, Nehaluddin Ahmad[2], LLD and Muhamad Hassan bin Ahmad[3], PhD

[1]Carrington Rand, Hong Kong SAR, Peoples Republic of China
[2]Faculty of Law, Sultan Sharif Ali Islamic University, Brunei
[3]Ahmad Ibrahim Kulliyyah of Laws, International Islamic University, Kuala Lumpur, Malaysia

Abstract

In 2020, the Securities and Futures Commission of Hong Kong banned a former China Bank relationship manager for life from coming back into the banking industry. The ban was announced 1 year after his fraud conviction by a Hong Kong magistrate. The regulator determined he was "not a fit and proper person to be licensed or registered to carry on regulated activities as a result of his criminal conviction." Therefore, pursuant to the significance of this event, and its severe consequences, the objective of this chapter is to examine critically the concept of being "fit and proper," to discover the term's use and meaning. In the 2016 case of *Re "A,"* in the High Court of Hong Kong, "A" applied under s. 27 of the *Legal Practitioners Ordinance, Cap 159 (Ordinance)*, for admission as a barrister of the High Court of Hong Kong. The question for the court was if the Applicant was a "fit and proper person" for admission as a barrister, a requirement under s. 27(1) of the Ordinance, and were not about the private rights of any parties. Australian, New Zealand and Hong Kong cases, and English rules, apply in Hong Kong. The principle of "fit and proper person" is Imperial legislation. The question is what meaning the term "fit and proper" imports into the general law of Hong Kong. The meaning of the term "fit and proper," in contrast to a well

* Corresponding Author's Email: carrington.rand@icloud.com.

In: Regulation of the Professions in East Asia
Editors: Gary I. Lilienthal and Muhamad Hassan bin Ahmad
ISBN: 979-8-88697-409-6

structured good character test, is insufficiently specific to be used as a set of criteria for admission to a profession. The research methodology of this critical literature review will be a legal narrative analysis. The parties to a "fit and proper" assessment are the court and members of the public, without the public ever participating in the assessment. A "fit and proper" assessment suggests a systemic inquiry against the applicant, inferring both bias and public denunciation.

Keywords: fit and proper, Imperial legislation, good character test, bias, denunciation

1. Introduction

In 2020, the Securities and Futures Commission of Hong Kong banned a former China Bank official for life from coming back into the banking industry. The ban was announced 1 year after his fraud conviction by a Hong Kong magistrate. The regulator determined he was "not a fit and proper person to be licensed or registered to carry on regulated activities as a result of his criminal conviction."[1] Therefore, pursuant to the significance of this event, and its severe consequences, the objective of this chapter is to examine critically the concept of being "fit and proper," to discover the term's use and meaning.

In the 2016 case of *Re "A,"*[2] in the High Court of Hong Kong, "A" applied under s. 27 of the *Legal Practitioners Ordinance, Cap 159 (Ordinance)*, for admission as a barrister of the High Court of Hong Kong.[3] The question for the court was if the Applicant was a "fit and proper person" for admission as a barrister, a requirement under s. 27(1) of the Ordinance,[4] and were not about the private rights of any parties. This had been the essence of the 2014 Hong Kong matter of *Re Mably*,[5] which approved in Hong Kong the 1992 High Court of Australia case of *Wentworth v NSW Bar Association*.[6] Since the public interest was of central issue, the Hong Kong Bar Association ought to assist the Court in assessing whether an applicant met the "fit and proper

---

[1] R Lawther, 'Hong Kong Regulator Bans Relationship Manager for Life', *International Advisor*, 28 Aug 2020.
[2] HCMP2079/2016.
[3] HCMP2079/2016 RE "A", [1].
[4] HCMP2079/2016 RE "A", [3].
[5] [2014] 1 HKLRD 627, §14, per Lam VP.
[6] (1992) 176 CLR 239, 250-251; HCMP2079/2016 RE "A", [4].

person" elements, as stated in the 2013 Hong Kong Court of First Instance matter of *Re Youh Alan Chuen Po*.[7] The Court held that there had been many such authorities coming from Hong Kong, as well as from other common law jurisdictions, from which the relevant legal principles of law could be traced.[8]

The Court offered its opinion that the matter had best been articulated by Lam JA, in the 2013 Hong Kong Court of First Instance case of *Re Youh Alan Chuen Po*,[9] stated in the following terms.

> The "fit and proper person" criterion is an important one. It is a criterion which an applicant has to satisfy beyond meeting the academic and legal training requirements. There is a considerable degree of public trust and confidence placed upon a barrister. A person admitted as a barrister has the privilege of practicing as a member of one of the most respected professions in our society. Members of the public, the Judiciary and other members of the legal profession expect members of the Bar to have integrity, honor, high professional standard, reasonably sound judgment and competence in their practice. In Hong Kong, the Bar can say with justifiable pride that by and large such expectations are met. The conduct of a barrister in his or her professional practice often has immense ramifications for the life of a client beyond the immediate outcome of a case. Such ramifications can be financial, emotional, political or social. What happens in litigation could affect the physical, emotional or psychological well-being of a client or those close to him or her. It is therefore necessary for the law to place importance on the "fit and proper person" criterion. Given that we have an adversarial system, unless the court and members of the public can have confidence that those practicing at the Bar are fit and proper persons, the administration of justice under our system will be severely hampered and the rule of law, a core value in our society, will be tarnished ....[10]

This implied some form of stasis between the Court, the public, and the applicant, leading to critical examination under stasis theory. Similarly, in the 1957 High Court of Australia case of *Ziems v Prothonotary of the Supreme Court of NSW*,[11] Kitto J stated as follows.

> Yet it cannot be that every proof which he may give of human frailty so disqualifies him. The ends which he has to serve are lofty indeed, but it is

[7] [2013] 2 HKLRD 485, §11, §59, per Lam JA (as he then was); HCMP2079/2016 RE "A" [5].
[8] HCMP2079/2016 RE "A", [37].
[9] [2013] 2 HKLRD 485.
[10] [2013] 2 HKLRD 485, §§9-10, per Lam JA (as he then was); HCMP2079/2016 RE "A", [39].
[11] (1957) 97 CLR 279, per Kitto J.

> with men and not with paragons that he is required to pursue them. It is not difficult to see in some forms of conduct, or in convictions of some kinds of offense, instant demonstration of unfitness for the Bar. Conduct may show a defect of character incompatible with membership of a self-respecting profession; or, short of that, it may show unfitness to be joined with the Bench and the Bar in the daily co-operation which the satisfactory working of the courts demands. A conviction may of its own force carry such a stigma that judges and members of the profession may be expected to find it too much for their self-respect to share with the person convicted the kind and degree of association which membership of the Bar entails.[12]

This confirmed that the Court itself was effectively a stakeholder in this kind of case, inferring the court was a judge in its own cause. The Hong Kong Court, in Re "A," cited the 2005 High Court of New Zealand case of *Re M*,[13] a deliberation on how to determine if an offending applicant had now reformed.[14] The English Inns' Conduct Committee held as follows.

> In general, any criminal conduct or other reprehensible behavior will be powerful evidence of the lack of one or more of [the essential qualities of a fit and proper person to practice at the English Bar].[15]

Thus, the Court held that this must also apply to the Hong Kong Bar.[16] In the light of these decisions, the principle of the "fit and proper person" is a long-standing term, a kind of Imperial legislation, which operates throughout much of the Commonwealth of Nations, and its old colonies. Thus, the question is what meaning of the term "fit and proper" is imported into the general law of Hong Kong. From an analysis of this, the meaning of the term "fit and proper," as opposed to a good character test, is not specific enough to derive a set of criteria for admission into a profession.

Since the research paradigm, stated above in the research objective, is to discover underlying norms that indicate meaning, the research methodology of this critical literature review will be a legal narrative analysis,[17] with relevant syntheses, structured as doctrinal research.

---

[12] (1957) 97 CLR 279, 298, per Kitto J; HCMP2079/2016 RE "A", [40].

[13] [2005] 2 NZLR 544.

[14] HCMP2079/2016 RE "A", [41].

[15] *Statements of Principles and Guidelines for the Inns' Conduct Committee*, 13 January 2015, §5.

[16] HCMP2079/2016 RE "A", [44].

[17] A cluster of chronological narratives grouped in logical order. Frank J D'Angelo, *Composition in the Classical Tradition*, University of Arizona Press, Tucson, 2000, p. 22.

This research is structured into the four main headings of: 1. Moral Character for Admission to a Profession; 2. Fitness and Propriety; 3. Critique of the "Fit and Proper Person" Construct; and, 4. The Fit and Proper Person in Practice. Main heading number 1 includes a sub-heading on Prediction of Future Behavior. Main heading number 3 includes sub-headings on 'Fit and Proper Person' as Self-Interest, Present Character and Future Behavior, Contradictory and Capricious Standards, Governance and Procedural Issues, and, Logistics Matters. Main heading number 4 includes sub-headings on Fitness and Propriety of Legal Practitioners, Fitness and Propriety of Migration Agents, Fitness and Propriety of Taxation Agents, Fitness and Propriety in Credit Matters, and, Disqualification of Lawyers and Licensed Conveyancers.

This chapter will conclude that the parties to a "fit and proper" assessment are the court and an ellipsis of members of the public, without the public ever knowing of the assessment. Obtaining strong external historical evidence rarely takes place, the courts tending to ignore the fact that the smallest alteration in contextual variables greatly alters leanings towards deceit, and that past facts rarely predict the future. A "fit and proper" assessment suggests a systemic inquiry against the applicant, inferring both real bias and an operation of public denunciation. Once assessors have constructed their judgments, they tend towards selectively assimilating only that information that confirms their early impressions.

2. Moral Character for Admission to a Profession

Late in the 19th century, and early in the 20th century, there was increased official attention to vocational character certification, not just for the law profession.[18] The then gatekeepers of many other professions also increased their entry restrictions,[19] establishing the licensing of occupations with new character conditions.[20] In the next 50 years, such character conditions began to be applied to "barbers, beauticians, embalmers, engineers, veterinarians, optometrists, geologists, shorthand reporters, commercial photographers,

[18] DL Rhode, 'Moral Character as a Professional Credential', *The Yale Law Journal*, vol. 45, no. 3, 1985, pp. 491-603, p. 498.

[19] CL Gilb, *Hidden Hierarchies: The Professions and Government*, Harper and Row, New York, 1966, pp. 61-64.

[20] LM Friedman, 'Freedom of Contract and Occupational Licensing 1890-1910: A Legal Social Study', *California Law Review*, vol. 53, 1965, pp. 487-534.

boxers, piano tuners, trainers of guide dogs for the blind, and-ironically enough-vendors of erotica."[21] Taken together, this raises a suggestion of professional society decisions of character based on an unsound analytic method.

Moral facets of character were generally considered as indicating stable personality traits. Rosenhan had reasoned, using the folk maxim "we expect people to practice what they preach," that people would behave dependably across a wide range of contexts.[22] Thus, using similar reasoning, law profession gatekeepers thought that any applicants displaying a lack of candor, or any lack of respect for the law, in one situation, would again act the same in another situation. They further reasoned that people who publicly acknowledged the wrongfulness of their previous conduct were much less likely to commit future violations.[23]

Rhode noted that because these character expectations had a long historical tradition, they therefore carried a widespread attraction.[24] Philosophers deliberating since the times of Aristotle had proposed a rigid ambit of character traits, each necessarily leading to either vicious or virtuous correlated behaviors.[25] Early psychology treatises developed the major premise that irreducible principles of personality traits always implied subsequent social styles of comportment.[26] There is, in this way, a prevailing public perception that ethical actions tend to be consistent, which rhetorically adds strength to a public intuition of plausibility, and thus predictability and self-control in a professional person, when making a wide range of professional judgments.[27] Plausibility comes from the internal consistency of

---

[21] DL Rhode, 'Moral Character as a Professional Credential', *The Yale Law Journal*, vol. 45, no. 3, 1985, pp. 491-603, p. 499.

[22] DL Rosenhan, 'Moral Character', *Stanford Law Review*, vol. 27, no. 3, 1975, pp. 925-935, p. 925.

[23] ibid.

[24] DL Rhode, 'Moral Character as a Professional Credential', *The Yale Law Journal*, vol. 45, no. 3, 1985, pp. 491-603, p. 556.

[25] Aristotle, *Nicomachean Ethics*, Book 2, §§ 5-6; A Macintyre, *After Virtue*, Bloomsbury, London, 2011; M Ossowska, *Social Determinants of Moral Ideas*, University of Pennsylvania Press, Philadelphia, 1971; J Pocock, *The Machiavellian Moment: Florentine Political Thought and The Atlantic Republican Tradition*, Princeton University Press, Princeton, 2016.

[26] G Allport, *Personality: A Psychological Interpretation*, H. Holt, Ann Arbor, 1937, p. 286.

[27] E Jones & R Nisbett, 'The Actor and Observer: Divergent Perceptions of The Causes of Behavior', in EE Jones, DE Kanouse, HH Kelley, RE Nisbett, S Valins & B Weiner (eds), *Attribution: Perceiving the causes of behavior* (pp. 79-94), General Learning Press, Morristown, 1972; R Nisbett & L Ross, *Human Inference: Strategies and Shortcomings of Social Judgment*, Prentice-Hall, New York, 1980, p. 31.

a narration and is therefore evidence through inference. In the context of default reasoning, or personal reasoning based on personal entrenched default positions, assessments based on measures of plausibility apply to those propositions that appear surprising, because they do not appear to follow from the person's expectations. "As a limiting case, plausibility also applies to propositions that follow from one's expectations. Such propositions enjoy maximal plausibility. They are all equally plausible, and more plausible than anything that contradicts the agent's expectations."[28] Thus, plausibility can provide proof at a sub-level of truth, such as for example a system of mere hegemony.[29] A want of plausibility implies an internal improbability, through confronting the unexpected, which may therefore be surmounted by stronger external historical evidence, suggesting likely errors of fact.

However, to the contrary, Rosenham and Mischel both thought that these pre-suppositions were mere objectives,[30] with any states of affairs built on character evidence necessarily lacking firm empirical bases. Up to the late 20th century, social science research had not found any evidence of consistency, over time, in character attributes.[31] These findings can be compared with the character-assessment techniques of Plutarch, reasoned as follows.

Any critical investigation of Plutarch's *Parallel Lives*,[32] where Plutarch matched the character traits of pairs of people with ostensibly parallel characters, begins with an analysis of Plutarch's structural styles. Aristotle's ethical doctrines were apparently the bases for Plutarch's dicta on character.[33] Plutarch's style was to articulate his conclusions on character and public persona, as he had inferred them from significant documentary evidence that he had traced meticulously. He usually made his preliminary points on the

---

[28] H Rott, 'Two Concepts of Plausibility in Default Reasoning', *Erkenntnis*, vol. 79, no. 6, 2014, pp. 1219-1252, p. 1222.

[29] Gaylen claimed that he had proved the brain to be the *hegemonikon* of the rational soul by an apodeictic proof, which provided a superior level of truth to the kind of argument derived merely from plausibility. The basis of Gaylen's apodeictic proof was his theory of transmission of hegemonical data in the brain by means of "pneuma", a hydraulic concept remarkable in its similarity to Freud's later theory of the plastic movements of the libido. J Rocca, *Gaylen on the Brain – Anatomical Knowledge and Physiological Speculation in the Second Century AD*, Brill, Boston, 2003, pp. 50, 51.

[30] DL Rosenhan, 'Moral Character', *Stanford Law Review*, vol. 27, no. 3, 1975, pp. 925-935, p. 926; W Mischel, *Personality and Assessment*, Erlbaum, Mahwah, 2016, pp. 23-26.

[31] RG Lawson, 'Credibility and Character: A Different Look at an Interminable Problem', *Notre Dame Lawyer*, vol. 50, no. 5, 1975, pp. 758-789, p. 776.

[32] Plutarch, *Plutarch's Lives of the Noble Grecians and Romans, Englished by Sir Thomas North Anno. 1579*, David Nutt, London, 1895.

[33] B Scardigli (ed.), *Essays on Plutarch's Lives,* Clarendon Press, Oxford, 1995, p. 81.

basis of the subject's early life education.[34] This process did not treat the subject's evolution. Instead, it concentrated on the innate character, after completion of the years of education, with any apparent changes in character being merely a progressive revelation of already latent characteristics, as a result of the contexts of chance and events.[35] This view of character served as a long-term preservative, and in the absence of such consideration, suggesting professional associations' exhibiting of apprehended or actual bias.

Plutarch's writing genre arose from the 4th century BCE structures of Isocrates and Xenophon.[36] Plutarch's standard form and arrangement for character assessment was stated and set out in nine divisions: ancestry; personality revealed in childhood anecdotes; campaigns as a boy; entry into politics; first main climax; in the wilderness in war and peace; second main climax; dramatic change of fortune; and, post-war governments, old age, death, funeral, children. Plutarch analyzed childhood by the device of anecdotes, which are either the building block units of, or complete statements of, the ancient *chreia* oratory, as stories based on amplification of a famous statement or action, or combination of statement and action.[37] He dealt with wartimes using the device of epitome, which was a point-by-point summary of an already written work, and therefore necessarily full of gaps, or elisions.[38]

Thus, Hartshorn and May's *Studies in the Nature of Character* found almost no correlation between integrity and self-control, in the context of conduct suggesting honesty in children. They concluded that moral behavior arose mainly from particular habits and settings, conjunctively, rather than from a range of general characteristics.[39] They found that lying and duplicitousness were not correlated, with the smallest alteration in contextual variables greatly altering leanings towards deceit. They concluded that

---

[34] ibid., p. 82.

[35] ibid., pp 84, 193.

[36] ibid., p. 86.

[37] Rainolde had set out three kinds of chreia: the saying kind; the action kind; and, the composite saying and action kind. He proposed that the most erudite form of the *chreia* comprised the following elements: a praise of the author; expounding the meaning of the saying; the reason for the saying; comparison by a contrary; gather the evidence of witnesses; conclusion. R Rainolde, *The Foundation of Rhetoric – 1563,* The Scholar Press Limited, Menston, 1972, folios xvi, xvii.

[38] ibid., p. 88.

[39] H Hartshorne & MA May, *Studies in the Nature of Character: Studies in Deceit*, Macmillan, New York 1928, Book 2, pp. 211-243; H Hartshorne & MA May, *Studies in the Nature of Character: Studies In The Organization of Character*, Macmillan, New York 1930, Book 2, pp. 153-212.

cheaters in one class could not be foreseen from cheating in another class.[40] Most subsequent studies have shown similar outcomes, stating that a person with "truly generalized conscience ... is a statistical rarity."[41] Because professional associations' assessors are people too, this suggests instances of improper purpose.

In both the studies of Burton and Cressey, they both observed, on the one hand, differing responses to temptation, but on the other hand, situational pressures having a marked effect on subjects' moral conduct without evidencing any general predisposition.[42] Mischel reported some studies, where "seemingly trivial situational differences may reduce [behavioral] correlations to zero,"[43] with the strength of situational factors reflected broadly in the social science scholarship. [44]A high proportion of professionals will either steal or cheat when the opportunities arise to gain without risk of any loss, and even more, they will decline to disclose such misconduct.[45] Aronfreed found that stress, competition, overbearing authority, or the influence of peers could quickly force divergences from established models of moral conduct.[46] The best example was that over 60% of subjects participating in Milgram's obedience experiment conformed with orders to deliver ostensibly life-threatening electric shocks to colleagues, in spite of their crying in pain.[47] In total, these issues strongly infer a form of finalized and unappealable denunciation under way.

---

[40] H Hartshorne & MA May, *Studies in the Nature of Character: Studies In Deceit*, Macmillan, New York 1928, Book 1, pp. 407-412; H Hartshorne & MA May, *Studies in the Nature of Character: Studies In Deceit*, Macmillan, New York 1928, Book 2, pp. 211-221; W Mischel, *Personality and Assessment*, Erlbaum, Mahwah, 2016, pp. 25-26; DJ Bem & A Allen, 'On Predicting Some of the People Some of the Time: The Search for Cross-Situational Consistencies in Behavior', *Psychological Review*, vol. 81, no. 6, 1974, pp. 506–520, pp. 506-507; DL Rosenhan, 'Moral Character', *Stanford Law Review*, vol. 27, no. 3, 1975, pp. 925-935, p. 926.

[41] W Mischel, *Personality and Assessment*, Erlbaum, Mahwah, 2016, p. 26; DL Rhode, 'Moral Character as a Professional Credential', *The Yale Law Journal*, vol. 45, no. 3, 1985, pp. 491-603, p. 557.

[42] RV Burton, 'Honesty and Dishonesty', in T Lickona (ed), *Moral Development and Behavior: Theory, Research and Social Issues*, Holt, Rinehart and Winston, New York, 1976, pp. 173, 176; DR Cressey, *Other People's Money; a Study in the Social Psychology of Embezzlement*, Patterson Smith, Montclair, 1973, pp. 142-43.

[43] W Mischel, *Personality and Assessment*, Erlbaum, Mahwah, 2016, p. 177.

[44] ibid.

[45] ibid.

[46] J Aronfreed, *Conduct and Conscience: The Socialization of Internalized Control Over Behavior*, Academic Press, New York, 2013, pp. 30-31, 40, 263.

[47] S Milgram, *Obedience To Authority: An Experimental View*, Harper & Row, New York, 1974, p. 35; S Milgram, 'Behavioral study of obedience', *Journal of Abnormal Social Psychology*, vol. 67, 1963, pp. 371-378.

This suggests that contextual stresses are critical in the manufacturing and moulding of conduct and apparent commitments.[48] Carlin's research into the Manhattan Bar, and Handler's study of small town legal practitioners, both clarified that a lawyer's preparedness to infringe professional or legal norms relies mostly on the magnitude of the temptation, pressures from clients and the views of collegiate peers' within the practice.[49]

2.1. Prediction of Future Behavior

The contextual nature of moral conduct implies that behavioral predictions are always uncertain in any context, with legal profession decision-making presenting some specific difficulties. One threshold arises from inherent limits to "clinical predictive techniques," inasmuch as they are grounded in non-statistical evidence. Monahan concluded that even practitioner mental health workers, psychologists and psychiatrists have lacked repeatable successes in predicting later deviancy, dishonest conduct, or other kinds of misconduct, when judged on the bases of analogous prior actions.[50] Clinical research has both proposed and proven that these professionals may get it wrong in 2 out of every 3 predictions of aggressive conduct, in cases of incarcerated mental illness patients,[51] with no available data allowing predictions for any white-collar violations.[52]

Despite most legal professional assessors' comfort with their own states of intuition, likes or dislikes, they may well not be more accurate than expert clinicians when predicting future conduct violations or any incapacities. These professional assessors, and also judges in courts, usually lack any clinical expertise, while at the same time, they are dealing with very constrained data

---

[48] DL Rhode, 'Moral Character as a Professional Credential', *The Yale Law Journal*, vol. 45, no. 3, 1985, pp. 491-603, p. 558.

[49] J Carlin, 'Lawyers Ethics: A Survey of The New York City Bar', *The Yale Law Journal*, vol. 76, no. 6, 1967, pp. 1252-1258; J Handler, *The Lawyer and The Community: The Practicing Bar In A Middle-Sized City*, University of Wisconsin Press, Madison, 1967, p. 155.

[50] J Monahan, *The Clinical Prediction of Violent Behavior*, US Government Printing Office, Washington DC, 1981.

[51] W Kaslow, 'Moral. Emotional and Physical Fitness for the Bar: Pondering (seeming) Imponderables', *Bar Examiner*, vol. 51, 1982, pp. 38-48, pp. 38, 41; J Monahan, 'Prediction of Crime and Recidivism', in J Dressler (ed), *Encyclopedia of Crime and Justice*, MacMillan, New York, 2001, pp. 1170, 1174-1175.

[52] Most of the published research has focused on identifying situational variables that may help in detecting or minimizing such offenses. DR Cressey, *Other People's Money; a Study in the Social Psychology of Embezzlement*, Patterson Smith, Montclair, 1973, pp. 153-54; G Nettler, *Lying, Cheating, Stealing*, Anderson Publishing Co, Cincinnati, 1982, p. 75.

sets. They often draw inferences about how people will fare under the temptations and pressures of uncertain contexts in future practices, based only on prior acts committed in different environments. One incident, or a number of actions, in differing social contexts provide insufficient bases for any reliable generalized conclusions.[53] For example, common sense and experience will not necessarily suggest that those violating drug laws or avoiding military service might commit professional indiscretions. Thus, applicants who have mismanaged their financial affairs cannot be judged as being predestined to steal client monies. Arguably, it is just as fallacious to assume that people prepared to acknowledge errors in their prior misconduct would be less likely to err in the future. Current research shows that people's struggles against temptation and their apparent remorse for their past errors are "completely independent or at best minimally interrelated."[54] Thus, the above examples infer strongly that legal professional organization character-based decision-making is limited by the coherence of the data, and also by inevitable personal biases during the evaluation, suggesting that such decision might well be mere denunciations. Predictions based on character assessments, relying on the assessors' intuitive judgments have again and again proved more inaccurate than assessments grounded in statistical analyses, because human inferences are preconditioned on apparently inescapable kinds of personal distortions.[55] One likely form of such distortion is the transference, described by Freud,[56] as follows.

> What are transferences? They are new editions or facsimiles of the tendencies and phantasies which are aroused and made conscious during the progress of the analysis; but they have this peculiarity, which is characteristic

---

[53] DJ Bem & A Allen, 'On Predicting Some of the People Some of the Time: The Search for Cross-Situational Consistencies in Behavior', *Psychological Review*, vol. 81, no. 6, 1974, pp. 506–520, pp. 506-507; RV Burton, 'Honesty and Dishonesty', in T Lickona (ed), *Moral Development and Behavior: Theory, Research and Social Issues*, Holt, Rinehart and Winston, New York, 1976, p. 193. Even the most sophisticated nonclinical predictive techniques have proven highly inadequate for identifying future criminal offenders unless they have high rates of recidivism.

[54] W Mischel, *Personality and Assessment*, Erlbaum, Mahwah, 2016, p. 26; DL Rhode, 'Moral Character as a Professional Credential', *The Yale Law Journal*, vol. 45, no. 3, 1985, pp. 491-603, p. 560.

[55] R Nisbett & L Ross, *Human Inference: Strategies and Shortcomings of Social Judgment*, Prentice-Hall, New York, 1980, pp. 140-41; RV Burton, 'Honesty and Dishonesty', in T Lickona (ed), *Moral Development and Behavior: Theory, Research and Social Issues*, Holt, Rinehart and Winston, New York, 1976, p. 183, which observes that the single most consistent measure of cheating is father's occupation.

[56] S Freud, *Dora – An Analysis of a Case of Hysteria*, Touchstone, New York, 1997.

> for their species, that they replace some earlier person by the person of the physician. To put it another way: a whole series of psychological experiences are revived, not as belonging to the past, but as applying to the person of the physician at the present moment. Some of these transferences have a content which differs from that of their model in no respect whatever except for the substitution. These, then—to keep to the same metaphor—are merely new impressions or reprints. Others are more ingeniously constructed; their content has been subjected to a moderating influence—to *sublimation,* as I call it— and they may even become conscious, by cleverly taking advantage of some real peculiarity in the physician's person or circumstances and attaching themselves to that. These, then, will no longer be new impressions, but revised editions.[57]

The question arises as to whether or not a current psychoanalysis, or the presence of the physician, are required elements of the transference. To this question, Freud had provided the following in his 1925 work *An Autobiographical Study*.[58] Here, while dealing with the element of suggestion in the transference, he characterised the transference as an intense emotional relationship, which replaces the patient's desire to be cured. He observed that transference is not created by analysis, but is merely uncovered and isolated by analysis, as a universal phenomenon of the mind. It is the same factor which hypnotists had called suggestibility.[59] Thus, the transference is a universal phenomenon of the mind, which can cause the assessor to replace the person under review with a new "reprint" of another person from the assessor's own past, that Freud called a "stereotype plate."[60] In what appears to be instances of transference, the scholarship reports that people often make assessments of character based on their own "stereotyped" views about certain social groups, their kinds of conduct, or relationships between some identified personality traits.[61] Thus, Burton showed that teachers' predictions of students' honesty correlated with the students' IQ test scores, their grades, and their socio-

---

[57] ibid., pp. 106-107.

[58] P Gay (ed.), *The Freud Reader,* Vintage, London, 1995.

[59] ibid., p. 26.

[60] *The Standard Edition of the Complete Psychological Works of Sigmund Freud Volume XII*, The Hogarth Press, London, 2001, p. 99.

[61] G Allport, *Personality: A Psychological Interpretation*, H Holt, Ann Arbor, 1937, pp. 499-509; R Nisbett & L Ross, *Human Inference: Strategies and Shortcomings of Social Judgment*, Prentice-Hall, New York, 1980, pp. 141-92; DJ Bem & A Allen, 'On Predicting Some of the People Some of the Time: The Search for Cross-Situational Consistencies in Behavior', *Psychological Review*, vol. 81, no. 6, 1974, pp. 506–520, p. 508.

economic class memberships.[62] Assessors at legal profession institutes appear to share these tendencies. An applicant's law school, the nature of the applicant's law firm affiliation, and his or her home living arrangements, have often swayed character predictions. The assessor/examiner's prejudices about alcohol, drugs, psychiatry and sex will also bias their views. Once they have formed their judgment, they tend towards selectively assimilating information confirming their original impressions, with conflicting data discarded and some rich personal information being distorted by overvaluation,[63] suggesting an investigation of bad faith, resulting in unappealable denunciation.

Allport had found that, generally, assessors allotted greater weight to unfavorable personal attributes than to the applicant's positive traits. They also tended to assess applicants on the basis of only one negative quality.[64] This leaves substantial room for inevitable and foreseeable error.[65]

3. Fitness and Propriety

The concepts of "fit and proper person" and "good character" are used in Australian regulatory law, and also in a range of Commonwealth jurisdictions around the world, and in Hong Kong. Few have argued that the "fit and proper" test is more appropriate than a "good character" assessment in informing decision-makers for withdrawing or granting professionals' registration.[66] Still fewer writers have made their own lists of traits and attributes for the interpretation of "fit and proper," and therefore, predicting recidivist conduct.[67] Many pieces of legislation use the "fit and proper" test, and a "character" test, as thresholds for applying government policies, such as conferral of Australian citizenship,[68] grants of migration visas,[69] regulating

---

[62] RV Burton, 'Honesty and Dishonesty', in T Lickona (ed), *Moral Development and Behavior: Theory, Research and Social Issues*, Holt, Rinehart and Winston, New York, 1976, p. 182.

[63] R Nisbett & L Ross, *Human Inference: Strategies and Shortcomings of Social Judgment*, Prentice-Hall, New York, 1980, p. 31.

[64] G Allport, *Personality: A Psychological Interpretation*, H Holt, Ann Arbor, 1937, pp. 520-21.

[65] DL Rhode, 'Moral Character as a Professional Credential', *The Yale Law Journal*, vol. 45, no. 3, 1985, pp. 491-603, p. 561.

[66] I Freckelton, '"Good character" and the Regulation of Medical Practitioners', *Journal of Law and Medicine*, vol. 16, no. 3, 2009, pp. 488-512.

[67] L Warfe, 'Determining the Risk of Recidivism in Previously De-registered Health Practitioners', *Journal of Law and Medicine*, vol. 21, no. 1, 2013, pp. 67-81.

[68] *Australian Citizenship Act 2007* s 21 (7) requirement for eligibility for Australian citizenship "is of good character".

[69] *Migration Act 1958* s. 501(1) subsection (6) defines the character test. The character test is defined in section 501(6) and includes that in addition to a criminal record, a person can

trades and professions, licensing for migration agents,[70] taxi drivers,[71] liquor sellers and managers of licensed premises,[72] legal practitioners,[73] liquidators[74] and health practitioners.[75] The term "fit and proper person" is used inductively when defining a practitioner's misconduct.[76] In the case of health practitioners, terms of registration include specific types of conduct, where the practitioner could cause risk to the public's health and safety, and to the public interest. The public interest includes the community's expectations, trust and confidence in the medical profession.[77]

The main two Australian judicial decisions on the term "fit and proper person" are in the 1955 High Court of Australia case of *Hughes and Vale Pty Ltd v New South Wales (No 2)*,[78] and in the 1990 High Court of Australia case of *Australian Broadcasting Tribunal v Bond*.[79] The holdings in *Hughes and Vale Pty Ltd v New South Wales (No 2)* [80] have been applied in subsequent cases, such as in the 2008 High Court of Australia case of *Shi v Migration Agents Registration Authority*,[81] concerning the cancelling of a migration agent's license, for not having integrity and not being a fit and proper person.

---

not pass the character test, if having regard to the person's past and present general conduct, the person is found to be not of good character, there is significant risk the person will engage in criminal conduct….

[70] *Shi v Migration Agents Registration Authority* [2008] HCA 31.

[71] *The Passenger Transport Act NSW* s 33(a) sets out that the authorised person is considered to be of good repute and in all other respects a fit and proper person to be the driver of a taxicab.

[72] Each Australian state and territory has legislation to regulate licensing of liquor sale, see for example *Liquor Act 2007* (NSW) s.68 (4), which refers to the requirement of "a fit and proper person" to manage licensed premises.

[73] Each Australian state and territory regulates legal practitioners through legislation see for example *Legal Profession Uniform Law 2014* (NSW) s 17 (1)(c) prerequisites for compliance certificates "is a fit and proper person to be admitted to the Australian Legal profession", s. 45 (2) with a prerequisite for grant or renewal of practising certificate of the "fit and proper person" to hold the certificate.

[74] *Corporations Act 2001* s532(4) that liquidators possess "sufficient moral integrity and rectitude of character" and s 1282(2) an applicant for registration as liquidator is "otherwise fit and proper person".

[75] *Health Practitioner regulation Act* 2009 No 86 (NSW) s. 55(h)(i) unsuitability to hold general registration "not a fit and proper person for general registration in the profession".

[76] Definition (c) of professional misconduct in the National Law: "conduct of the practitioner, whether occurring in connection with the practice of the health practitioner's profession or not, that is inconsistent with the practitioner being a fit and proper person to hold registration in the profession".

[77] Australian Health Practitioner Regulation Law (NSW) 2009, s. 150.. Suspension or conditions of registration to protect public.

[78] [1955] HCA 28; 93 CLR 127; 29 ALJR 129; [1955] ALR 525.

[79] [1990] HCA 33; 170 CLR 321; 94 ALR 11; 21 ALD 1; 5 BR 137.

[80] [1955] HCA 28; 93 CLR 127; 29 ALJR 129; [1955] ALR 525.

[81] [2008] HCA 31, 235 CLR 286; 82 ALJR 1147; 248 ALR 390.

Judicial interpretation of both the "fit and proper" person, and also of the term "character," suggests these terms are interchangeable, having in common the attributes of trustworthiness, knowledge, honesty, and, public perception of and confidence in the profession.[82] The High Court of Australia, in the 1955 case of *Hughes and Vale Pty Ltd v New South Wales (No 2)*,[83] had given the term "fit and proper person" a very broad formulation, as follows.

> … while it includes concepts of honesty, knowledge and ability, it cannot be restricted and should allow the import of matters which may be legitimately enquired into, as well as for special circumstances and a judgment on a case by case basis, in other words allowing for a broad judgment and room for rejection.[84]

This suggests a systemic inquiry against the applicant, inferring bias. Thus, "a very wide discretion is allowed for" by the phrase "fit and proper person."[85] *Hughes and Vale Pty Ltd v New South Wales (No 2)*[86] was the seminal Australian case to discuss the import of the term "fit and proper." Section 12 of the *State Transport (Co-ordination) Act* 1931-1954 (NSW) ('the Act') provided that nobody should operate a public vehicle in inter-State trade unless the vehicle was licensed under the Act. Section 17 of the Act covered granting the licenses. Section 17(4)(a) provided that the Commissioner might refuse the application if satisfied that the applicant was not a fit and proper person to hold the license.[87] When interpreting the Act, the High Court, comprising Dixon CJ, McTiernan and Webb JJ, held unanimously that the intention behind the term "fit and proper" was to allow the widest possible scope for either judgment or for rejection

> 9. Sub-section (4) provides that the Commissioner for Road Transport may refuse the application if satisfied of one of the things set out in certain lettered paragraphs. By par. (a) the wide ground is given that the applicant is not a fit and proper person to hold the license…

---

[82] *CJE v Medical Board of Australia* [2019] VCAT 1619, confirming the decision in the Supreme Court of Victoria Court of Appeal in *Medical Practitioners Board of Victoria v Lal* [2009] VSCA109.

[83] [1955] HCA 28; 93 CLR 127; 29 ALJR 129; [1955] ALR 525.

[84] *Hughes and Vale Pty Ltd v New South Wales (No 2)* [1955] HCA 28; 93 CLR 127; 29 ALJR 129; [1955] ALR 525.

[85] *Re Percival and ASC* (1993) 30 ALD 280, [48].

[86] [1955] HCA 28; 93 CLR 127; 29 ALJR 129; [1955] ALR 525.

[87] 93 CLR 127, 127.

> The expression "fit and proper person" is of course familiar enough as traditional words when used with reference to offices and perhaps vocations. But their very purpose is to give the widest scope for judgment and indeed for rejection. "Fit" (or "idoneus") with respect to an office is said to involve three things, honesty knowledge and ability: "honesty to execute it truly, without malice affection or partiality; knowledge to know what he ought duly to do; and ability as well in estate as in body, that he may intend and execute his office, when need is, diligently, and not for impotency or poverty neglect it.[88]

The High Court of Australia, later, in 1990, held in *Australian Broadcasting Tribunal v Bond*[89] as follows.

> it does indicate that, in certain contexts, character (because it provides indication of likely future conduct) or reputation (because it provides indication of likely future conduct) may be sufficient to ground a finding that a person is not fit and proper to undertake the activities in question.[90]

Thus, the scholarship disagrees with the rationale for this judgment, suggesting errors of fact. In the 1990 High Court of Australia case of *Australian Broadcasting Tribunal v Bond*,[91] it was alleged that Mr. Bond purposefully gave misleading evidence to the Australian Broadcasting Tribunal, and subsequently, the Tribunal found Mr. Bond to be not a "fit and proper person" to hold a broadcasting license under the Broadcasting Act (Cth) (1942) s. 88. Two High Court Justices, Toohey and Gaudron JJ, held as follows.

> The expression "fit and proper person," standing alone, carries no precise meaning. It takes its meaning from its context, from the activities in which the person is or will be engaged and the ends to be served by those activities. The concept of "fit and proper" cannot be entirely divorced from the conduct of the person who is or will be engaging in those activities. However, depending on the nature of the activities, the question may be whether improper conduct has occurred, whether it is likely to occur, whether it can be assumed that it will not occur, or whether the general community will have confidence that it will not occur. The list is not exhaustive, but it

---

[88] ibid., 157.

[89] [1990] HCA 33; 170 CLR 321; 94 ALR 11; 21 ALD 1; 5 BR 137.

[90] *Australian Broadcasting Tribunal v Bond* [1990] HCA 33; 170 CLR 321; 94 ALR 11; 21 ALD 1; 5 BR 137, [36] per Toohey and Gaudron JJ.

[91] [1990] HCA 33, [36].

> does indicate that, in certain contexts, character (because it provides indication of likely future conduct) or reputation (because it provides indication of likely future conduct) may be sufficient to ground a finding that a person is not fit and proper to undertake the activities in question.[92]

In the same case, Chief Justice Mason stated subsequently, as follows.

> The question whether a person is fit and proper is one of value judgment. In that process the seriousness or otherwise of particular conduct is a matter for evaluation by the decision maker. So too is the weight, if any, to be given to matters favoring the person whose fitness and propriety is under consideration.[93]

In the 2018 Victorian Civil and Administrative Tribunal case of *Mr. Chooks Halal Chicken Pty Ltd v Primesafe (Review and Regulation)*,[94] the applicant was an operator of a business under the Meats Industry Act, 1993 (Vic).

Wentworth (Senior Member) stated as follows.

> For the reasons which follow, I have found that Mr. Taleb is not a fit and proper person for the purposes of the Act. I find that he lacks the necessary honesty, understanding, character and integrity to be a licensee or nominated operator in the meat industry. This is not to say that he is an inherently bad person or incapable of working in some other capacity in the meat industry.[95]

This articulation of judgment evinces an internal inconsistency, suggesting a defective prior determination of stasis. In reaching that decision, Wentworth (Senior Member) referred to the *Meats Industry Act, 1993* (Vic), thus.

> 16. Fit and proper person - operator and applicant
>
> 1. This section does not limit the circumstance in which a person may be considered not to be fit and proper person to be nominated as, or to be an operator or to be granted a license.
>
> 2. For the purposes of this Act, a person must be taken not to be a fit and proper person to be an operator or to be granted a license if-

---

[92] *Australian Broadcasting Tribunal v Bond* [1990] HCA 33, [36].

[93] ibid., [63].

[94] [2018] VCAT 1932.

[95] ibid., [11].

> a. the person, or an associate of the person is not of good repute having regard to character, honesty and integrity;[96]

Determining whether conduct was dishonest was considered in the 1998 High Court of Australia case of *Peters v R*,[97] in which the Court held as follows.

> In a case in which it is necessary for a jury to decide whether an act is dishonest, the proper course is for the trial judge to identify the knowledge, belief or intent which is said to render that act dishonest and to instruct the jury to decide whether the accused had that knowledge, belief or intent and, if so, to determine whether, on that account, the act was dishonest. ... If the question is whether the act was dishonest according to ordinary notions, it is sufficient that the jury be instructed that that is to be decided by the standards of ordinary, decent people. [98]

The Court's opinion suggested evidence by inference, further suggesting judgment by plausibility, further suggesting errors of fact. The term "dishonest" was considered in the 2003 Supreme Court of Victoria, Court of Appeal case of *Harle v Legal Practitioners Liability Committee*,[99] which held as follows.

> an assessment of a person's honesty under the Act for the purposes of the fit and proper person test, should use the ordinary meanings of the words honesty and dishonesty, containing a consideration of the mental state - the knowledge, belief or intention - of the person concerned,[100]

Further when assessing whether a person was "fit and proper," the 1990 High Court of Australia in *Australian Broadcasting Tribunal v Bond*[101] referred to the conduct of the person, past, present and future.[102] Thus, in the 2009 Supreme Court of Victoria Court of Appeal case of *Medical Practitioners Board of Victoria v Lal,*[103] the Court held as follows.

---

[96] *Meats Industry Act, 1993* (Vic), s. 16(1), (2)(a).
[97] *Peters v R* [1998] HCA 7; (1998) 192 CLR 493:
[98] *Peters v R* [1998] HCA 7, [18]; (1998) 192 CLR 493, per Toohey and Gaudron JJ.
[99] [2003] VSCA 133.
[100] [2003] VSCA 133, at [29].
[101] [1990] HCA 33 [63].
[102] [1990] HCA 33; (1990) 94 ALR 11 [36] per Toohey and Gaudron JJ.
[103] [2009] VSCA 109.

> The public interest is a protean concept. What is relevant to the public interest depends on the statutory context in which the concept is used. Its content cannot be confined by reference to any predetermined generic criteria. Sound registration practices also confer an indirect form of public protection, through the establishment and the maintenance of public confidence in the medical profession. If the public at large have confidence in doctors, they are more likely to seek medical advice and treatment when the need arises. This is conducive to the general health of the community.[104]

Declaring a concept to be protean, but nevertheless proceeding to formulate a judgment based on that concept, suggests the operation of a decision based on alterity. More recently, in the 2019 Victorian Civil and Administrative Tribunal case of *CJE v Medical Board of Australia*,[105] *the* Victorian Civil and Administrative Tribunal noted with approval the 2018 Victorian Civil and Administrative Tribunal case of *TGH v Secretary to the Department of Justice and Regulation (Review and Regulation)*,[106] in which the Tribunal had adopted the following propositions.

> Like the goodwill which attaches to a business, however, public confidence in the medical profession is not turned on and off like a switch. Public confidence is won – or lost – gradually, as the cumulative effect of the experiences of thousands of individuals in their dealings with medical practitioners over many years. The decision to register a particular person to practise medicine is unlikely, in our view, to have any material or lasting effect on the established reputation of the medical profession as a whole. It is not irrelevant that the standing of the medical profession in this community is very high.[107]

This suggests strongly an onus on the profession to prove its high standing in the community, as an inherent factor in making a "fit and proper" determination, in respect of the applicant, either to join or to continue in the profession, implying a defect in assessment of stasis.

---

[104] [2009] VSCA 109 from [56].

[105] [2019] VCAT 1619, confirming the decision in the Supreme Court of Victoria Court of Appeal in *Medical Practitioners Board of Victoria v Lal* [2009] VSCA109.

[106] [2018] VCAT 110.

[107] ibid.

4. Critique of the "Fit and Proper Person" Construct

4.1. 'Fit and Proper Person' as Self-Interest

The objective of the 'fit and proper person' test to enhance the honor of the profession, is seen by some as illegitimate. Even if this goal was evaluated objectively and repeatably, it is unclear how it could be better than improving the profession's actual trustworthiness by legislating exacting practice standards.[108] Its rationale for excluding new entrants is also unclear,[109] with subsisting suspicions of the profession's desire for monopoly and autonomy.[110]

4.2. Present Character and Future Behavior

Woolley's analysis concluded that the fundamental premise of the "fit and proper" person demand is that character is the 'well-spring of professional conduct in lawyers.'[111] Nevertheless, recent social psychology studies have concluded how contexts and situations determine behavior. They have constructed the fact that a person proving honest in one situation may not correlate with their likely honest behavior in a different situation.[112] For example, Martin Luther King, Mahatma Gandhi and Franklin Roosevelt all had significant personal faults, but all worked hard and effectively in the interests of justice in their world.[113] This means that professional bodies must

---

[108] H Breakey, C Sampford & J Rogers, *Fit and Proper Person Test,* Professional Standards Councils, Sydney, 2020, p. 3.

[109] DL Rhode, 'Moral Character as a Professional Credential', *The Yale Law Journal*, vol. 45, no. 3, 1985, pp. 491-603, pp. 493, 512; A Woolley, 'Tending the Bar: The "Good Character" Requirement for Law Society Admission', *Dalhousie Law Journal*, vol. 70, 2007, pp. 27-78, p. 60.

[110] This criticism has its roots in the 1970s writings of M Larson, *The Rise of Professionalism: Monopolies of Competence and Sheltered Markets*, Transaction Publishers, New Brunswick, 2013.

[111] A Woolley, 'Tending the Bar: The "Good Character" Requirement for Law Society Admission', *Dalhousie Law Journal*, vol. 70, 2007, pp. 27-78, p. 30.

[112] A Woolley, 'Tending the Bar: The "Good Character" Requirement for Law Society Admission', *Dalhousie Law Journal*, vol. 70, 2007, pp. 27-78, pp. 63-66; H Breakey, 'Building Ethics Regimes: Capabilities, Obstacles and Supports for Professional Ethical Decision-Making', *University of New South Wales Law Journal*, vol. 40, no. 1, 2017, pp. 322-352, p. 344.

[113] C Menkel-Meadow, 'Private Lives and Professional Responsibilities? The Relationship of Personal Morality to Lawyering and Professional Ethics', *Pace Law Review*, vol. 21, no. 2, 2000, pp. 365-393, p. 393.

not attribute to candidates generalized virtues and vices, but rather, must focus on the specific traits required for appropriate professional actions.

Using good character criteria for disciplinary measures also has its problems. The stakes of an adverse finding are high, constituting a public denunciation, suggesting that this might always have been the goal.[114] This means standards must be both publicly stated, and internally consistent.[115] Conversely, a profession member's violation of standards of professional conduct infers greater power of prediction of likely future breaches, compared to historical indiscretions in differing contexts.[116] This suggests that the public's perception of safety, and trustworthiness within the profession, ought to be assessed by more effective inspection of practitioners.[117] Professional organizations tend to judge existing members to a lower standard than that applying to applicants. This policy tends to excuse members' indiscretions, and also tends to limit market competition by new entrants. It is inevitable that allegations of double standards could abound.[118]

4.3. Contradictory and Capricious Standards

The commentators have documented wide variations in standards, both across jurisdictions,[119] and also with the same institutions.[120] The test is not 'value

---

[114] The commonplace oratory could access people's hatred for non-criminal errors, when stated in the public domain as maxims. When embedded within a judicial denunciation, commonplace served as a criminal judgment without a crime. Although it is said to be unnecessary to make an account of an acknowledged crime or error, commonplace had instead a goal of amplifying only what has been already acknowledged. As such, it assumes guilt regardless of the overwhelming circumstances. GA Kennedy, (trans), *Progymnasmata: Greek Textbooks of Prose Composition and Rhetoric*, Society of Biblical Literature, Atlanta, 2003, pp. 202, 203.

[115] This is particularly important in some professions, such as teaching. Queensland College of Teachers, *Professional Boundaries: A Guideline for Queensland Teachers*, The Queensland College of Teachers, Brisbane, 2017.

[116] H Breakey, C Sampford & J Rogers, *Fit and Proper Person Test,* Professional Standards Councils, Sydney, 2020, p. 4.

[117] DL Rhode, 'Moral Character as a Professional Credential', *The Yale Law Journal*, vol. 45, no. 3, 1985, pp. 491-603, p. 546.

[118] ibid., pp. 547-549, 585.

[119] F Bartlett & L Haller, 'Disclosing Lawyers: Questioning Law and Process in the Admission of Australian Lawyers', *Federal Law Review*, vol. 41, no. 2, 2013, pp. 227-263.

[120] DL Rhode, 'Moral Character as a Professional Credential', *The Yale Law Journal*, vol. 45, no. 3, 1985, pp. 491-603, p. 591; A Woolley, 'Tending the Bar: The "Good Character" Requirement for Law Society Admission', *Dalhousie Law Journal*, vol. 70, 2007, pp. 27-78; C Menkel-Meadow, 'Private Lives and Professional Responsibilities? The Relationship

neutral' and tends to change over time.[121] Thus, not paying income tax was not relevant to an assessment of good character until more recently. Now also, applicants are required to disclose mental health concerns, in the context of many instances of psychological upsets among current professionals, as well as students in professional degrees programs. It is now unclear, whether professional admission boards are supposed primarily to protect the public, or to sustain their own membership.[122] It seems to be for protecting the public, with evidence of correlation between professional violations and symptoms of mental disease such as addiction.[123] However, mental health status cannot evidence conduct implying any incapacity to do the job,[124] this kind of status more likely to be a discriminatory obstacle to entry,[125] with applicants being asked to give personal disclosures from their lives.[126]

4.4. Governance and Procedural Issues

There are arbitrary standards, leading to uncertainty about what must be disclosed, followed by unpredictability in the assessor's decision. There is also a lack of transparency, about the applicable standards, how assessors will weigh up countervailing factors, such as the quality of complaints, and whether the outcome will be confidential.[127] Decisions are frequently unappealable, and can diverge from the original purposes of the requirements.[128]

---

of Personal Morality to Lawyering and Professional Ethics', *Pace Law Review*, vol. 21, no. 2, 2000, pp. 365-393, p. 370.

[121] F Bartlett & L Haller, 'Disclosing Lawyers: Questioning Law and Process in the Admission of Australian Lawyers', *Federal Law Review*, vol. 41, no. 2, 2013, pp. 227-263.

[122] ibid., p. 247.

[123] ibid., p. 247.

[124] ibid., p. 248.

[125] ibid., pp. 252-255.

[126] ibid., p. 235; H Breakey, C Sampford & J Rogers, *Fit and Proper Person Test,* Professional Standards Councils, Sydney, 2020, p. 5.

[127] F Bartlett & L Haller, 'Disclosing Lawyers: Questioning Law and Process in the Admission of Australian Lawyers', *Federal Law Review*, vol. 41, no. 2, 2013, pp. 227-263, p. 262.

[128] A Woolley, 'Tending the Bar: The "Good Character" Requirement for Law Society Admission', *Dalhousie Law Journal*, vol. 70, 2007, pp. 27-78, p. 39.

4.5. Logistics Matters

Professional organizations administering the "fit and proper" person test for admission often have little time, assistance or sources of information, suggesting possible instances of bad faith, contributing to unpredictable outcomes and a lack of transparency. Also, the timing of the testing comes before applicants have endured the pressures of practice, but after years of education.[129]

5. The Fit and Proper Person in Practice

The expression 'fit and proper' person, on its own, has no precise meaning.[130] It takes its meaning from its factual context,[131] thus suggesting the term is an argument based on facts, triggering a requirement to discuss stasis theory, to examine critically the strength and character of the term.[132] 'Fit and proper' person follows from an assessment of a person's personal qualities and conduct while discharging professional responsibilities, with the central characteristics being knowledge, honesty and ability: "honesty to execute truly without malice, affection or partiality; knowledge to know what one ought duly to do; and the ability to execute one's office diligently."[133] The idea of a fit and proper person is not limited to assessment only within the legal

[129] DL Rhode, 'Moral Character as a Professional Credential', *The Yale Law Journal*, vol. 45, no. 3, 1985, pp. 491-603, p. 515; A Woolley, 'Tending the Bar: The "Good Character" Requirement for Law Society Admission', *Dalhousie Law Journal*, vol. 70, 2007, pp. 27-78, p. 75; H Breakey, C Sampford & J Rogers, *Fit and Proper Person Test,* Professional Standards Councils, Sydney, 2020, p. 6.

[130] *Australian Broadcasting Tribunal v Bond* (1990) 170 CLR 321, [380].

[131] ibid.

[132] Ancient Greek concepts of motion gave classical rhetoricians an abstract framework for the analysis and conduct of rational argument. Otto Alvin Loeb Dieter, 'Stasis', Speech Monographs, XVII (November 1950), pp. 345-369. The various 'grounds', on which contrary motions came to a 'rest', (stasis) were borrowed from the philosophic studies of kinesis, or, 'movements', and *metabolai*, or, 'changes in Being'. Using these ideas, rhetoricians described the 'moving apart' of opposing assertions. Stasis theory thus allowed the rhetorician to judge whether or not a conflict of wills really existed, and if so, in what ways. This paradigm allowed an anticipation of the central question to be resolved, which the Greeks called the *krinomenon*, the likely opposing accusatory and defence strategies, and consequently, how best to win the clash. D Goodwin, 'Controversiae Meta-Asystatae and the New Rhetoric', *Rhetoric Society Quarterly*, vol. 19, no. 3, 1989, pp. 205-216, p. 205.

[133] *Hughes and Vale Pty Ltd v State of NSW (No 2)* (1955) 93 CLR 127, [156].

profession, its general principles being the same across many vocations and fields.[134] In the 1965 case of *Maxwell v Dixon*,[135] Hale J observed:

> Clearly different qualifications are needed by e.g., lawyers, transport operators, hotel keepers and land agents …[136]

These measures have been applied, among many others, for granting broadcasting licenses,[137] customs licensing for importing drugs,[138] Air Navigation Regulations licensing.[139] Thus, "fit and proper" can be considered to be a genus, rather than a specification, suggesting decisions based on alterity.

5.1. Fitness and Propriety of Legal Practitioners

Seeking admission as a legal practitioner means satisfying the admissions board[140] as being a 'fit and proper' person, and suitable for admission into the law profession. This happens for first admission, and also, for people renewing annually their Australian practicing certificates.[141]

The admissions board can take into account many disparate factors,[142] to decide if an applicant is a 'fit and proper person.' These factors include whether the applicant:[143] (a) is at the time of application of good fame and

---

[134] ibid.

[135] [1965] WAR 167, [169].

[136] *Maxwell v Dixon* [1965] WAR 167, [169]; N Ng, 'Fitness and Propriety, Spent Convictions and Technology: Lessons from ASIC Investigations', *Australian Institute of Administrative Law Forum*, vol. 92, 2018, pp. 1-112, p. 71.

[137] *Australian Broadcasting Tribunal v Bond* (1990) 170 CLR 321.

[138] *Re Dowling and Secretary to Department of Health* [1985] AATA 237; (1985) 8 ALD 171.

[139] *Re Taylor and Department of Transport* [1978] AATA 64; (1978) 1 ALD 312.

[140] In Victoria and New South Wales, lawyers and law practices are subject to the same framework of Legal Profession Uniform Rules made by the Legal Services Council — in Victoria, the Victorian Legal Admissions Board; in New South Wales, the Legal Profession Admission Board.

[141] *Legal Profession Uniform Law*, s 45(2). The Uniform Law applies as if it were an act: see *Legal Profession Uniform Law Application Act 2014* s 4. The Uniform Law is in force in New South Wales by application of the *Legal Profession Uniform Law Application Act 2014*. The Uniform Rules also apply to Australian-registered foreign lawyers.

[142] *Legal Profession Uniform Admission Rules 2015*.

[143] *Legal Profession Uniform General Rules 2015* r 13(1), in force in Victoria and New South Wales.

character;[144] (b) is currently, or has ever been, bankrupt;[145] (c) was found guilty of a criminal offense, including any spent offense, either in Australia or in an overseas country, with regard to the kind of offense, when it was committed, and the candidate's age at the time of commission of the offense;[146] or, (d) was subject to any disciplinary action in Australia or an overseas jurisdiction, in any profession, or vocation,[147] whether or not there had been an unfavorable finding against the applicant.[148] These factors suggest a pre-judicial form of denunciation.[149] Assessors may ask if the candidate can currently carry out the requirements for practice, as a legal practitioner.[150] There is now no case law interpreting this specific point.

Analysis now turns to a critical examination of the 2002 Victoria Supreme Court case of *Frugtniet v Board of Examiners*.[151] At the outset of Frugtniet's 2001 application for admission as a legal practitioner, his affidavit of disclosure included details of his 1997 conviction in the Broadmeadows Magistrates' Court, but not his UK convictions, perjury charges against him, or further charges related to the ANZ bank.[152] When these finally emerged, the Board of Examiners rejected his application.[153]

Frugtniet appealed the Board's decision. Pagone J heard his appeal in the Supreme Court of Victoria, but without success. Pagone J criticized Frugtniet's significant omissions, when not disclosing his UK convictions.[154] The judge held that Frugtniet was obliged to:

> inform the decision-maker of everything that could bear upon the judgement that needed to be made about … his character … not to select and

[144] ibid., r 10(1)(f). The equivalent provision for a renewal of practicing certificate is the *Legal Profession Uniform General Rules 2015* r 13(1)(a).

[145] *Legal Profession Uniform Admission Rules 2015* r 10(1)(g). The equivalent provision for a renewal of practising certificate is the *Legal Profession Uniform General Rules 2015* r 13(1)(b)(i).

[146] ibid., r 10(1)(h). The equivalent provision for a renewal of practising certificate is the *Legal Profession Uniform General Rules 2015* r 13(1)(c).

[147] ibid., r 10(1)(i).

[148] ibid., r 10(1)(j). The equivalent provision for a renewal of practising certificate is the *Legal Profession Uniform General Rules 2015* rr 13(1)(g)(i), (ii).

[149] Refer to research gap 5, in section 2.0 as below.

[150] *Legal Profession Uniform Admission Rules 2015* r 10(1)(k). The equivalent provision for a renewal of practicing certificate is the *Legal Profession Uniform General Rules 2015* r 13(1)(m).

[151] [2002] VSC 140.

[152] *Frugtniet v Board of Examiners* [2002] VSC 140, [3] and [5].

[153] *Frugtniet v Board of Examiners* [2005] VSC 332, [17].

[154] *Frugtniet v Board of Examiners* [2002] VSC 140, [3] and [5].

edit from his life's experiences'[155] and that he should have been, but was not, the 'source of the Board's and the Court's knowledge' of the matters.[156]

Pagone J stated:

> the way in which details of perjury charges, the ANZ charges and, more particularly, the UK convictions [came] to light in [the] proceedings [does not] leave [me] with sufficient confidence in the applicant[157] ... I am not satisfied that [the failure to volunteer the facts which had given rise to the convictions] have been satisfactorily explained or justified by the applicant.[158]

Pagone J stated that it was not the Court's task to find affirmatively that Frugtniet was 'not a fit and proper person for admission to practice,'[159] but while based on the materials before the Court, Frugtniet could not satisfy the Court he was fit and proper for admission.[160] Thus, the Court was not satisfied, but did not hold he was not "fit and proper," suggesting commonplace denunciation.

Assessing the candidate as a fit and proper person to practice law must be determined at the time of the admission.[161] While great weight can be apportioned to historical events, old offenses, even those involving measures of dishonesty, do not necessarily bar admission, if the candidate can show evidence of reform. Frugtniet made a further application for admission, but was again refused. He appealed this decision to the Supreme Court of Victoria.

Justice Gillard described the criteria for satisfying the Court that an applicant with a history of prior transgressions had reformed, as "demonstration that his past character or past outlook have changed,[162] usually by evidencing a long period of blameless, honest life."[163]

The more serious the past transgressions, the longer the period of time will be necessary to demonstrate rehabilitation. The person claiming to have been

---

[155] ibid., [11].
[156] ibid., [14].
[157] ibid., [11].
[158] ibid., [13].
[159] ibid., [15].
[160] N Ng, 'Fitness and Propriety, Spent Convictions and Technology: Lessons from ASIC Investigations', *Australian Institute of Administrative Law Forum*, vol. 92, 2018, pp. 1-112, p. 69.
[161] *Re B* [1981] 2 NSWLR 372, [381].
[162] *Frugtniet v Board of Examiners* [2002] VSC 140, [31].
[163] ibid., [32].

reformed must prove, on the balance of probabilities, that there was contrition and that he or she would not stray from the required high professional standards.[164]

Gillard J described Mr. Frugtniet as 'a man who is loose with the truth and prepared to distort [it] if he thinks it will help him';[165] 'a witness whose first move was to think of an answer which would help his cause rather than being frank and honest';[166] and 'went off on some tangent seeking to minimize his criminality in the past.'[167] Gillard J questioned Frugtniet's credibility, calling Frugtniet's claims 'humbug.'[168] Thus, the Court rejected Frugtniet's claims of contrition or reform, holding that Frugtniet had refused to admit candidly his past level of honesty,[169] and also, that Frugtniet 'carries … a massive bag of dishonest conduct.'[170]

Justice Gillard considered it unlikely that Frugtniet would ever meet the required standard of a fit and proper person, so that Frugtniet's failure to prove he was fit and proper for admission into the legal profession effectively nullified the likelihood of his ever practicing as a legal practitioner.[171] In other applications, he also fell short of criteria to practice in credit activities,[172] tax agency,[173] immigration assistance,[174] or, as a licensed conveyancer.[175]

5.2. Fitness and Propriety of Migration Agents

Frugtniet was registered as a migration agent in 1996, applying for repeat registration every year after that time.[176] In 2014, the Migration Agents Registration Authority ('MARA') cancelled Frugtniet's registration, deciding he was not a person of integrity or was otherwise not a fit and proper person

164 *Stasos v Tax Agents' Board of New South Wales* [1990] FCA 379.
165 *Frugtniet v Board of Examiners* [2002] VSC 140, [68].
166 ibid., [37].
167 ibid., [68].
168 ibid., [65].
169 ibid., [66].
170 ibid., [67].
171 ibid; *Frugtniet v Board of Examiners* [2005] VSC 332; *Frugtniet v Law Institute of Victoria Ltd* [2012] VSCA 178.
172 *National Consumer Credit Protection Act 2009* (Cth) s 37(2).
173 *Tax Agent Services Act 2009* (Cth) s 20.15.
174 *Migration Act 1958* (Cth) s 303(1)(f).
175 By virtue of being deemed a 'disqualified person': *Conveyancers Act 2006* (Vic) ss 5(c), 11(c).
176 *Frugtniet v Migration Agents Registration Authority* [2016] AATA 299, [1].

to give immigration assistance,[177] and also, because of possible untrue affirmations submitted to the MARA. Frugtniet appealed the cancellation decision to the Administrative Appeals Tribunal ('AAT') in 2016.[178]

Under the *Migration Act 1958* (Cth), MARA "must not register an applicant if the applicant is not a fit and proper person to give immigration assistance."[179] When determining an applicant's fitness and propriety, MARA considers whether the applicant has been convicted of a relevant criminal offense,[180] and any investigation or inquiry into the applicant,[181] or any disciplinary action against the applicant.[182] MARA can also consider any other matter that may be relevant to the applicant's fitness to render immigration assistance.[183]

Referring to the record of Frugtniet's history, and that he still showed neither contrition nor remorse, declining to admit candidly his dishonesty,[184] the AAT found that Frugtniet did not show the behavior of a fit and proper person and a person of integrity.[185]

Forgie DP stated as follows:

> The responsibilities of a registered migration agent are, to a large extent, codified ... but, for all that, they are little different from those described by Pagone J as those of a legal practitioner ... While the focus of a migration agent will be much narrower than that of a legal practitioner, the same commitment to honesty is required as is candor and frankness irrespective of self-interest and embarrassment.[186]

5.3. Fitness and Propriety of Taxation Agents

The Tax Practitioners Board ('the Tax Board') investigated three client complaints about Frugtniet's conduct, and in 2013, decided to terminate

---

[177] ibid.

[178] N Ng, 'Fitness and Propriety, Spent Convictions and Technology: Lessons from ASIC Investigations', *Australian Institute of Administrative Law Forum*, vol. 92, 2018, pp. 1-112, p. 73.

[179] *Migration Act 1958* (Cth), s. 290(1).

[180] ibid., ss 290(2)(c), (d).

[181] ibid., ss. 290(2)(e), (f).

[182] ibid., s. 290(2)(g).

[183] ibid., s. 290(2)(h).

[184] *Frugtniet v Board of Examiners* [2005] VSC 332, [566].

[185] *Frugtniet v Migration Agents Registration Authority* [2016] AATA 299, [136].

[186] ibid.

Frugtniet's registration. This was on the basis that he did not meet the requirement of being a fit and proper person.[187] The income tax laws applied the fit and proper person standards for registration as a tax agent,[188] in order to prepare income tax returns lawfully.[189] The legislation refers to 'good fame, integrity and character.'[190] In the 1982 AAT case of *Su v Tax Agents' Board of South Australia* the Tribunal stated as follows:

> A person is a fit and proper person to handle the affairs of a client if he is a person of good reputation ... He should be a person of such competence and integrity that others may entrust their taxation affairs to his care. He should be a person of such reputation and ability that officers of the Taxation Department may proceed upon the footing that the taxation returns lodged by the agent have been prepared by him honestly and competently.[191]

When applying for registration as a migration agent, Frugtniet stated that he had never had a professional body membership or registration 'refused, cancelled or suspended.' The Tax Board decided this was false or misleading.[192] They also attached significant weight to the 2002 and 2005 Supreme Court of Victoria decisions, in which Frugtniet was found to be not a fit and proper person to be admitted as a legal practitioner. On appeal in the AAT, Senior Member Fice affirmed the Tax Board's determination, stating that Mr. Frugtniet's 'disgraceful conduct [as] a registered tax agent'[193] proved he was not a fit and proper person to be a tax agent.[194]

5.4. Fitness and Propriety in Credit Matters

Under the *National Credit Act 2009* (Australia), a fit and proper person for engaging in credit activities is a person with the attributes of: "good character, diligence, honesty, integrity and judgement."[195] The decision of the Australian

---

[187] *Frugtniet and Tax Practitioners Board* [2014] AATA 766, [12].
[188] *Tax Agent Services Act 2009* (Cth.), s 20-5(1)(a).
[189] *Income Tax Assessment Act 1936* (Cth), s. 251BC(1).
[190] ibid., s. 251BC(1)(d).
[191] *Su v Tax Agents' Board of South Australia* [1982] AATA 127, [4] and [5].
[192] *Frugtniet and Tax Practitioners Board* [2014] AATA 766, [108].
[193] ibid., [104].
[194] ibid., [106].
[195] *Australian Securities and Investments Commission Regulatory Guide* 204.177; N Ng, 'Fitness and Propriety, Spent Convictions and Technology: Lessons from ASIC Investigations', *Australian Institute of Administrative Law Forum*, vol. 92, 2018, pp. 1-112, p. 74.

Securities and Investments Commission ('ASIC') banned Frugtniet, because they believed that Frugtniet was not a fit and proper person to engage in credit activities,[196] due to his persistent contraventions,[197] and due to his adverse disciplinary history.

5.5. Disqualification of Lawyers and Licensed Conveyancers

In 2010, Frugtniet was at Werribee Magistrates' Court, and deliberately and falsely represented himself as a legal practitioner appearing on behalf of one of the parties,[198] whereas, at no time had he ever been an Australian legal practitioner. Thus, the Law Institute of Victoria applied to the Victorian Civil and Administrative Tribunal ('VCAT') designating Frugtniet as a disqualified person under the *Legal Profession Act 2004* (Vic).[199] This disqualification would prevent him acting as an associate in a law practice, without prior approval from the Legal Services Board.[200] VCAT observed that Frugtniet 'failed to demonstrate any insight into his behavior' and 'failed to express any responsibility or remorse'[201] and therefore, it imposed on him a 3-year disqualification order.

During the hearing at VCAT, Frugtniet denied he represented himself as a legal practitioner, claiming that he relied on a general power of attorney for his appearance in the Werribee Magistrates Court. He tendered a document, apparently signed and stamped by a Registrar at the Magistrates Court of Victoria on the Werribee hearing date, however the signatory registrar was not at work at Werribee on that day.[202] There was no copy of the power of attorney either filed or found at the Werribee court. The VCAT Vice President, Judge Jenkins, observed a contrast between Frugtniet's evidence and employees' evidence from the Magistrates' Court. He concluded:

---

196 *National Consumer Credit Protection Act 2009* (Cth) s 80(f).

197 *Australian Securities and Investments Commission Regulatory Guide* 218.55, Table 2.

198 *Frugtniet v Australian Securities and Investments Commission* [2017] FCAFC 162, [22].

199 Pursuant to div 3 of pt 2.2. of the *Legal Profession Act 2004* (Cth) (the applicable legislation at that time).

200 *Law Institute of Victoria Limited v Frugtniet (Legal Practice)* [2011] VCAT 596; *Callychurn v Australian Securities and Investments Commission* [2017] FCAFC 137, [3]; *Callychurn v Australian Securities and Investments Commission* [2017] FCA 29, [9]; *Frugtniet v Australian Securities and Investments Commission* [2017] FCAFC 162, [25].

201 *Law Institute of Victoria Limited v Frugtniet (Legal Practice)* [2011] VCAT 596, [163].

202 ibid., [62].

> I have grave reservations about the veracity of his evidence in a number of respects, but in particular his evidence that he filed the original power of attorney with the Court Registry ...[203]

Jenkins J also noted that:

> the circumstances reveal that there appears to have been some degree of planning undertaken by Mr. Frugtniet in order to get around the limitation which he faced.[204]

Frugtniet appealed the VCAT decision,[205] and in 2012, his appeal was heard by Warren CJ, Nettle JA and Beach AJA in the Supreme Court of Victoria, Court of Appeal. Frugtniet argued that the Law Institute of Victoria could seek a disqualification order, only against a person who already purported to act as a lay associate, and also, that the Law Institute of Victoria had to establish that, except for the operation of a disqualification order, it would be probable that this person would have acted as an associate.[206]

The Court of Appeal[207] rejected these submissions, saying that the disqualification order could be sought whether or not the person was already a lay associate when the order was issued.[208] This was to prevent the wrong people purporting to act as lay associates:

> given the evident legislative purpose of preventing inappropriate persons from acting as associates of solicitors, it is unrealistic to suppose that Parliament intended to limit the scope of the delegation to taking action against existing associates of solicitors.[209]

Frugtniet then applied for special leave to appeal the Court of Appeal decision to the High Court of Australia, this special leave application being

---

[203] ibid., [152].

[204] *Frugtniet v Law Institute of Victoria Ltd* [2011] VCSA 184, 20.

[205] *Rudy Noel Frugtniet v Law Institute of Victoria Ltd* [2011] VSCA 176.

[206] N Ng, 'Fitness and Propriety, Spent Convictions and Technology: Lessons from ASIC Investigations', *Australian Institute of Administrative Law Forum*, vol. 92, 2018, pp. 1-112, p. 75.

[207] *Frugtniet v Law Institute of Victoria Ltd* [2012] VSCA 178.

[208] *Rudy Noel Frugtniet v Law Institute of Victoria Ltd* [2011] VSCA 178, [22] and [29]; *Callychurn v Australian Securities and Investments Commission* [2017] FCAFC 137, [3]; *Callychurn v Australian Securities and Investments Commission* [2017] FCA 29, [8]; *Frugtniet v Australian Securities and Investments Commission* [2017] FCAFC 162, [25].

[209] *Frugtniet v Law Institute of Victoria Ltd* [2012] VSCA 178, [29].

refused by Hayne and Crennan JJ,[210] predicting that such 'an appeal … would enjoy no prospect of success.'[211]

This disqualification under the Legal Profession Act also disqualified Frugtniet under the *Conveyancers Act 2006* (Vic),[212] and made him ineligible for a conveyancing license. The Court held that in circumstances where the conveyancer must deal with trust moneys, it would be sensible and logical that this person who is already disqualified from the legal profession must also be disqualified from conveyancing.[213] The consequence of this decision is that the Conveyancers Act had the same honesty and fit and proper person criteria as did the Legal Profession Act.[214] In summation, Frugtniet had been publicly denounced for life, implying an egregious instance of commonplace denunciation.

Conclusion

The chapter's research question asked what meaning the term "fit and proper" might have imported into the general law of the Hong Kong Special Administrative Region. Chapter argument has sought to sustain the proposition that the meaning of the term "fit and proper," in contrast to a well structured good character test, was insufficiently specific to be used as a set of criteria for admission to a profession.

The sources agree that it is both the court and members of the public who must have confidence that those practicing at the Bar are fit and proper persons. This suggests some kind of stasis between the Court as a party, members of the public, and the applicant, inferring a further critical examination under stasis theory. Complicating this search for stasis, character pre-conditions had begun to apply to "barbers, beauticians, embalmers, engineers, veterinarians, optometrists, geologists, shorthand reporters, commercial photographers, boxers, piano tuners, trainers of guide dogs for the blind, and-ironically enough-vendors of erotica." The sheer breadth of scope in these vocations, and their apparently unrelated fields, suggests decisions of

[210] *Rudy Noel Frugtniet v Law Institute of Victoria Ltd* [2012] HCASL 162.

[211] ibid.

[212] *Conveyancers Act 2006* (Vic) s 5; *Frugtniet v Law Institute of Victoria Ltd* [2011] VSCA 184, [18].

[213] *Frugtniet v Law Institute of Victoria Ltd* [2011] VSCA 184, [18].

[214] N Ng, 'Fitness and Propriety, Spent Convictions and Technology: Lessons from ASIC Investigations', *Australian Institute of Administrative Law Forum*, vol. 92, 2018, pp. 1-112, p. 76.

character based on a defective analytic method. In this kind of analytic method, a judgment against a person for want of plausibility implied an internal improbability of expectation, which might therefore be surmounted by stronger external historical evidence, which rarely takes place, suggesting issues of bad faith and errors of fact. Thus, a judgment containing errors of fact would imply a bare denunciation, without due recourse to the scholarship on character assessment.

The Plutarchian process of character assessment did not treat the subject's evolution. Instead, it concentrated on his or her innate character, after his completion of the years of education, with any apparent changes in character being merely a progressive revelation of already latent characteristics, as a result of the interplays between the contexts of chance and events. This view of character served as a long-term preservative, and suggested that professional associations were exhibiting either apprehended or actual bias.

The scholarship shows that lying and duplicitousness are not correlated, with the smallest alteration in contextual variables greatly altering leanings towards deceit. They concluded that cheaters in the one class could not be foreseen from cheating in the other. Most subsequent studies have shown similar outcomes, stating that a person with "truly generalized conscience ... is a statistical rarity." Because professional associations' assessors are people too, and must know their own nature to a large extent, this suggests possible instances of improper purpose. High proportions of professionals will either steal or cheat when the opportunities arise to gain without risk of any loss, and more, they will decline to disclose such misconduct. Aronfreed found that stress, competition, overbearing authority, or the influence of peers could quickly force divergences from established models of correct moral conduct. The best example was that over 60% of subjects participating in Milgram's obedience experiment conformed with orders to deliver ostensibly life-threatening electric shocks to colleagues, in spite of the colleagues crying in pain. In total, these issues suggested a form of creation of subalterity by denunciation under way.

Thus, the above examples suggest strongly that legal professional organization character-based decision-making is limited by the coherence of the data, and also by inevitable biases during the evaluation. In what appears to be instances of transference, the scholarship reports that people often make alterity assessments of character based on their own "stereotyped" views about certain social groups, their kinds of conduct, or relationships between some identified personality traits. Once assessors have formed their judgment, they tend towards selectively assimilating information confirming their original impressions, with conflicting data discarded and some rich personal information being distorted by overvaluation, again suggesting instances of bad faith.

The concepts of "fit and proper person" and "good character" are used in Australian regulatory law, and also in a wide range of Commonwealth jurisdictions around the world, and in Hong Kong. Few have argued that the "fit and proper" test is more appropriate than a "good character" assessment, in informing decision-makers for withdrawing or granting professionals' registration. Also, the term "fit and proper person" construct is used inductively, rather than deductively, when defining a practitioner's misconduct. While it includes concepts of honesty, knowledge and ability, it cannot be restricted and should allow the import of matters which may be legitimately enquired into, as well as for special circumstances and a judgment on a case by case basis, in other words allowing for a broad judgment and room for rejection. This suggests a systemic inquiry against the applicant, inferring inherent bias.

The High Court of Australia has said, arguably erroneously, that the "fit and proper" test does indicate that, in certain contexts, character (because it provides indication of likely future conduct) or reputation (because it provides indication of likely future conduct) may be sufficient to ground a finding that a person is not fit and proper to undertake the activities in question. Thus, the scholarship disagrees with the rationale for this judgment, suggesting errors of fact, no doubt based on the hidden stasis between the court and the appellant.

The Court had found Mr. Taleb to be not a fit and proper person for the purposes of the Act, because he lacked the necessary honesty, understanding, character and integrity to be a licensee or nominated operator in the meat industry. However, the Court went on to say that this was not to say that he was an inherently bad person or incapable of working in some other capacity in the meat industry. Arguably, the public mind would only see a denunciation. Thus, this articulation of judgment evinces an internal inconsistency, suggesting a defective prior determination of the matter's stasis.

If the question is whether the act was dishonest according to ordinary notions, and it was sufficient that the jury be instructed that that it was to be decided by the standards of ordinary, decent people, whatever that means, then the Court was advocating evidence by inference, thus encouraging the jury to judge facts by plausibility, further suggesting an outcome of errors of fact.

The public interest is a protean concept. Declaring a concept to be protean, but nevertheless proceeding to formulate a judgment based on that concept, suggests the operation of a decision based on alterity, despite an onus on the profession to prove its own high standing in the community, as an inherent factor in making a "fit and proper" determination. The expression 'fit and proper' person, on its own, has no precise meaning. It takes its meaning from its factual context, thus suggesting the term is a conjectural argument based on facts, triggering a requirement to discuss stasis theory, to examine critically the strength and character of the term.

Clearly different qualifications are needed by, for example, lawyers, transport operators, hotel keepers and land agents. The concept of "fit and proper" had been applied for granting broadcasting licenses, customs licensing for importing drugs, Air Navigation Regulations licensing. Thus, the term "fit and proper" can be considered rather to be a genus, than as a specification, suggesting defective logic to ground decisions based on alterity.

Pagone J had stated that it was not the Court's task to find affirmatively that Frugtniet was 'not a fit and proper person for admission to practice,' but while based on the materials before the Court, Frugtniet could not satisfy the Court he was fit and proper for admission. Thus, the Court was not satisfied, but did not hold he was not "fit and proper," suggesting commonplace denunciation. Justice Gillard considered it unlikely that Frugtniet would ever meet the required standard of a fit and proper person, so that Frugtniet's failure to prove he was fit and proper for admission into the legal profession effectively nullified the likelihood of his ever practicing as a legal practitioner. It appears the Court requires a commitment to honesty, candor and frankness, whether or not this forces the applicant into public embarrassment. In summation, Frugtniet had been publicly denounced for life, implying an egregious instance of commonplace denunciation.

In extended synthesis, the parties to a "fit and proper" assessment are the court and members of the public, yet the public never participates in the assessment. Such a judgment against a person, for effectively a want of plausibility, implies an internal improbability, which may therefore be surmounted by stronger external historical evidence, but which rarely takes place. In fact, the courts tend to ignore that the smallest alteration in external contextual variables greatly alters leanings towards deceit, and that past facts rarely predict the future. A "fit and proper" assessment suggests a systemic inquiry against the applicant, inferring both bias and public denunciation. Once assessors have formed their judgment, they tend towards selectively assimilating only that information that confirms their original impressions.

References

Allport, G, *Personality: A Psychological Interpretation*, H. Holt, Ann Arbor, 1937.

Aristotle, *Nicomachean Ethics*.

Aronfreed, J, *Conduct and Conscience: The Socialization of Internalized Control Over Behavior*, Academic Press, New York, 2013.

Australian Broadcasting Tribunal v Bond [1990] HCA 33; 170 CLR 321; 94 ALR 11; 21 ALD 1.

Australian Broadcasting Tribunal v Bond 5 BR 137.

Australian Citizenship Act 2007.

Australian Health Practitioner Regulation Law (NSW) 2009.

Australian Securities and Investments Commission Regulatory Guide.

Bartlett, F & L Haller, 'Disclosing Lawyers: Questioning Law and Process in the Admission of Australian Lawyers,' *Federal Law Review*, vol. 41, no. 2, 2013, pp. 227-263.

Bem, J & A. Allen, 'On Predicting Some of the People Some of the Time: The Search for Cross-Situational Consistencies in Behavior,' *Psychological Review*, vol. 81, no. 6, 1974, pp. 506–520.

Breakey, H, 'Building Ethics Regimes: Capabilities, Obstacles and Supports for Professional Ethical Decision-Making,' *University of New South Wales Law Journal*, vol. 40, no. 1, 2017, pp. 322-352.

Breakey, H, C Sampford & J Rogers, *Fit and Proper Person Test,* Professional Standards Councils, Sydney, 2020.

Burton, RV, 'Honesty and Dishonesty,' in T Lickona (ed), *Moral Development and Behavior: Theory, Research and Social Issues*, Holt, Rinehart & Winston, New York, 1976.

Callychurn v Australian Securities and Investments Commission [2017] FCAFC 137.

Carlin, J, 'Lawyers Ethics: A Survey of The New York City Bar,' *The Yale Law Journal*, vol. 76, no. 6, 1967, pp. 1252-1258.

CJE v Medical Board of Australia [2019] VCAT 1619.

Conveyancers Act 2006 (Vic).

Corporations Act 2001.

Cressey, DR, *Other People's Money; a Study in the Social Psychology of Embezzlement*, Patterson Smith, Montclair, 1973.

D'Angelo, FJ, *Composition in the Classical Tradition*, University of Arizona Press, Tucson, 2000.

Dieter, OAL, 'Stasis,' *Speech Monographs*, XVII (November 1950), pp. 345-369.

Fischer, CT, 'Levels of Cheating Under Conditions of Informative Appeal to Honesty, Public Affirmation of Value, and Threats of Punishment,' *The Journal of Educational Research*, vol. 64, no. 1, 1970, pp. 12-16.

Freckelton, I, '"Good character" and the Regulation of Medical Practitioners,' *Journal of Law and Medicine*, vol. 16, no. 3, 2009, pp. 488-512.

Freud, S, *Dora – An Analysis of a Case of Hysteria*, Touchstone, New York, 1997.

Friedman, LM, 'Freedom of Contract and Occupational Licensing 1890-1910: A Legal Social Study,' *California Law Review*, vol. 53, 1965, pp. 487-534.

Frugtniet and Tax Practitioners Board [2014] AATA 766.

Frugtniet v Australian Securities and Investments Commission [2017] FCAFC 162.

Frugtniet v Board of Examiners [2002] VSC 140.

Frugtniet v Law Institute of Victoria Ltd [2012] VSCA 178.

Frugtniet v Migration Agents Registration Authority [2016] AATA 299.

Gay, P (ed.), *The Freud Reader*, Vintage, London, 1995.

Gilb, CL, *Hidden Hierarchies: The Professions and Government*, Harper and Row, New York, 1966, pp. 61-64.

Goodwin, D, 'Controversiae Meta-Asystatae and the New Rhetoric,' *Rhetoric Society Quarterly*, vol. 19, no. 3, 1989, pp. 205-216.

Handler, J, *The Lawyer and The Community: The Practicing Bar In A Middle-Sized City*, University of Wisconsin Press, Madison, 1967.

Harle v Legal Practitioners Liability Committee [2003] VSCA 133.

Hartshorne, H & MA May, *Studies in the Nature of Character: Studies in Deceit*, Macmillan, New York 1928.

Health Practitioner Regulation Act 2009.

Hetherington, EM & SE Feldman, 'College Cheating as a Function of Subject and Situational Variables,' *Journal of Educational Psychology*, vol. 55, no. 4, 1964, pp. 212-218.

Hughes and Vale Pty Ltd v New South Wales (No 2) [1955] HCA 28; 93 CLR 127; 29 ALJR 129; [1955] ALR 525.

Income Tax Assessment Act 1936 (Cth).

Jones, E & R Nisbett, 'The Actor and Observer: Divergent Perceptions of The Causes of Behavior,' in EE Jones, DE Kanouse, HH Kelley, RE Nisbett, S Valins & B Weiner (eds), *Attribution: Perceiving the causes of behavior* (pp. 79-94), General Learning Press, Morristown, 1972.

Kaslow, W, 'Moral. Emotional and Physical Fitness for the Bar: Pondering (seeming) Imponderables,' *Bar Examiner*, vol. 51, 1982, pp. 38-48.

Kennedy, GA (trans), *Progymnasmata: Greek Textbooks of Prose Composition and Rhetoric*, Society of Biblical Literature, Atlanta, 2003.

Kohlberg, L, 'Stage and Sequence: The Cognitive-Developmental Approach to Socialization,' in D Goslin (ed), *Handbook of Socialization Theory and Research*, (pp. 347-480), Rand McNally Chicago, 1969.

Larson, M, *The Rise of Professionalism: Monopolies of Competence and Sheltered Markets*, Transaction Publishers, New Brunswick, 2013.

Law Institute of Victoria Limited v Frugtniet (Legal Practice) [2011] VCAT 596.

Lawson, RG, 'Credibility and Character: A Different Look at an Interminable Problem,' *Notre Dame Lawyer*, vol. 50, no. 5, 1975, pp. 758-789.

Lawther, R, 'Hong Kong Regulator Bans Relationship Manager for Life,' *International Advisor*, 28 Aug 2020.

Lee, SLJ, 'Making a Case for the Duty to Act for Proper Purposes,' *Singapore Journal of Legal Studies*, July 2014, pp. 79-97.

Legal Profession Act 2004 (Cth).

Legal Profession Uniform Admission Rules 2015.

Legal Profession Uniform General Rules 2015.

Legal Profession Uniform Law 2014 (NSW).

Legal Profession Uniform Law Application Act 2014.

Liquor Act 2007 (NSW).

Macintyre, A, *After Virtue*, Bloomsbury, London, 2011.

Maxwell v Dixon [1965] WAR 167.

McQueen, R, 'Examination Deception as a Function of Residual, Background, and Immediate Stimulus Factors,' *Journal of Personality*, vol. 25, 1957, pp. 643-650.

Meats Industry Act, 1993 (Vic).

Medical Practitioners Board of Victoria v Lal [2009] VSCA 109.

Menkel-Meadow, C, 'Private Lives and Professional Responsibilities? The Relationship of Personal Morality to Lawyering and Professional Ethics,' *Pace Law Review*, vol. 21, no. 2, 2000, pp. 365-393.

Migration Act 1958 (Cth).

Milgram, S, 'Behavioral Study of Obedience,' *Journal of Abnormal Social Psychology*, vol. 67, 1963, pp. 371-378.

Milgram, S, *Obedience To Authority: An Experimental View*, Harper & Row, New York, 1974.

Mischel, W, *Personality and Assessment*, Erlbaum, Mahwah, 2016.

Monahan, J, 'Prediction of Crime and Recidivism,' in Joshua Dressler (ed), *Encyclopedia of Crime and Justice*, MacMillan, New York, 2001.

Monahan, J, *The Clinical Prediction of Violent Behavior*, US Government Printing Office, Washington DC, 1981.

Mr. Chooks Halal Chicken Pty Ltd v Primesafe (Review and Regulation) [2018] VCAT 1932.

National Consumer Credit Protection Act 2009 (Cth).

Nettler, G, *Lying, Cheating, Stealing*, Anderson Publishing Co, Cincinnati, 1982.

Ng, N, 'Fitness and Propriety, Spent Convictions and Technology: Lessons from ASIC Investigations,' *Australian Institute of Administrative Law Forum*, vol. 92, 2018, pp. 1-112.

Nisbett, R & L Ross, *Human Inference: Strategies and Shortcomings of Social Judgment*, Prentice-Hall, New York, 1980.

Olowofoyeku, AA, 'Regulating Supreme Court Recusals,' *Singapore Journal of Legal Studies*, July 2006, pp. 60-85.

Ossowska, M, *Social Determinants of Moral Ideas*, University of Pennsylvania Press, Philadelphia, 1971.

Peters v R [1998] HCA 7, [18]; (1998) 192 CLR 493.

Plutarch, *Plutarch's Lives of the Noble Grecians and Romans, Englished by Sir Thomas North Anno. 1579*, David Nutt, London, 1895.

Pocock, J, *The Machiavellian Moment: Florentine Political Thought and The Atlantic Republican Tradition*, Princeton University Press, Princeton, 2016.

Pozen, DE, 'Constitutional Bad Faith,' *Harvard Law Review*, vol. 129, no. 4, 2016, pp. 885-955.

Queensland College of Teachers, *Professional Boundaries: A Guideline for Queensland Teachers*, The Queensland College of Teachers, Brisbane, 2017.

Rainolde, R, *The Foundation of Rhetoric – 1563,* The Scholar Press Limited, Menston, 1972.

Re "A" HCMP2079/2016.

Re B [1981] 2 NSWLR 372, [381].

Re Dowling and Secretary to Department of Health [1985] AATA 237; (1985) 8 ALD 171.

Re M [2005] 2 NZLR 544.

Re Mably [2014] 1 HKLRD 627.

Re Percival and ASC (1993) 30 ALD 280, [48].

Re Taylor and Department of Transport [1978] AATA 64; (1978) 1 ALD 312.

Re Youh Alan Chuen Po [2013] 2 HKLRD 485.

Reyes, GM, 'Memory and Alterity: The Case for an Analytic of Difference,' *Philosophy & Rhetoric*, vol. 43, no. 3, 2010, pp. 222-252.

Rhode, DL, 'Moral Character as a Professional Credential,' *The Yale Law Journal*, vol. 45, no. 3, 1985, pp. 491-603.

Rocca, J, *Gaylen on the Brain – Anatomical Knowledge and Physiological Speculation in the Second Century AD*, Brill, Boston, 2003, pp 50, 51.

Rosenhan, DL, 'Moral Character,' *Stanford Law Review*, vol. 27, no. 3, 1975, pp. 925-935.

Rott, H, 'Two Concepts of Plausibility in Default Reasoning,' *Erkenntnis*, vol. 79, no. 6, 2014, pp. 1219-1252, p. 1222.

Rudy Noel Frugtniet v Law Institute of Victoria Ltd [2011] VSCA 176.

Sartre, J-P, *Being and Nothingness*, Hazel E. Barnes (trans.), Washington Square Press, New York, 1992.

Scardigli, B (ed.), *Essays on Plutarch's Lives*, Clarendon Press, Oxford, 1995.

Shi v Migration Agents Registration Authority [2008] HCA 31, 235 CLR 286; 82 ALJR 1147; 248 ALR 390.

Shi v Migration Agents Registration Authority [2008] HCA 31.

Stasos v Tax Agents' Board of New South Wales [1990] FCA 379.

Statements of Principles and Guidelines for the Inns' Conduct Committee, 13 January 2015.

Su v Tax Agents' Board of South Australia [1982] AATA 127.

Tax Agent Services Act 2009 (Cth).

TGH v Secretary to the Department of Justice and Regulation (Review and Regulation) [2018] VCAT 110.

The Passenger Transport Act (2014) NSW.

The Standard Edition of the Complete Psychological Works of Sigmund Freud Volume XII, The Hogarth Press, London, 2001.

Warfe, L, 'Determining the Risk of Recidivism in Previously De-registered Health Practitioners,' *Journal of Law and Medicine*, vol. 21, no. 1, 2013, pp. 67-81.

Wentworth v NSW Bar Association (1992) 176 CLR 239.

Woolley, A, 'Tending the Bar: The "Good Character" Requirement for Law Society Admission,' *Dalhousie Law Journal*, vol. 70, 2007, pp. 27-78.

Ziems v Prothonotary of the Supreme Court of NSW (1957) 97 CLR 279.

Chapter 2

The 'Fit and Proper Person' in Malaysia and Singapore

Ashgar Ali Ali Mohamed[1], PhD,
Muhamad Hassan bin Ahmad[1], PhD
and Gary I. Lilienthal[2,*], PhD

[1]Ahmad Ibrahim Kulliyyah of Laws, International Islamic University, Kuala Lumpur, Malaysia
[2]Carrington Rand, Hong Kong SAR, Peoples Republic of China

Abstract

A person to be admitted in Malaysia into any professional body such as architect, medical, engineer, or legal must, besides having the requisite professional qualifications from a recognized university, be assessed in terms of his character. The Board of Architects, Medical Council, Board of Engineers, and the Malaysian Bar are the professional bodies established pursuant to the *Registration of Engineers Act 1967* (Malaysia), *Architects Act 1967* (Malaysia), *Medical Act 1971* (Malaysia), and *Legal profession Act 1976* (Malaysia). The tasks of the above-mentioned bodies include ensuring that the members are better regulated with higher standards of practice. The requirement to be 'fit and of good character' also reflects the growing importance of issues concerning the problems within the profession and maintaining integrity and honor of the profession. In Singapore, any person who wishes to be admitted to the Singapore Bar shall be a 'qualified person' as specified in the *Legal Profession Act 1966* (Singapore), the *Legal Profession*

* Corresponding Author's Email: carrington.rand@icloud.com.

In: Regulation of the Professions in East Asia
Editors: Gary I. Lilienthal and Muhamad Hassan bin Ahmad
ISBN: 979-8-88697-409-6

(Qualified Persons) Rules (Singapore), and the *Legal Profession (Admission) Rules 2011* (Singapore).

Keywords: professional qualifications, character, practice, fit and proper, integrity, honor

1. Introduction

Significantly, Malaysia and Singapore both follow the English system of fitness and propriety for regulation of key professions. Thus, the research objective is to examine the extent to which this doctrine applies in the two jurisdictions. The *Registration of Engineers Act 1967* (Malaysia), *Architects Act 1967* (Malaysia), *Medical Act 1971* (Malaysia), and *Legal Profession Act 1976* (Malaysia) allow admission of a qualified person into their profession so long as the applicant besides fulfilling the educational requirements, is a fit and proper person for admission. Section 14(1)(c)[1] and Section 14B(1)(d)[2] of the *Medical Act 1971* as amended by the *Medical (Amendment) Act 2012* (Malaysia) for example, provide that a person is entitled to full, and specialist registration, respectively, with the Medical Council if he has proven to the satisfaction of the Council that he is 'fit and of good character'. Further, the professional bodies under the aforementioned statutes are empowered to take disciplinary action against the registered members when it is proven that their action or conduct has been 'infamous' or 'disgraceful'.

Section 15(2)(d) of the *Architects Act 1967* (Malaysia) for example provides that the Disciplinary Committee may order the issuance of a written reprimand to, the imposition of a fine not exceeding one hundred thousand ringgit on, the suspension for a period not exceeding three years of, the cancellation of the registration of, any Architect, Graduate Architect or a

---

[1] Section 14(1) of the *Medical Act 1971* as amended by the *Medical (Amendment) Act 2012* provides that: 'Subject to this Act, no person shall be entitled to be fully registered as a medical practitioner under this Act unless –
(a) he has been provisionally registered under section 12;
(b) he has submitted a certificate issued under subsection 13(2); and
(c) he has proven to the satisfaction of the Council that he is fit and of good character'.

[2] Section 14B of the *Medical Act 1971* as amended by the *Medical (Amendment) Act 2012* provides that: 'A person is entitled to be registered as a specialist under this Act if –
(a) he has been fully registered under section 14;
(b) he has attended specialized training in that specialty in a recognized training institution;
(c) he holds a recognized specialist qualification; and
(d) he has proven to the satisfaction of the Council that he is fit and is of good character'.

foreign architect when he is found guilty by the Disciplinary Committee of any act or conduct which in the opinion of the Disciplinary Committee is infamous or disgraceful. Likewise, section 29(2)(b) of the *Medical Act 1971* (Malaysia) provides that the Medical Council may exercise disciplinary jurisdiction over any registered person who has been guilty of infamous conduct in any professional respect. The infamous or disgraceful conduct is to be judged according to the rules, written or unwritten, governing the profession.[3] In *Dr Koay Cheng Boon v. Majlis Perubatan Malaysia*,[4] upon an inquiry into this complaint, the respondent, Malaysian Medical Council found the appellant guilty of infamous conduct in a professional respect under s 29(2)(b) of the *Medical Act 1971* (Malaysia). In this case, a complaint was lodged against the appellant, a medical practitioner, for engaging in a sexual relationship with a patient, the wife of the complainant. Having said the above, this chapter discusses the 'fit and proper person tests with reference to the legal profession in Malaysia.

The research question is: How does the fit and proper test operate in Malaysia and Singapore? Argument proposes that the fit and proper test operate in Malaysia and Singapore on statutory bases.

At this juncture, it is worthwhile to note that Malaysia administers a mixed legal system or a pluralistic legal system namely, the Common Law System and Islamic Legal System. The civil courts and the Syariah courts established under the above two systems, respectively are independent of each other. The recognition of the Syariah courts is based on Article 121(1A) of the Federal Constitution which excluded the jurisdiction of the civil courts in respect of any matters within the jurisdiction of the Syariah courts.[5] The legal profession in Malaysia has its roots from the UK legal practice where this country was ruled by the British for almost one hundred and fifty years from 1786 to 1957. A body which resembles the Malaysian Bar today was established as early as 1914 through the enforcement of the Advocates and Solicitors Ordinance 1914. The ordinance aimed to regulate legal practitioners in the Federated

---

[3] In *Marzaini Zainuddin v. Majlis Peguam* [2007] 10 CLJ 339, it has also been decided that members of the same profession are in the best position to decide as they know and appreciate better than anyone else the standards of conduct expected of the legal profession.

[4] [2012] 3 MLJ 173.

[5] Article 121(1A) provides: 'The courts referred to in Clause (1) shall have no jurisdiction in respect of any matter within the jurisdiction of the Syariah courts'. See *Subashini Rajasingam v. Saravanan Thangathoray & other appeals* [2008] 2 CLJ 1, FC. It is noteworthy that the Syariah court's jurisdiction is only over persons professing the religion of Islam or a Muslims and on Muslim personal law and minor offences against the precepts of the religion of Islam under the relevant Syariah enactments of the states.

Malay States. It was later replaced by the Advocates and Solicitors Ordinance in 1940. The legal practice in the Unfederated Malay States was regulated by different ordinances – Johor was regulated by the Advocates and Solicitors Enactment of Johor and the Strait Settlements were regulated by the Advocates and Solicitors Ordinance of the Straits Settlement. After the second world war, all the ordinances and enactments were repealed and replaced by one ordinance, the Advocates and Solicitors Ordinance 1947.

2. Legal Profession

The legal profession in the civil courts in Malaysia is regulated by the *Legal Profession Act 1976 (LPA)* (Malaysia)[6] which Act came into effect on 1 June 1977 replacing the *Advocates and Solicitors Ordinance 1947* (Malaya). This Act however only applicable to the states in West Malaysia. In relation to the states in East Malaysia, namely the states of Sabah and Sarawak, they have a separate set of laws regulating the legal profession namely, the *Advocates Ordinance (Sabah) (Cap. 2)* and *Advocates Ordinance (Sarawak) (Cap. 110).* Being the main regulation to regulate the lawyers in West Malaysia, the LPA has undergone many amendments since 1977 to suit the changes in legal development in the country. The LPA provides inter alia, for the establishment of the Legal Profession Qualifying Board, the Malaysian Bar, the Bar Council and the State Bar Committees. Further, the Act deals with admission requirements to the Bar as well as the professional practice, etiquette, conduct and discipline of an advocate and solicitor.

Meanwhile, the Syarie legal profession is contained in the *Syarie Legal Profession (Federal Territories) Act 2019* (Malaysia), a statute passed by Parliament for the Federal Territories in relation to Syarie matters enumerated in List II of the 9th Schedule to the Federal Constitution. It allows for the establishment of the *Syarie* Legal Profession Qualifying Board, *Badan Peguam Syarie* and *Majlis Peguam Syarie*. Further, the admission requirements of a *Peguam Syarie* as well as their professional practice, etiquette, conduct and discipline are also featured therein. Having said the above, only fit and proper person is admitted into the legal profession which is further explained below with reference to in practiced in the ordinary courts

---

[6] Section 2 of LPA clearly states that the LPA covers Malaysia as a whole: 'This Act shall apply throughout Malaysia but shall only be made applicable to Sabah and Sarawak with such modifications as the Yang di-Pertuan Agong may by order make; and such Order shall be published in the Gazette'.

of law or commonly also terms as civil courts and the Shariah courts in the Federal Territories.

2.1. Admission in Civil Courts

The admission and qualifications requirements for admission to the Malaysian Bar are contained part 2 of the LPA namely, sections 10 to 19, as well as the gazette notifications made from time to time under section 3 thereof. This is subject to section 3[7] which further sets other possible entry into the Legal Profession and this would be admission prior to the passing of this Act. In the context of section 3, the term advocate and solicitor of the High Court must satisfy section 10[8] of the LPA where he/she must either be a qualified person[9] or an articled clerk. A 'qualified person' under section 3 not only includes a person who has passed the final examination from the faculties of laws in Malaysia[10] but also foreign Universities that are recognized by the Act and the

---

[7] Section 3 provides that: "In this Act unless the context otherwise requires - 'advocate and solicitor', and 'solicitor' where the context requires means an advocate and solicitor of the High Court admitted and enrolled under this Act or under any written law prior to the coming into operation of this Act."

[8] Section 10 provides that: "The High Court may at its discretion and subject to this Act admit as an advocate and solicitor of the High Court -

(a) any qualified person; and

(b) any articled clerk who has complied with section 25: Provided that no person who is a qualified person by reason of his having passed the final examination for the degree or other qualification which makes him a qualified person under paragraph (a), (b) or (c) of the definition of 'qualified person' in section 3 shall be admitted as an advocate and solicitor before the degree or other qualification has been conferred upon him."

[9] Section 3 defines the phrase 'qualified person' as "any person who -

(a) has passed the final examination leading to the degree of Bachelor of Laws of the University of Malaya, the University 16 Laws of Malaysia ACT 166 of Malaya in Singapore, the University of Singapore or the National University of Singapore;

(b) is a barrister-at-law of England; or

(c) is in possession of such other qualification as may by notification in the Gazette be declared by the Board to be sufficient to make a person a qualified person for the purposes of this Act."

[10] Section 3 states that: 'Faculty of Law' means "the Faculty of Law of a University established under the *Universities and University Colleges Act 1971 [Act 30]*, the Faculty of Law of the Universiti Teknologi MARA established under the *Universiti Teknologi MARA Act 1976 [Act 173]* and the Kuliyyah of Law of the International Islamic University of Malaysia established pursuant to the *Companies Act 1965 [Act 125]*."

decision-making power is vested with the Legal Professional Qualifying Board (LPQB)[11] as provided by section 5 of the LPA.[12]

Generally, a person who has passed the final examination leading to the degree of Bachelor of Laws from the public universities as listed in the relevant Gazette Notifications is a qualified person for the purposes of admission to the Bar as an Advocate and Solicitor pursuant to the *Legal Profession Act 1976* (Malaysia). However, holders of LL.B degrees from other universities will be required to sit and pass the Certificate in Legal Practice (CLP) examination before they can be deemed qualified for admission to the Bar in Malaysia. The requirement of passing the CLP examination is made obligatory only for candidates who are: (a) Malaysian citizens or holding permanent resident status; (b) citizens of Brunei; (c) who obtained law degrees in universities in Australia, New Zealand, and the United Kingdom recognised by the Legal Profession Qualifying Board Malaysia (the Board), Bachelor of Jurisprudence (B. Juris) in the University of Malaya and Bachelor of Legal Studies in UiTM. The Board is responsible to conduct the CLP examination.

A lawyer prayer's as espoused by St Thomas More[13] preached much ethics and virtues[14] are also reflected in section 11 of the LPA where one of

---

[11] Section 4 states that there is established a body to be called the Legal Profession Qualifying Board (LPQB).

[12] Section 5 sets out the functions of Board. The above section states: "The Board shall have the following functions:

(a) to prescribe the qualifications required for the entry of any person into articles with a view to his admission as an advocate and solicitor;

(b) to provide courses of instruction for, and to regulate the training and instruction of, articled clerks;

(c) to provide for the examination of articled clerks wishing to become qualified persons;

(d) to decide on the qualifications, if any, other than those set out in paragraphs (a) and (b) of the definition of 'qualified person' in section 3, which may entitle a person to become a qualified person for the purposes of this Act;

(e) to provide courses of instruction for, and for the examination of, persons whose qualifications are not sufficient to make them qualified persons for the purposes of this Act except after undergoing the courses and passing the examination;

(f) to provide for the management and conduct of the Bahasa Malaysia Qualifying Examination."

[13] Sir Thomas More (7 February 1478–6 July 1535).

[14] Thomas More, counselor of law and statesman of integrity, merry martyr and most human of saints:

'Pray that, for the glory of God and in the pursuit of His justice, I may be trustworthy with confidences, keen in study, accurate in analysis, correct in conclusion, able in argument, loyal to clients, honest with all, courteous to adversaries, ever attentive to conscience. Sit with me at my desk and listen with me to my clients' tales. Read with me in my library and stand always beside me so that today I shall not, to win a point, lose my soul. Pray that my family may find in me what yours found in you: friendship and courage, cheerfulness and

the criteria for admission to the Bar is that the qualified person must be of 'good character'. In particular, section 11(1) provides inter alia, that a qualified person may be admitted as an advocate and solicitor if he or she fulfilled the following requirements: (a) has attained the age of eighteen years; (b) is of good character; and (i) has not been convicted in Malaysia or elsewhere of a criminal offense as would render him unfit to be a member of his profession, and in particular, but not limited to, an offense involving fraud or dishonesty; (ii) has not been adjudicated bankrupt and has not been found guilty of any of the acts or omissions mentioned in the *Insolvency Act 1967* (Malaysia); (iii) has not done any other act which, if being a barrister or solicitor in England, would render him liable to be disbarred, disqualified or suspended from practice; or (iv) has not been, or is not liable to be, disbarred, disqualified or suspended in his capacity as a legal practitioner in any other country; (c) is either a Federal citizen or a permanent resident of Malaysia; (d) has satisfactorily served in Malaysia the prescribed period of pupillage for qualified persons.

The pupillage period is currently fixed for a term of 9 months and it must be done with a master having at least seven years standing in practice as an Advocate and Solicitor. Generally, the pupils will be involved in handling civil and criminal litigations and non-litigation works. The Bar Council *vide* its Pupillage Handbook, has provided valuable guidelines for pupils to plan and manage their time effectively at the law firm throughout their pupillage. Further, section 13(4) provides that a qualified person who has served in the Judicial and Legal Service for at least one year shall be exempted from serving any period of pupillage provided his application for admission as an advocate and solicitor is supported by a certificate from the Attorney General to the effect that he is a fit and proper person to be admitted as an advocate and solicitor. As for Sabah and Sarawak, admission to the profession also requires completion of pupillage, not nine but for 12 months.[15] Candidates must also meet up certain specific criteria as set out in the Advocates Ordinance of Sabah and Advocates Ordinance of Sarawak. Such criteria include that the candidate must have connection to Sabah or Sarawak, whether by birth, marriage with a resident in Sabah or Sarawak or continuous residence of five or more years; he must currently be domiciled in Sabah or Sarawak; and must serve a three

---

charity, diligence in duties, counsel in adversity, patience in pain—their good servant, and God's first. Amen'.

[15] Sarawak State Attorney General Chambers; The State Attorney-General's Chambers, Sabah.

to six months of pupillage in Sabah or Sarawak.[16] In *Re Judy Blacious AF Pereira; Petitioner,*[17] it was noted that the Bar Council has a public statutory duty to ensure that only persons of 'good character' are admitted as an advocate and solicitor. A person's 'good character' means 'both his disposition and reputation, so that if the petitioner appears either to lack the qualities of integrity, honesty and the like which an advocate and solicitor ought to possess, or to have a bad reputation in these respects, he will be shown to want that 'good character'.[18] In *Voon Lee Shan v. Richard Malanjum,*[19] before the petition for admission and application for exemption from pupilage were heard, the plaintiff, a Sarawakian lawyer, applied to intervene in those matters. In allowing the application including for exemption, it was noted that the petitioner was a person of good character and fit and proper to be admitted and enrolled as an advocate of the High Court in Sabah and Sarawak. While admitting that the law applies to everyone regardless of their rank or position, the Court was a bit puzzled why anyone, let alone a practicing lawyer, would have any issue with a former Chief Justice and long-serving Chief Judge of Sabah and Sarawak being exempted from pupilage.

As the legal profession is an honorable profession, its members are expected to conduct themselves honorably. When there is a public complaint against any of its members, the matter is referred to the Disciplinary Committee which comprises of senior members of the profession to determine whether the accused person is guilty of misconduct in his practice as advocate and solicitor. As the respondent in *Majlis Peguam Malaysia v. Krishnasamy a/l Bhaktavatsalu,*[20] had been struck off the Roll for grossly improper conduct, to reinstate him back to the roll, he must necessarily be subject to stricter scrutiny than that of a new entrant to the legal profession who has no adverse record. The law too does not envisage that an advocate and solicitor who had been struck off the Roll must be totally barred from returning to the profession.

In an application for reinstatement to the roll as an advocate and solicitor, the onus is on the applicant to show that there has been such a change in his character as to make him a fit and proper person to resume practice at the Bar, he is truly penitent; and he has made restitution.[21] In *Majlis Peguam Malaysia*

---

[16] Candidate who intends to practise in Sabah must complete a mandatory six months pupillage in Sabah.

[17] [2015] 6 CLJ 1127.

[18] See *Re B Surinder Singh Kanda* [1964] MLJ 135 and *Re SRC Augustin* [1973] MLJ 208.

[19] [2022] MLJU 436.

[20] [2020] 12 MLJ 438.

[21] See *Che Man bin Che Mud v. Majlis Peguam Malaysia* [2022] 8 MLJ 961.

v. Ahmad Rushdi bin Omar,[22] it is clear that an applicant in a restoration application must demonstrate to the court that he is fully rehabilitated as the court must not only be concerned with the individual interest only but the interest of the public at large as well as the interest of the profession. Another crucial consideration is whether the applicant has made restitution. The court, however, noted that the plaintiff had not satisfied the court that it is 'fair and reasonable' for the plaintiff to be restored to the Roll.

Again, in *Re S.R.C. Augustin,*[23] and *Majlis Peguam Malaysia & Anor v. Judy Blacious s/o AF Pereira,*[24] the court had allowed the readmission of the petitioners into practice as an advocate. It was stated that in the above cases, the applicants had learned a bitter lesson from their past misconduct, and should their petitions be dismissed it would in effect be saying that they suffer from an incurable and ineradicable defect of character. In *Darshan Singh Atma Singh v. Majlis Peguam Malaysia,*[25] the court stated that in relation to remorsefulness or penitence, this can be clearly inferred from the circumstances, specifically the averments deposed to by the applicant in both his affidavits. Again, in *Patrick Samuel a/l Joseph Sebastian v. Majlis Peguam Malaysia,*[26] the High Court found that the application for restoration to the roll filed almost ten years after the applicant therein has ceased practiced and three years after he was struck off the roll was sufficient for him to be readmitted and resumed practice.

Be that as it may, one interesting aspect covered and emphasised in the LPA is the requirement of professional practice, etiquette, conduct and discipline of advocates and solicitors. As much as a judge is bound by a certain code of ethics, lawyers are equally bound by certain ethics which require them to act professionally, particularly on matters relating to their clients. As an officer of the court, the member of the profession 'had an avowed duty to prevent the administration of justice from being imperilled and brought into disrepute.'[27] The ethical aspect of a practising lawyer is emphasised from the very beginning in the law schools and during the period of pupillage. This is where the future lawyers are being taught to act professionally and ethically toward their clients, the judges, and fellow lawyers.

---

[22] [2017] 6 MLJ 70.
[23] [1973] 1 MLJ 208.
[24] [2016] MLJU 1116.
[25] [2015] 4 CLJ 1083.
[26] [2014] 9 MLJ 479.
[27] See *S Ashok Kandiah & Anor v. Dato' Yalumallai Muthusamy & Anor* [2011] 1 CLJ 460, CA.

The *Legal Profession (Practice and Etiquette) Rules 1978* (Malaysia) (the 1978 Rules) is a set of rules made by the Bar Council in ensuring that lawyers meet the standard and ethics expected in the profession. It is made pursuant to s. 77 of the *Legal Profession Act 1976* (Malaysia) which grants the Bar Council the power to make rules to regulate the practice. The Rules are binding upon each lawyer and failure to comply would result in disciplinary action.[28] The 1978 Rules list down a number of rules that basically intend to regulate the relationship between lawyer and client, the requirement to act independently and professionally, the requirement to respect the court and other important regulations. These rules are binding upon each lawyer. Failure to comply would result in disciplinary action.[29]

2.2. Admission in Syariah Courts

The admission requirements as Syarie lawyer (Peguam Syarie) for a qualified person[30] in the Federal Territories[31] are set out in section 12(1) of the 2019 Act namely, the applicant has attained the age of twenty-one years;[32] is a

---

[28] The disciplinary proceedings are elaborated in Part VII of the *Legal Profession Act 1976*. The Bar Council has also set up rules to elaborate on the proceeding in the Legal Profession (Disciplinary Board) (Procedure) Rules 1994, Legal Profession (Disciplinary Proceedings) (Investigating Tribunal and Disciplinary Committee) Rules 1994 and Legal Profession (Disciplinary Proceedings) (Appeal) Rules 1994.

[29] The disciplinary proceedings are elaborated in Part VII of the *Legal Profession Act 1976*. The Bar Council has also set up rules to elaborate on the proceeding in the Legal Profession (Disciplinary Board) (Procedure) Rules 1994, Legal Profession (Disciplinary Proceedings) (Investigating Tribunal and Disciplinary Committee) Rules 1994 and Legal Profession (Disciplinary Proceedings) (Appeal) Rules 1994.

[30] Section 11 of the 2019 Act defines a 'qualified person' as 'any person who –
(a) possesses any qualification prescribed by the Board; or
(b) is an advocate and solicitor and has any additional qualification in the syariah field or judicial Syarie as prescribed under section 12'.

[31] Malaysia is a federation in which the country is formed by a group of 13 independent states. Those states are Johor, Kedah, Kelantan, Melaka, Negeri Sembilan, Pahang, Pulau Pinang, Perak, Perlis, Sabah, Sarawak, Selangor and Terengganu. Malaysia also has three Federal Territories. The Federal Territories are Kuala Lumpur, which was formerly part of the state of Selangor, Labuan, which was part of Sabah and Putrajaya, which was also part of Selangor.

[32] Section 53 of the *Interpretation Acts 1948 and 1967* provides that: 'In computing years of age for the purposes of any written law, a person shall be regarded as having completed a year of age on the expiration of the day preceding the anniversary of his birth, reckoned according to the Gregorian calendar: Provided that for the purposes of this section the anniversary of the birth of a person born on 29 February shall, in a year which is not a leap year, be taken as 1 March'.

Muslim; either a citizen or permanent resident of Malaysia;[33] is of good character; has not been convicted in Malaysia or elsewhere of any criminal offense; has not been adjudicated as an undischarged bankrupt;[34] has attended and passed the courses of instruction, training, education, interview or examination prescribed by the Board, where applicable; and has served the period of pupillage as required under section 13 which currently set at six months.[35] A pupil shall serve his period of pupillage with a master who is and has been in an active practice in the Federal Territories for a total period of not less than seven years immediately preceding the date of commencement of his pupillage.[36] The Majlis Peguam Syarie may however exempt any qualified person who has served as a Syariah officer for a period of at least one year from serving any period of pupillage under section 13.[37]

---

[33] Malaysian citizenship is acquired either by registration or by naturalization and the requirements of the above are contained in Part III, chapter I (articles 14 to 22) of the Federal Constitution. Generally, a person born in Malaysia or outside of Malaysia to Malaysian parents is entitled to citizenship by operation of law. If he is born in Malaysia and any one of his parents is a Malaysian citizen, the child is also deemed a citizen, see *Madhuvita Janjara Augustin (Suing through Next Friend, Margaret Louisa Tan) v. Augustin Lourdsamy & Ors* [2018] 4 CLJ 758. Citizenship may also be acquired by a foreign woman whose husband is a citizen of the Federation with the marriage registered according to Malaysian law. However, if the birth of the person is outside Malaysia, he would not be entitled to citizenship under the operation of law if at the time of the birth the child's father was not a citizen of the Federation. Again, a child of foreign parents who are not Malaysian who gives birth in Malaysia does not acquire citizenship by operation of law. Meanwhile, a permanent resident refers to a person who has been granted the right to live in a particular country for an indefinite period while he continues to remain a citizen of another country. The term 'permanent resident' is defined in section 3 of the *Courts of Judicature Act 1964* as 'a person who has permission granted without limit of time under any federal law to reside in Malaysia, and includes a person treated as such under any written law relating to immigration'. This provision describes the conditions as recognised by the law before a person is regarded as a permanent resident. In Malaysia, a permanent resident holds a 'red' identity card.

[34] For the disability of an undischarged bankrupt, see section 38(1) of the *Insolvency Act 1967*.

[35] Section 12 of the 2019 Act.

[36] During the pupillage, a pupil should not, unless special leave in writing is first obtained from the Majlis Peguam Syarie, hold any office or engage in any employment of any kind, whether full time or otherwise. The Majlis Peguam Syarie may on special grounds allow a pupil to serve his period of pupillage with a Peguam Syarie who is practising in other States or has been practising less than seven years (section 14(1)). The Majlis may also allow any qualified person to serve different parts of his period of pupillage with different masters (section 14(2) of the 2019 Act). Any qualified person who has served as a syariah officer for a period of at least one year may be given exception from serving any period of pupillage under section 13 (section 14(3) of the 2019 Act).

[37] Section 14(3) of the 2019 Act. The Syariah officer is however, required to submit to the Majlis Peguam Syarie a certificate from the Director General of Department of Syariah Judiciary Malaysia or respective head of service, as the case may be, stating his period of service as a syariah officer, see s 14(4) of the 2019 Act.

An application for admission as Peguam Syarie under the 2019 Act shall be made to the Syariah High Court.[38] The application shall be supported by an affidavit exhibiting the certified copies of any documentary evidence showing that he is a qualified person, two recent certificates as to his good character; a certificate of diligence from his master with whom he served his pupillage; a certificate signed by the Secretary to the Board that the applicant has attended the courses of instruction, training, education, interview or examination prescribed by the Board, where applicable; and certified copies of any documentary evidence showing that the applicant has attained the age of twenty one years, is a Muslim and is either a citizen or permanent resident of Malaysia.

The applicant shall then serve a copy of his application for admission as a Peguam Syarie on the Board, the Chief Syariah Prosecutor and the *Majlis Peguam Syarie* within a period not less than thirty days before the date fixed for the hearing of the application for admission or such shorter period as ordered by the Syariah High Court.[39] Upon receiving the application for admission, the *Majlis Peguam Syarie* shall make or cause to be made full inquiries into the character of the applicant and submit a confidential report of the result of such inquiries to the Chief Registrar.[40] If the report is unfavorable to the applicant, the Chief Registrar shall submit the said report to the Chief Syarie Judge who may, if he thinks fit and reasonable, direct the report to be filed in the Syariah High Court and a copy of the report to be served on the applicant and, subject to such directions as the Syariah High Court may give, such report shall be taken into consideration on the hearing of the application.[41]

Upon receiving a copy of the application for admission as Peguam Syarie, section 19 empowers the Chief Syariah Prosecutor or the *Majlis Peguam Syarie* to raise objection to the application by filing a notice of objection which shall specify in brief terms the grounds of the objection. The notice of objection shall then be filed in the Chief Registrar's Office and served on the applicant within the period of not less than three days or any shorter period as the Syariah High Court may order before the date fixed for the hearing of the application for admission. Further, section 20 provides that any person other than the Chief Syariah Prosecutor or the *Majlis Peguam Syarie* may enter an objection to object the application for admission as a Peguam Syarie.

[38] Section 15 of the 2019 Act.
[39] Section 17 of the 2019 Act.
[40] Section 18(1) of the 2019 Act.
[41] Section 18(2) of the 2019 Act.

Likewise, the objection should be filed in the Chief Registrar's Office and shall contain the full name, occupation and address of the person objecting the application for admission, a brief statement of the grounds of his objection and an address for service. Upon such objection being filed, the application for admission shall not be heard unless a notice of hearing of not less than three days has been served on the person objecting the application for admission.

The Syariah High Court may, after considering the application under section 15, the inquiry report under section 18 and objection under sections 19 or 20 if any, admit the applicant as a Peguam Syarie.[42] Any person who is aggrieved by the decision of the Syariah High Court may, within thirty days of the date of the decision, appeal to the Syariah Appeal Court.[43] Upon admission, the Peguam Syarie must apply to the Chief Registrar[44] for the issuance of certificate of Peguam Syarie[45] and if he wishes to be active in Syariah legal practice, apply for an Annual Practicing Certificate.[46] The Chief Registrar shall keep and maintain a Register of Peguam Syarie. The name and the date of admission of a Peguam Syarie shall be entered in the Register and the Register shall be open for inspection by any person without payment unless the application is an extract or a copy of the Register which shall be subject to a prescribed fee.[47] Section 25 provides that the name of the Peguam Syarie may be removed from the Register if it can be shown to the satisfaction of the Syariah High Court that the affidavit, acknowledgement or other document filed by the Peguam Syarie contains false or misleading statement in its substance or a suppression of any material fact.

It is noteworthy that any unauthorized person who acts as a Peguam Syarie or an agent for any party to a proceedings or in any capacity, other than as a party to an action in which he himself is a party, commences, carries on, solicits or defends any action, suit or other proceedings in the name of any other person in any of the Syariah court or draws or prepares any instrument relating to any proceedings in any Syariah court or willfully or falsely pretends

---

[42] Section 21 of the 2019 Act.

[43] Section 22 of the 2019 Act.

[44] Section 45 of the *Administration of Islamic Law (Federal Territories) Act 1993* provides that the Yang di-Pertuan Agong may, on the advice of the Chief Syariah Judge, appoint, from amongst members of the general public service of the Federation, a Chief Registrar of the Syariah Appeal Court, a Registrar of the Syariah High Court, and Assistant Registrars of the Syariah Subordinate Courts. e Chief Registrar of the Syariah Appeal Court is the chief administrative arm of the Syariah judiciary and directly responsible to the Chief Syariah Judge.

[45] Section 23 of the 2019 Act.

[46] Section 28 of the 2019 Act.

[47] Section 24 of the 2019 Act.

to be, or takes or uses any name, title, addition or description implying that he is duly qualified or authorized to act as a Peguam Syarie, or that he is recognized by law as so qualified or authorized, commits an offense and shall, on conviction, be liable to a fine not exceeding five thousand ringgit or to imprisonment for a term of not exceeding three years or to both.[48]

The Badan Peguam Syarie of the Federal Territories is established pursuant to section 42 of the Act and among whose function as provided in section 43(4) are to maintain the integrity and status of the Peguam Syarie as well as to avoid unlawful, dishonest and unethical practices among Syariah law practitioners. Further, pursuant to section 59(4), the Majlis Peguam Syarie is empowered, pursuant to section 64(1) to make rules for regulating the professional practice, etiquette, conduct, and discipline of the Peguam Syarie. Any Peguam Syarie who fails to comply with any rules made thereunder shall be subjected to disciplinary proceedings. The practice and etiquette rules which are currently applicable to Peguam Syarie in the Federal Territories is the *Amalan dan Etika Peguam Syarie (Wilayah-Wilayah Persekutuan)* 2000 whose contents are similar to the *Legal Profession (Practice and Etiquette) Rules 1978* as discussed above.

It may be added that section 77(1) of the 2019 Act provides that the Majlis Peguam Syarie shall have disciplinary authority over all Peguam Syarie and pupil, and may exercise disciplinary jurisdiction over any complaint concerning the misconduct involving either of them. The term ‘misconduct’ is defined in section 77(4) to mean any conduct of, or omission to act by, a Peguam Syarie in a professional capacity or otherwise which amounts to grave impropriety and includes –

a) conviction of a criminal offense which makes him unfit to be a member of his profession;
b) breach of duty to a Syariah court including any failure by him to comply with an undertaking given to the Syariah court;
c) dishonest or fraudulent conduct in the performance of his duties;
d) breach of any rules of practice and etiquette of the profession made by the Majlis Peguam Syarie under this Act or otherwise;
e) being an adjudicated bankrupt;
f) the tendering or giving of any gratification to any person for having procured the employment in any Syariah legal business of himself or any other Peguam Syarie;

[48] Section 35(1) of the 2019 Act.

g) directly or indirectly procuring or attempting to procure the employment of himself or any other Peguam Syarie through or by the instruction of any person to whom any remuneration for obtaining such employment has been given by him or agreed or promised to be so given;
h) accepting employment in any Syariah legal business through a tout;
i) allowing any unauthorized person to carry on Syariah legal business in his name without his direct and immediate control as principal or without proper supervision;
j) the carrying on by himself, directly or indirectly, of any profession, trade, business or calling which is incompatible with the Syariah legal profession or being employed for reward or otherwise in any such profession, trade, business or calling;
k) the breach of any provision of this Act or any rules made under this Act or any direction or decision of the Majlis Peguam Syarie;
l) the removal or the striking off of his name from the Register, suspension or censure in his capacity as a Peguam Syarie in any other States or being guilty of misconduct which would render him to be punished in any other States;
m) the charging, in the absence of a written agreement, in respect of the professional services rendered to a client, of fees or costs which are grossly excessive in all the circumstances;
n) gross disregard of his client's interests; and
o) acting in any matter which is unbefitting of a Peguam Syarie or which brings or is calculated to bring the Syariah legal profession into disrepute.

Further, the Majlis is empowered to establish a mechanism, including the establishment of a Disciplinary Board to deal with the complaint or information received against a Peguam Syarie and any other committees to assist the Disciplinary Board. Section 78(1) provides that any complaint of misconduct against any Peguam Syarie or pupil made to the Disciplinary Board shall be in writing. The Syariah Court Judge or Syariah Prosecutor may also refer any complaints against any Peguam Syarie or pupil to the Disciplinary Board.[49]

Where a complaint to the Disciplinary Board is against a firm, section 79(1) provides that the complaint shall be deemed to be made: (i) in the case

---

[49] Section 78(2) of the 2019 Act.

of a sole proprietorship, against the Peguam Syarie who was at the material time the sole proprietor of the firm; and (ii) in the case of a partnership, against all the Peguam Syarie who were at the material time partners of the firm, unless the firm satisfies the Disciplinary Board of the identity of the Peguam Syarie in the firm against whom the complaint has arisen. If at any stage of the proceedings, the Disciplinary Board is satisfied that a complaint made against a firm shall be directed against a particular Peguam Syarie, the Disciplinary Board shall forthwith replace the name of the firm with the name of the Peguam Syarie concerned.

A complaint of misconduct against the Peguam Syarie or any pupil shall not be inquired into by the Disciplinary Board after the expiration of six years from the date on which the right of action accrued. The exception however is where the complaint is based upon the fraud of the Peguam Syarie or his agent or of any person through whom the Peguam Syarie or his agent claims, or where the right of action to bring the complaint is concealed by the fraud of the Peguam Syarie or of his agent or any person through whom he or his agent claims. In such cases, the period of limitation shall not begin to run until the complainant has discovered the fraud, or could with reasonable diligence have discovered it.[50]

After the conclusion of the disciplinary proceedings, should the misconduct be established against the Peguam Syarie or the pupil, the Disciplinary Board may impose the following penalties or punishments: (i) the recording of a reprimand or censure against the name of the Peguam Syarie in the Register; (ii) impose a fine not exceeding fifty thousand ringgit; (iii) suspending the Peguam Syarie from practice for such period not exceeding five years; or (iv) the striking off the name of the Peguam Syarie from the Register.[51] The punishment meted out against the Peguam Syarie or the pupil must be proportionate with the nature and gravity of the misconduct committed. In determining the appropriate punishment, the Board may consider the serious nature of the misconduct and the extenuating circumstances such as the remorsefulness for his misconduct and pleading of guilty immediately after the reading of the charge, among others.

Further, section 83(1) provides that 'if a Peguam Syarie –

---

[50] Section 80 of the 2019 Act.

[51] Section 82 of the 2019 Act.

a) has been found guilty by a court of law of any offense involving dishonesty, misuse or misappropriation of any money or property of a client or of any other person;
b) has been struck off his name from the Register;
c) has been barred, suspended, reprimanded or censured in his capacity as Peguam Syarie in any other States;
d) is the subject of a complaint concerning any dishonest act committed by him in his capacity as a Peguam Syarie;
e) has left the country or has not attended his office in such circumstances that the Majlis Peguam Syarie may reasonably presume that he has absconded; or
f) is otherwise incapable from infirmity of body or mind or any other cause of effectively performing the functions of a Peguam Syarie, and the Majlis Peguam Syarie considers that it would be in the public interest or in the interest of his clients or of the profession that the Peguam Syarie be suspended from practice, the Majlis Peguam Syarie may apply to the Disciplinary Board for an order suspending the Peguam Syarie from practice until further notice is given.'

Any person who is aggrieved by any order or decision made against him by the Disciplinary Board in the exercise of its disciplinary jurisdiction may appeal to the Syariah High Court within thirty days of the receipt of the notification of the order or decision.[52]

3. Special Reference to Legal Profession in Singapore

In Singapore, any person who wishes to be admitted to the Singapore Bar shall be a 'qualified person' as specified in the *Legal Profession Act 1966* (Singapore), the *Legal Profession (Qualified Persons) Rules* (Singapore), and the *Legal Profession (Admission) Rules 2011* (Singapore). A 'qualified person' is defined under the *Legal Profession Act 1966* (Singapore) as any person who:

> "(a) possesses such qualifications as the Minister may prescribe under subsection (2), or may deem under section 14(2) or (3) to be so prescribed,

[52] Section 84 of the 2019 Act.

and satisfies such requirements as the Minister may prescribe under subsection (2);

(b) was approved by the Board of Legal Education as a qualified person under section 7 in force immediately before 9 October 2009; or

(c) is approved by the Minister as a qualified person under section 15A(1) of this Act as in force immediately before 3 May 2011 or under section 14(1)."[53]

Accordingly, the *Legal Profession Act 1966* (Singapore) empowers the Minister for Law,[54] in consultation with the Board of Directors[55] of the Singapore Institute of Legal Education,[56] to make rules to prescribe the qualifications, education, training, and any other requirements that must be satisfied by person desired to be a qualified person for the legal profession.[57]

Generally, a 'qualified person' can be admitted as an advocate and solicitor if he or she:

"(a) has attained 21 years of age;

(b) is of good character;

(c) has satisfactorily served the practice training period[58] applicable to him or her;

(d) has attended and satisfactorily completed such courses of instruction[59] as the Board of Directors of the Institute may prescribe under section 10;[60] and

---

[53] Section 2(1) of the *Legal Profession Act 1966*.

[54] Ministry of Law Singapore, "Our Management" available at <https://www.mlaw.gov.sg/about-us/our-management/> (accessed on 08 July 2022).

[55] Section 5(3) of the *Legal Profession Act 1966* provides that the Board of Directors of the Institute consists of the following members:
(a) the Attorney-General;
(b) the president of the Society;
(c) the Dean of the Faculty of Law of the National University of Singapore;
(d) the Dean of the School of Law of the Singapore Management University;
(da) the Dean of the School of Law of the Singapore University of Social Sciences;
(e) not less than 8 and not more than 12 other members, all of whom must be appointed by the president of the Academy, after consulting the Senate, for such period and on such terms and conditions as the president of the Academy may determine.

[56] See also Sections 2(1), 3, 4, 5 of the *Legal Profession Act 1966*.

[57] Section 2(2) of the *Legal Profession Act 1966*.

[58] Rule 14(2) of the Legal Profession (Admission) Rules 2011 provides that: "[T]he practice training period applicable to a qualified person shall be (6) months."

[59] See also Rule 3 of the Part II of the Legal Profession (Admission) Rules 2011 for the courses prescribed for purposes of Section 13(1)(d) of the *Legal Profession Act 1966*.

[60] Section 10(2) of the *Legal Profession Act 1966* provides that the Board of Directors of the Institute may, after consulting the Minister and the Council, make rules:

(e) has passed such examinations[61] as the Board of Directors of the Institute may prescribe under section 10."[62]

However, a person who just passed the final examination for a law degree in any recognized institution of higher learning[63] will not be admitted as an advocate and solicitor before the law degree is conferred upon him or her.[64]

(a) with respect to the supervised training in relation to the practice of Singapore law which a practice trainee must receive before he or she can be admitted as an advocate and solicitor;
(b) to prescribe the duration of the practice training period applicable to a practice trainee (including different durations for different classes of practice trainees), and to regulate the manner in which a practice trainee is to serve his or her practice training period;
(c) to prescribe the courses of instruction which a qualified person must attend and satisfactorily complete before the qualified person can be admitted as an advocate and solicitor, the conditions for entry to such a course and the subjects in such a course, and to regulate the conduct of a qualified person while attending such a course (including through disciplinary measures for any misconduct);
(d) to prescribe the examinations which a qualified person must pass before the qualified person can be admitted as an advocate and solicitor and the conditions for sitting for such an examination, and to regulate the conduct of a qualified person during such an examination (including through disciplinary measures for any misconduct);
(e) to provide for the courses of instruction which a foreign lawyer must attend and satisfactorily complete before the foreign lawyer can be registered under section 36B, including the conditions for entry to such a course and the subjects in such a course, and to regulate the conduct of a foreign lawyer while attending such a course (including through disciplinary measures for any misconduct);
(f) to provide for the examinations which a foreign lawyer must pass before the foreign lawyer can be registered under section 36B, including the conditions for sitting for such an examination, and to regulate the conduct of a foreign lawyer during such an examination (including through disciplinary measures for any misconduct);
(g) to prescribe the procedure by which a qualified person is admitted as an advocate and solicitor of the Supreme Court;
(h) to prescribe the forms to be used and the fees to be paid for the purposes of this Part, Part 2A, section 25(1)(ca) and any rules made under subsection (1) or this subsection;
(i) to prescribe the requirements relating to continuing professional development that must be satisfied by advocates and solicitors and by foreign lawyers registered under section 36B (including different requirements for different classes thereof), and the measures which may be taken to verify whether those requirements have been complied with and to enforce compliance with those requirements; and
(j) to provide for the waiver of any requirement referred to in paragraph (*i*), in relation to any advocate and solicitor or foreign lawyer referred to in that paragraph, by such person or persons as the Board of Directors of the Institute may appoint.

[61] See also Rule 4 of the Part II of the Legal Profession (Admission) Rules 2011 for the examinations prescribed for purposes of Section 13(1)(e) of the *Legal Profession Act 1966*.

[62] Section 13(1) of the *Legal Profession Act 1966*.

[63] See the Legal Profession (Qualified Persons) Rules: Rules 4, 5AA, 5A, 6 of the Part II for the graduates from institutions of higher learning in Singapore; and Rules 8, 9, 9A, 10, 11 of the Part III for the graduates from institutions of higher learning outside Singapore. See also 1st to 5th Schedules of the Legal Profession (Qualified Persons) Rules.

[64] Section 13(2) of the *Legal Profession Act 1966*.

The *Legal Profession Act 1966* (Singapore) confers vast powers to the Minister for Law in relation to admission requirements of advocates and solicitors in Singapore. Once a person who is entitled to be a 'qualified person' make an application to be admitted as an advocate and solicitor, the Minister may approve by issuing a written notice to that person if he or she thinks that the person possesses qualification or expertise to contribute, promote or enhance the quality of legal services in Singapore. Besides, the Minister may impose any conditions that he or she thinks fit to such an approval for admission.[65] Normally, the Minister may assume that a person has required qualification if the applicant's qualification is conferred by any recognized institution of higher learning.[66] Even if the applicant's qualification is recognized by a foreign authority which has power to permit the person to practice law in a state or territory other than Singapore, the Minister may still deems that the person's qualification is equivalent to any qualification conferred by any recognized institution of higher learning. Of course, this can only be done after the consultation with the Board of Directors of the Singapore Institute of Legal Education.[67]

Furthermore, the Minister may exempt any 'qualified person' from the practice training period applicable to him or her; complete the courses of instruction; and examinations as the Board of Directors of the Singapore Institute of Legal Education.[68] The Minister may also abridge the practice training period applicable to any qualified person. Again, this can only be done after the consultation with the Board of Directors of the Singapore Institute of Legal Education.[69]

Nevertheless, in exceptional circumstances, the *Legal Profession Act 1966* (Singapore) empowers the Minister to make such a decision without requiring the consultation with the Board of Directors of the Singapore Institute of Legal Education if the Minister is of the opinion that "the qualified person is, by reason of his or her standing and experience or for any other cause, a 'fit and proper person' to be so exempted or to have his or her practice training period abridged, as the case may be."[70] Such a special approval not

---

[65] Section 14(1) of the *Legal Profession Act 1966*.
[66] Section 14(2) of the *Legal Profession Act 1966*.
[67] Section 14(3) of the *Legal Profession Act 1966*.
[68] See Section 13(1)(c), (d), (e) and Section 10(2)(a), (b), (c), (d) of the *Legal Profession Act 1966*.
[69] Section 14(4) of the *Legal Profession Act 1966*.
[70] Section 14(5) of the *Legal Profession Act 1966*.

only required to be notified in writing to the person but also need not be published in the *Gazette*.[71]

In addition, the *Legal Profession Act 1966* (Singapore) also confers power to the court[72] to admit a person who possesses special qualifications or experience for the purpose of appearing in any particular case on *ad hoc* basis.[73] Such a person does not need to reside in Singapore or Malaysia as his or her intention to come to Singapore is just to appear for the purpose of that particular case only.[74] The court normally can admit a person to practice as an advocate and solicitor if he or she holds Her Majesty's Patent as Queen's Counsel; or any appointment of equivalent distinction of any jurisdiction.[75]

Conclusion

Malaysia

A person to be admitted in Malaysia into any professional body such as architect, medical, engineer, or legal must, besides having the requisite professional qualifications from a recognized university, be assessed in terms of his character. The Board of Architects, Medical Council, Board of Engineers, and the Malaysian Bar are the professional bodies established pursuant to the *Registration of Engineers Act 1967* (Malaysia), *Architects Act 1967* (Malaysia), *Medical Act 1971* (Malaysia), and *Legal profession Act 1976* (Malaysia). The tasks of the above-mentioned bodies include ensuring that the members are better regulated with higher standards of practice. The requirement to be 'fit and of good character' also reflects the growing importance of issues concerning the problems within the profession and maintaining integrity and honor of the profession.

Singapore

In Singapore, any person who wishes to be admitted to the Singapore Bar shall be a 'qualified person' as specified in the *Legal Profession Act 1966*

---

[71] Section 14(6) of the *Legal Profession Act 1966*.

[72] Section 2(1) of the *Legal Profession Act 1966* defines "court" as "the General Division of the High Court or a Judge sitting in open court in the General Division of the High Court."

[73] Section 15(1)(c) of the *Legal Profession Act 1966*.

[74] Section 15(1)(b) of the *Legal Profession Act 1966*.

[75] Section 15(1)(a) of the *Legal Profession Act 1966*.

(Singapore), the *Legal Profession (Qualified Persons) Rules* (Singapore), and the *Legal Profession (Admission) Rules 2011* (Singapore).

References

Administration of Islamic Law (Federal Territories) Act 1993 (Malaysia).
Advocates and Solicitors Ordinance 1947 (Malaya).
Advocates Ordinance (Sabah) (Cap. 2).
Advocates Ordinance (Sarawak) (Cap. 110).
Amalan dan Etika Peguam Syarie (Wilayah-Wilayah Persekutuan) 2000.
Architects Act 1967 (Malaysia).
Che Man bin Che Mud v. Majlis Peguam Malaysia [2022] 8 MLJ 961.
Darshan Singh Atma Singh v. Majlis Peguam Malaysia [2015] 4 CLJ 1083.
Dr Koay Cheng Boon v. Majlis Perubatan Malaysia [2012] 3 MLJ 173.
Insolvency Act 1967 (Malaysia).
Interpretation Acts 1948 and 1967 (Malaysia)
Legal Profession (Admission) Rules 2011 (Singapore).
Legal Profession (Practice and Etiquette) Rules 1978 (Malaysia).
Legal Profession (Qualified Persons) Rules (Singapore).
Legal Profession Act 1966 (Singapore).
Legal Profession Act 1976 (Malaysia).
Madhuvita Janjara Augustin (Suing through Next Friend, Margaret Louisa Tan) v. Augustin Lourdsamy & Ors [2018] 4 CLJ 758.
Majlis Peguam Malaysia & Anor v. Judy Blacious s/o AF Pereira [2016] MLJU 1116.
Majlis Peguam Malaysia v. Ahmad Rushdi bin Omar [2017] 6 MLJ 70.
Majlis Peguam Malaysia v. Krishnasamy a/l Bhaktavatsalu [2020] 12 MLJ 438.
Marzaini Zainuddin v. Majlis Peguam [2007] 10 CLJ 339.
Medical Act 1971 (Malaysia).
Medical (Amendment) Act 2012 (Malaysia).
Patrick Samuel a/l Joseph Sebastian v. Majlis Peguam Malaysia [2014] 9 MLJ 479.
Re B Surinder Singh Kanda [1964] MLJ 135.
Re Judy Blacious AF Pereira; Petitioner [2015] 6 CLJ 1127.
Re S.R.C. Augustin [1973] 1 MLJ 208.
Registration of Engineers Act 1967 (Malaysia).
S Ashok Kandiah & Anor v. Dato' Yalumallai Muthusamy & Anor [2011] 1 CLJ 460, CA.
Sarawak State Attorney General Chambers.
Subashini Rajasingam v. Saravanan Thangathoray & other appeals [2008] 2 CLJ 1, FC.
Syarie Legal Profession (Federal Territories) Act 2019 (Malaysia).
Voon Lee Shan v. Richard Malanjum [2022] MLJU 436.

Chapter 3

The Origin of the Professions

Gary I. Lilienthal[1,*], PhD
and Nehaluddin Ahmad[2], LLD
[1]Carrington Rand, Hong Kong SAR, Peoples Republic of China
[2]Faculty of Law, Sultan Sharif Ali Islamic University, Brunei

Abstract

The term, "profession" first appeared in the 16th Century, applying to the so-called learned professions of theology, law and medicine. A profession consists of a range of characteristics: "prolonged, specialized, intellectual training, a technique, either scientific or institutional, based on natural science or study of human institutions, remuneration for professional service in the form of fee and not salary, a sense of responsibility to the client, formation of associations to test competence and maintain ethical codes." The research objective of this chapter is to investigate critically the sources of regulation of the professions. Licensure is a procedure for screening candidates for admission to a profession, to review the qualifications of existing practitioners, to work to establish ethical standards, to maintain, advance and enhance the profession's standards, and to assure fair dealing with the members of the public. The professional licensing of members originated in the gilds of the middle-ages. Admission to the gild was the equivalent of modern licensure and was the gild's specific monopoly. The phases and terminologies of modern professional education still follow much the organizational skeleton of the medieval gilds and professions. Freedom of the city of London could be acquired only by one of the original three pathways of patrimony, apprenticeship, or by redemption from the court of aldermen. Pulling wrote that from ancient Saxon times the power of

* Corresponding Author's Email: carrington.rand@icloud.com.

In: Regulation of the Professions in East Asia
Editors: Gary I. Lilienthal and Muhamad Hassan bin Ahmad
ISBN: 979-8-88697-409-6

conferring the freedom of the city was independent of the crown. People not free of the city were designated as foreigners or strangers, in accordance with the ancient law of Rome. The freedom of the City of London was essential for commercial activity. Up to 1835, every person who wished to become a city freeman first had to become a freeman of one of the City. The research question asks how professional recognition is structured, and for what purposes. Argument seeks to sustain the view that maintenance of societal hegemony has been the purpose of the professions since the times of the middle ages gilds. The research paradigm is psychoanalytic, in that it deploys both historiographic method and historical narrative analysis in order to construct its syntheses. In today's western capitalist state, the bourgeois rule by both domination and by hegemony, where domination is rule by force and hegemony is rule by consent, coordinated by professional advice to subaltern masses, a transmission of bourgeois ideology, where the advice is set up to have essential value to them. The "historical bloc" is a structural conception that coordinates society just as a king used to do, by use of references to bundles of myths as historical forces. Now, the dominant bourgeoisie must form a unified ideology to articulate this unified ideology to the masses and project onto them what they have learned in their years of higher education. When the masses nevertheless fail to consent, either actively or passively, the state exercises coercive power over them by legally enforcing discipline onto such recalcitrant groups. Similarly, the king had power to create and dismantle professions, by means of proceedings in *quo warranto*. The freedom of the city was the device by which the right to make a professional level of living was enforced. Through this process and structure, the mercantile gilds became today's hegemonic professions. The historical bloc forming a superstructure to keep these professional groups in this hierarchy was public fear of deceit in the trades.

Keywords: hegemony, professional advice, subaltern masses, king's power, mercantile gilds, hegemonic professions, historical bloc

1. Introduction

The term, "profession" is not to be found in the Greek or Latin languages. The term, "profession" first appeared in the 16th Century, applying to the so-called learned professions of theology, law and medicine. Until this time, university teaching was described as sciences or studies.[1] A profession consists of a range

[1] John S Brubacher, 'The Evolution of Professional Education', in *Education for the Professions*, University of Chicago Press, Chicago, 1962, p. 50.

of characteristics: "prolonged, specialized, intellectual training, a technique, either scientific or institutional, based on natural science or study of human institutions, remuneration for professional service in the form of fee and not salary, a sense of responsibility to the client, formation of associations to test competence and maintain ethical codes."[2] Yet, many other activities, such as accountancy and even management, are also known as professions. In the light of this statement of significance, the research objective of this chapter is to investigate critically the sources of regulation of the professions.

Licensure is a procedure for screening candidates for admission to a profession, to review the qualifications of existing practitioners, to work to establish ethical standards, to maintain, advance and enhance the profession's standards, and to assure fair dealing with the members of the public. Certification is similar to licensure, but is often limited to assuring a minimum level of competence for the purposes of professional practice, and with less attention to those aspects required for ethical standards and regulations of practice.[3]

The term "licensing" is considered in connection with the healing arts, such as medicine, nursing, osteopathy, dentistry and similar. The term "certification," however, applies to those such as accountants, teachers, architects, land-surveyors, engineers Lawyers are neither licensed nor certified, but "admitted" by the controlling courts in each jurisdiction.[4]

In their certifying and licensing functions, states regulate professional admissions. The various professional associations establish professional regulations and standards to guide state licensing and certification procedures.[5] There is also a third significant force, which is called "professional membership," where the various professional associations set membership and practice standards for operation within their specific professional associations.[6]

---

[2] Alexander M Carr-Saunders & PA Wilson, *The Professions*, Frank Cass, London, 1964, pp. 284-289.

[3] John J Ahern, *An Historical Study of the Professions and Professional Education in the United States*, Loyola University, Chicago, 1971, p. 146.

[4] G Lester Anderson, & Merton W Ertell, 'Extra-institutional forces affecting professional education', in Education for the Professions, National Society for the Study of Education, Chicago, 1962, p. 238.

[5] John J Ahern, *An Historical Study of the Professions and Professional Education in the United States*, Loyola University, Chicago, 1971, p. 146.

[6] G Lester Anderson, & Merton W Ertell, 'Extra-institutional forces affecting professional education', in Education for the Professions, National Society for the Study of Education, Chicago, 1962, p. 239.

The professional licensing of their members originated in the gilds of the middle-ages. Admission to the gild was the equivalent of modern licensure and was the gild's specific monopoly. The phases and terminologies of modern professional education still follow much the organizational skeleton of the medieval gilds and professions. Today's publicly announced purpose of licensure is "protection of the public through assurance of minimum level of competence," and appears to have had the effect of continually recreating the medieval monopolies, but for stated avowed purposes of public good.[7]

From ancient times, freedom of the city of London could be acquired only by one of the original three pathways of patrimony, apprenticeship, or by redemption from the court of aldermen.[8] Pulling wrote that from ancient Saxon times the power of conferring the freedom of the city was independent of the crown.[9] People not free of the city were designated as foreigners or strangers, in accordance with the ancient law of Rome.[10]

The freedom of the City of London was essential for commercial activity and functioned as follows. Only city freemen could vote in Parliamentary elections, vote in civic elections for councilmen and alderman, be exempt from all tolls payable on animals brought into the City for sale, be exempt from all market tolls payable anywhere in the country, be exempt from naval conscription, and enjoy the right to claim freedom from prosecution except in the city's courts.[11]

Up to 1835, every person who wished to become a city freeman first had to become a freeman of one of the City livery companies. These were mercantile successors to the medieval trade and craft gilds. The freedom of a livery company was merely an ordinary membership. A person wishing to become a senior member of a livery company had to be first a freeman both of that company and of the City of London. A person who was a freeman of both the City and a livery company was named, referred to, and thus identified as "Citizen and [Livery Company name] of London."[12] Without this freedom of the city, the person could not function as an independent professional. Thus, modern licensure depends on recognition by public authorities, sufficient to

---

[7] ibid., p. 236.

[8] 2 Brownlow 286; 4 Inst 250; 2 and 276-7; 2 Bulstr 189-190; 3 Keb 225; 8 Co 112 b; 4 Mod 145.

[9] Alexander Pulling, *The Laws, Customs, Usages and Regulations of the City and Port of London*, William Henry Bond and Wildy and Sons, London, 1854, p. 59.

[10] Cicero, *De Offi* 1, 12.

[11] Vivienne Aldous, *Research Guide 1: City Freedom Archives*, Corporation of London Records Office, London, 1999.

[12] ibid.

retain membership of a profession, and the question therefore arises as to how this recognition is structured, and for what purposes. Argument seeks to sustain the view that maintenance of societal hegemony has been the purpose of the professions since the times of the middle ages gilds, where Gramsci had found that the western dominant class, known as the bourgeoisie, ruled with the subordinate masses' consent, despite massive contradictions, and which he called "the hegemony of the bourgeoisie."[13]

The research paradigm is psychoanalytic, in that it deploys both historiographic method and historical narrative analysis in order to construct its syntheses. The structure of this research is divided into four main sections. The first is entitled Hegemony, covering: Bourgeois Hegemony; The Material Base for Exercising Hegemony; The Historical Bloc; and, Formation of the Capitalist State. The second is entitled The King's Power, covering: The King's Power of Quo Warranto; The City of London Legal System; Nature of the Jurisdiction of the Courts of the City of London; The City of London Control over the Economy; and, Freedom of the City. The third is entitled The Relationship between Commerce, The Economy and The Gilds, covering: Gild Formation; Gild Ordinance Structure; and, Collapse of Gild Independence. The fourth is entitled The Position of The Workers, covering: City of London Protection of the Masters; and, The Pressing of The Trades into a Crown System of Commercial Ranks.

The likely research outcome will be that, in a western capitalist state, the bourgeois rule by both domination and by hegemony, where domination is rule by force and hegemony is rule by consent, coordinated by professional advice to subaltern masses, a transmission of bourgeois ideology, where the advice is set up to have essential value to them. The dominant class may sustain the material bases of this economic compromise, only by being the most dominant force, directing the field of production, while the subordinate classes must never be incentivized to withdraw consent to the rule of the hegemonic class. The "historical bloc" is a structural conception that coordinates society just as a king used to do, by use of references to bundles of myths as historical forces. Now, the dominant bourgeoisie must form a unified ideology to articulate this unified ideology to the masses and project onto them what they have learned in their years of higher education. Their success as hegemons depends on a validating truth in the bourgeois hegemonic ideology in people's daily lives, such as when their advice conforms to

[13] Antonio Gramsci, *Selections from the Prison Notebooks of Antonio Gramsci*, International Publishers, New York, 1971, p. 57.

satisfying the exigencies of daily life. When the masses nevertheless fail to consent, either actively or passively, the state exercises coercive power over them by legally enforcing discipline onto such recalcitrant groups. In this paradigm, force and consent are the equivalent of each other. Similarly, the king had, for many centuries, the power to create and dismantle professions, by means of proceedings in *quo warranto*. The freedom of the city was the device by which the right to make a professional level of living was enforced. Without it, the worker reverted to the ancient form of slavery. The oath of freedom of the city summarized those interests which professionals had given up, in order to retain their bourgeois positioning. Through this, the mercantile gilds became today's professions. The historic bloc forming a superstructure to keep these professional groups in this hierarchy was that of deceit in the trades. The crown wanted to be atop this professional hierarchy, by continuing and strict supervisory processes, should it have desired to control the stamping out of deceit in the trades. Now, the bourgeoisie exercises his function juridically.

2. Hegemony

According to orthodox Marxian interpretations, a socialist revolution is the inevitable consequence of the developments of contradictions within the capitalist schema for production. Thus, according to this dictum, the proletariat is the universal class of the post-capitalist era and it will necessarily win all revolutionary fights with the bourgeoisie. However, the western historical experience has shown that capitalism survives even in its periods of severe economic crises, with the possibility of any proletarian revolutions neither universal nor permanent, suggesting that these repeating contradictions were a form of stability.

> From Gramsci's theoretical work there emerges a structural dualism that combines factory councils and soviets as organs of popular socialist democracy with the revolutionary party as a mechanism of coordination and leadership. Rooted in the innovative and heroic practice of the Turin proletariat itself, his systematic integration of the council movement into the Marxist tradition lent concreteness to Gramsci's unique strategy - to his notion of counter-hegemonic struggle, to his critique of bourgeois party and union structures and of the elitist centralism implicit in the concept of "dictatorship of the proletariat." Through his understanding of the councils

as the prefiguration of the new order within bourgeois society, Gramsci raised the theoretical attack upon bureaucracy to a more positive level . . . .[14]

After several defeats in the Factory Council Movement and other similar kinds of revolutionary movements, Gramsci's main problem, while in Mussolini's prison, was to explain capitalism's resilience, while finding a sounder theoretical basis for the proletariat's counter-strategy. The key theoretical conception he elaborated, while in prison, was "hegemony." Before Gramsci, Lenin also applied the concept of hegemony, but Lenin's ideas were restricted to the political fields, specifically the political leadership of the proletarian alliances with the peasantry.[15] Gramsci found that the western dominant class, known as the bourgeoisie, ruled with the subordinate masses' consent, despite massive contradictions, and which he called "the hegemony of the bourgeoisie."[16]

2.1. Bourgeois Hegemony

According to Gramsci's views, a class's supremacy works in two ways: by domination and by hegemony. Domination is rule by force and hegemony is rule by consent. For Gramsci, the dominant bourgeoisie's maintaining of power, in capitalist societies, is usually by organization of consent, rather than by naked force. Hegemony, which is the organizing of the consent of the subordinate masses, is based on the dominant social groups' ability to represent those universal interests subsisting in the entire society, for a particular time, in which these interests would be interpreted through ideological foundations.

According to Engels' original formulation of the term, 'ideology' could be described in detail as follows:

> Ideology is a process accomplished by the so-called thinker consciously . . . but with a false consciousness. The real motive forces impelling him remain unknown to him; otherwise, it simply would not be an ideological process.

---

[14] Carl Boggs, Jr., 'Gramsci's Theory of the Factory Councils: Nucleus of the Socialist State', *Berkeley Journal of Sociology*, vol. 19, 1974-1975, pp. 171-187, p. 171.

[15] Perry Anderson, 'The Antinomies of Antonio Gramsci', *New Left Review*, no. 100, 1976-77, pp. 15-18; Christine Buci-Glucksmann, *Gramsci and the State*, Lawrence and Wishart, London, 1980.

[16] Antonio Gramsci, *Selections from the Prison Notebooks of Antonio Gramsci*, International Publishers, New York, 1971, p. 57.

> Hence he imagines false or seeming motive forces. Because it is a process of thought, he derives its form as well as its content from pure thought, either his own or that of his predecessors. He works with mere thought material, which he accepts without examination as the product of thought, and does not investigate further for a more remote source independent of thought; indeed, that is a matter of course for him, because, as all action is mediated by thought, it appears to him to be ultimately based upon thought.[17]

Representation of universal interests may not be settled by ideological inculcation, or by the *marche de dupes*[18] of western elections, but only by realizing the subordinate masses' interests concretely.[19] No ideology can coordinate concrete interests between dominant classes and subordinate groupings, unless validated in some material form, because ideology's instability of false consciousness implies the emergence of contradictions. Although consent can be induced by "false consciousness" or "mass delusion," this kind of consent cannot subsist for long without material content.[20] In the result, moral and intellectual leadership cannot be secured only by ideological methodologies. Rather, the dominant socio-economic formation sets up the objective conditions, by which ideological leadership could develop,[21] such as by a bourgeois professional class giving "advice" to members of the less educated masses.

Although Gramsci articulated the role of ideas and consciousness in forming socio-political relations, he did not characterize hegemony in merely superstructural terms. He stressed that hegemony, as arranging consent, had material bases: "Though hegemony is ethical-political, it must also be economic, must necessarily be based on the decisive function exercised by the leading group in the decisive nucleus of economic activity."[22] Thus, only a fundamental class at the level of economy could become a force of hegemony. A social group may rule, for a limited time, without being the leading

---

[17] Marx and Engels, *Selected Correspondence*, Foreign Language Publishing House, Moscow, no date, p. 541.

[18] Literally, a fool's bargain.

[19] Antonio Gramsci, *Selections from the Prison Notebooks of Antonio Gramsci*, International Publishers, New York, 1971, p. 182.

[20] Adam Przeworski, 'Material Bases of Consent: Economics and Politics in a Hegemonic System', in *Political Power and Social Theory*, vol. 1, JAI Press, Greenwich, 1980, p. 24.

[21] Antonio Gramsci, *Selections from the Prison Notebooks of Antonio Gramsci*, International Publishers, New York, 1971, p. 161.

[22] ibid.

economic force, as already shown in the instance of the Italian bourgeoisie in its period of Risorgimento.[23]

As Salomone had clarified about the Risorgimento:

> Was not the Italian liberals' claim to have made Italy in the likeness and image of European *sacro egoismo* of an authoritarian, class-conscious elite of landed magnates, upper-bourgeois "rich men," and the influential intellectual and professional classes? Had not the lower classes been simply used and exploited and then forgotten or excluded in the wake of a national spoils system that had been instituted under the pretext of the independence, unity and liberty of Italy.[24]

However, Gramsci did not see even this as hegemony in the formal sense, as it was a bourgeoisie forming a new state despite the material interests of the people to the contrary. He regarded the ideological and political leadership, exercised by the Italian bourgeoisie over the subordinate masses, as a "bastard" hegemony, due to its insufficient material basis.[25]

2.2. The Material Base for Exercising Hegemony

Gramsci held that the organizing of consent started from an economic compromise between the dominant class and the various subordinate classes. The dominant class may achieve hegemony by concrete coordination of its interests with those of the subordinate classes. In order to do this, the dominant class must be careful not to sacrifice the real interests of the subordinate classes, but instead, partially to realize the subordinate classes' interests by forgoing some of its own material interests. They transfer and project some bourgeois interests onto the masses. In consequence of this, the dominant class may sustain the material bases of this economic compromise, only by being the most dominant force in the field of production. Developing and organizing the material forces of production provides the objective basis for establishing

[23] Hyug Baeg Im, 'Hegemony and Counter-Hegemony in Gramsci', *Asian Perspective*, vol. 15, no. 1, 1991, pp. 123-156, p. 127.

[24] A William Salomone, 'The Risorgimento between Ideology and History: The Political Myth of rivoluzione mancata', *The American Historical Review*, vol. 68, no. 1, 1962, pp. 38- 56, p. 42.

[25] Antonio Gramsci, *Selections from the Prison Notebooks of Antonio Gramsci*, International Publishers, New York, 1971, pp. 90, 120; John A Davis (ed.), *Gramsci and Italy's Passive Revolution*, Croom and Helm, London, 1979.

a dominant class's hegemony. In this way, to manufacture hegemony continuously, the dominant class must continually reproduce the subsisting mode of production. Despite all this, dominant class concessions to the subordinate classes should have the prescribed limit that "such a compromise cannot touch the essential" economic order.[26]

Thus the hegemonic class must be in a controlling position to create and maintain an equilibrium between its own interests and those interests of the subordinate classes, without touching the dominant mode of production. The subordinate classes must never be incentivized to withdraw consent to the rule of the hegemonic class.[27]

> We are able to construct a scheme of six classes over time: self-declared entrepreneurs, self-employed running a company; professionals, self-employed active in an officially recognized profession; managers, dependent employees but with considerable autonomy. These three groups are taken together in most analyses and called bourgeoisie .... [28]
>
> The other three classes are the white collars, dependent workers with a medium level of autonomy who tend to have stable, long-term employment contracts; traditional self-employed, or petty bourgeoisie, running their own independent small business, as shopkeepers, craftsmen and so on; the blue collars, or working class, including workers in dependent (or pseudo self-employed) positions who may or may not have long-term working contracts. The latter class also includes low-skilled, non-manual jobs in the tertiary sector.[29]

From this, bourgeoisie hegemony is not conceivable without the operation of a capitalist economy, in which the entrepreneurs, professionals and managers project their knowledge onto the masses, ideological reframed as a benefit to the masses. Having this main role and positioning in the capitalist economy provides an objective basis for bourgeoisie hegemony. In a capitalist economy, the bourgeoisie is the fundamental class, allowing it to decide how to allocate products as wages and profits, with some certain constraints. Excesses in profits, relative to the level of wages, harms bourgeois rule over a

---

[26] Antonio Gramsci, *Selections from the Prison Notebooks of Antonio Gramsci*, International Publishers, New York, 1971, p. 161.

[27] ibid., p.120; Davis 1979; Hyug Baeg Im, 'Hegemony and Counter-Hegemony in Gramsci', *Asian Perspective*, vol. 15, no. 1, 1991, pp. 123-156, p. 128.

[28] G Ballarino & A Cobalti, *Mobilità sociale*, Carocci, Roma, 2003.

[29] Gabriele Ballarino & Stefani Scherer, 'More investment – less returns? Changing returns to education in Italy across three decades', *Stato e mercato*, vol. 99, no. 3, 2013, pp. 359-388, pp. 370-371.

capitalist society, because excesses in profits result in reduced wages, causing workers to withdraw their voluntary consent to bourgeois rule. At the same time, profits must not fall below a level sufficient to maintain the capitalist economic system, with these profits then used for providing a necessary investment fund used for reproducing capitalist production. Thus in order to exercise their hegemony, the bourgeoisie must realize material interests of the proletariat, while guarding the essentials of the basic bourgeoisie class interests.[30] The exercising of bourgeois hegemony is "conditioned and limited by the capitalist accumulation process."[31] The bourgeois system of hegemony is thus based on unstable equilibria, where neither the basic bourgeoisie class interests nor the proletariat's economic interests should be dishonored.

The leading role and positioning in the economy does not, of itself, generate a class's hegemony. It is a necessary but insufficient condition for establishing hegemony. Although the bourgeoisie is the dominant capitalist economic force, it could not create hegemony over subordinate classes if it only wanted to pursue corporative interests without sharing.[32] According to Gramsci's view, to be a hegemonic class, it must "transcend the corporate limits of purely economic class" and be a "universal" class, able to project its own class interests onto those of subordinate groups.[33]

Sigmund Freud articulated the concept of projection, in his letters to Wilhelm Fliess.[34] Karl Abraham and Anna Freud further refined it. Freud stated that, in projection, motivations, thoughts, feelings and desires that cannot be accepted as arising in oneself, are placed into the outside world and attributed to another person.[35] What the ego refused to accept would be split off and put into another person,[36] so that bourgeois learning can be privatized, reframed as a benefit to the proletariat, and sold to them as controlling advice.

To be a universal class, an economically fundamental class must deploy this political, intellectual and moral leadership, at the level of so-called superstructures. Thus, Gramsci stated that a genuinely hegemonic phase takes

---

[30] Adam Przeworski, 'Material Bases of Consent: Economics and Politics in a Hegemonic System', in *Political Power and Social Theory*, vol. 1, JAI Press, Greenwich, 1980, p. 30.

[31] Bob Jessop, *The Political Indeterminacy Marxism and Democracy*, Lawrence and Wishart, London, 1980, p. 64.

[32] Hyug Baeg Im, 'Hegemony and Counter-Hegemony in Gramsci', *Asian Perspective*, vol. 15, no. 1, 1991, pp. 123-156, p. 129.

[33] Antonio Gramsci, *Selections from the Prison Notebooks of Antonio Gramsci*, International Publishers, New York, 1971, p. 181.

[34] Jean-Michel Quinodoz, *Reading Freud: A Chronological Exploration of Freud's Writings*, Routledge, London, 2005, p. 24.

[35] Sigmund Freud, *Case Histories II*, Penguin, London, 1991, p. 210.

[36] Otto Fenichel, *The Psychoanalytic Theory of Neurosis*, Routledge, Oxford, 1946, p. 146.

place at the moment of the decisive passing from the structure to complex superstructure,[37] meaning that in a hegemonic system, the political and ideological superstructure also must sustain the same kind of economic compromise in place at the base. For Gramsci, the political and ideological spheres are the loci of class struggles, appearing as contradictions, formed continually through the dialectic outcomes of these struggles. For continuous reproduction of a hegemonic systems, the political and ideological superstructure must be compatible with economic compromises at the base. This means that all the superstructures, such as culture, politics, family systems, religions, law, school systems and public opinion, must be organized to facilitate class compromise. The formation of an entire hegemonic system is complete when the fundamental class unifies political, economic and ideological hegemony.[38]

2.3. The Historical Bloc

The "historical bloc"[39] is the central concept, in Neo-Gramscian theory that unifies the connections between society and state, international and domestic, and subaltern and dominant socioeconomic vectors, from which hegemonic relationships develop. This conception covers the social, political and economic connections, arrayed both internationally and domestically, between the coercive and administrative instrumentalities of the state. It also includes social groupings inside supportive civil society, in which leading capitalist forces establish their own ascendancy over others by assimilating them into the instrumentalities of governance and the state, as subaltern supporters.[40] Thus, the historical bloc is the integration by inter-networking of many class interests, propagated through society to promote a wide moral and cultural

---

[37] Antonio Gramsci, *Selections from the Prison Notebooks of Antonio Gramsci*, International Publishers, New York, 1971, p. 181.

[38] ibid., p. 182.

[39] "In Sorel's work there is no reference to the concept of "historical bloc." Valentino Gerratana has suggested that Gramsci, who in prison did not have access to Sorel's *Reflections on Violence*, had in mind Sorel's references to myths, and in particular Sorel's insistence that these images *should be taken as a whole, as historical forces*, probably from a reference in a book by Giovanni Malagodi." Panagiotis Sotiris, 'Gramsci and the Challenges for the Left: The Historical Bloc as a Strategic Concept', *Science & Society*, vol. 82, no. 1, 2018, pp. 94–119, p. 97, citing Antonio Gramsci, *Quaderni di Carcere*, Valentino Gerratana (ed.), Einaudi, Torino, 1977, p. 2632.

[40] Richard Saull, 'Hegemony and the Global Political Economy', in Robert A Denemark (ed.), *The International Studies Encyclopedia*, vol. V, Wiley-Blackwell, Oxford, 2010, p. 3285.

unity.[41] The historical bloc, as a hierarchical coercive arrangement of social classes, reproduces itself through a wide articulation of consciousness, ideas and identity, by those participating parts of civil society.[42] Thus, class interests indicating what a class has to lose, the historical bloc integrates material forces with ideological thinking.

Gramsci articulated the concept of "historical bloc" as "the complex, contradictory, and discordant ensemble of the superstructure and the structure."[43] This concept of "historical bloc" leads to the correct reading of Gramsci's idea of hegemony, yet the concept of historical bloc neither provides a sound superstructural nor a sound materialistic reading of Gramsci.[44] Rather, the concept of a "historical bloc" emphasizes the necessity for unity of economic, ideological and political unity within a hegemonic realm, welded together by ideologically-based historiographic narratives. Although dominance in economic positioning is the necessary precondition for hegemony, organized ideology and politics are also required for establishing a hegemonic system. This is because they act to cement and to unify hegemonic relations within the economic system, raising the domination of a social group onto a "universal plane." The most appropriate political and ideological system, available for the hegemonic bourgeoisie to organize is bourgeois democracy, because it actualizes and consolidates capitalist productive relations on the political plane by individualizing the subordinate classes into "citizens" or separate people,[45] on the bases of ideologically-based historical narratives.

This individualization of the subordinate masses, into "citizens" or "people," disorganizes the subordinate classes. Each individual in a class no longer acts as a member of that class, acting instead as people or citizen. Anyone is permitted to participate in bourgeois democracy generators like parliaments, trade unions, political parties and other representational political institutions, and anyone will then be represented not as a class member but as an individual voter or citizen with no power base[46] In a democratic system, the

---

[41] Adam Morton, *Unravelling Gramsci: Hegemony and Passive Revolution in the Global Economy*, Pluto, London, 2007, p. 118.

[42] Stephen Gill, *Power and Resistance in the New World Order*, Palgrave, Basingstoke, 2003, p. 58.

[43] Antonio Gramsci, *Selections from the Prison Notebooks of Antonio Gramsci*, International Publishers, New York, 1971, p. 366.

[44] Hyug Baeg Im, 'Hegemony and Counter-Hegemony in Gramsci', *Asian Perspective*, vol. 15, no. 1, 1991, pp. 123-156, p. 130.

[45] Nicos Poulantzas, *Political Power and Social Classes*, New Left Books, London, 1973.

[46] Bob Jessop, *The Political Indeterminacy Marxism and Democracy*, Lawrence and Wishart, London, 1980, p. 59.

participatory outcomes are not decided by positioning within the production system, which are class positions, and consequently, no group ever feels the certainty that its interests will ever be realized. This indeterminacy and uncertainty is the distinguishing indicium of institutionalized competition within bourgeois democracy, although all constituents only have a mere opportunity to realize some of their material exigencies through political competition.[47] As individual citizens, but not producers, wage earners can merely articulate claims to improvements in their material conditions via democratic institutions within the confines of capitalism, which sets up the illusion of freedom of speech. Bourgeois hegemony is possible only when the ruling bourgeoisie reduces politics, in the sole form of bourgeois democracy, to a situs of a contradiction-laden struggle for corporate economic interests.[48]

In this bourgeois democracy, the subordinate classes are now tolerable and therefore urged to participate in democratic institutions in exchange for their consent to rule by the bourgeois paradigm of capital. Bourgeois democracy positions the bourgeois class to represent the society's universal interests, which is the sustaining of the capitalist system, and makes all members of the subordinate classes pursue corporate economic interests.[49] In order to be a national hegemonic class, the bourgeoisie have to create "a new type of politics" and construct "a new type of civilization," purpose-built to ensure bourgeois hegemony at cultural and ideological levels. Gramsci stated that hegemony required "not only a unison of economic and political aims, but also intellectual and moral unity."[50] Hegemony based on class compromise on the economic plane must also extend to the ideology by which "men gain consciousness of conflicts in the world of economy." Thus, the realization of the subordinate classes' material interests must be concentrated in organizing ideological hegemony. The consequence of this is that bare "corporate consciousness" can never become a hegemonic ideology, because it does not concern the realization of the subordinate classes' ideological interests. Nevertheless, the hegemonic bourgeoisie must generate kinds of consciousness in the minds of the subordinate masses, which reach

---

[47] Adam Przeworski, 'Material Bases of Consent: Economics and Politics in a Hegemonic System', in *Political Power and Social Theory*, vol. 1, JAI Press, Greenwich, 1980, p. 30.

[48] Hyug Baeg Im, 'Hegemony and Counter-Hegemony in Gramsci', *Asian Perspective*, vol. 15, no. 1, 1991, pp. 123-156, p. 131.

[49] This is why Lenin believed that the bourgeoisie democracy is "the best possible political shell" for capitalism. V Lenin, 'The State and Revolution', in *Selected Works*, Progress Publishers, Moscow, 1963, p. 296.

[50] Antonio Gramsci, *Selections from the Prison Notebooks of Antonio Gramsci*, International Publishers, New York, 1971, p. 181.

equilibrium in a position of subordination, and it was this semi-stable equilibrium that Gramsci called "corporate consciousness."[51] In the result, ideological hegemony raises the bourgeoisie consciousness to the level of "identifying the interests and the requirements common to all the national forces."[52]

However, the search for specific interests of individual members of the bourgeoisie cannot become part of a hegemonic ideology, meaning they must form profession-like groupings. Thus, to establish ideological hegemony, the dominant bourgeoisie must form a unified ideology through transcending the operative corporate consciousness of individual members of the bourgeoisie. For example, in a profession, many members give up their right to litigate against each other, apparently making the profession a unified group to serve the public, rather than its own interests. This unifying ideology must be in a category of ideology, which can represent the general interests of the whole "people-nation."[53] For Gramsci, the bourgeoisie can never retain its hegemony through any "false consciousness," imposed by the bourgeoisie to deceive and defraud workers or even to distort the practicalities and procedures of domination.[54] Mass acquiescence in the bourgeois hegemonic system depends on a validating truth in the bourgeois hegemonic ideology in people's daily lives,[55] such as in the exigencies of daily life.

2.4. Formation of the Capitalist State

Gramsci saw the function of ideology as being to "organize human masses, and create the terrain on which men move, acquire consciousness of their position, struggle etc.," in the economic world.[56] It is within the ambient

---

[51] Stuart Hall, Bob Lumley & Gregor McLennan, 'Politics and Ideology: Gramsci', *Working Papers in Cultural Studies*, no 10, 1977, pp. 45–76, p. 49.

[52] Antonio Gramsci, *Selections from the Prison Notebooks of Antonio Gramsci*, International Publishers, New York, 1971, p. 78.

[53] Hyug Baeg Im, 'Hegemony and Counter-Hegemony in Gramsci', *Asian Perspective*, vol. 15, no. 1, 1991, pp. 123-156, p. 132.

[54] Gramsci asserted that "men become consciousness of fundamental conflicts on the level of ideology is not psychological or moralistic in character but structural and epistemological." For him, the ideological hegemony cannot be accomplished through neither "continuous marche de dupes" nor "swindles" Antonio Gramsci, *Selections from the Prison Notebooks of Antonio Gramsci*, International Publishers, New York, 1971, p. 164).

[55] Stuart Hall, Bob Lumley & Gregor McLennan, 'Politics and Ideology: Gramsci', *Working Papers in Cultural Studies*, no 10, 1977, pp. 45–76, p. 53.

[56] Antonio Gramsci, *Selections from the Prison Notebooks of Antonio Gramsci*, International Publishers, New York, 1971, p. 377.

ideology that the subaltern masses live out their consent to the political power and authority of the bourgeoisie in their daily lives. Since ideology cannot function alone as a suite of spiritual realities, it always has to be made material in practice,[57] with material forces providing the means for validating ideology:

> Precisely material forces are the content and ideologies are the form, though this distinction between form and content has purely didactic value, since the material forces would be conceivable historically without form and the ideologies would be individual fancies without material force.[58]

A Gramscian conception of the state arises from this. The state is an institution defined carefully, "on the juridical plane," to organize the entire society for forming class compromises in the midst of unstable equilibria between the interests of the basic group and the subordinate groups.[59] These equilibria are unstable, as contradictions, in the economic, political and ideological fields:

> It is true that the State is seen as the organ of one particular group, destined to create favorable conditions for the latter's maximum expansion. But the development and expansion of the particular groups are conceived of, and presented, as being the motor force of a universal expansion, of a development of all national energies. In other words, the dominant group is coordinated concretely with the general interests of the subordinate groups, and the life of the State is conceived of as a continuous process of formation and superseding of unstable equilibria (on the juridical plane) between the interests of the fundamental groups and those of the subordinate groups - equilibria in which the interests of the dominant group prevail, but only up to a certain point, i.e., stopping short of narrowly corporate economic interest.[60]

Gramsci reasoned that the capitalist state was not merely the instrument of the dominant bourgeois class, but more, was the instrument for producing

---

[57] Chantall Mouffe, 'Hegemony and Ideology in Gramsci', in Chantall Mouffe (ed.), *Gramsci and Marxist Theory*, Routledge & Kegan Paul, London, 1979, p. 186.

[58] Antonio Gramsci, *Selections from the Prison Notebooks of Antonio Gramsci*, International Publishers, New York, 1971, p. 377.

[59] Hyug Baeg Im, 'Hegemony and Counter-Hegemony in Gramsci', *Asian Perspective*, vol. 15, no. 1, 1991, pp. 123-156, p. 133.

[60] Antonio Gramsci, *Selections from the Prison Notebooks of Antonio Gramsci*, International Publishers, New York, 1971, p. 182.

that kind of class compromise required for continuing bourgeois hegemony.[61] Thus, the main purpose of the capitalist state is the continuing reproduction of capitalist social relationships in the political, economic and ideological fields. The capitalist state does things that "raise the great masses of the population to a particular cultural and moral level, a level which corresponds to the productive force for development,"[62] in such a way as to form favorable circumstances for class compromises for resolving capitalist contradictions, between the hegemonic bourgeoisie and the subordinate subaltern masses.

Through these resolutions, Gramsci regarded the capitalist state as "the organizer of consent" in the bourgeois hegemonic apparatus.[63] Thus, every institution that helps the state to arrange this consent, may be included in the Gramscian categorization of the state. Therefore, the Gramscian concept of the state may be stated as "state = political society + civil society."[64] Civil institutions such as the churches, schools, and the newspapers, all function to conform the morality and culture of the masses to the requirements of the capitalist economy.[65]

> Educative and formative role of the state. Its aim is always that of creating new and higher type of civilization, of adapting the 'civilization" and the morality of the broadest popular masses to the necessities of the continuous development of the economic apparatus of production; hence of evolving even physically new types of humanity.[66]

However, bourgeois hegemony cannot be maintained and reproduced by both active and voluntary consent arising from the subordinate masses, because, when the masses "do not 'consent' either actively or passively," the state apparatus of coercive power "legally" enforces discipline onto recalcitrant groups.[67] Bourgeois hegemony is forever "protected by the armor

---

[61] Anne Showstack Sassoon, 'Hegemony and Political Intervention', in Sally Hibbin, (ed.), *Politics, Ideology and the State*, London 1978, p. 31.

[62] Antonio Gramsci, *Selections from the Prison Notebooks of Antonio Gramsci*, International Publishers, New York, 1971, p. 258.

[63] Hyug Baeg Im, 'Hegemony and Counter-Hegemony in Gramsci', *Asian Perspective*, vol. 15, no. 1, 1991, pp. 123-156, p. 134.

[64] Antonio Gramsci, *Selections from the Prison Notebooks of Antonio Gramsci*, International Publishers, New York, 1971, p. 263.

[65] Developing Gramsci's thesis, Louis Althusser conceptualized 'ideological state apparatuses'; Louis Althusser, 'Ideology and Ideological State Apparatuses', in *Lenin and Philosophy and Other Essays*, New Left Books, London, 1977.

[66] Louis Althusser, 'Ideology and Ideological State Apparatuses', in *Lenin and Philosophy and Other Essays*, New Left Books, London, 1977, p. 242.

[67] ibid., p. 12.

of coercion."[68] Thus, provision for coercion is always inherent to, but latent within, hegemony. Coercion remains latent within hegemony, until popular consent is insufficient to reproduce capitalist relationships. Althusser deduced that, for Gramsci, "hegemony and dictatorship is indistinguishable, force and consent are simply equivalent,"[69] as the ultimate contradictions.

3. The King's Power

So far, argument has only covered the hegemony of the bourgeoisie. However the bourgeoisie is a middle class, with its monarchical ruling class theoretically removed since the onset of the French Revolution. Since the French Revolution, the British Crown has arguably behaved more as a constitutional monarchy, leaving all the rule-making to the bourgeoisie. Thus, argument ought to investigate critically what the crown had put in place.

3.1. Quo Warranto

The king had for many centuries the power to create and dismantle professions. In the 1846 case of *Darley v The Queen*,[70] its judges were summoned to the House of Lords to give their opinion on the nature of *quo warranto*, at a time before the House of Lords possessed a judicial arm. Tindal CJ stated to the House of Lords the general rule as to the proper defendant in proceedings in *quo warranto*, as follows.

> The procedure by *quo warranto* is appropriate wherever there has been a usurpation of any office, whether created by charter alone or by the Crown with the consent of Parliament; provided the office be of a public nature and a substantive office, not merely the function or employment of a deputy or servant held at the will and pleasure of others.[71]

---

[68] ibid., p. 263.
[69] ibid., p. 271; Hyug Baeg Im, 'Hegemony and Counter-Hegemony in Gramsci', *Asian Perspective*, vol. 15, no. 1, 1991, pp. 123-156, p. 135.
[70] 12 C L & F 541, 542.
[71] John Shortt, *Informations (Criminal and Quo Warranto) Mandamus and Prohibition*, The Blackstone Publishing Company, Philadelphia, 1888, p. 148.

Shortt collated the following list of gild officers, who had been held to be proper defendants in *quo warranto* proceedings, when the usurpation of office was inferred by improper performance in office. The list included the master of a city company, such as that of Merchant Taylors' Company, or the Coopers' Company, or the Patton Makers' Company. The list also included the master of the Company of Tailors at Lichfield, and, the assistant of the Saddlers' Company.[72] Any of these officers acting in derogation of the crown was therefore subject to a possible *quo warranto* judicial inquiry. In theory, this perceived threat could color the way these professional officials both structured their positions and executed their duties within their gilds. They would want to avoid an action in *quo warranto*.

The king maintained his positioning atop the goods manufacturing and mercantile hierarchies, control of the very means of production, by means of proceedings in *quo warranto*. In this way the king could construct his own hierarchies. He could specify who would occupy the positions of lords, who would owe fealty or exact homage[73] or own in socage,[74] from one to the other. In the same way, arguably the king could remove entire charters. After the Norman Conquest of 1066, manufactured goods were produced and sold by way of a power granted in a crown franchise. A franchise, created by royal charter, was always subject to the king's pleasure. No franchise could be relied upon as permanent.[75]

The king had an ancient power in respect of the forfeiture of the charters and franchises of a corporation aggregate.[76] By this power, he could seize

---

[72] ibid., pp. 150, 151.

[73] Coke described homage as follows. "Homage is the most honorable service, and most humble service of reverence, that a franktenant may do to his lord. For when the tenant shall make homage to his lord, he shall be ungirt, and his head uncovered, and his lord shall sit, and the tenant shall kneele before him, on both his knees, and hold his hands jointly together between the hands of his lord, and shall say thus: I become your man from this day forward of life and limbe, and of earthly worship, and unto you shall be true and faithfull, and beare to you faith for the tenements that I claim to hold of you, saving the faith that I owe unto our soveraigne lord the king; and then the lord so sitting shall kisse him." Eduardo Coke, *The First Part of the Institutes of the Laws of England or a Commentary upon Littleton*, J & W Clarke; Saunders & Benning; A. Maxwell; S. Sweet; H. Butterworth; Stevens & Sons; R. Pheney; and J. Richards, London, 1832, 64a.

[74] For definitions and discussion of these concepts, see Sir Thomas Littleton, *Littleton's Tenures in English*, John Byrne & Co, Washington, 1903.

[75] J Kidgell, *Power of the Kings of England to examine the charters of particular corporations and companies: exemplified by the statutes and laws of this realm*, John Kidgell Printer, London, 1684, p. 1.

[76] A corporation consisting of two or more persons.

franchises and liberties and examine charters.[77] This power was based on the doctrine that, when the King granted a franchise, there was an ancient condition in law that he should do right to all parties concerned, otherwise the franchise should be seized.[78] That condition in law derived from an ancient statement of the purpose of making corporations. In the time of William the Conqueror this had been implied as conditions into charters. It provided that corporations were erected for, first, the conservation of the dignities and pre-eminences of the crown and the laws of the land, second, for defense of the king's subjects and for keeping the king's peace in time of sudden uproars, and third, for defense of the realm against outward and inward hostility.[79]

The single exception to this statement of law appears to have been in the case of the City of London. The liberties of the City of London could not be taken into the king's hands, but continued both its own customs[80] and the ancient Roman Imperial Law.[81] Stolte reported, from a telephone interview that he conducted with Professor J. H. Baker on 21 October 1997, that a "custom" was a type of legal action heard by local or municipal courts as opposed to common law courts.[82] The common law courts frequently adopted the "customs" of prominent cities and counties such as London and incorporated them into the common law of the realm. Crown charters continued the ancient franchises and Customs of London. These crown charters were of gifts, grants and confirmations. Although these grants of continuation might still be forfeited if they were somehow abused or misused, the king could never act summarily in this way.[83] The reason was that crown summary action would be ineffective against any local customary law already established by prescription, and thus, the crown got around the power of

[77] J Kidgell, *Power of the Kings of England to examine the charters of particular corporations and companies: exemplified by the statutes and laws of this realm*, John Kidgell Printer, London, 1684, p. 1.

[78] ibid., p. 6, citing 20 E 4 fol 5, 6.

[79] ibid.

[80] Keith M Stolte, 'How Early Did Anglo-American Trademark Law Begin? An Answer to Schechter's Conundrum', *Trademark Reports*, vol. 88, 1998, pp. 564-606, p. 592n.

[81] J Kidgell, *Power of the Kings of England to examine the charters of particular corporations and companies: exemplified by the statutes and laws of this realm*, John Kidgell Printer, London, 1684, p. 9, citing Rot. Parl. I E. 3. Authoritate Parliament, Injt. Part 4. Fol. 253.

[82] Keith M Stolte, 'How Early Did Anglo-American Trademark Law Begin? An Answer to Schechter's Conundrum', *Trademark Reports*, vol. 88, 1998, pp. 564-606.

[83] J Kidgell, *Power of the Kings of England to examine the charters of particular corporations and companies: exemplified by the statutes and laws of this realm*, John Kidgell Printer, London, 1684, p. 9.

established custom by use of an administrative action in *quo warranto* against the Mayor and Commonalty and Citizens of the City.[84]

For example, during the reign of Edward I,[85] the franchise of returning members to parliament was conferred on many towns, most of which were incorporated. This franchise was executed by writ of a bailiff or other chief officer, which by this process gained a certain regal authority. The crown saw the need to strengthen its control over franchise holders. It devised and implemented the common law writ of *quo warranto*. By this writ, the judges were empowered to inquire by what warrant all who claimed any franchise, in derogation of the crown, maintained their title to this franchise.[86] This form of action assumed strictly that the claimant had wrongly claimed a franchise against the interests of the crown.[87]

In theory, *quo warranto* proceedings also could overturn any ranking system of officials. In this way, it could control the commercial activities of anyone inferior in title to that of the king. This included those producing goods for sale at the lower levels of commercial ranks. So in the statute 18 Edward I of 1290, entitled *Statutum De Quo Warranto Novum*, the king's position over the towns was considerably strengthened by making *quo warranto* more specific. It was enacted in the following terms.

> Concerning the writ that is called *quo warranto*, our lord the king at the feast of Pentecost, in the eighteenth year of his reign, hath established, that all those who claim to have quiet possession of any franchise before the time of king Richard, without interruption, and can show the same by lawful inquest, shall well enjoy their possession, and in case that such possession be demanded for cause reasonable, our lord the king shall confirm it by title. And those that have old charters of privileges shall have the same charters adjudged according to the tenor and form of them: And those that have lost their liberties since Easter last past by the aforesaid writ, according to the course of pleading in the same way writ heretofore used, shall have restitution of their franchise lost, and from henceforth they shall have according to the nature of this present constitution.[88]

---

[84] ibid.
[85] 1272-1307.
[86] JW Willcock, *The Law of Municipal Corporations, together with a brief sketch of their history, and a treatise on mandamus and quo warranto*, John S Little, Philadelphia, 1836, p. 4.
[87] ibid.
[88] 1 *Statutes of the Realm* 1235-1377, p. 107.

This statutory provision provided guidance for *quo warranto* proceedings. It allowed long-held claims to stand by confirmation of the king, it provided that old charters should be judged by their tenor and form, and it appeared to appease those who had more recently lost their franchises by restoring them with statutory force. The allowance of judging a charter by tenor and form apparently allowed the court more depth of examination, and suggested a presumption in favor of long-held office, suggesting a genesis of today's professions.

Proceedings in *quo warranto* commenced with the old common law writ were purely civil, and judgment against the defendant might include the remedy of the king seizing the franchise. The king could grant it out again, however he pleased.[89] This was presumably only for public purposes, using the king's ancient power of forfeiture of charters and franchises, as discussed above.

4. The City of London Legal System

4.1. Nature of the Jurisdiction of the Courts of the City of London

The City of London had its own ancient mercantile style of jurisdiction, and therefore had its own courts of law within the walls of the City of London. The Court of Hustings was the highest court of judicature in London, presided over by the mayor and sheriffs. This court had jurisdiction over all real and mixed actions except ejectment. It had jurisdiction in actions *in personam* only by appeal from the sheriff's court.[90] In matters of appeal, the Town Clerk could make out orders in prohibition, certiorari and procendendo.[91] This effectively gave the Hustings control over the action in replevin. In theory, replevin could remove goods into the hands of the plaintiff at the outset of an action for unlawful possession of goods.[92]

---

[89] John Shortt, *Informations (Criminal and Quo Warranto) Mandamus and Prohibition*, The Blackstone Publishing Company, Philadelphia, 1888, p. 138.

[90] Alexander Pulling, *The Laws, Customs, Usages and Regulations of the City and Port of London*, William Henry Bond and Wildy and Sons, London, 1854, p. 171.

[91] ibid., p. 173.

[92] The term "passed off" is used in this sense without the hyphen as a factual rather than legal circumstance.

Indicative of administrative reverse onus in property matters, the Court of Hustings maintained a register of all real and personal property in London.[93] Arguably, this allowed it full administrative and supervisory control of all property in London. In theory, title to property could be changed administratively, just by amending the property register.

Both the procedural[94] and the substantive law in London were arguably customary law in character. Pulling, speaking of the most ancient legal usages of London, stated that long before the court of chancery was established, the lord mayor's court, also called the court of aldermen, was a court of record of law and equity.[95] More relevantly, it had powers of the widest kind over property. The Recorder of the City of London was in fact the sole presiding judge. The Recorder's record of the oral customs of the court, rather than those of the community, became the authority for judging disputes.[96]

This London system appeared to have been widespread in other English jurisdictions. For example, all people, freemen and non-freemen could sue in the court of aldermen. Later, litigants resorted to the court of chancery while the court of aldermen fully retained its equitable jurisdiction.[97] If for some reason the defendant did not appear, or was found to be outside the jurisdiction of the court, the remedy of foreign attachment applied. By this remedy, the plaintiff could instantly attach any property or debts owing to the defendant from any person within the jurisdiction.[98] An action previously commenced in the superior courts, however, acted as a bar to the remedy of attachment in the mayor's court.[99] This customary mode of commencing an action also applied in other ancient English cities and towns such as Bristol, Exeter, Lancaster, as well as in Scotland and Jersey.[100]

Similarly, the court was seized of jurisdiction in the powerful remedy of sequestration. Suggesting how a creditor might out-rank an alleged debtor, if a debtor absconded leaving goods in a house or warehouse, a creditor could apply for the subject goods to be sequestered.[101] The remedies of foreign

---

[93] Alexander Pulling, *The Laws, Customs, Usages and Regulations of the City and Port of London*, William Henry Bond and Wildy and Sons, London, 1854, p. 176.

[94] Procedural rules of the court.

[95] Alexander Pulling, *The Laws, Customs, Usages and Regulations of the City and Port of London*, William Henry Bond and Wildy and Sons, London, 1854, p. 177.

[96] ibid.

[97] ibid., p. 181.

[98] ibid., p. 188.

[99] ibid., p. 192, citing 2 Show 374; 1 Rol Abr 552, g.

[100] Alexander Pulling, *The Laws, Customs, Usages and Regulations of the City and Port of London*, William Henry Bond and Wildy and Sons, London, 1854, p. 189.

[101] ibid., p. 192.

attachment and sequestration were arguably open to abuse. Hypothetically, a debtor could either be chased away, or kidnapped, or worse, so that his goods could be either attached or sequestered or both. In this way, title to his working capital and stock could be transferred out of the debtor's hands.

Actions commenced in London were unlikely to be appealed or removed to royal courts in Westminster. Suggesting a procedure for perpetual investigation, and therefore permanent and continuing reverse onus, an action in the lord mayor's court remained in force forever, just as in investigations within today's professions. This could be so, even without the commencement of formal proceedings. In this way, the Court exercised a supervisory jurisdiction. Such actions could be removed to a superior court at Westminster only by the prerogative actions of *habeas corpus* or *certiorari*, except where the action lay by the custom of London, in which case they could not be removed at all.[102]

Making removal to royal courts even more unlikely, the lord mayor's court was an appeal court, and in its equitable jurisdiction could stay all other kinds of action.[103] The lord mayor's power to stay actions was quite advantageous to many wealthy and privileged defendants. For example: in the sheriff's court, by ancient custom of London, a losing party might apply, at a time after verdict and before judgment, to have the matter "marked" by the lord mayor. This process was known as markment and allowed the mayor to bar the complaint and stay enforcement proceedings. The defendant entered into a mere recognizance[104] for double the amount of the verdict, rather than suffering a damaging judgment.[105]

4.2. The City of London Control over the Economy

This section investigates how the City of London might have used both its County Palatine form[106] over the weaker status of chartered cities, and its strict

---

102 ibid., p. 193.

103 ibid., p. 198.

104 Recognizance. A bond by which a person undertakes before a court or magistrate to observe some condition, especially to appear when summoned. *Oxford English Dictionary*, Clarendon Press, 2nd edn., Oxford, 1989.

105 Alexander Pulling, *The Laws, Customs, Usages and Regulations of the City and Port of London*, William Henry Bond and Wildy and Sons, London, 1854, p. 203.

106 A County Palatine was one ruled by a petty sovereign who was not bound by the English Acts of Parliament and which held its own parliament, and civil and criminal courts. *Remains*

control over the gilds, as the forerunners to today's professions, to make the influence of its oral customary laws spread in England.

Royal Charter[107] declared the following ancient custom of London. "The mayor and aldermen for the time being ought to record all their ancient customs by word of mouth as often as anything should be moved in act or question before any judges or justices touching their customs."[108] An official holding the office and title of Recorder performed this recording process.[109] The records of the Recorder were subject to being proved in Court, by the evidential procedure of judicial notice, with only the Recorder himself appearing at the bar of the Court.[110]

Royal charters set up many counties and cities. London was the most significant exception to this rule, with law by ancient prescription being more powerful than royal charter. Charters were a species of letters patent from the crown. They conferred franchises and made regulations for local governments, such as the constitutional arrangements allowed the crown to grant.[111] However, the main formal difference between charters and letters patent was that, while the letter patent usually bore a simple *teste meipso*,[112] the charter declared itself to have been delivered by the king or by his chancellor. This was in the presence of many witnesses whose names were given within it. The charter was attended upon by a public gathering for the announcement and was emblematic of the king's will.[113] Arguably, this kind of will of the king was a public good.

Charters set up the constitutions of civic gilds or companies. Arguably, charters were based on accepted practice based on long-standing custom. Charters regulated the proceedings of local courts, and conferred upon the corporations their own power to administer justice, the privileges of holding

---

Historical and Literary Connected with the palatine Counties of Lancaster and Chester, Volume XXXVII, Chetham Society, Manchester, 1856, p. 3.

[107] Charter of Edward IV of 9th November 1463.

[108] Alexander Pulling, *The Laws, Customs, Usages and Regulations of the City and Port of London*, William Henry Bond and Wildy and Sons, London, 1854, p. 4.

[109] ibid.

[110] Year Book, 21 Edw IV 74, 78; 22 Edw IV 30; Co Litt 74; 2 Inst 126; 2 Roll Aor 579; Cro Car 516; *Player v Hutchins*, O Brid Com Dig *Exoins*, D.

[111] Alexander Pulling, *The Laws, Customs, Usages and Regulations of the City and Port of London*, William Henry Bond and Wildy and Sons, London, 1854, p. 9.

[112] Medieval Latin *teste meipso* (or *seipso*), by my (or his) own witness, indicating the witnessing or concluding clause of an instrument. James Morwood (ed.), *The Oxford Latin Mini Dictionary*, Oxford University Press, Oxford, 1995.

[113] FW Maitland, 'History from the Charter Roll', *The English Historical Review*, vol. 8, no. 32, 1893, pp. 726-733, p. 726.

markets, collecting tolls, fines, and forfeitures.[114] The London trading companies had charters of their own. These defined their powers over their members and their trade.[115] This suggested that the power of commerce was divided between the City and County corporations at the higher level of prestige as constituters of markets, and the companies or gilds at a lower level of prestige as regulators of their own members.

The City of London had no gild-like form of charter of establishment. Its royal charters were confined to a mere continuing of its ancient system of government, recognized under the ancient Roman Imperial law. Its customary laws were not subject to desuetude, so that when the king's force to the contrary was removed, the ancient prescriptions automatically returned to operation.[116] Arguably, the king had to struggle to prevail in the City of London.

4.3. Freedom of the City

Freedom of the city was the administrative procedure that controlled hierarchies in the workplace. Any breach of it was dealt with without the requirement for proof of *mens rea*. It was equivalent to immigration status conferred on those people who had been either foreigners or strangers to the City. It created subservient ranks of master craftsmen, lawful journeymen and apprentices. This micro-hierarchy was subservient to the City and County, which in turn, was subservient to the king. The freedom system allowed those higher up in the hierarchy to take action against those of lower rank for misrepresenting their rank.

The freedom of the city was the device by which the right to make a professional level of living was enforced. Without it, the worker reverted to the ancient form of slavery. From early Saxon times, membership in the gilds depended on full citizenship. However, the exclusion of strangers could not be explained by any political activist tendency by the crafts. Non-citizens, whether they were aliens or mere strangers, occupied a precarious position in medieval England. On their arrival in town, they were required to lodge in the house of one of the burgesses assigned to them as host, and who would be

114 Alexander Pulling, *The Laws, Customs, Usages and Regulations of the City and Port of London*, William Henry Bond and Wildy and Sons, London, 1854, p. 10.

115 ibid.

116 Alexander Pulling, *The Laws, Customs, Usages and Regulations of the City and Port of London*, William Henry Bond and Wildy and Sons, London, 1854, p. 13.

responsible for their good behavior. The burgess answered for the stranger and this situated the stranger in a lowly hierarchical position. The period of the stranger's sojourn was often limited by the immigration laws of the day to forty days. They were allowed to trade only with citizens or members of the applicable merchant gild.[117] At the trade fairs, strangers were subject to separate tribunals, such as the piepowder courts. In all cases, heavy fines were imposed.[118]

A court of Piepowders was a special court in England arranged by a borough for a fair or market. This court's jurisdiction was for events taking place in the market, including disputes between merchants, theft, and acts of violence. Punishments typically included fines and the possibility of being held in a pillory or being drawn in a tumbrel in order to humiliate the offender. The court of Piepowder had its own position within the system of the common law. *Doctor and Student* situated the Court of Piepowder within the legal system, by noting that common law marketplace issues of a pre-statutory nature could be dealt with in courts of Piepowder.[119]

Seligman noted that the distinction between freeman and foreigner was strongly accentuated in the general law. It was also accentuated in all the city

---

[117] Edwin RA Seligman, 'Two Chapters on the Mediaeval Guilds of England', *Publications of the American Economic Association*, vol. 2, no. 5, 1887, pp. 9-113, pp. 69, 70.

[118] ibid.

[119] The Common law is taken three manner of ways. First, it is taken as the law of this realm of England, dissevered from all other laws. And under this manner taken it is oftentimes argued in the laws of England, what matters ought of right to be determined by the Common law, and what by the admiral's court, or by the spiritual court: and also if an obligation bear date out of the realm, as in Spain, France, or such other, it is said in the law, and truth it is, that they be not pleadable at the Common law. Secondly, the Common law is taken as the king's courts, of his Bench, or of the Common Place: and it is so taken when a plea is removed out of ancient demesne, for that the land is frank-fee, and pleadable at the Common law, that is to say, in the king's court, and not in ancient demesne. And under this manner taken, it is oftentimes pleaded also in base courts, as in Courts-Barons, the County, and the court of Piepowders, and such other, this matter or that, etc., ought not to be determined in that court, but at the Common law, that is to say, in the king's courts, etc. Thirdly, by the Common law is understood such things as were law before statute made in that point that is in question; so that that point was holden for law by the general or particular customs and maxims of the realm, or by the law of reason, and the law of God, no other law added to them by statute, nor otherwise, as is the case before rehearsed in the first chapter, where it is said, that at the Common law, tenant by the courtesy and tenant in dower were punishable of waste, that is to say, that, before any statute of waste made, they were punishable of waste by the grounds and maxims of the law used before the statute made in that point. But tenant for term of life, ne for term of years, were not punishable by the said grounds and maxims, till by the statute remedy was given against them; and therefore it is said, that at the Common law they were not punishable of waste. William Muchall (ed.), *Doctor and Student*, James Moore, 18th edn., London, 1792, dialog 2, chapter 2.

regulations, such as those of Worcester, Bristol, Winchester, Ipswich, and the Cinque Ports.[120] He stated that the exclusion of non-freemen from the crafts was not so much the result of any independent action of the gilds, but was a principle of the early common law.[121]

Freedom was arguably a specious term. It did not really mean that the person was free. The meaning of this kind of freedom was far from today's meaning of the absence of necessity, coercion, or constraint in choice or action. From ancient times, freedom of the city of London could be acquired only by one of the original three pathways of patrimony, apprenticeship, or by redemption from the court of aldermen.[122] Pulling wrote that from ancient Saxon times the power of conferring the freedom of the city was independent of the crown.[123] People not free of the city were designated as foreigners or strangers, in accordance with the ancient law of Rome.[124]

The freedom of the City of London was essential for commercial activity and functioned as follows. Only city freemen could vote in Parliamentary elections, vote in civic elections for councilmen and alderman, be exempt from all tolls payable on animals brought into the City for sale, be exempt from all market tolls payable anywhere in the country, be exempt from naval conscription, and enjoy the right to claim freedom from prosecution except in the city's courts.[125]

Up to 1835, every person who wished to become a city freeman first had to become a freeman of one of the City livery companies. These were mercantile successors to the medieval trade and craft gilds. The freedom of a livery company was merely an ordinary membership. A person wishing to become a senior member of a livery company had to be first a freeman both of that company and of the City of London. A person who was a freeman of both the City and a livery company was named, referred to, and thus identified as "Citizen and [Livery Company name] of London."[126]

Freedom by servitude was when a person had to complete an apprenticeship of at least 7 years' duration to a City freeman. Freedom by

---

120 Edwin RA Seligman, 'Two Chapters on the Mediaeval Guilds of England', *Publications of the American Economic Association*, vol. 2, no. 5, 1887, pp. 9-113, pp. 69, 70.

121 ibid.

122 2 Brownlow 286; 4 Inst 250; 2 and 276-7; 2 Bulstr 189-190; 3 Keb 225; 8 Co 112 b; 4 Mod 145.

123 Alexander Pulling, *The Laws, Customs, Usages and Regulations of the City and Port of London*, William Henry Bond and Wildy and Sons, London, 1854, p. 59.

124 Cicero, *De Offi* 1, 12.

125 Vivienne Aldous, *Research Guide 1: City Freedom Archives*, Corporation of London Records Office, London, 1999.

126 ibid.

patrimony was open only to the legitimate and natural children of a male freeman who were born after their parent's own freedom admission. Redemption, or purchase, was obtainable by "presentation" by a corporation officer or other person who had been granted the right of presenting a limited number of candidates in lieu of salary or as a reward for services. The intending freeman usually had to pay the officer for presenting him.[127]

Livery was an underlying customary norm to public representation of professional commercial rank. A public breach of this customary arrangement was arguably a misrepresentation of fact, which would have been complete without *mens rea*. With these customs, those with the freedom of the city were represented publicly first by their livery. This meant their special uniform as worn by a servant, an official, or a member of a City company. People could have an honorary freedom acclaimed by the citizenry as a public act, a completed apprenticeship of 7 years, by lawfully recognized patrimony, or by paying an official essentially for recognition. In fact, to be admitted on the livery of a company was technically called 'having the clothing'.[128]

Breaching the freedom of the city by non-freemen, or arguably passing oneself off as a freeman, was discussed in the following case. In this case, the defendants' pleadings were the sole basis for judgment, suggesting the reverse onus system of an administrative hearing.

> 31 Aug. 1306. Wednesday after the Feast of the Decollation of St John the Baptist [29 Aug.] before John de Wengrave, deputy of the Mayor. John de Coppedok, Geoffrey Giffard, John Brid, John de Rodbourne, and Hamo atte Barre, poulterers, were attached to answer the Commonalty, for buying poultry within the City to sell it outside, as though they were freemen, thus producing a scarcity of poultry to the damage of the citizens. The defendants pleaded that they bought poultry in the markets of Kyngeston, Berkingg, St Albans and other places far and near, paying custom there, and brought it to the City and sold it there to the profit of the City, and that they paid the bailiffs murage and other customs; and they demanded a jury. Afterwards John de Redbourne (*sic*) and Hamo atte Barre paid a fine to the Commonalty to have the freedom, and went quit. A jury of John Burel and others gave a verdict in accordance with the defendants' pleading. They were mainprised by John de Sabrichesworth, John atte Barre, John Burel and Roger Prior, poulterers, to hear judgment on Saturday. Afterwards the defendants made

[127] ibid.

[128] William Herbert, *The History of the Twelve Great Livery Companies, Vol I*, William Herbert, London, 1887, p. 60.

> satisfaction to the Commonalty and were admitted and sworn to the freedom of the City.[129]

The most significant privileges for the citizen with freedom of the city were two. Freemen enjoyed freedom from tolls throughout the realm, whenever they travelled outside their home city. There was also the freeman's right to claim freedom from prosecution, except in the city's courts. As this freedom was gained either by public honour, heredity, apprenticeship or redemption, admission to these privileges was a means by which the city could exercise control over the flow of trade immigrants. In order to formalize this control into an administrative methodology, the City needed a system of registration. It therefore turned to the misteries[130] for administrative support, because only they had control over their own membership registries.[131]

The freedom of the city was designed to identify foreigners and apprentices as prospective economic threats to both the master craftsmen and the taxation system. The meaning of this freedom within the administrative structure was suggested in the earliest surviving City of London Ordinance as to the freedom of London, dated circa 1230, as follows. It maintained the anti-vagrant policy devised and enacted under King Athelstan,[132] apparently to deal with conflicts arising from the presence of unauthorized people. Under this rule, people were prohibited from traveling unless there was a Lord to answer for them.

> Because many persons of the City traveling throughout England claim to belong to the liberty of London, whereby disputes and tumults arise, in order that it may be known whom of the City to defend as freemen, it is provided that no foreigner nor any apprentice departing from his lord shall enjoy the liberties of the City, nor sell retail in the City, unless they are found to have been enrolled. . . . because by the taking of apprentices many contentions and discords arise owing to the ambiguity of their covenants, and in order that such ambiguities may henceforth be removed, it is provided that no one receive an apprentice unless they cause the covenant to be enrolled . . .[133]

---

129 *Calendar of Early Mayor's Court Rolls: 1298-1307, Calendar Roll H 12 December 1305 - 12 November 1306* (1924), 228 - 252.

130 Also known as gilds, guilds, companies.

131 AF Sutton, 'The Silent Years of London Guild History before 1300: the Case of the Mercers', *Historical Research*, vol. 81, no. 175, 1998, pp. 121-141, p. 137.

132 Carl Stephenson, 'The Anglo-Saxon Borough', *The English Historical Review*, vol. 45, no. 178, 1930, pp. 177-207, pp. 198, 199.

133 Corporation of London Records Office, *Liber Ordinacionum* fo 173 For other suits prosecuted in 1299 by the clerks of the chamber on behalf of the commonalty of the city against those

Only masters with the freedom of the City could take on apprentices. Apprentices had to be sworn and enrolled as freemen before they could practice their craft as masters. Otherwise they would have to continue as a servant/employee to a master. Both master and apprentice were bound together by a private contract. Either the Chamberlain of the City or the mayor's court would enforce this contract. They could either specifically enforce it, or annul it. Thus, the outward representational sign of this gild power to identify and control members was the bestowing of a communal cognizance and livery.[134]

Freedom of the City was enforced by the terms of an oath. On 10 December 1830, the common council settled an amended form of the oath to be sworn upon being admitted to the freedom of the city of London. The oath was amended to accommodate contemporary variations in religious principles. Thus, any natural born subject became admitted to the freedom automatically at that date.[135] Otherwise, the oath wordage remained unchanged since former and ancient times. The oath was worded as follows.

> Ye shall swear that ye shall be good and true to our Sovereign Lady Queen Victoria; obeysant and obedient ye shall be to the mayor and ministers of this city; the franchises and customs thereof ye shall maintain, and the city keep harmless in that in you is. Ye shall be contributing to all manner of charges within this city, as summons, watches, contributions, taxes, talliages, lot and scot, and to all other charges, bearing your part as a freeman ought to do. Ye shall colour no foreigner's goods under or in your name, whereby the Queen or this city might or may lose their customs or advantages. Ye shall take none apprentices for any less term than for seven years, without fraud or deceit, and within the first year ye shall cause him to be enrolled, or else pay such fine as shall reasonably be imposed upon you for omitting the same; and after

---

who infringed the freedom, in the courts of the chamberlain and the mayor, see Arthur Hermann Thomas, *Calendar of Early Mayor's Court Rolls, City of London (England) Lord Mayor's Court, City of London (England) Court of Common Council*, The University Press, London, 1924.

[134] AF Sutton, 'The Silent Years of London Guild History before 1300: the Case of the Mercers', *Historical Research*, vol. 81, no. 175, 1998, pp. 121-141; Cognizance and Livery. In Heraldry. a device by which a person or a person's servants or property can be recognized, such as by a badge or uniform; a special uniform worn by a servant, an official, or a member of a City Company. The original sense was 'the dispensing of food, provisions, or clothing to servants', and the sense of a special uniform arose because medieval nobles provided matching clothes to distinguish their own servants from those of others. *Oxford English Dictionary*, Clarendon Press, 2nd edn., Oxford, 1989.

[135] Alexander Pulling, *The Laws, Customs, Usages and Regulations of the City and Port of London*, William Henry Bond and Wildy and Sons, London, 1854, p. 61.

> the term's end, within convenient time (being required) ye shall make him free of this city, if he have well and truly served you. Ye shall also keep the Queen's peace in your own person. Ye shall know no gatherings, conventicles, nor conspiracies made against the Queen's peace, but ye shall warn the mayor thereof, or let it to your power. All these points and articles ye shall well and truly keep, according to the laws and customs of the city, to your power.[136]

The newly amended wordage of the oath contained the following key requirements. The first was a duty to carry out unspecified charges using language of the common good. The second prohibited the use of the freeman's name on the goods of a foreigner or stranger. The third conferred responsibility on the freeman for keeping the queen's peace and reporting any breaches to the mayor. The fourth ensured no freedoms to apprentices. The fifth required apprentices to be registered, forced to serve seven years, and, given freedom only if they well and truly served.

5. The Relationship between Commerce, the Economy and the Gilds

5.1. Gild Formation

'Gild', 'guild', 'mistery', 'company': all refer to the same concept in its historical development. The meaning of the word *gild* has passed through several phases.[137] First, it originally meant the sacrificial meal convened out of the common contributions. Later, it meant a sacrificial banquet in general, and lastly it came to mean a society. It was a socially cohesive force for its members.[138]

Traces of old gilds were also found around the English countryside, importing a certain system of customary servitude. One was said to have existed in Winchester in 856 C.E., and although nothing was told about its

---

[136] ibid., pp. 61, 62.

[137] The word itself, less commonly, but more correctly, written *gild*, was derived from the Anglo-Saxon *gildan* meaning "to pay," whence came the noun *gegilda*, "the subscribing member of a gild." In its origin the word *guild* is found in the sense of "idol" and also of "sacrifice," which has led some writers to connect the origin of the gilds with the sacrificial assemblies and banquets of the heathen Germanic tribes. E Burton, The Catholic Encyclopedia, *Guilds*, Robert Appleton Company, 1910.

[138] Toulmin Smith (ed.), *English Gilds*, Oxford University Press, Oxford, 1870, p. xviii.

nature, it was probably the same as the Cnighten-gild mentioned in Domesday. Similarly, there were several other Cnighten-gilds at Canterbury, London, and Nottingham.[139] However, Seligman suggested it might have been preserved in the Tenure by Knights Service, as explained in Littleton's Tenures. Littleton explained that tenure by homage, fealty and *escuage*, which were of heraldic origin indicating a right to form military structures, were all forms of holding title by knight's service. The obligations of Knight's service included strict control over the tenant's marital rights, inheritance and the holding of property by the lord before the age of becoming *sui juris*. It was uncertain what these Cnighten or Knights were. However, it may be inferred that this kind of service, signified by its heraldic art, was part of the military structure of the realm. The word "Cnighten" originally had the meaning of a servant, and frequently occurred in the sense of a subordinate member of a nobleman's retinue. It was apparently used in this sense in the gild statutes of Exeter and Cambridge, where the Knight contributed less money than the full member, and where his lord was responsible if he were to draw a weapon or wound another. The Knights' rank and importance, however, increased until at the Conquest they became the equals of the Thanes, or nobles.[140]

Gilds began as groups for crown policing of some unlawful activities. Gross noted that King Athelstan's gilds were units for the social control of property.[141] This was done by classifying men either as riders or workers, and governing them by a church style of organization, inside the gilds, and by military style of organization in the field. Under Athelstan there were statutes of a fully developed frithguild recorded in the *Judicia Civitatis Londoniae*.[142] This was a combination of associations of one hundred men, subdivided into smaller groups of ten, subject to common rules, but otherwise independent of each other.[143] In the time of King Athelstan, the gilds had already developed their own very rudimentary system of justice against theft, administered by both the reeve and the bishop. The *Judicia Civitatis Londoniae*,[144] provided as follows. "This is the ordinance which the bishops and reeves who belong to

---

139 Sir Thomas Littleton, *Littleton's Tenures in English*, John Byrne & Co, Washington, 1903, pp. 39-111.

140 Edwin RA Seligman, 'Two Chapters on the Mediaeval Guilds of England', *Publications of the American Economic Association*, vol. 2, no. 5, 1887, pp. 9-113, pp. 15, 16.

141 *Athelstan was the first king of all England, and Alfred the Great's grandson. He reigned between 925 and 939.*

142 Charles Gross, *The Guild Merchant, Vol I*, The Clarendon Press, Oxford, 1890, p. 178.

143 Edwin RA Seligman, 'Two Chapters on the Mediaeval Guilds of England', *Publications of the American Economic Association*, vol. 2, no. 5, 1887, pp. 9-113, pp. 13, 14.

144 A collection of laws made in the time of King Athelstan. Charles Gross, *The Guild Merchant, Vol I*, The Clarendon Press, Oxford, 1890.

London borough have agreed upon." After repeating Athelstan's recent enactments concerning cattle thieves, the ordinance proceeded to describe the protective association, called the frithgild, formed to help in enforcing the enactments. Offenders were to be rigorously pursued. No pursuit was to be abandoned on either side of the Thames River, before every gildsman with a horse had ridden out. The man who owned no horse was to keep at work until his lord returned. If any group members were to protect a thief and prove strong enough to defy the gild, then the presiding reeve was to call out the gild's full strength and send for aid from the reeves on both adjoining sides. When a trail was followed from one such district into another, the fullest co-operation of the reeves concerned was mandatory. In this way, people were classified as either "men with horses" or "men as workers."[145]

Thus, the ordinance was that one either protected property or tended to it. The only forms of property that were likely to be stolen, and for which compensation could be claimed, were horses, oxen, cows, pigs, sheep, and slaves.[146] King Athelstan's most important enactment controlled individuals who wandered around the country, without either property or a lord to answer for them. These wanderers were a form of property, to be held by inference by relevant Lords. Two indicia of servitude together defined the qualifications for being a member of the state. They were property and status within an overlord system of rank. The close relatives of the wandering vagrants were commanded to place their wandering relatives under a lord, who, were they to be accused, should present them for justice.[147]

Sutton stated that the 1200s were a pivotal period in the work-life of London. It was a century, which saw the growth of restrictive regulations by towns. It was a period witnessing the rise of closed shops and closed towns as privileges were gathered, written down and arrayed against competitors. Craft[148] gilds, such as for example the Weavers, coalesced as groupings of powerful craftsmen in English towns, from the early twelfth century.[149] These

---

145 Charles Gross, *The Guild Merchant, Vol I*, The Clarendon Press, Oxford, 1890.

146 Carl Stephenson, 'The Anglo-Saxon Borough', *The English Historical Review*, vol. 45, no. 178, 1930, pp. 177-207, pp. 198, 199.

147 ibid.

148 The word 'craft' is related to the Latin *astus*, meaning astute or good at making shrewd judgments. James Morwood (ed.), *The Oxford Latin Mini Dictionary*, Oxford University Press, Oxford, 1995.

149 AF Sutton, 'The Silent Years of London Guild History before 1300: the Case of the Mercers', *Historical Research*, vol. 81, no. 175, 1998, pp. 121-141, p. 126.

craft gilds were called *mestier, métier, ministerium,*[150] and from this, derived the English 'mistery', or 'mystery', simply meaning a handicraft or trade.[151]

Eventually, the gild system fractured into mercantile gilds and artisan gilds, the former with a higher commercial rank, or professional status, than that of the latter. Immediately prior to 1266, there appeared to be an economic transition where the classes of the poor coalesced with the classes of the craftsmen. The poor were excluded originally from merchant gild association for their lack of any property possession.[152] This transition gave birth to a gild statute creating merchant gilds for the first time, merely by excluding practicing craftsmen coming from the artisan gilds. It provided that no person "with dirty hands or with blue nails,"[153] or who hawked his wares in the streets, such as did peddlers, could become a member of the gild, and that craftsmen must have foresworn their trade for at least a year before being admitted to the gild.[154] This suggested a tendency to populate these new mercantile gilds with those of higher status, rather than with artisans or salesmen of lower status. It suggested that artisans, in comparison with mercantile gild members, were limited in their ability to trade in their own name.

Toulmin-Smith illustrated this development with the instance of the Gild of Berwick. He reasoned inductively that they were representative of a national social movement.[155] The Gild of Berwick was a merchant gild, where its members only traded, rather than worked, in wool or hides. Formerly this trade was undoubtedly carried on with that of the butchers. After craftsmen had been excluded from the gilds, butchers working outside the purview of this gild were forbidden to carry on the trade practiced by current gild members.[156] This was enacted into Article 25 of the Statutes of Berwick. The article said "No butcher, while he follows that calling, shall buy wool or hides."[157] This meant that no butcher, while carrying on his trade of cutting

---

[150] From the Latin, meaning 'service'. James Morwood (ed.), *The Oxford Latin Mini Dictionary*, Oxford University Press, Oxford, 1995.

[151] AF Sutton, 'The Silent Years of London Guild History before 1300: the Case of the Mercers', *Historical Research*, vol. 81, no. 175, 1998, pp. 121-141, p. 126.

[152] Toulmin Smith (ed.), *English Gilds*, Oxford University Press, Oxford, 1870, p. cvii.

[153] The suggestion is that a person with dirty hands or with blue fingernails would have been a craftsman, rather than a merchant, and was so identified for purposes of exclusion of gild membership.

[154] Toulmin Smith (ed.), *English Gilds*, Oxford University Press, Oxford, 1870, p. cvii.

[155] ibid., p. 343.

[156] ibid., p. cviii.

[157] ibid., p. 343.

and preparing meat, was allowed to deal in wool or hides unless he gave up cutting and preparing meat.[158]

However, every artisan was permitted to carry on his trade provided he joined and submitted himself to the regulation of the relevant craft gild, but not a mercantile gild. The principal publicly stated purposes of craft gild rules were to secure sound quality work, to act as a police authority on behalf of the public, and as well, to secure the welfare of the members. Admission to a trade was via a long apprenticeship, typically of some seven years in duration. Admission of an apprentice was a public event of a contractual nature. It was held in the Guildhall and presided over by the Chamberlain of the City. They instructed the apprentice in his solemn moral and trade duties, and then publicly executed the indentures of apprenticeship.[159]

5.2. Gild Ordinance Structure

Toulmin-Smith indicated that the available records of the Gild of Tailors of Exeter gave an instructive example of the character, workings, and usefulness of a middle-ages craft gild in England.[160] This gild was erected by the Charter of Edward IV,[161] in which the king commanded that gild members were to wear livery,[162] hold feasts, make ordinances, be a body corporate and have a common seal. The charter also commanded that the master and wardens were to have control over tailors and others of the gild.[163] This suggested the creation of ever-tightening rules for the control of manufacture of goods.

Significant ordinances of this gild were set out as follows. The indenture of each apprentice had to be enrolled in a gild registry within 12 months, or else the master could lose his freedom permanently.[164] The registry was an effective means for controlling the apprentices and their work. Newly created freemen were limited in how many servants they could have.[165] Arguably,

[158] ibid., p. cvii.
[159] ibid., p. cxxix.
[160] ibid., p. 299.
[161] Reigned 1461-1483.
[162] A form of uniform, whose colours and style were unique to each guild. Note the signifying effect of uniform as similar in effect to that of a seal, heraldic shield or trademark. *Oxford English Dictionary*, Clarendon Press, Oxford, 2nd edn., 1989.
[163] Toulmin Smith (ed.), *English Gilds*, Oxford University Press, Oxford, 1870, p. 301.
[164] ibid., p. 316.
[165] ibid.

their capacity for production, and competition with senior masters, was limited by this provision.

Each craftsman tailor had to swear an oath to the fraternity. Perhaps, this oath illustrated the nature of gild covenants among the fraternity. Each element of the oath dealt with a proscribed act. The most significant elements of the oath were as follows.

> To be true to the fraternity;[166] To obey the master and wardens, disobedience to authority suggesting insubordination;[167] Not to disclose the affairs of the craft, suggesting a prohibition against making public the secrets of the craft;[168] Not to counsel or to encourage any foreigner either to dwell within the franchises or to use the craft;[169] To show the indentures of the apprentices and to bring them in at the end of their terms;[170] Not to hire or entice any worker or apprentice away;[171] Not to take a shop until admitted as a freeman;[172] Not to entice customers away, by any means, from the master of from any brother;[173] Not to leave the gild, but to uphold it according to the brother's estate;[174] Not to sue any brother of the craft without license from the master.[175]

It is of note in these rules that failure to obey an authority suggested an act of insubordination. Toulmin Smith recorded that in the event of disputes among members of a gild, it was a requirement that gild-brothers had to bring their case before the gild court of the master and wardens for settlement, before considering a court of law. This was in order to attempt reconciliation before the matter went further. However, the gild only dealt with such matters by way of compensation, fines and expulsion, as it had never assumed either a right of members' life and limb, or a judicial role.[176]

---

166 ibid.
167 ibid., p. 317.
168 ibid.
169 ibid.
170 ibid.
171 ibid.
172 ibid.
173 ibid., pp. 8, 317.
174 Toulmin Smith (ed.), *English Gilds*, Oxford University Press, Oxford, 1870, p. 317.
175 ibid.
176 ibid., p. ciii.

5.3. Collapse of Gild Independence

One version of the Evil May-day riot[177] commences with an account by a chronicler named Edward Hall. Hall noted that anti-alien sentiments had been mounting in the capital, London, for some time. In early April of 1517, a peddler[178] named John Lincoln convinced a minister of religion, called Dr. Bell, to introduce his sermon at St Paul's Cross on Easter Tuesday with an exhortation stated in the following terms. "Englishmen to cherish and defend themselves, and to hurt and grieve aliens for the common weal."[179] Dr. Bell read the complaint to a crowd in the following terms.

> To all you, the Worshipful Lords and Masters of this City, that will take compassion on the poor people, your neighbors; as also, of the great and insufferable hurts, losses, and hindrances, whereof proceedeth the extreme poverty to all the Kings Subjects that inhabit within this City and the suburbs thereof; for so it is, that the Aliens and Strangers eat the bread from the fatherless children, and take the living from the artificers, and the intercourse from all merchants, whereby poverty is so increased, that everyone bewaileth the misery of the other; for crafts-men be brought to beggary, and merchants to neediness; wherefore the premises considered, the redress must be of the Commons, knit and united to one part; and as the hurt and damages grieveth all men, that they set their willing power for the remedy, and not suffer the Aliens so highly in their wealth, and the natural born men of this kingdom to come to poverty.[180]

Scattered attacks were mounted against aliens over the ensuing two weeks, and there were rumors that, on the very next May Day, a so-called spontaneous riot was expected to erupt. Aware of these rumors of impending riot, the aldermen imposed a 9.00 pm curfew on the eve of the expected riot. They did not announce the curfew until 8.30 pm. One hour before the curfew was to commence, one alderman John Mundy had a street altercation with a youth. This altercation precipitated a riot of about 1000 apprentices, in the

177 Steve Rappaport, *Worlds Within Worlds: Structures of Life in Sixteenth-Century London*, Cambridge University Press, Cambridge, 1989, pp. 15, 16.

178 Note the relationship between mercers and peddlers and the fact that peddlers were likely not subject to gild control.

179 Steve Rappaport, *Worlds Within Worlds: Structures of Life in Sixteenth-Century London*, Cambridge University Press, Cambridge, 1989, p. 15.

180 *Forfeitures of Londons Charter or an impartial account of the several Seisures of the City Charter*, Daniel Brown at the Black Swan and Bible without Temple Bar and Thomas Benskin in St Brides Church Yard, London, 1682.

ensuing 2 hours. The rioting apprentices descended upon the wealthy neighborhood of St Martin le Grand, where many aliens lived, within the walls, near St Paul's Cathedral.[181]

The under-sheriff of London met them. He had almost succeeded in convincing them to return to their homes when the residents of St Martin le Grand began to throw stones at them. Residents poured hot water on them from their windows. An official was apparently wounded, at which he yelled 'down with them'.[182] This unleashed the mob on the alien community of St Martin le Grand. Three hundred people were arrested. The king later pardoned most of them. However, 13 rioters, including John Lincoln, were convicted of treason and were executed. The king hanged several aristocrats, and as well, gave supervisors the power to give orders to workers, for the first time expanding the bourgeoisie by creating a new class of managers.[183]

Resolving the conflicts of Evil May Day did little to resolve the underlying cause of attacks on London's aliens. In April of 1518, the Merchant Taylors complained to the Common Council of London that strangers, who were licensed to work as only menders of clothing, were making clothes. The complaint was drafted in the following terms.

> A great multitude of strangers and aliens born out of this realm, not being freemen of this city, daily resort, multiply, increase and inhabit within this city and liberties thereof and in the same presume to work and do work in houses, chambers, alleys and in other places, as well secret as open . . . in the name of botchers, which is only to amend old apparel and garments; by colour whereof they work and make new apparel to the great loss, hurt and damage of the freemen of the handicraft or mystery of Merchant Taylors.[184]

The result came in 1523 through an Act of Parliament stopping all strangers from hiring, as an apprentice, any person not born in England. It placed further limits on the hiring of non-English born journeymen. For the companies of London, the third section of the Act was the most significant, because it gave them direct control of all strangers living in the city. It was drafted in the following terms.[185]

---

[181] Steve Rappaport, *Worlds Within Worlds: Structures of Life in Sixteenth-Century London*, Cambridge University Press, Cambridge, 1989, p. 16.
[182] ibid.
[183] ibid.
[184] ibid., p. 43.
[185] ibid., p. 45.

> All manners of persons being aliens born using any manner of handicraft, be they denizens or not denizens, and inhabited within the city of London or suburbs of the same . . . or within two miles compass . . . shall be under the search and reformation of the [companies'] wardens . . . with one substantial stranger being a householder of the same craft by the same wardens to be chosen.[186]

In this way, the companies were given operational crown authority to regulate the economic activities of all Londoners practicing crafts and trades within a radius of two miles of the city. The wardens were given full power and authority to search, view and reform all kinds of wares and workmanship made by alien-born handicraftsmen.

In 1529, the crown intervened again, with an action in Star Chamber by a group of craftsmen. King Henry VIII's Lord Chancellor, Cardinal Wolsey, instigated the action. He charged a group of Flemings with violations of the Act of 1523. The outcome was a decree against the Flemings and a new Act of Parliament in the following year. This Act provided that no stranger, artificer, or handicraftsman should set up or keep any house, shop, shops, or chamber in England, in which they would exercise any handicraft. They were exempt from this if they were a denizen.[187] Denization occurred by a grant of letters patent, as an exercise of the royal prerogative. Denizens paid a fee and took an oath of allegiance to the crown. The denizen was neither a citizen nor an alien, but had a status akin to today's permanent residency. Sir William Blackstone stated the following. "A denizen is a kind of middle state, between an alien and a natural-born subject, and partakes of both."[188]

In 1549, the terms of a new statute[189] forbade conspiracies of handicraftsmen to sell their wares at unreasonable prices, in an apparent attempt to protect consumers from oppressive market behavior such as of over-pricing and poor identification of product sources. The Statute also

---

[186] ibid., pp. 208-209.

[187] ibid., pp. 297-301.

[188] The denizen was not a citizen because he did not have any political rights: he could not be a member of parliament or hold any civil or military office. However, the status of denizen allowed a foreigner to purchase property, although a denizen could not inherit property. Historically, paying for letters patent was thus a requirement of foreign land ownership in England. Sir William Blackstone, *Commentaries on the Law of England*, Childs & Peterson, Philadelphia, 1860, Book 1, Chapter X, p. 374.

[189] Penalties on butchers, bakers, etc conspiring to sell victuals only at certain prices; and on artificers conspiring as to prices or times of work . . . . Act 2nd and 3rd Edw VI c 15; 4 *Statutes of the Realm* 1547-1624, pp. 58, 59.

proscribed intermeddling in each other's work, to finish another person's already-started work.[190]

In 1641 the apprentices petitioned Parliament pleading to restrict the activities and rights of settlement of foreign craftsmen.[191]

> And first we beseech your honours to take into consideration the intolerable abuse of our apprentices, for where we by coercion are necessarily compelled to serve seven or eight years at least, before we can have the immunity and freedom of this city to trade in: those which are mere strangers do snatch this freedom from us, and pull the trades out of our hands, so that by these means, when our times are fully expired, we do then begin in a manner to suffer a second apprenticeship to them, who do thus domineer over us in our own trades, &c.[192]

Rappaport said that the issue was now fully clarified, saying it was as to who should and could lawfully dominate craftsmen in their own trade. One argument as to the methodology for resolution of this serious social problem, suggested that the crown, the City and the companies began an unprecedented cooperation by means of legislation and charters to limit the rights of Londoners without the freedom. He reported that these new crown restrictions had to be enforced by the City authorities, and through the City's powers, the companies were then given operational crown authority to regulate the economic activities of all Londoners.[193]

6. The Position of the Workers

6.1. City of London Protection of the Masters

It was considered a good custom in London for the governing officers of a trade to have the power to seize ill and unserviceable goods, which were exposed to sale, and then to remove them to Guildhall. This suggested that a breach of custom could be dealt with summarily as an argument based on fact. It also suggested the possibility of the exercise of an administrative discretion

---

[190] Toulmin Smith (ed.), *English Gilds*, Oxford University Press, Oxford, 1870, p. clvii.
[191] ibid., p. cl.
[192] ibid., p. cl footnote.
[193] Steve Rappaport, *Worlds Within Worlds: Structures of Life in Sixteenth-Century London*, Cambridge University Press, Cambridge, 1989, p. 44.

on a reverse-onus basis by the governing officers of a trade. At Guildhall, these officers could impanel a jury to render their verdict, and as a result, to restore or destroy these goods. This custom arguably served as the basis for city companies making by-laws for general regulation of their trades, and for the discipline of the individual members.[194]

The City of London reacted with its customary jurisdiction to the king's exercise of power to allow the entry of foreign merchants. This was because it was not in the interests of the London inhabitants to be flooded with non-loyal and non-tax-paying foreigners. By the Act of common council of 15 April 1606,[195] it was found that there was a custom from time immemorial that no person, not being free of the City of London, should either by himself or his agent, show or sell his wares by means of retail, within the city or its liberties. The penalty for breach of this regulation was £5 for each offense. The act further provided as follows.

> . . . that no person, not free of the city, could "by any colour, way, or means whatsoever, directly or indirectly, by himself or by any other" keep any shop or other place whatsoever, inward or outward, for show, sale, or putting to sale of any wares or merchandise whatsoever by way of retail, or use any art, trade, occupation, mystery, or handicraft whatsoever within the said city or the liberties thereof," under the same penalty.[196]

These were declared not to exclude the keeping of apprentices under 21 years of age, or employ strangers who were feltmakers, cap-thickers, carders, spinners, knitters, or brewers, or to employ non-freemen if freemen could not be found.[197] The prohibitory part of these by-laws was stated in very remarkably similar terms to that set out in the *Wagoner's case*,[198] extracted below.

In the 1610 Case of *Wagoner v Finch*, known as *Wagoner's Case, the Case of the City of London*,[199] Mr. Wagoner was already in custody for non-payment of a fine for unlawfully plying his trade and for keeping an unlawful shop. The fine was levied by the City of London as a reverse onus procedure.

---

194 Alexander Pulling, *The Laws, Customs, Usages and Regulations of the City and Port of London*, William Henry Bond and Wildy and Sons, London, 1854, p. 388.

195 Priv. Lond. 160.

196 ibid.

197 Alexander Pulling, *The Laws, Customs, Usages and Regulations of the City and Port of London*, William Henry Bond and Wildy and Sons, London, 1854, pp. 385, 386.

198 8 Co 125; Cro Eliz 352, 353.

199 *Wagoner v Fish* Hil 7 Jacobi I, 4 Coke Rep 121b.

His legal representatives brought an action in *habeas corpus* as against the Mayor, Aldermen and Sheriffs of London regarding his incarceration.[200] The City of London submitted a reply to the action, making key arguments, as follows.

> . . . where by the ancient charters, customs, franchises, and liberties of the city of London, confirmed by sundry acts of Parliament, no person not being free of the city of London, may or ought to sell or put to sale any wares or merchandizes within the said city, or the liberties of the same, by retail, or keep any open or inward shop, or other inward place or room, for show, sale, or putting to sale of any wares or merchandizes, or the use of any art, occupation, mystery, or handicraft within the same. And whereas also Edward, sometime King of England, of famous memory, the third of that name, by his charter made and granted to the said city in the fifteenth year of his reign, confirmed also by Parliament, amongst other things granted, that if any customs in the said city before that time obtained and used, were in any part hard or defective, or any things in the same city newly arising, where remedy before that time was not ordained, should need amendment, the Mayor and Aldermen of the said city, and their successors, with the assent of the Commonalty of the same city, might put and ordain thereunto fit remedy, as often as it should seem expedient to them, so that such ordinance should be profitable to the King, for the profit of the citizens, and other his people repairing to the said city, and agreeable to reason.[201]

The first key issue in the reply was that it cited certain charters, customs, franchises, and liberties of the city of London, apparently confirmed by several acts of Parliament.[202] The Court stated that the following was evident from *The Prince's Case* of 1606[203] "[A] Charter having the authority and force of parliament is sufficient in itself without any other act."[204] The *Rhetorica ad Herennium* described legal custom as that which, in the absence of any statute, was endowed by usage with the force of statute law.[205] Taken together, this raises the issue of whether the custom of London, as a species of statute, so cited might and should be read as good and operative law.

The second key issue was that the Court noted that one might become free of the city, or, a freeman of the City of London, in only three ways, as follows.

---

200 4 Coke Rep 122a.
201 4 Coke Rep 122a,b.
202 ibid.
203 *The Prince's Case* (1606) 8 Rep 1; 4 Coke Rep 168.
204 ibid.
205 Cicero, *Rhetorica Ad Herennium*, Harvard University Press, Cambridge, 2004, p. 93.

The first was by service such as by an apprenticeship. The second was by birthright, such as for example the son of a freeman. The third was by redemption by way of allowance by the Court of the Mayor and Aldermen. These three methods were customary in character, and neither charter nor command of the king could create the status of the freeman of the City.[206] Thus, passing off oneself as a freeman was arguably a breach of ancient customary law.

The court held further that strangers and foreigners had devised and practiced, by sinister and subtle means, ways of defrauding the charters, liberties, customs, good orders and ordinances of London. From this might be inferred the possibility that a sinister and subtle breach of customary laws might have been indicative of fraud. The inference could run thus: people without a historical connection to a customary rule, or not bound by such a customary law, acted without proper approval or supervision as if they were of equal rank or status to those approved and properly supervised people paying their taxes, and therefore damaged these properly approved and supervised people.

The holding continued, by particularizing its suggestion of fraud. It was alleged they had sold and presented for sale their wares and merchandises in private and secret places, probably suggesting a failure to operate in market overt. The allegation also stated they had used arts, trades, occupations, mysteries, and handicrafts to the detriment and hurt of the inhabitants of the city. It added that the local inhabitants had to pay scot and lot, bore offices and underwent other charges, which foreigners and strangers did not have to do.[207] This reasoning suggested that while all the locals had to pay burdensome taxes and circumscribe their lives with certain prohibitive rules, a foreign person, not so constrained, caused apparent detriment to the local inhabitants. Therefore the city made by-laws forcing strangers to become free of the city. These by-laws required them to show their wares in public, so that regulatory authorities could supervise them.

Coke's Reports wrote that the court held as follows.

> In this case it was resolved, that the said custom of London, that no person whatsoever, not being free of the city of London, shall by any colour,[208] way,

[206] 4 Coke Rep 126b.
[207] 4 Coke Rep 122a.
[208] Colour of right in equity, to confer the impression that title in property, or goods, is held by someone when that is not in fact the case. *Encyclopaedic Australian Legal Dictionary*, LexisNexis, Sydney [2012], online.

> or mean whatsoever, directly or indirectly, by himself or any other, keep any shop or any other place whatsoever, inward or outward, for show or putting to sale of any wares or merchandizes whatsoever by way of retail, or use any trade, occupation, mystery, or handicraft, for hire, gain, or sale, within the City of London, is, upon the whole matter disclosed in the return, a good custom; and that such constitution made according to the custom alleged in the return, upon pain of forfeiture of 5l, was also good.[209]

This suggested that strangers were considered as diverters of business away from lawful freemen. In other words, it could be argued as a corollary of forestalling of goods that strangers were unfair competitors.

The court also resolved that a city's custom and a charter granted to a city were different in effect. This was because customs could only be good by the very nature of custom. However, a custom could not be effective by grant, unless deemed so by an act of parliament,[210] because trade could not be maintained or enhanced without proper government. Therefore, the king could lawfully counteract a custom by erecting a new *guildam mercatoriam*, or, mercantile gild.[211] All members of this mercantile gild were to pay scot and lot. Seligman noted that freemen, or citizens, of the city and gild members were not the same. The freeman was the inhabitant householder who paid scot and bore lot. This meant that the freeman contributed his proportion to the taxes, bore his share of the civic burdens and was enrolled at the Court Leet. On the other hand, gild members were recruited from strangers as well as from local inhabitants. While the guild members might reside outside the city, the citizen in general could not. While the citizen needed to have a house, the guild member did not.[212] This suggested a judgment establishing a superior commercial rank of the freemen over other citizens.

In practice, the city limited itself to restricting retail dealers or tradespersons in those trades requiring more than the ordinary surveillance of the civic authorities.[213] Thus, when the power of the city and county corporations became more strictly exercised, the main wholesale transactions

[209] 4 Coke Rep 124b, 125a.
[210] 4 Coke Rep 125a.
[211] ibid.
[212] Edwin RA Seligman, 'Two Chapters on the Mediaeval Guilds of England', *Publications of the American Economic Association*, vol. 2, no. 5, 1887, pp. 9-113, pp. 36, 37.
[213] Alexander Pulling, *The Laws, Customs, Usages and Regulations of the City and Port of London*, William Henry Bond and Wildy and Sons, London, 1854, p. 386.

took place in fairs and markets, and it was in these venues that the city concentrated its control.[214]

In the 1675 case of *Hutchins v Player, Chamberlain of London*,[215] the court stated that the corporation of the City of London could generally restrain persons in places for public buying and selling, the times in which they could buy and sell, the trades with which they could meddle, and the trades with which they should not intermeddle.

Thus, in this 1675 case of *Hutchins v Player*,[216] the court considered the issue of the claim by non-freemen to deal by wholesale within the jurisdiction of the City of London. The reported facts referred to an Act for the better regulating of the old and new drapery in Blackwell Hall and Leadenhall. It appeared that Samuel Hutchins had been arrested and was in Sheriffs' custody in a London gaol, for an apparently unpaid fine. He was fined under an Ordinance of the City. It stated that all broad cloths should be pitched and harboured in Blackwell Hall and Leadenhall, and that they should be duly entered with both hallage[217] and duty to be paid. It was also enacted that no person should be a broker, factor or buyer in those Halls unless first approved by the mayor and aldermen and entered into a recognizance in the King's Court.[218]

Sir Orlando Bridgman then stated, *inter alia*, the following holdings. They suggested that a *prima facie* case of a breach of City Custom was sufficient for the City to act by levying a fine and confiscating goods.

> A fuller statement of the relevant custom than that which is reproduced in *Wagoner's Case*[219] is as follows. The ordinance of Common Council had stated that many freemen pretended to be immediate buyers, but were really agents and brokers for strangers and foreign men. This was contrary to the custom of London and the privileges of the City, and that such practices were

---

214 ibid., p. 387.

215 Hargr. MSS. No. 26, 48, quoted in S Bannister (ed.), Hargraves Manuscripts, *Reports of Judgments Delivered by Sir Orlando Bridgman when Chief Justice of the Common Pleas from Mich 1660 to Trin 1667*, Butterworths, London, 1823.

216 Hargr. MSS. No 55. fol. 153.

217 Hallage. A fee or toll paid for goods sold in a hall. *Webster's Revised Unabridged Dictionary*, C & G Merriam Co., Springfield, 1913.

218 Hargraves Manuscripts, *Reports of Judgments Delivered by Sir Orlando Bridgman when Chief Justice of the Common Pleas from Mich 1660 to Trin 1667*, Butterworths, London, 1823, pp. 273, 274.

219 4 Coke Rep 121b.

> coloring of foreigners' goods and contrary to the oath of a freeman. Therefore all such commodities bought and sold were to be forfeit to the City.[220]
>
> For the factors, buying is in the markets. Therefore he should not be permitted to exercise a by-trade[221] of his own in the same commodities whereby he is the clothier's servant. If the factor buys for himself, it is in his power to undo the clothier. For example: a clothier sends twelve cloths to his factor to sell for him. The factor likes them and buys them all for himself, or he culls out the best colors and cloths, then leaves the refuse to an uncertain market. This factor may then make the clothier pay factorage for the cloths he has culled out for himself, thereby under-buying any other man. He might keep the cloths unsold until the rates are low so that he may buy them at his own price. If the factor trades for himself in this way, no man can buy goods except at second hand.[222]

The legislature enacted the Statute of Elizabeth,[223] specifically to adopt this custom of the City of London, on a nation-wide basis. This statute enacted that a prior apprenticeship was required to carry on trade in any part of the kingdom,[224] in the following terms.

> AND bee it further enacted by the authoritee aforesaid, That after the first daye of Maie next coming, it shall not be lawfull to any person or persons, other then suche as nowe doo laufully use or exercise any Arte Misterye or Occupation, nowe used or occupied within the Realme of Englande or Wales, Excepte he shall have been brought uppe therin Seaven yeares at the least as Apprentice, in maner and fourme abovesaid, nor to set anye person on woorck in suche Misterye Arte or Occupation, being not a Worckman at this Day, excepte he shall have bene Apprentice as ys aforesaid, orels having served as an Apprentice as is aforesaid, shall or will become a Journeymen, or be hyred by the yere; upon payne that every person willingly offending or doing the contrary, shall forfeite and lose for every Defaulte fourtye shillinges for every monethe.[225]

---

[220] Hargraves Manuscripts, *Reports of Judgments Delivered by Sir Orlando Bridgman when Chief Justice of the Common Pleas from Mich 1660 to Trin 1667*, Butterworths, London, 1823, pp. 289, 290.

[221] Presumably a trade ancillary to that of the clothier.

[222] Hargraves Manuscripts, *Reports of Judgments Delivered by Sir Orlando Bridgman when Chief Justice of the Common Pleas from Mich 1660 to Trin 1667*, Butterworths, London, 1823), pp. 313, 314.

[223] 5 Eliz. C 4, s 24.

[224] Alexander Pulling, *The Laws, Customs, Usages and Regulations of the City and Port of London*, William Henry Bond and Wildy and Sons, London, 1854, p. 481.

[225] 4 *Statutes of the Realm* 1547-1624, p. 420.

Further, in accordance with an old custom of London, a person who had served a seven-year apprenticeship to a trade of buying and selling, might give up that trade and take up another.[226] This custom was considered to apply to every trade in which the Statute of Elizabeth[227] specifically required an apprenticeship.[228]

The principal crafts had become incorporated, during the time of King Henry VI,[229] this incorporation executed directly by the crown.[230] However, in the 1830 case of *Clark v Denton*,[231] it was held, citing the same principles enunciated in *Wagoner's Case*,[232] that the real meaning of the custom that no person should keep a shop or place for use of any art or trade, was specifically that people should not carry on business as masters, unless they were masters. If the defendant could prove that he acted in the trade as a journeyman or apprentice only, it would be a defense.[233] This suggested that a person of lower commercial rank than master was presumed legally incompetent to sell in market overt on his own account.

6.2. The Pressing of the Trades into a Crown System of Commercial Ranks

As for commercial rank, at the conclusion of the reign of Edward II[234] it had been established that a certain twelve of the companies were the "wisest" and most self-sufficient, and therefore, they should be the most active in advising the city. These companies were, in descending order of precedence and therefore also presumably in descending order of wisdom and prerogative, or rank, as follows: mercers; grocers; drapers; fishmongers; goldsmiths; skinners; merchant tailors; haberdashers; salters; ironmongers; vintners, and, the cloth workers.[235]

---

226 *Allen v Tolley* BR 12 Jac I, Calth Rep 9, 48.
227 5 Eliz. c 4.
228 *Allen v Tolley* BR 12 Jac I, Calth Rep 9, 48.
229 1547-1555.
230 Alexander Pulling, *The Laws, Customs, Usages and Regulations of the City and Port of London*, William Henry Bond and Wildy and Sons, London, 1854, p. 485.
231 1 Barn & Ad 92; (1830) 109 ER 721.
232 4 Coke Rep 121b.
233 *Clark v Denton* 1 Barn & Ad 92, 97.
234 1307–1327.
235 Alexander Pulling, *The Laws, Customs, Usages and Regulations of the City and Port of London*, William Henry Bond and Wildy and Sons, London, 1854, p. 78.

The London court of aldermen enacted an ordinance,[236] probably in 1356, establishing and confirming the custom as follows.

> . . . all the mysteries should be faithfully ruled and governed, each according to its nature, and in such a manner, that no deceit should be found in any of their works or trades; that in each mystery, there should be chosen four or six, or more, or less, according to the needs of the mystery; which persons, so chosen and sworn, should have full power from the mayor to will and faithfully to do and perform the same.[237]

This ordinance suggests that deceit in the trades was inconsistent with very powerful supervision. It could be expected, as a natural consequence, that the crown would want to be atop this hierarchy, should it have desired to control the stamping out of deceit. The royal reaction to this ranking of the companies by the city appeared to have been to bring its tenets more under the king's jurisdiction, by enacting the following statute.[238]

> . . . the Masters Wardens and People of every such Guild Fraternity or Company incorporate, betwixt this and the Feast of Saint Michael next coming, shall bring and do all their Letters Patents and Charters to be registered of Record before the Justices of Peace in the Counties, or before the Chief Governors of the said Cities, Boroughs, and Towns where such Guilds, Fraternities, and Companies be . . . no such Masters, Wardens, nor People make nor use no Ordinance which shall be to the Disherison or Diminution of the [King's Franchises] or of other, nor against the common Profit of the People . . . .[239]

This situation was further clarified,[240] using a recital of the substance of the statute 15 Hen. VI. c. 6, as above, and noting that the statute 15 Hen. VI. c. 6 had expired. It provided as follows.

> . . . divers and many ordinances had been made by divers and many private bodies corporate within their cities, towns, and boroughs, contrary to the king's prerogative, his laws, and the common weal of his subjects: it was therefore enacted, that no masters, wardens, and fellowships of crafts or mysteries, nor any of them, nor any rulers, or gilds, or fraternities, should

---

[236] 39 Edward III.
[237] 2 Rep. MC 13.
[238] 15 Henry VI c 6, probably in 1437.
[239] 2 *Statutes of the Realm* 1377-1504, pp. 298, 299.
[240] 19 Hen. VII c 7, probably in 1504.

> make any acts or ordinances in disinheritance of the prerogative of the king, nor of none others, nor against the common profit of the people . . . .[241]

This statute explicitly set the prerogative of the king above anyone else's prerogative. It set the common profit of the people as being equal to a sole right in the king, and appeared to remove any management prerogative from within the gilds, unless approved by the crown.

Conclusion

The research question asked how professional recognition is structured, and for what purposes. Argument has sought to sustain the view that maintenance of societal hegemony has been the purpose of the professions since the times of the middle ages gilds.

The western historical experience has shown that capitalism survives even in its periods of severe economic crises, with the possibility of any proletarian revolutions neither universal nor permanent, suggesting that these repeating contradictions were a form of stability. Gramsci found that this was because the western dominant class, known as the bourgeoisie, ruled with the subordinate masses' consent, despite massive contradictions, and which he called "the hegemony of the bourgeoisie." They ruled by both domination and by hegemony, where domination is rule by force and hegemony is rule by consent.

Ideology being a process accomplished by the so-called thinker consciously, but with a false consciousness, no ideology could coordinate concrete interests between dominant classes and subordinate groupings, unless validated in some material form. Rather, the dominant socio-economic formation sets up the objective conditions, by which ideological leadership could develop, such as by a bourgeois professional class giving "advice" to members of the less educated masses. Professional advice is thus transmission of ideology to subaltern groups, where the advice is set up to have essential value to them.

The dominant class may achieve hegemony by this kind of concrete coordination of its interests with those of the subordinate classes. In order to do this, the dominant class must be careful not to sacrifice the real interests of the subordinate classes, but instead, partially to realize the subordinate classes'

---

[241] 19 Hen. VII c 7, probably in 1504.

interests by forgoing some of its own material interests. Professional give up some of their freedoms, in order to organize and secure their bourgeois positioning. They transfer and project some bourgeois interests onto the masses, inevitably those interests they are least likely to worry about losing, such a right to hard manual work. In consequence of this, the dominant class may sustain the material bases of this economic compromise, only by being the most dominant force, directing field of production.

This hegemonic class must be in a controlling position to create and maintain an equilibrium between its own interests and those interests of the subordinate classes, without touching or sacrificing control of the dominant mode of production, while the subordinate classes must never be incentivized to withdraw consent to the rule of the hegemonic class.

The scheme of three dominant bourgeois classes: self-declared entrepreneurs, self-employed running a company; professionals, self-employed and active in an officially recognized profession; and, managers, dependent employees but with considerable autonomy. The political and ideological superstructure, formerly run and ruled by the monarch, must be compatible with economic compromises at the base. This means that all the superstructures, such as culture, politics, family systems, religions, law, school systems and public opinion, must be organized to facilitate class compromise. The "historical bloc" is the central concept, in Neo-Gramscian theory that unifies the connections between society and state, international and domestic, and subaltern and dominant socioeconomic vectors, from which hegemonic relationships develop. It is a structural conception that coordinates society like a king. Gramsci likely had in mind, as the historical bloc, the use of references to myths as historical forces.

Historical blocs provide an epideictic mythical narrative, to generate hegemony by representing people's inner beliefs. This representation individualizes the subordinate masses into "citizens" or "people," while thoroughly disorganizing the subordinate classes. Each individual in a class no longer acts as a member of that class, acting instead as individual people or citizens. As individual citizens, but not producers, wage earners can merely articulate claims to improvements in their material conditions via representative democratic institutions, within the confines of capitalism, which sets up the illusion of freedom of speech.

However, to the contrary, the search for specific interests of individual members of the bourgeoisie cannot ever become part of a hegemonic ideology, otherwise they would be seen to be selfish and unrepresentative. Instead, they must form profession-like groupings, to project bourgeois ideology onto the masses as "advice. Thus, to establish ideological hegemony, the dominant bourgeoisie must form a unified ideology through transcending the operative corporate consciousness of individual members of the bourgeoisie. They articulate this unified ideology to the masses and project what they have learned in their years of higher education. Mass acquiescence in the bourgeois hegemonic system depends on a validating truth in the bourgeois hegemonic ideology in people's daily lives, such as when they conform to satisfying the exigencies of daily life.

Thus, the main purpose of the capitalist state is the continuing reproduction of capitalist social relationships in the political, economic and ideological fields. The capitalist state does things that raise the great masses of the population to a particular cultural and moral level, a level which corresponds to the productive force for development, in such a way as to form favorable circumstances for class compromises, resolving capitalist contradictions between the hegemonic bourgeoisie and the subordinate subaltern masses.

Despite this equilibrium, when the masses fail to consent, either actively or passively, the state exercises coercive power by legally enforcing discipline onto recalcitrant groups. This is the synthesis of bourgeois ideology expressed as juridical rules, and, administrative or police coercive power. Althusser deduced that, for Gramsci, hegemony and dictatorship were indistinguishable, with force and consent being equivalent as the ultimate contradictions.

The king had for many centuries the power to create and dismantle professions, maintaining his positioning atop the goods manufacturing and mercantile hierarchies, control of the very means of production, by means of proceedings in *quo warranto*. In theory, *quo warranto* proceedings also could overturn any ranking system of officials. In this way, it could control the commercial activities of anyone inferior in title to that of the king. This included those producing goods for sale at the lower levels of commercial ranks, and therefore included direct control of professionals. For example, actions commenced in London were unlikely to be appealed or removed to royal courts in Westminster. Suggesting a procedure for perpetual investigation, and therefore permanent and continuing reverse onus, an action in the lord mayor's court remained in force forever, just as in administrative investigations within today's professions. This could be so, even without the commencement of formal proceedings. In this way, the London Court exercised a jurisdiction of constant monitoring and supervision.

The London trading companies had charters of their own. These defined their powers over their members and their trade. This suggested that the power of commerce was divided between the City and County corporations at the higher level of prestige as constituters of markets, and the companies or gilds at a lower level of prestige as regulators of their own members. The freedom of the city was the device by which the right to make a professional level of living was enforced. Without it, the worker reverted to the ancient form of slavery. From early Saxon times, membership in the gilds depended on full citizenship. However, the exclusion of strangers could not be explained by any political activist tendency by the crafts.

Freedom was arguably a specious term. It did not really mean that the person was free. From ancient times, freedom of the city of London could be acquired only by one of the original three pathways of patrimony, apprenticeship, or by redemption from the court of aldermen. People not free of the city were designated as foreigners or strangers, in accordance with the ancient law of Rome. The freedom of the City of London was essential for commercial activity and functioned as follows. Only city freemen could vote in Parliamentary elections, vote in civic elections for councilmen and alderman, be exempt from all tolls payable on animals brought into the City for sale, be exempt from all market tolls payable anywhere in the country, be exempt from naval conscription, and enjoy the right to claim freedom from prosecution except in the city's courts. In order to formalize this control into an administrative methodology, the City needed a system of registration. It therefore turned to the misteries for administrative support, because only they had control over their own membership registries.

The newly amended wordage of the oath of freedom of the city contained the following key requirements. The first was a duty to carry out unspecified charges using language of the common good. The second prohibited the use of the freeman's name on the goods of a foreigner or stranger. The third conferred responsibility on the freeman for keeping the queen's peace and reporting any breaches to the mayor. The fourth ensured no freedoms to apprentices. The fifth required apprentices to be registered, forced to serve seven years, and, given freedom only if they well and truly served. This sounded remarkably like those interests which professionals had given up, in order to retain their bourgeois positioning.

Eventually, the British gild system fractured into mercantile gilds and artisan gilds, the former with a higher commercial rank, or professional status, than that of the latter. Immediately prior to 1266, there appeared to be an economic transition where the classes of the poor coalesced with the classes of the craftsmen. The poor were excluded originally from merchant gild association for their lack of any property possession. This transition gave birth to a gild statute creating merchant gilds for the first time, merely by excluding practicing craftsmen coming from the artisan gilds. It provided that no person "with dirty hands or with blue nails," or who hawked his wares in the streets, such as did peddlers, could become a member of the gild, and that craftsmen must have foresworn their trade for at least a year before being admitted to the gild. This suggested a tendency to populate these new mercantile gilds with those of higher status, rather than with artisans or salesmen of lower status. A person of lower commercial rank than master was presumed legally incompetent to sell in market overt on his own account. Mercantile gilds were the professions. It was a requirement that gild-brothers had to bring their case before the gild court of the master and wardens for settlement, before considering a court of law. They had given up their rights to litigate. After the riots in London of 1517, the king hanged several aristocrats, and as well, gave supervisors the power to give orders to workers, for the first time expanding the bourgeoisie by creating a new class of managers.

As for commercial rank, at the conclusion of the reign of Edward II it had been established that a certain twelve of the companies were the "wisest" and most self-sufficient, and therefore, they should be the most active in advising the city. These companies were, in descending order of precedence and therefore also presumably in descending order of wisdom and prerogative, or rank, as follows: mercers; grocers; drapers; fishmongers; goldsmiths; skinners; merchant tailors; haberdashers; salters; ironmongers; vintners, and, the cloth workers. The historic bloc forming a superstructure to keep these professional groups in this hierarchy was that of deceit in the trades. The myth was deceit was inconsistent with very powerful supervision. It could be expected, as a natural consequence, that the crown wanted to be atop this hierarchy, by strict supervisory processes, should it have desired to control the stamping out of deceit in the trades.

In summary, in a western capitalist state, the bourgeois rule by both domination and by hegemony, where domination is rule by force and hegemony is rule by consent, coordinated by professional advice to subaltern masses, a transmission of bourgeois ideology, where the advice is set up to have essential value to them. The dominant class may sustain the material bases of this economic compromise, only by being the most dominant force, directing the field of production, while the subordinate classes must never be incentivized to withdraw consent to the rule of the hegemonic class. The "historical bloc" is a structural conception that coordinates society just as a king used to do, by use of references to bundles of myths as historical forces. Now, the dominant bourgeoisie must form a unified ideology to articulate this unified ideology to the masses and project onto them what they have learned in their years of higher education. Their success as hegemons depends on a validating truth in the bourgeois hegemonic ideology in people's daily lives, such as when their advice conforms to satisfying the exigencies of daily life. When the masses nevertheless fail to consent, either actively or passively, the state exercises coercive power over them by legally enforcing discipline onto such recalcitrant groups. In this paradigm, force and consent are the equivalent of each other. Similarly, the king had, for many centuries, the power to create and dismantle professions, by means of proceedings in *quo warranto*. The freedom of the city was the device by which the right to make a professional level of living was enforced. Without it, the worker reverted to the ancient form of slavery. The oath of freedom of the city summarized those interests which professionals had given up, in order to retain their bourgeois positioning. Through this, the mercantile gilds became today's professions. The historic bloc forming a superstructure to keep these professional groups in this hierarchy was that of deceit in the trades. The crown wanted to be atop this professional hierarchy, by continuing and strict supervisory processes, should it have desired to control the stamping out of deceit in the trades. Now, the bourgeoisie exercises his function juridically.

References

1 *Statutes of the Realm* 1235-1377.
12 C L & F 541, 542.
15 Henry VI c 6, probably in 1437.
19 Hen. VII c 7.
2 And 276-7.
2 Brownlow 286.
2 Bulstr 189-190.
2 Inst 126.
2 Rep. MC 13.
2 Roll Aor 579.
2 *Statutes of the Realm* 1377-1504.
22 Edw IV 30.
3 Keb 225.
39 Edward III.
4 Coke Rep 121b.
4 Coke Rep 122a.
4 Coke Rep 124b.
4 Coke Rep 125a.

4 Coke Rep 126b.
4 Coke Rep 168.
4 Inst 250.
4 Mod 145.
4 *Statutes of the Realm* 1547-1624.
5 Eliz. c 4.
8 Co 112 b.
8 Co 125.
Act 2nd and 3rd Edw VI c 15.
Ahern, John J, *An Historical Study of the Professions and Professional Education in the United States*, Loyola University, Chicago, 1971.
Aldous, Vivienne, *Research Guide 1: City Freedom Archives*, Corporation of London Records Office, London, 1999.
Allen v Tolley BR 12 Jac I, Calth Rep 9.
Althusser, Louis, 'Ideology and Ideological State Apparatuses', in *Lenin and Philosophy and Other Essays*, New Left Books, London, 1977.
Anderson, G Lester, & Merton W Ertell, 'Extra-institutional forces affecting professional education', in *Education for the Professions*, National Society for the Study of Education, Chicago, 1962.
Anderson, Perry, 'The Antinomies of Antonio Gramsci', *New Left Review*, no. 100, 1976-77, pp. 15-18.
Ballarino, G, & A Cobalti, *Mobilità sociale*, Carocci, Roma, 2003.
Ballarino, Gabriele, & Stefani Scherer, 'More investment – less returns? Changing returns to education in Italy across three decades', *Stato e mercato*, vol. 99, no. 3, 2013, pp. 359-388.
Bannister, S, (ed.), Hargraves Manuscripts, *Reports of Judgments Delivered by Sir Orlando Bridgman when Chief Justice of the Common Pleas from Mich 1660 to Trin 1667*, Butterworths, London, 1823.
Barn & Ad 92.
Blackstone, Sir William, *Commentaries on the Law of England*, Childs & Peterson, Philadelphia, 1860.
Boggs, Jr, Carl, 'Gramsci's Theory of the Factory Councils: Nucleus of the Socialist State', *Berkeley Journal of Sociology*, vol. 19, 1974-1975, pp. 171-187.
Brubacher, John S, 'The Evolution of Professional Education', in *Education for the Professions*, University of Chicago Press, Chicago, 1962.
Buci-Glucksmann, Christine, *Gramsci and the State*, Lawrence and Wishart, London, 1980.
Burton, E, The Catholic Encyclopedia, *Guilds*, Robert Appleton Company, 1910.
Calendar of Early Mayor's Court Rolls: 1298-1307, Calendar Roll H 12 December 1305 - 12 November 1306 (1924), 228 - 252 http://www.british-history.ac.uk/report.aspx?compid=31974&strquery=FreedomoftheCity.
Carr-Saunders, Alexander M, & PA Wilson, *The Professions*, Frank Cass, London, 1964.
Charter of Edward IV of 9th November 1463.
Cicero, *De Offi*.
Cicero, *Rhetorica Ad Herennium*, Harvard University Press, Cambridge, 2004.
Clark v Denton 1 Barn & Ad 92.

Co Litt 74.

Coke, Eduardo, *The First Part of the Institutes of the Laws of England or a Commentary upon Littleton*, J & W Clarke; Saunders & Benning; A. Maxwell; S. Sweet; H. Butterworth; Stevens & Sons; R. Pheney; and J. Richards, London, 1832.

Corporation of London Records Office, *Liber Ordinacionum* fo 173.

Cro Car 516.

Cro Eliz 352, 353.

Davis, John A (ed.), *Gramsci and Italy's Passive Revolution*, Croom and Helm, London, 1979.

Encyclopaedic Australian Legal Dictionary, LexisNexis, Sydney [2012], online.

Fenichel, Otto, *The Psychoanalytic Theory of Neurosis*, Routledge, Oxford, 1946.

Forfeitures of Londons Charter or an impartial account of the several Seisures of the City Charter, Daniel Brown at the Black Swan and Bible without Temple Bar and Thomas Benskin in St Brides Church Yard, London, 1682.

Freud, Sigmund, *Case Histories II*, Penguin, London, 1991.

Gill, Stephen, *Power and Resistance in the New World Order*, Palgrave, Basingstoke, 2003.

Gramsci, Antonio, *Quaderni di Carcere,* Valentino Gerratana (ed.), Einaudi, Torino, 1977.

Gramsci, Antonio, *Selections from the Prison Notebooks of Antonio Gramsci*, International Publishers, New York, 1971.

Gross, Charles, *The Guild Merchant, Vol I*, The Clarendon Press, Oxford, 1890.

Hall, Stuart, Bob Lumley & Gregor McLennan, 'Politics and Ideology: Gramsci', *Working Papers in Cultural Studies*, no 10, 1977, pp. 45–76.

Hargr. MSS. No 55. fol. 153.

Hargr. MSS. No. 26.

Herbert, William, *The History of the Twelve Great Livery Companies, Vol I*, William Herbert, London, 1887.

Im, Hyug Baeg, 'Hegemony and Counter-Hegemony in Gramsci', *Asian Perspective*, vol. 15, no. 1, 1991, pp. 123-156.

Jessop, Bob, *The Political Indeterminacy Marxism and Democracy*, Lawrence and Wishart, London, 1980.

Kidgell, J, *Power of the Kings of England to examine the charters of particular corporations and companies: exemplified by the statutes and laws of this realm*, John Kidgell Printer, London, 1684.

Lenin, V, 'The State and Revolution', in *Selected Works*, Progress Publishers, Moscow, 1963.

Littleton, Sir Thomas, *Littleton's Tenures in English*, John Byrne & Co, Washington, 1903.

Maitland, FW, 'History from the Charter Roll', *The English Historical Review*, vol. 8, no. 32, 1893, pp. 726-733.

Marx and Engels, *Selected Correspondence*, Foreign Language Publishing House, Moscow, no date.

Morton, Adam, *Unravelling Gramsci: Hegemony and Passive Revolution in the Global Economy*, Pluto, London, 2007.

Morwood, James (ed.), *The Oxford Latin Mini Dictionary*, Oxford University Press, Oxford, 1995.

Mouffe, Chantall, 'Hegemony and Ideology in Gramsci', in Chantall Mouffe (ed.), *Gramsci and Marxist Theory*, Routledge & Kegan Paul, London, 1979.

Muchall, William (ed.), *Doctor and Student*, James Moore, 18th edn., London, 1792.

Oxford English Dictionary, Clarendon Press, 2nd edn., Oxford, 1989.

Player v Hutchins, O Brid Com Dig *Exoins*, D.

Poulantzas, Nicos, *Political Power and Social Classes*, New Left Books, London, 1973.

Przeworski, Adam, 'Material Bases of Consent: Economics and Politics in a Hegemonic System', in *Political Power and Social Theory*, vol. 1, JAI Press, Greenwich, 1980.

Pulling, Alexander, *The Laws, Customs, Usages and Regulations of the City and Port of London*, William Henry Bond and Wildy and Sons, London, 1854.

Quinodoz, Jean-Michel, *Reading Freud: A Chronological Exploration of Freud's Writings*, Routledge, London, 2005.

Rappaport, Steve, *Worlds Within Worlds: Structures of Life in Sixteenth-Century London*, Cambridge University Press, Cambridge, 1989.

Remains Historical and Literary Connected with the palatine Counties of Lancaster and Chester, Volume XXXVII, Chetham Society, Manchester, 1856.

Salomone, A William, 'The Risorgimento between Ideology and History: The Political Myth of rivoluzione mancata', *The American Historical Review*, vol. 68, no. 1, 1962, pp. 38- 56.

Sassoon, Anne Showstack, 'Hegemony and Political Intervention', in Sally Hibbin, (ed.), *Politics, Ideology and the State*, London 1978.

Saull, Richard, 'Hegemony and the Global Political Economy', in Robert A Denemark (ed.), *The International Studies Encyclopedia*, vol. V, Wiley-Blackwell, Oxford, 2010.

Seligman, Edwin RA, 'Two Chapters on the Mediaeval Guilds of England', *Publications of the American Economic Association*, vol. 2, no. 5, 1887, pp. 9-113.

Shortt, John, *Informations (Criminal and Quo Warranto) Mandamus and Prohibition*, The Blackstone Publishing Company, Philadelphia, 1888.

Smith, Toulmin (ed.), *English Gilds*, Oxford University Press, Oxford, 1870.

Sotiris, Panagiotis, 'Gramsci and the Challenges for the Left: The Historical Bloc as a Strategic Concept', *Science & Society*, vol. 82, no. 1, 2018, pp. 94–119.

Stephenson, Carl, 'The Anglo-Saxon Borough', *The English Historical Review*, vol. 45, no. 178, 1930, pp. 177-207.

Stolte, Keith M, 'How Early Did Anglo-American Trademark Law Begin? An Answer to Schechter's Conundrum', *Trademark Reports*, vol. 88, 1998, pp. 564-606.

Sutton, AF, 'The Silent Years of London Guild History before 1300: the Case of the Mercers', *Historical Research*, vol. 81, no. 175, 1998, pp. 121-141.

The Prince's Case (1606) 8 Rep 1.

Thomas, Arthur Hermann, *Calendar of Early Mayor's Court Rolls, City of London (England) Lord Mayor's Court, City of London (England) Court of Common Council*, The University Press, London, 1924.

Wagoner v Fish Hil 7 Jacobi I, 4 Coke Rep 121b.

Webster's Revised Unabridged Dictionary, C & G Merriam Co., Springfield, 1913.

Willcock, JW, *The Law of Municipal Corporations, together with a brief sketch of their history, and a treatise on mandamus and quo warranto*, John S Little, Philadelphia, 1836.

Year Book, 21 Edw IV 74.

Chapter 4

The Fitness and Propriety of Subaltern Groups

Gary I. Lilienthal[1,*], PhD
and Muhamad Hassan bin Ahmad[2], PhD

[1]Carrington Rand, Hong Kong SAR, Peoples Republic of China
[2]Ahmad Ibrahim Kulliyyah of Laws, International Islamic University, Kuala Lumpur, Malaysia

Abstract

Jacques Lacan's theory of the mirror stage demonstrates a kind of alterity, occurring during early childhood development. The mirror stage conjures an original image or reflection the "ego ideal," which becomes the child's imaginary self, as he or she tries in vain to reconnect with the ego ideal. In Lacanian terms, this formation of the subject, as a child, sees a splitting of the self into "self" and "other." In the light of the significance of this struggle for the ego ideal, for propriety of the self, the objective of this research is to examine critically the underlying operation of alterity within the conjunctive conception of fitness and propriety. The research question asks how the alterity, that is inherent in the "fit and proper test," might generate the subaltern groups of fit and proper professions, clients and others. Argument seeks to sustain the view that the fit and proper professions are priestly enterprises of manipulated public memory, by commanding descending chains of the meanings of technical terms, so that the subaltern groups of clients and the general public are somehow morally obliged, inferring a duty, to the institutions of the professions. The research is doctrinal research, based on library research, working with evidentiary sources from the best available analyses of the scholarship. Thus, the research is set out in the structure

[*] Corresponding Author's Email: carrington.rand@icloud.com.

In: Regulation of the Professions in East Asia
Editors: Gary I. Lilienthal and Muhamad Hassan bin Ahmad
ISBN: 979-8-88697-409-6

of five identifiable key themes, in the structure of a legal narrative analysis. The outcomes of the research will conclude that the *mysterium tremendum*, as a great or profound protean mystery, provides an opportunity for public manipulation of reality. There is therefore an inferred non-priestly subaltern mass of assumed religious adherents, whose reality is controlled by public practices of forced remembrance, but with operative alterity really having existed prior to the commanding group's cognizing its own apparent moral superiority. If emerging language placed alterity into a structure of existence, then there must have been a second level of alterity, where the one level forever corrected the other, with the first other imagining it had a right from birth to correct the second "fallen" other by altering the canonization of the meaning of words. In this way, Luther had used gospels to replace, and alter at will, the deity itself, rendering the deity protean, suggesting the construction of a descending chain of meanings between the deity and the gospels. This implies a subaltern group is somehow morally obliged to the commanding social group through the commanders' moral altitude. To stabilize this social paradigm, women are structured as unifying signifiers, subject at any time to command alteration of the doxa within their significations, to bind together both alterity and the confected religious institution version of the ancient custom of matrimony, in order to command the entire human project of propriety.

Keywords: alterity, otherness, fitness and propriety, subaltern groups, priestly enterprises, protean deity

1. Introduction

Jacques Lacan's theory of the mirror stage demonstrates a kind of alterity, occurring during early childhood development. The mirror stage conjures a scene in which infants first see their reflection in a mirror. Lacan called this original image or reflection the "ego ideal," which becomes the child's imaginary self, as he or she tries in vain to reconnect with the ego ideal. In Lacanian terms, this formation of the subject, as a child, sees a splitting of the self into "self" and "other." From this story of early childhood development, the internal struggle for the ego ideal alters any simple conception of alterity, as defined only by difference in interpersonal relationships.[1] In the light of the

[1] Jacques Lacan, 'The Mirror Stage As Formative of the Function of the I As Revealed in Psychoanalytic Experience,' in Jacques Lacan, *Écrits: A Selection*, Alan Sheridan (trans.), WW Norton and Company, New York, 1977.

significance of this struggle for the ego ideal, for propriety of the self, the objective of this research is to examine critically the underlying operation of alterity within the conjunctive conception of fitness and propriety. Alterity is thus a fundamental aspect of being human. It is absolute otherness in a natural structure of existence. Misunderstanding of this structure has been misused in the life of humanity, when hierarchical groupings have purported to command and control, with power, groups they themselves define as subaltern.[2]

In the 2016 High Court of Hong Kong case of *Re "A,"*[3] the Applicant, "A," applied under s. 27 of the *Legal Practitioners Ordinance, Cap 159 (Ordinance)*, to be admitted as a barrister of the High Court of Hong Kong.[4] The issue was whether the Applicant was considered to be a "fit and proper person" to be admitted as a barrister, which was a requirement pursuant to s. 27(1) of the Ordinance.[5] The Court stated that admission proceedings were for protecting the public interest. They did not constitute any resolution of the private rights of parties in disagreement, and that this was the gist of the 2014 Hong Kong case of *Re Mably*,[6] which cited with approval the 1992 High Court of Australia case of *Wentworth v NSW Bar Association*.[7] Since public interest was at issue, the Hong Kong Bar Association must assist the Court to assess whether an applicant satisfied the "fit and proper person" criteria, as was stated in the 2013 Hong Kong Court of First Instance case of *Re Youh Alan Chuen Po*.[8] The Court stated that there were many authorities emanating from Hong Kong, and also, from other common law jurisdictions, out of which the relevant legal principles of law could be derived. The decision was thus one for the Court's judgment, in the light of these precepts.[9] In the 2009 Supreme Court of Victoria Court of Appeal case of *Medical Practitioners Board of Victoria v Lal*,[10] the Court held as follows.

> The public interest is a protean concept. What is relevant to the public interest depends on the statutory context in which the concept is used. Its content cannot be confined by reference to any predetermined generic criteria. Sound registration practices also confer an indirect form

---

[2] William Blake, *The Marriage of Heaven and Hell*, Oxford University Press, Oxford, 1988.
[3] HCMP2079/2016.
[4] HCMP2079/2016 RE "A", [1].
[5] ibid., [3].
[6] [2014] 1 HKLRD 627, §14, per Lam VP.
[7] (1992) 176 CLR 239, 250-251; HCMP2079/2016 RE "A", [4].
[8] [2013] 2 HKLRD 485, §11, §59, per Lam JA (as he then was); HCMP2079/2016 RE "A" [5].
[9] HCMP2079/2016 RE "A", [37].
[10] [2009] VSCA 109.

of public protection, through the establishment and the maintenance of public confidence in the medical profession. If the public at large have confidence in doctors, they are more likely to seek medical advice and treatment when the need arises. This is conducive to the general health of the community.[11]

With this entire dictum apparently protean in structure, especially including the court's reasoning about the public interest, no valid argument could yet proceed beyond this point without developing an incisive understanding of the term "protean." In this respect, O'Nolan had posited that Proteus was a god of human extraction with no background. He seemed to be a late arrival among the gods, whose credentials had not been very carefully checked. The first identifiable account of Proteus was Homer's. He described "an old man of the sea," who was a keeper of seals, who sought a daily siesta on the island of Pharos with his ungainly flock. He was a prophet who, if seized, would change his shape, becoming a tree, or a river, or fire, or assuming various beastly shapes, in his efforts to escape his captor. If he were to be held physically, he would eventually resume his own shape and divulge his prophetic knowledge. This was reminiscent of how the various animal headpieces worn ceremonially by ancient Egyptian kings gave rise to the shape-changing legend of Proteus. The seal held a peculiar place in European folk tradition, in which at certain times seals might change their appearance and take on human shape. Generally this was managed by laying aside their skins. If the temporarily discarded skin was taken, the seal to whom it belonged followed the taker and appeared to be in his power.[12] Book Four of the Homer Chronicles recorded the difficulties of the hero Menelaus who was stranded on the island of Naxos. Menelaus sought advice from the god Proteus, who when approached, changed from shape to shape, thus eluding the inquirer. Menelaus found that when he grasped Proteus tightly through each astounding transformation, the god would take on his own form and then submit to questioning.[13] Referring to Lucian's treatise *On the Dance*, Lawler reported the view that the ancient Egyptian Proteus was nothing but a dancer, portraying a lion, a panther, then a branch of a tree, with superb mimetic artistry. As the story of this metamorphic skill was received from antiquity, it

---

[11] Ibid., from [56].

[12] K O'Nolan, 'The Proteus Legend,' *Hermes*, vol. 88, no. 2, 1960, pp. 129-138, pp. 129, 132, 134, 137.

[13] Jessica Lane, 'The Poetics of Legal Interpretation,' *Columbia Law Review*, vol. 87, no. 1, 1987, pp. 197-216, p. 197.

turned into a tale of actual metamorphosis. Lawler stated that Proteus was either an Egyptian king or a Greek sea-divinity who, when seized, changed into flame, water, and a variety of animals, one after the other; but if his assailant held him fast, Proteus resumed his own shape and foretold the future. Lawler suggested that in this strange legend there was probably a combination of several elements, one of which might have been an old ritual dance, perhaps to a sea or river divinity, in which a prominent individual, or a priest, or a priest-king, portrayed a sequence of ideas such as "lion," "fire," "serpent," and "water." Such dances were common to all primitive races and were offered to divinities of all sorts, invariably accompanied by an illusion of spiritual "possession" or identification of the dancer with a god or with the animal or thing portrayed.[14] Beloe recorded that the successor of King Pheron of Egypt was a citizen of Memphis, whose name in the Greek tongue was Proteus. Proteus was an Egyptian title of the deity, under which he was worshipped, both in the Pharos and at Memphis. He was the same as Osiris and Canobus, and particularly the god of mariners, who confined his department to the sea,[15] suggesting his jurisdiction was over the non-spatial conception of neither a public nor a private domain.

Declaring a concept to be protean, apparently as a genus rather than a specification, but nevertheless proceeding to formulate a judgment based on that concept, suggests the operation of a decision based not so much on alterity but on the basis of a constructed specification, namely that of subalterity. The idea of a fit and proper person is not limited to assessment only within the legal profession, its general principles having spread across many vocations and fields.[16] In the 1965 case of *Maxwell v Dixon*,[17] Hale J observed:

> Clearly different qualifications are needed by e.g., lawyers, transport operators, hotel keepers and land agents …[18]

[14] Lillian B Lawler, 'Proteus Is a Dancer,' *The Classical Weekly*, vol. 36, no. 10, 1943), pp. 116-117, pp. 116, 117.

[15] William Beloe (transl.), *The History of Herodotus*, Leigh and Sotheby, London, 1741, p. 344, fn 197.

[16] Ibid.

[17] [1965] WAR 167, [169].

[18] *Maxwell v Dixon* [1965] WAR 167, [169]; Nathalie Ng, 'Fitness and Propriety, Spent Convictions and Technology: Lessons from ASIC Investigations,' *Australian Institute of Administrative Law Forum*, vol. 92, 2018, pp. 1-112, p. 71.

These measures have been applied, among many others, for granting broadcasting licenses,[19] customs licensing for importing drugs,[20] Air Navigation Regulations licensing.[21] Thus, "fit and proper" can be considered to be a genus, rather than a specification, suggesting mundane decisions based on subalterity. In the light of these issues, the question arises as to how the alterity, that is inherent in the "fit and proper test," might generate the subaltern groups of fit and proper professions, clients and others. Argument seeks to sustain the view that the fit and proper professions are priestly enterprises of manipulated public memory, by commanding descending chains of the meanings of technical terms, so that the subaltern groups of clients and the general public are somehow morally obliged, inferring a duty, to the institutions of the professions.

The research in this chapter is doctrinal research, based on library research, working with evidentiary sources from the best available analyses of the scholarship. Thus, the research is set out in the structure of five identifiable key themes, in the structure of a legal narrative analysis.[22] The first theme is Alterity, and the Theory of Religion, which also covers Originary Alterity, and, Blake's Interiority. The second key theme is Wittgenstein, Aliens and Aquinas. The third is Memory and Alterity: An Analytic of Difference. The fourth theme is Reciprocity and Alterity in Lévy-Strauss, which also covers The Semantic Field of Alterity. Finally, the fifth theme is The Strangeness of Alterity, which also covers Stranger, Other and Alterity.

The outcomes of the research will conclude that the *mysterium tremendum*, as a great or profound protean mystery, provides an opportunity for public manipulation of reality. There is therefore an inferred non-priestly subaltern mass of assumed religious adherents, whose reality is controlled by public practices of forced remembrance, but with operative alterity really having existed prior to the commanding group's cognizing its own apparent moral superiority. If emerging language placed alterity into a structure of existence, then there must have been a second level of alterity, where the one level forever corrected the other, with the first other imagining it had a right from birth to correct the second "fallen" other by altering the canonization of the meaning of words. In this way, Luther had used gospels to replace, and

---

[19] *Australian Broadcasting Tribunal v Bond* (1990) 170 CLR 321.

[20] *Re Dowling and Secretary to Department of Health* [1985] AATA 237; (1985) 8 ALD 171.

[21] *Re Taylor and Department of Transport* [1978] AATA 64; (1978) 1 ALD 312.

[22] For a description of the structure and purpose of 'legal narrative,' as a cluster of chronological narratives grouped in logical order to create a state of affairs, see Frank J D'Angelo, *Composition in the Classical Tradition*, University of Arizona Press, Tucson, 2000, p. 22.

alter at will, the deity itself, rendering the deity protean, suggesting the construction of a descending chain of meanings between the deity and the gospels. This implies a subaltern group is somehow morally obliged to the commanding social group through the commanders' moral altitude. To stabilize this social paradigm, women are structured as unifying signifiers, subject at any time to command alteration of the doxa within their significations, to bind together both alterity and the confected religious institution version of the ancient custom of matrimony, in order to command the entire human project of propriety.

2. Alterity, and the Theory of Religion

2.1. Originary Alterity

Beginning with William Blake,[23] who was a poetic master of imagination and alterity, we read from his *The Marriage of Heaven and Hell*:[24]

> The ancient Poets animated all sensible objects with Gods or Geniuses, calling them by the names and adorning them with the properties of woods, rivers, mountains, lakes, cities, nations, and whatever their enlarged and numerous senses could perceive. And particularly they studied the genius of each city and country, placing it under its mental deity; Till a system was formed, which some took advantage of, and enslaved the vulgar by attempting to realize or abstract the mental deities from their objects: thus began Priesthood; Choosing the forms of worship from poetic tales. And at length they pronounced that the Gods had ordered such things. Thus men forgot that All deities reside in the Human breast.[25]

Blake's theory is thus one of primal animism, but more, it is a theory of poetry and the corporal enlivening permitted by the enhanced and various senses of an innocent and unspoiled moment, taking place before the fall of

---

[23] William Blake, (1757 –1827), was an English poet, printmaker and painter. Blake was a seminal figure in poetry and the visual arts during the Romantic Age. Northrop Frye and Robert D Denham, *Collected Works of Northrop Frye*, University of Toronto Press, Toronto, 2006, pp 11–12. He produced diverse works, embracing imaginative impressions of "human existence itself". Mona Wilson, *The Life of William Blake*, The Nonesuch Press, Nonesuch Press, London, 1927, p. 167.

[24] William Blake, *The Marriage of Heaven and Hell*, Oxford University Press, Oxford, 1988.

[25] ibid., p. 38.

man. In Blake's view, the fall of man is a fleeing from concreteness towards abstraction as well as the slavery caused by the veiling of socially-based concepts. The forgetting that all deities live in the human breast is the same as saying that the so-called binding implemented by religion is a binding off of humanity's imagination. Blake's views are pregnant with meaning, one string of his text concerning the origin of religion through a braiding of history and existence. Another such string concerns an inferred interior character by deities residing in the human breast. Yet another concerns the humanism of the poets and scholars, in their skepticism toward religion.

The very conception of any kind of origin of religion can be understood in both phenomenological and historical senses, or otherwise stated, in an existential and temporal sense. In this way, an origin of religion can be linked to the historical blocs that create the subaltern public acquiescence in hegemony.[26] Similarly, the word "moment," as it existed at the point of the fall of man, may mean a small quota of time or importance in either effect or influence. In these senses, alterity may be understood as the phenomenological genesis of religion, by which people are constrained within a large social group, to the exclusion of those who do not profess such a religion.

The seeking of assistance on this topic, in an anthropological context, shows there may be no help from the contemporary masters, such as Victor Turner,[27] Clifford Geertz,[28] and Mary Douglas.[29] Although their analyses were

---

[26] "In Sorel's work there is no reference to the concept of "historical bloc." Valentino Gerratana has suggested that Gramsci, who in prison did not have access to Sorel's *Reflections on Violence*, had in mind Sorel's references to myths, and in particular Sorel's insistence that these images *should be taken as a whole, as historical forces*, probably from a reference in a book by Giovanni Malagodi." Panagiotis Sotiris, 'Gramsci and the Challenges for the Left: The Historical Bloc as a Strategic Concept,' *Science & Society*, vol. 82, no. 1, 2018, pp. 94–119, p. 97, citing Antonio Gramsci, *Quaderni di Carcere,* Valentino Gerratana (ed.), Einaudi, Torino, 1977, p. 2632.

[27] Victor Witter Turner, (1920 –1983), was a British cultural anthropologist whose work was on symbols, rites of passage and rituals. He attended University College in 1946 focussing on anthropology, and later pursuing postgraduate studies in anthropology at Manchester University. Jerry D Moore, *Victor Turner: Symbols, Pilgrims, and Drama: Visions of Culture*, Alta Mira Press, Lanham, 2012, pp. 224-234; Edith Turner, 'The Literary Roots of Victor Turner's Anthropology,' in Kathleen M Ashley (ed.), *Victor Turner and the Construction of Cultural Criticism*, Indiana University Press, Indianapolis, 1990, pp. 163–169.

[28] Clifford James Geertz, (1926 –2006), was an American literary critic and anthropologist, who influenced the field of cultural symbols. He was professor emeritus at the Institute for Advanced Study, at Princeton University. Richard A Shweder & Byron Good (eds.), *Clifford Geertz by His Colleagues*, University of Chicago Press, Chicago, 2005.

[29] Mary Douglas, (1921 –2007), was a British social anthropologist, who wrote on symbolism and human culture. Douglas followed Émile Durkheim and was a noted proponent of structuralist analysis. She had a strong interest in comparative religion. Richard Fardon,

penetrating, their considerations of religion were not attempts to understand religion at its source. Religion puts forward sure and persuasive symbolic descriptions and rules of behavior, reflecting much about social life and cultures. Thus, argument turns instead to two scholars who actually penetrated the character of religion. These are Weston La Barre[30] and Roy Rappaport.[31] Their master works on religion had concern for its origins. La Barre's *Ghost Dance* has a subtitle *The Origins of Religion*,[32] and Rappaport's posthumous major work was *Ritual and Religion in the Making of Humanity*.[33] Both were concerned with the nature of humanity, as seen through the lens of religion.[34] Both referred to notions of the numinous, developed by Rudolf Otto,[35] and meaning arousing spiritual or religious emotion, mysterious, or awe-inspiring, and also to the *mysterium tremendum*, meaning a great or profound mystery, with Rappaport treating them more favorably than La Barre. The *mysterium tremendum* clearly provides an open opportunity for public manipulation of reality. Both sought the origins of religion and holiness, in the field of biology. From this, there is a correspondence between evolutionary origin through biology and an existential origin through embodiment, this point of correspondence being the nub of alterity.

In La Barre's interpretation, a religious reaction is distinctively both human and alien to animals, since "the context is the universally human

---

'Immortality yet? Or, the permanence of Mary Douglas,' *Anthropology Today*, vol. 34, no. 4, 2018, pp. 23–26.

[30] Raoul Weston La Barre, (1911-1996), was an American anthropologist, working in ethnobotany. He applied psychiatric and psychoanalytic precepts to ethnography. In 1954, he published *The Human Animal*, which was his psychoanalytical approach to culture and psychology. Gabriel Ward Lasker, 'The Human Animal. Weston la Barre,' *American Anthropologist*, vol. 57, no. 2, 1955, pp. 377–378.

[31] Roy A Rappaport, (1926–1997), was an American anthropologist, in the fields of ritual and ecological anthropology. Rappaport articulated the distinction between a people's cognized and *operational environments*, as how people understand the consequences of their actions in the world, as distinguished from how the anthropologist might interpret this environment through observation and measurement. Roy A Rappaport, 'Ritual Regulation of Environmental Relations among a New Guinea People,' *Ethnology*, vol. 6, no. 1, 1967, pp. 17–30.

[32] Weston La Barre, *The Ghost Dance: The origins of religion*, Dell, New York, 1970.

[33] Roy A Rappaport, *Ritual and religion in the making of humanity*, Cambridge University Press, Cambridge, 1999.

[34] Thomas J Csordas, 'Asymptote of the Ineffable: Embodiment, Alterity, and the Theory of Religion,' *Current Anthropology*, vol. 45, no. 2, 2004, pp. 163-185, p. 164.

[35] Rudolf Otto, (1867-1937), was an eminent Lutheran theologian, comparative religionist and philosopher. He was best known for his concept of the *numinous*, a certain emotional experience constituting the pith of the world's religions. Joseph Adler, *Rudolf Otto's Concept of the Numinous*, Kenyon College, Gambier, 2016.

nuclear family, the condition is individual human neoteny."[36] Neoteny is that human condition of being born in an immature state. As opposed to other animals, humans have a large brain, at birth that continues to grow afterward, instinct-less learning process, and an extended adolescence. For "the extravagantly heightened mammalian dependency of the unfinished organism,"[37] "human neoteny not only provides conditions for learning both of group culture and individual character, but also forms the experiential matrix for magic and religion, and indeed for the scientific world-view as well."[38] In the biological context, the human baby's environment is that created by other people. "The biologically infantilized human learns his humanity from infancy onward. This humanity arises in the psychological experiences of his particular animal milieu. The emotional reality of magic and religion lies precisely in these experiences."[39]

For La Barre, feelings of power and dependency begin in the experience of infantile omnipotence and the parents later omnipotence, especially that of the father. His psychoanalytic argument, beginning from neoteny, is a way to ground alterity, as the state of being "other" or "different" in the human body and to incorporate the otherness of religion to the other of the father, thereby attaching the authority of the father to the power of the priesthood, suggesting that non-priestly subaltern mass of assumed adherents. Rappaport also argued this topic of infantile dependency. Although he began from the works of Erik Erikson,[40] he preferred the context of the child's experience of the mother, rather than of its father. He also noted the "pseudo-infancy" conjured in some rituals, inferring it may have "its ontogenetic origin in the relationship of preverbal infants to their mothers,"[41] where where ontogeny is the origination and development of the organism, both psychological and physical, from the time of fertilization to adult. Earlier he had cited Bates' citing of Aldous

[36] Weston La Barre, *The Ghost Dance: The origins of religion*, Dell, New York, 1970, p. 12.
[37] ibid., p. 94.
[38] ibid., p. 87.
[39] ibid., p. 357.
[40] Erik Homburger Erikson, (1902-1994), was a developmental psychologist and psychoanalyst. He was known for his theory of psychological development of human beings. Steven J Haggbloom, Renee Warnick, Jason E Warnick, Vinessa K Jones, Gary L Yarbrough, Tenea M Russell, Chris M Borecky, Reagan McGahhey, John L Powell, Jamie Beavers, Emmanuelle Monte, 'The 100 Most Eminent Psychologists of the 20th Century,' *Review of General Psychology*, vol. 6, no. 2, 2002, pp. 139–152.
[41] Roy A Rappaport, *Ritual and religion in the making of humanity*, Cambridge University Press, Cambridge, 1999, p. 390.

Huxley,[42] on comprehending a state of holiness or grace, "the holy" being for Rappaport a union of discursive and non-discursive facets of human experience, or, stated in his terms, a union of the numinous and the sacred:

> ... the communication and behavior of animals has a naiveté, simplicity, which man has lost. Man's behavior is corrupted by deceit, even self-deceit, by purpose, and by self-consciousness. As Aldous saw the matter, man has lost the 'grace,' which animals still have."[43]

Animal grace and pseudo-infancy do not correspond to each other. The one is preverbal and the other nonverbal. The infant already has a powerful other, and the animal has none. Rappaport posited that, for such a human fall from grace, we must consider the evolution of language and the splitting of parts of the psyche that it causes. This emergence of language implied a preceptual rupture, which constituted a deep alterity, characterized by coexisting otherness and fallen otherness. He often cited the argument of Martin Buber,[44] that the genesis of evil is the human dual capability to both lie and pose alternatives. He concludes that they were caused by the advent of language. He also proposed "the sacred is inconceivable in the absence of language," as unique to humans, but contrariwise, that "language could not have emerged in the absence of religion," as they have the same time of origin.[45] Both the sacred and language "emerged together in a process of mutual causation formally similar to, and in all likelihood concurrent with, that which is said to have organized the interdependent evolution of human intelligence and human technology."[46] Thus, if emerging language placed alterity into a structure of existence, then there must have been a second level of alterity, where the one level forever corrects the other, the one other

---

[42] Aldous Leonard Huxley, (1894 –1963), was an English philosopher and writer. He authored some 50 books, as well as other essays, and poems. Donald Watt (ed.), *Aldous Huxley*, Routledge, London, 1975, p. 366.

[43] Roy A Rappaport, *Ritual and religion in the making of humanity*, Cambridge University Press, Cambridge, 1999, p. 384.

[44] Martin Buber, (1878 –1965), was an Austrian Jewish and Israeli philosopher best known for his philosophy of dialogue, a form of existentialism centered on the distinction between the I–Thou relationship and the I–It relationship. Martin Buber, *I and Thou*, Charles Scribner's Sons, New York, 1970.

[45] Roy A Rappaport, *Ecology, meaning, and religion*, North Atlantic Books, Richmond, 1979, p. 201; Roy A Rappaport. 'Logos, liturgy, and the evolution of humanity,' in Astrid Beck, Andrew Bartlet, Paul Raabe & Chris Franke (eds.), *Fortunate the eyes that see: Essays in honor of David Noel Freedman*, pp. 601–32, WD Eerdmans, Grand Rapids, 1995, p. 602.

[46] Roy A Rappaport, *Ritual and religion in the making of humanity*, Cambridge University Press, Cambridge, 1999, p. 418.

imagining it had a right from birth to correct a "fallen" other. For adaptation, which Rappaport considered as processes by which living beings maintained themselves against perturbations,[47] meaning the onsets of mental unease:

> … sanctity has made it possible for associations of organisms to persist in the face of increasing threats posed to their orderly social life by the increasing ability of their members to lie[48] …. The innumerable possibilities inherent in words and their combinations are constrained, reduced, and ordered by the unquestionable Word enunciated in ritual's apparently invariant canon. Sanctity orders a versatility that otherwise might spawn chaos."[49]

Rappaport thought there was a catastrophic rupture, generating a possibility for chaos in language, with direct connection from language to logos, logos meaning principles or order and knowledge.[50] His enhanced understanding of logos was as a principle of order that underlay the ritual, the sacred, sanctity and religious foundations of humanity. He states that the "epochal significance of language for the world beyond the species in which it appeared .... Language has ever more powerfully reached out from the species in which it emerged to reorder and subordinate the natural systems in which populations of that species participate."[51] Rappaport's view gave language its own intent, forming an alterity construed in human experience as logos. This construction unveiled alterity within language, as a human other above a natural other, a split pitting logos and sanctity, against alternatives and lies.[52] Finally, there was a third level of alterity, showing that, as logos and lie, it appeared in both facets of the holy, namely the non-discursive numinous and the discursive sacred.[53]

---

[47] ibid., p 408.
[48] ibid., p 416.
[49] ibid., p 418.
[50] FE Peters, *Greek Philosophical Terms*, New York University Press, New York, 1967.
[51] Roy A Rappaport. 'Logos, liturgy, and the evolution of humanity,' in Astrid Beck, Andrew Bartlet, Paul Raabe, and Chris Franke (eds.), *Fortunate the eyes that see: Essays in honor of David Noel Freedman*, pp. 601–32, WD Eerdmans, Grand Rapids, 1995, pp. 606-607.
[52] Thomas J Csordas, 'Asymptote of the Ineffable: Embodiment, Alterity, and the Theory of Religion,' *Current Anthropology*, vol. 45, no. 2, 2004, pp. 163-185, p. 165.
[53] ibid.

2.2. Blake's Interiority

Blake's second issue was the apparent "interiority," arising from his articulation of deities residing in the human breast. In so saying, William James[54] had based his own study of religion on a most intense and radical interior, namely the personal and solitary spiritual flashes of religious intellects, those looking for the core of religious occurrences in those "which are most one-sided, exaggerated, and intense."[55] The contrary approach of pursuing the smallest measure of religious occurrence, that phenomenological kernel at the origin of the religious symbol, institution and sentiment, might be equally productive. Rather than examining the limits of religious moments for the most religious person, this method sought to know the most marginal religious instances of the minimally religious person. Two prominent anthropologists addressed these insights of James during the *William James Lecture on the Varieties of Religious Experience*, at James's alma mater of Harvard University. Clifford Geertz delivered the lecture of 1998, in which he shifted the ground of discussion away from the solitary towards the public. He proposed that our era needed "firmer, more determinate, more transpersonal, extravert" terms than "experience," terms such as "meaning," "identity," and "power."[56] Nevertheless, he acknowledged that James's senses were still relevant in our time of great religious change, in that it provided "circumstantial accounts of the personal inflections of religious engagement that reach far beyond the personal" and echoed an "openness to the foreign and unfamiliar, the particular and incidental, yes, even the extreme and the brainsick"[57]

Such openness to the unfamiliar other reveals the thread along which the link between personal experience and, in Geertz's words, the "conflicts and dilemmas of our age" can be traced.[58] In the *William James Lecture* of 1997, Arthur Kleinman[59] had already taken an opposite path, by embracing the

---

[54] William James, (1842 – 1910), was an American psychologist. He was the first to offer a psychology course in the United States. Ralph Barton Perry, *The Thought and Character of William James*, vol. 1, Vanderbilt University Press, Nashville, 1996, p. 228.

[55] William James, *The varieties of religious experience*, Collier Books, New York, 1961.

[56] Clifford Geertz, 'The pinch of destiny: Religion as experience, meaning, identity, power,' in *Available light: Anthropological reflections on philosophical topics*, University Press, Princeton, 2000, p. 175.

[57] ibid., p. 185.

[58] ibid.

[59] Arthur Michael Kleinman, (1941-), is an American psychiatrist, psychiatric anthropologist and a professor of medical anthropology and cross-cultural psychiatry at Harvard University. He is well known for his work on mental illness in Chinese culture. In 1976, he founded

anthropology of experience. Kleinman's point of conjunction between the anthropology of experience and the investigation of religion was that of suffering, not in the sense of the vindication of divine providence in view of the existence of evil, but more in the sense of constituting "the stuff of experience that summons inquiry."[60] While discussing the Weberian paradigm,[61] which Geertz argued to some extent, Kleinman felt guided "to speak almost of a tyranny of meaning,"[62] that subdued the "fragmentary, contradictory, changing, unexpressed, and inexpressible" facets of sensory circumstances, aesthetic and moral senses, muscular action and agency, and, social memories and relations. In citing both Primo Levi[63] and Veena Das,[64] he observed that the process of making meaning could be a distorting, inadequate and inhuman "apolitical tool that reworks experience so that it conforms to the demands of power,"[65] implying that a perception of experience could be distorted by external power, such that a person's experience could simply be ignored. Kleinman posited that the intense otherness of human suffering could be understood only if one understood that

---

the journal *Culture, Medicine and Psychiatry*, and was its Editor-in-Chief until 1986. MJ Delvecchio Good & BJ Good, 'Culture, medicine and psychiatry: Twenty years and more,' *Culture, Medicine and Psychiatry*, vol. 20, no. 1, 1996, pp. vii–xi.

[60] Arthur Kleinman, 'Everything that really matters: Social suffering, subjectivity, and the remaking of human experience in a disordering world,' *Harvard Theological Review*, vol. 90, 1997, pp. 315–335, p. 316.

[61] Maximilian Karl Emil Weber, (1864 – 1920), was a German sociologist, jurist, historian and political economist. Weber argued that power could take three forms: shown in the social order through their status; in the economic order through class; and, in the political order through party. These constitute the distribution of power within a community. Charles E Hurst, *Social Inequality: Forms, Causes, and Consequences*, Allyn and Bacon, Boston, 2007.

[62] Arthur Kleinman, 'Everything that really matters: Social suffering, subjectivity, and the remaking of human experience in a disordering world,' *Harvard Theological Review*, vol. 90, 1997, pp. 315–335, p. 317.

[63] Primo Michele Levi, (1919 – 1987), was an Italian writer, chemist, partisan and Jewish Holocaust survivor. He authored several books, the best known of which included *If This Is a Man* (1947), as his account of the year he was a prisoner in the Auschwitz concentration camp in Poland. Ian Thomson, *Primo Levi*, Picador, London, 2019, pp. 17-18, 138; Carole Angier, *The Double Bond: Primo Levi: A Biography*, Penguin, London, 2002, p. 35.

[64] Veena Das, (1945-), is Professor of Anthropology at Johns Hopkins University in the United States. Her specialisations include the anthropology of violence, social suffering, and the state. Linda Green, 'Reviewed work: Social Suffering, Arthur Kleinman, Veena Das, Margaret Lock,' *Medical Anthropology Quarterly*, vol. 13, no. 3, 1999, pp. 375–377; Veena Das and Deborah Poole (eds.), *Anthropology in the Margins: Comparative Ethnographies*, SAR Press, Santa Fe, 2004.

[65] Arthur Kleinman, 'Everything that really matters: Social suffering, subjectivity, and the remaking of human experience in a disordering world,' *Harvard Theological Review*, vol. 90, 1997, pp. 315–335, p. 318.

"experience is both within and without the boundary of the body-self, crossing back and forth as if that body was permeable,"[66] and that the making of meaning is optimally consequential only as a connection between transpersonal processes and cultural representations, in the first instance, and embodied subjectivity and bodily processes, in the second instance.

This shared theme of otherness sustains a phenomenological kernel within religion. The most incisive understanding of this kernel arises in the works of the phenomenologists of religion, but not so much in the more widely read Mircea Eliade,[67] as in the less familiar works of Rudolf Otto and Gerardus van der Leeuw.[68] As an anthropologist, van der Leeuw is somewhat unknown, and colleagues tend to regard Otto as representing the more anachronistic religious theories. In the 1970s, students learned of the scholarship of the study of religion, in an anthropological context, recognizing certain scholarly precursors, whose ideas were central but outmoded. Among these precursor scholars were Sir James George Frazier,[69] Max Muller,[70] Edward Tylor,[71] Numa-Denis Fustel de Coulanges,[72] and Rudolf Otto. Otto continued to be

---

[66] ibid., p. 326.

[67] Mircea Eliade, (1907 –1986), was a historian of religion and philosopher at the University of Chicago. He was a leading interpreter in the field of religious experience. See Mircea Eliade, *Shamanism: Archaic Techniques of Ecstasy*, Princeton University Press, Princeton, 2004, p. xiii.

[68] Gerardus van der Leeuw, (1890 – 1950), was a Dutch historian and philosopher of religion, politician and ordained minister and. At Leiden University, he studied theology, and egyptology. In 1918, he became professor of history of religion at the University of Groningen. Gerardus van der Leeuw, *Einführung in die Phänomenologie der Religion*, Ernst Reinhardt, München, 1925.

[69] Sir James George Frazer, (1854 – 1941), was a Scottish social anthropologist and folklorist influential in the studies of mythology and comparative religion. Mary Beard, 'Frazer, Leach, and Virgil: The Popularity (and Unpopularity) of the Golden Bough,' *Comparative Studies in Society and History*, vol. 34, no. 2, 1992, pp. 203–224.

[70] Friedrich Max Müller, (1823 –1900), was a philologist and orientalist. He was one of the founders of the disciplines of Indian studies and religious studies. RCC Fynes, 'Müller, Friedrich Max (1823–1900),' in *Oxford Dictionary of National Biography*, Oxford University Press, Oxford, 2004.

[71] Sir Edward Burnett Tylor, (1832 –1917), was an English anthropologist, the founder of cultural anthropology. In 1883, Tylor was appointed Keeper of the University Museum at Oxford, and, from 1884 to 1895, was the first Reader in Anthropology. In 1896 he was appointed first Professor of Anthropology at Oxford University. Hugh Chisholm (ed.), 'Tylor, Edward Burnett,' *Encyclopædia Britannica*, vol. 27, Cambridge University Press, Cambridge, 1911, p. 498.

[72] Numa Denis Fustel de Coulanges, (1830 –1889), was a French historian. His first great book, *The Ancient City* (1864), was based on his in-depth knowledge of religion as the sole factor in the evolution of ancient Greece and Rome. Joseph M McCarthy, 'Fustel de Coulanges, Numa,' in Kelly Boyd (ed.), *Encyclopedia of historians and historical writing* (1999), Taylor & Francis, London, 1999, vol. 1, pp. 429-30.

read seriously, in those times, in some quarters of religious studies, as his view posed that the object of the direction of the numinous consciousness was a *mysterium tremendum et fascinans*, which he described as follows:[73]

> Taken in the religious sense, that which is "mysterious" is—to give it perhaps the most striking expression—the "wholly other," that which is quite beyond the sphere of the usual, the intelligible, and the familiar, which therefore falls quite outside the limits of the "canny" and is contrasted with it, filling the mind with blank wonder and astonishment .... the essential characteristic ... lies in a peculiar "moment" of consciousness, to wit, the *stupor* before something "wholly other."... [74]

Although this invocation of blank wonder, astonishment and stupor is significant, the phenomenon of the "wholly other" points to how Otto thought about the "limits of the 'canny,'" canny meaning shrewd judgment. Van der Leeuw observed similarly about the object of religion:[75]

> The first affirmation we can make about the Object of Religion is that it is a highly exceptional and extremely impressive "Other." Subjectively, again, the initial state of man's mind is amazement; and, as Söderblom[76] has remarked, this is true not only for philosophy but equally for religion. As yet, it must further be observed, we are in no way concerned with the supernatural or the transcendent: we can speak of "God" in a merely figurative sense; but there arises and persists an experience which connects or unites itself to the "Other" that thus obtrudes .... this Object is a departure from all that is usual and familiar; and this again is the consequence of the power it generates.[77]

This formulation is more temperate than Otto's, grounded in the serious pronouncements of Söderblom's leveling link between religion and philosophy, as it pinpoints amazement as the original state of the human mind.

---

[73] Rudolf Otto, *The idea of the holy*, Oxford University Press, Oxford, 1923.

[74] ibid., pp. 26–27.

[75] Gerardus van der Leeuw, *Religion in essence and manifestation (1938)*, Princeton University Press, Princeton, 1986, p. 23.

[76] Lars Olof Jonathan Söderblom, (1866 –1931), was the Church of Sweden Archbishop of Uppsala, from 1914 to 1931, and was recipient of the Nobel Peace Prize in 1930. See Klas Hansson, 'Nathan Söderblom's ecumenical cope: A visualization of a theological and ecumenical concept,' *Studia Theologica – Nordic Journal of Theology*, vol. 66, no. 1, 2012, pp. 62-79.

[77] Gerardus van der Leeuw, *Religion in essence and manifestation (1938)*, Princeton University Press, Princeton, 1986, p. 23.

It also speaks of the transcendent and supernatural as secondary to the primary encounter with otherness.[78]

Following these links in the chain of argument is the issue of power, which van der Leeuw elaborated as a sublimating potency, and sustained with familiar, and therefore plausible, ethnographic illustrations of *mana* and *orenda*, where *mana* is power or prestige, and, *orenda* is a mystical power pervading all things. Otto also evoked the conception of power, but more dramatically, elaborated it as an overwhelming "aweful majesty."[79] In viewing these sources for comprehension of alterity, it is of note that strong opposition to these phenomenologists of religion persists. For example, just as William James might have triggered some category of degenerative progression, the philosopher Giorgio Agamben[80] identified Otto as embodying a culmination of psychologizing the religious experience, as Agamben had argued that, with Otto's

> ... concept of the sacred that completely coincides with the concept of the obscure and the impenetrable, a theology that had lost all experience of the revealed word celebrated its union with a philosophy that had abandoned all sobriety in the face of feeling. That the religious belongs entirely to the sphere of psychological emotion, that it essentially has to do with shivers and goose bumps—this is the triviality that the neologism 'numinous' had to dress up as science.[81]

In a different way, Donald Wiebe[82] identifies van der Leeuw's work as a religio-cultural quest that depreciates and undermines any scientific study into religion.[83] Wiebe cites van der Leeuw's view of comprehending phenomena through the lens of their spiritual content, and his assertion that all comprehension is, in the end, religious such that "all significance sooner or later leads to ultimate significance."[84] Nevertheless, in religious studies,

---

78 Thomas J Csordas, 'Asymptote of the Ineffable: Embodiment, Alterity, and the Theory of Religion,' *Current Anthropology*, vol. 45, no. 2, 2004, pp. 163-185, p. 166.

79 Rudolf Otto, *The idea of the holy*, Oxford University Press, Oxford, 1923, p. 20.

80 Giorgio Agamben, (1942-), is an Italian philosopher who investigated the concepts of the state of exception, the form-of-life and *homo sacer*. Leland de la Durantaye, *Giorgio Agamben: A Critical Introduction*, Stanford University Press, Stanford, 2009, p. 53.

81 Giorgio Agamben, *Homo sacer: Sovereign power and bare life*, Stanford University Press, Stanford, 1995, p. 78.

82 Donald Wiebe is Professor of the Philosophy of Religion at Trinity College, at the University of Toronto. He has argued for a clear line between Religious Studies and Theology. Donald Wiebe, *The Science of Religion: A Defence, Essays by Donald Wiebe*, Brill, Leiden, 2019.

83 Donald Wiebe, *The politics of religious studies*, Palgrave, New York, 1999.

84 ibid., p. 180.

science is pitted against theology, and to agree that religion exists *sui generis*, forces a theological conclusion.[85] In anthropology, causal accounts are pitted against the interpretive ones, with the issue being the comparative merits of hard and soft methods. Anthropologists avoid the debate on whether religion is *sui generis*, seeing it more as a matter of theory than theology. The problem with these formulations is a methodological one, coming from reifying alterity, or put otherwise, reifying otherness as that kind of object, where we can be "in its presence." If this reification can be suspended, for a moment, one reaches the observation of Charles Long,[86] that "Otto is telling us that it is possible to experience apart from the categorical schema," that is, to have "experience of reality as a priori, as a datum that has not yet become a structure of the human project."[87] In short, reality is very simply other.

Thus arises the argument that alterity is a fundamental aspect of being human, a plain structure of existence, and misunderstanding this has caused both misery and creativity in the life of humanity, when hierarchical groupings purport to control with power the human project itself. This formulation coincides with what Blake articulated in *The Marriage of Heaven and Hell*.[88]

3. Wittgenstein, Aliens and Aquinas

The considering of alterity has, as has already been seen, too many paths of approach. The oldest and most cogent is called the existential approach. First, consider the Other, that Augustine spoke of as "more intimately present to me than my innermost being (*Tu autem eras interior intimo meo et superior*

---

[85] Charlotte Allen, 'Is nothing sacred?,' *Lingua Franca*, November 1996, pp. 30–40.

[86] Charles Houston Long, (1926 - 2020), was a cultural historian, religious studies scholar, and essayist in the fields of religion, theology, and modernity studies. He was an academician at the University of Chicago, UNC Chapel Hill, Syracuse University, Duke University, and the University of California Santa Barbara. Jennifer Reid & David Carrasco (eds.), *With This Root about My Person: Charles H. Long and New Directions in the Study of Religion*, University of New Mexico Press, Santa Fe, 2020.

[87] Charles Long, 'The oppressive elements in religion and the religions of the oppressed,' *Harvard Theological Review*, vol. 59, 1976, pp. 397–412, p. 402.

[88] William Blake, *The Marriage of Heaven and Hell*, Oxford University Press, Oxford, 1988; Thomas J Csordas, 'Asymptote of the Ineffable: Embodiment, Alterity, and the Theory of Religion,' *Current Anthropology*, vol. 45, no. 2, 2004, pp. 163-185, p. 167.

summo meo)."[89] Alternately, Martin Luther[90] warned Erasmus[91] to turn one's mind more to the compassionate and preached will of God, as demanded by the gospels, rather than to the veiled and aweful will of the deity, as a demonstration of Luther's use of gospels to replace, and alter at will, the deity. This of course would be the methodology of any simplistic and natural theology. The latter, warned Luther, "is not to be inquired into, but reverently adored, as by far the most inspiring secret of the Divine Majesty, reserved for himself alone and forbidden to us."[92] Luther was far from alone in articulating those dark excesses of God. Descartes articulated it too,[93] although, in his Enlightenment spirit, the stated excesses became constituted by light rather than by darkness. In his *Third Meditation on First Philosophy*,[94] Descartes was not so much providing a proof of the existence of God, as being overwhelmed by it:

> I clearly understand that there is more reality in an infinite substance than in a finite one, and hence that my perception of the infinite, that is God, is in some way prior to my perception of the finite, that is, myself. For how could I understand that I doubted or desired that is, lacked something and that I was not wholly perfect, unless there was in me some idea of a more perfect being which enabled me to recognize my own defects by comparison?[95]

---

[89] Augustine, 'The Confessions III,' in John E. Rotelle (ed.), *The Works of St. Augustine: A Translation for the 21st Century*, Maria Boulding (trans.), vol. 1/1, New City Press, New York, 1997, p. 8.

[90] Martin Luther, (1483 –1546), was a German priest, theologian, author, composer, former Augustinian friar, and is best known as a seminal figure in the Protestant Reformation and as the namesake of Lutheranism. Martin Luther, *Lectures on Genesis: Chapters 45–50*, Jaroslav Jan Pelikan, Hilton C Oswald, and Helmut T Lehmann (eds.), vol. 8, *Luther's Works*, Concordia Publishing House, Saint Louis, 1999, 5:326.

[91] Desiderius Erasmus Roterodamus, (1466 –1536), was a Dutch philosopher and Catholic priest, considered one of the greatest scholars within the northern Renaissance. He was a significant figure in classical scholarship, writing in the pure Latin style. Harry Vredeveld, 'The Ages of Erasmus and the Year of his Birth,' *Renaissance Quarterly*, vol. 46, no. 4, 1993, pp. 754–809.

[92] Martin Luther, 'The Bondage of the Will,' in Helmut T. Lehmann (ed.), *Luther's Works*, Philip S Watson & Benjamin Drewery (trans.), vol. 33, Fortress Press, Philadelphia, 1972, p. 139.

[93] René Descartes, (1596 –1650), was a French philosopher, scientist and mathematician, who invented analytic geometry. Descartes' *Meditations on First Philosophy*, (1641), is still a standard text in many university philosophy departments. René Descartes, *Meditations on First Philosophy*, J Cottingham (trans.), Cambridge University Press, Cambridge, 1996.

[94] René Descartes, *Meditations on First Philosophy*, J Cottingham (trans.), Cambridge University Press, Cambridge, 1996.

[95] René Descartes, 'Meditations on First Philosophy with Selections from the Objections and Replies,' in Karl Ameriks (ed.), *Cambridge Texts in the History of Philosophy*, John Cottingham (trans.), Cambridge University Press, Cambridge, 1996, p. 31. Juxtaposing

If alterity is the absolute fertility that circumscribes humanity, and philosophy attacks itself by rejecting whatever lies beyond a thinking self, then escapades into the alterity of discourse are the sole possible styles of project for modern philosophy. The deconstructions of Derrida[96] are premised on permitting différance its voice, where "différance" is the endless deferring of any final meaning of a sentence or word, because of the likely infinite series of other and equally uncertain signs or words.[97] Any infinite series thus may be turned into a power hierarchy, turning alterity into subalterity, constructed from subaltern groups. This is because only a silent interlocutor, a paradox in itself, can prevent the preeminence of logocentricism. Derrida is correct, because if mere conjecture is removed, only différance can enhance discourse. As Caputo noted, "The point of the play of différance and on this point différance is to be compared to Wittgenstein's language games and to Heidegger's[98] Unter-Schied is precisely to provide for multiple varieties of discourse while delimiting the hegemonic power of the single discourse."[99]

Mark Taylor[100] distinguishes two modern groups of thinkers: the "modernist postmodernists," who prefer Nietzschian freedom and deny grace; and, "poststructural post-modernists," who are the disquieted who are disturbed by grace. Taylor has further written:

Luther and Descartes, the respective scions of faith and reason, illumines a fundamental feature of philosophic alterity. It is always in inundation of a system; the logical coordinates that form the system are of secondary importance. Thus God may coherently be considered as absolute darkness or light. What counts is the systemic-excess of the absolute; Terrance W Klein, 'Adventures In Alterity: Wittgenstein, Aliens, Anselm and Aquinas,' *New Blackfriars*, vol. 88, no. 1013, 2007, pp. 73-86, p. 73.

[96] Jacques Derrida, (1930 –2004), was a French philosopher who developed a kind of semiotic analysis called deconstruction. He is one of the major scholars associated with post-structuralism and postmodern philosophy. Vincent B Leitch, *Postmodernism: Local Effects, Global Flows*, State University of New York Press, Albany, 1996, p. 27.

[97] Alan Bass (trans.), 'Différance,' in *Margins of Philosophy*, Chicago University Press, Chicago, 1982, p. 5.

[98] Martin Heidegger, (1889 –1976), was a 20th century German philosopher. He has been best known for his contributions to hermeneutics, phenomenology and existentialism. Matthew Sharpe, 'On Reading Heidegger—After the "Heidegger Case"?,' *Critical Horizons*, vol. 19, no. 4, 2018, pp. 334–360.

[99] John D Caputo, 'God Is Wholly Other - Almost: Différance and the Hyperbolic Alterity of God,' in Orrin F Summerell (ed.), *The Otherness of God*, University Press of Virginia, Charlottesville, 1998, p. 195.

[100] Mark C Taylor, (1945-), is a postmodern cultural and religious critic. He has published works on metaphysics, theology, architecture, art, media, economics, technology and postmodernity. See Mark C Taylor, *Erring: A Postmodern A/theology*, University of Chicago Press, Chicago, 2013.

> Modernist post-modernists interpret the ostensible absence of the real as the lack of what we never had in the first place. The real is a chimera fabricated to make us believe that there is something beyond the play of simulacra. Once we have been disabused of this illusion, we are free to enjoy the passing moment. When what is, is what ought to be, there is need for neither critique or resistance. For poststructural postmodernists, the absence of the real is the trace of a lack that can never be overcome. This lack is no simple absence but is instead the elusive margin of difference that allows appearances to appear and disappear. Since a non-absent absence repeatedly disrupts the present and defers the enjoyment of presence, what is, is never what ought to be. Consequently, critique and resistance are not only possible but unavoidable.[101]

Derrida's différance might be a secularized form of theology, for seeking grace in a religion-free world. Although Derrida denies any negative theology, his denial could well cancel itself.[102] Still, Derrida's deconstruction shares the adjectival, but insubstantial, formulation of Aquinas.[103] Aquinas' dictum was stated as: "concerning God, we cannot grasp what he is, but only what he is not, and how other beings stand in relation to him."[104] Putting the two parts of this dictum together, Aquinas permits the human project to cognize the deity through a chain of subaltern groupings, each subaltern level absolutely not being the next level up. The Fathers of the Fourth Lateran Council could well have been doing deconstruction, when they opined that "between creator and creature there can be noted no similarity so great that a greater dissimilarity cannot be seen between them?"[105] This implies the question as to what dynamic in the human spirit explains our perpetual disquietude at what has come before us. As Emmanuel Lévinas[106] asked, that "one can define the

---

101 Mark Taylor, 'Postmodern Times,' in Orrin F Summerell (ed.), *The Otherness of God*, University Press of Virginia, Charlottesville, 1998, p. 186.

102 Jacques Derrida, 'How to Avoid Speaking,' in Harold Coward & Toby Foshay (eds.), *Derrida and Negative Theology*, Ken Frieden (trans.), SUNY Press, Albany, 1992, pp. 73-142; Jacques Derrida, 'Sauf le nom,' in Thomas Dutoit (ed.), *On the Name*, John P. Leavey Jr. (trans.), Stanford University Press, Stanford, 1995, pp. 35-85; Jacques Derrida, 'Faith and Knowledge,' in *Religion*, Samuel Weber (trans.), Stanford University Press, Stanford, 1996, pp. 1-78.

103 Terrance W Klein, 'Adventures In Alterity: Wittgenstein, Aliens, Anselm and Aquinas,' *New Blackfriars*, vol. 88, no. 1013, 2007, pp. 73-86, p. 76.

104 *Catechism of the Catholic Church*, Our Sunday Visitor, Publishing Division, United States, 2000, #43.

105 1215 CE.

106 Emmanuel Lévinas, (1906 –1995), was a French philosopher known for his work in Jewish philosophy, phenomenology and existentialism, specialising in the relationships between

human by the desire for the new and by the capacity for renewal."[107] This necessarily requires a reexamination of the bases of modern discourse. Must discourse use deconstruction for its own fertility? Is discourse always severed from anything except itself, except absence?

This series of evolving questions can be reasoned through three thinkers: Ludwig Wittgenstein,[108] who removed the word "Being" from today's discourse; Martin Heidegger who made discourse serve the creation of Being; and Thomas Aquinas who said that self becomes self, becomes Being, by way of egress and return (*reditio completa inseipsum*). All of these dicta suggest entire epics concerning alterity. There are those who read Wittgenstein as cleansing a very temple of thought from metaphysical frauds, focussing on his *Tractatus Logico-Philosophicus*.[109] In *Tractatus*, Wittgenstein attempted to explain the relationship between three realms of language, thought and reality, up to that time thought to be merely parallel. After all, without knowing a word's meaning, one cannot use that word to exploit reality.[110] Wittgenstein thus issues a veiled warning that language and thought could manipulate reality by seizing power over canonized meanings of words.

4. Memory and Alterity: An Analytic of Difference

The relationship between collective identity and public memory tends to coalesce, around the idea of Hannah Arendt,[111] that public practices of

---

metaphysics, ethics, and ontology. Bettina Bergo, 'Emmanuel Levinas,' in Edward N Zalta (ed.), *The Stanford Encyclopedia of Philosophy*, Stanford University, Palo Alto, 2015.

107 Emmanuel Lévinas, 'The Old and the New,' in *Time and the Other*, Duquesne University Press, Pittsburgh, 1987, p. 121.

108 Ludwig Josef Johann Wittgenstein, (1889 –1951), was a philosopher who worked primarily in the philosophy of mind, logic, the philosophy of mathematics and the philosophy of language. He is considered to be one of the most famous philosophers in modern times. Nuno Venturinha, *The Textual Genesis of Wittgenstein's Philosophical Investigations*, Routledge, 2013, p. 39.

109 Ludwig Wittgenstein, *Tractatus Logico-Philosohicus*, DF Pears & BF McGuinness (trans.), Routledge, London, 1961.

110 Terrance W Klein, 'Adventures In Alterity: Wittgenstein, Aliens, Anselm and Aquinas,' *New Blackfriars*, vol. 88, no. 1013, 2007, pp. 73-86, p. 77.

111 Hannah Arendt, (1906 – 1975), wrote on intellectual history, developing insights into totalitarian movements and their threat to human freedom through bourgeois morality and scientific abstraction. She was an independent thinker keeping separate from schools of thought, or ideology. Elisabeth Young-Bruehl, Hannah Arendt: For Love of the World, Yale University Press, 2004; Wayne F Allen, 'Hannah Arendt: existential phenomenology and political freedom,' *Philosophy & Social Criticism*, vol. 9, no. 2, 1982, pp. 170–190.

remembrance are the lifeblood of the city form of state. It appears that without remembrance, collective identity and historical responsibility essentially disappear,[112] raising the question of whether such collectivity is nothing more than the legislated remembering of what the person has never experienced, this kind of false memory being a catastrophic move to subaltern status. The scholars Maurice Halbwachs,[113] Benedict Anderson[114] and Peter Novick[115] have highlighted this link between collective identity and public memory, all holding an interest in the capacity of public memory to constitute national, transnational and localized identities.[116] These scholars view remembrance as an activity bringing collective identity into being, emerging through the other's call of the collective to remember.[117]

In intersubjective paradigms of identity, difference appears as a mere obstacle, rather than as a valuable part of collective identity. Alterity is obliterated in those discourses of memory that appropriate personal views,[118] suggesting that subalterity might only be maintained by memories the person has never had. The most common meaning of difference is found in its contrarietal position to sameness, explaining the use of the term within constructions such as "different-from," or "different-than." This allows people to speak about such differences, in contrast to the similarities of the entities or concepts.[119]

However, difference carries an alternate meaning in relation to alterity, not so much defined by its own opposite as by what Heidegger called "the opening," and for which his student, Hannah Arendt, coined the term "natality." Her term means the arising of something absolutely new, with

---

112 Indeed, for Arendt, in her work Hannah Arendt, *The Origins of Totalitarianism*, Harcourt, Brace, New York, 1968, a central element of totalitarianism is the total control of public memory via the practices of remembrance.

113 Maurice Halbwachs, *On Collective Memory,* University of Chicago Press, Chicago, 1992

114 Benedict Anderson, *Imagined Communities: Reflections on the Origin and Spread of Nationalism,* Verso, New York, 1991.

115 Peter Novick, *The Holocaust in American Life,* Houghton Mifflin, Boston, 1999.

116 G Mitchell Reyes, 'Memory and Alterity: The Case for an Analytic of Difference,' *Philosophy & Rhetoric*, vol. 43, no. 3, 2010, pp. 222-252, p. 222.

117 Siobhan Kattago, *Ambiguous Memory: The Nazi Past and German National Identity*, Praeger, Westport, 2001; Michael Kammen, *Mystic Chords of Memory: The Transformation of Tradition in American Culture*, Knopf, New York, 1991; John R. Gillis (ed.), *Commemorations: The Politics of National Identity*, Princeton University Press, Princeton, 1994; John Bodnar, *Remaking America: Public Memory, Commemoration, and Patriotism in the Twentieth Century*, Princeton University Press, Princeton, 1992.

118 Diane Davis, 'Addressing Alterity: Rhetoric, Hermeneutics, and the Nonappropriative Relation,' *Philosophy and Rhetoric*, vol. 38, no. 3, 2005, pp. 191–212.

119 G Mitchell Reyes, 'Memory and Alterity: The Case for an Analytic of Difference,' *Philosophy & Rhetoric*, vol. 43, no. 3, 2010, pp. 222-252, p. 223.

novelty, and indeterminate, in this sense closely related to alterity.[120] Whereas many scholars have considered a relationship between identity and memory, few of them have reflected on what connects memory and alterity, such an exploration most probably offering public memory scholars fresh ways to consider remembrance. In the light of alterity, public memory transforms from a governance method for creating collective identities, to an arena in which identity and alterity can interact, so that identity can be introjected into the collective as that which its members are not. Several public memory scholars have already started to explore the dimensions of remembrance, for other reasons.

Jeffrey Olick has developed a process approach to remembrance,[121] Charles Scott has sought to understand the development of memory through its appearance,[122] and Barbie Zelizer[123] has examined the character of interwoven texts of visual memory.[124] The work of Bradford Vivian[125] comes

---

[120] Jeffrey Nealon, *Alterity Politics: Ethics and Performative Subjectivity*, Duke University Press, Durham, 1998; Gilles Deleuze, *Difference and Repetition*, Columbia University Press, New York, 1994; Jacques Derrida, *Limited Inc.*, Northwestern University Press, Evanston, 1988; Diane Davis, 'Addressing Alterity: Rhetoric, Hermeneutics, and the Nonappropriative Relation,' *Philosophy and Rhetoric*, vol. 38, no. 3, 2005, pp. 191–212.

[121] Jeffrey K Olick, *The Politics of Regret: On Collective Memory and Historical Responsibility*, Routledge, New York, 2007.

[122] Charles Scott, *The Time of Memory*, State University of New York Press, Albany, 1999; Charles Scott, 'The Appearance of Public Memory,' in *Framing Public Memory*, Kendall Phillips (ed.), pp. 147–156, University of Alabama Press, Tuscaloosa, 2004.

[123] Barbie Zelizer, 'The Voice of the Visual in Memory,' in Kendall Phillips (ed.), *Framing Public Memory*, pp. 157–86, University of Alabama Press, Tuscaloosa, 2004.

[124] A representative sample of scholars who have also attended to the performative dimensions of remembrance includes Edward E Casey, *Remembering: A Phenomenological Study*, Indiana University Press, Bloomington, 2000; Robert Hariman and John Lucaites 'Performing Civic Identity: The Iconic Photograph of the Flag Raising on Iwo Jima,' *Quarterly Journal of Speech*, vol. 88, no. 4, 2002, pp. 363–92; Greg Dickinson, 'Memories for Sale: Nostalgia and the Construction of Identity in Old Pasadena,' *Quarterly Journal of Speech*, vol. 83, no. 1, 1997, pp. 1–27; James V Wertsch *Voices of Collective Remembering*, Cambridge University Press, Cambridge, 2002; Jan Assmann, 'Collective Memory and Cultural Identity,' *New German Critique*, vol. 65, 1995, pp. 125–33; Diana Taylor, *The Archive and the Repertoire: Performing Cultural Memory in the Americas*, Duke University Press, Durham, 2003. It should be noted that scholars who are interested in the performative do not necessarily dismiss intersubjectivity. Assmann's work illustrates the point: while he regards remembrance as an active process, he still sees it as constituting collective identities intersubjectively: "We can refer to the structure of knowledge in this case as the 'concretion of identity.' With this we mean that a group bases its consciousness of unity and specifi city upon this knowledge and derives formative and normative impulses from it, which allows the group to reproduce its identity" Jan Assmann, 'Collective Memory and Cultural Identity,' *New German Critique*, vol. 65, 1995, pp. 125–33, p. 128.

[125] Bradford Vivian is a professor in the Department of Communication Arts and Sciences at Penn State University. His research and teaching focuses on theories of rhetoric (or the art

closest to a necessary critical shift. In his *'A Timeless Now': Memory and Repetition*,[126] Vivian explores repetition to develop a conception of public memory as itinerant. In his essay *Jefferson's Other*, he traces ghostly counterparts to Thomas Jefferson's alternate and public identity, as articulated in popular national texts.[127] In tracing the various others into Jefferson's official image, Vivian shifts from the either/or binary logic of remembering and forgetting, to an "either/or, or, or" logic of alterity,[128] raising the issue of whether public identities are created by metonymic chains of signifiers. In the case of poetry, as an example of public discourse, the terms metonymy and metaphor are not used as figures of speech but rather, as tropes of pervasive forces used for organizing language.

> Theorists have differed in defining this term, and any single definition would be prescriptive. Such consensus as there is wants trope to mean a figure that changes the meaning of a word or words, rather than simply arranging them in a pattern of some sort. . . . Some theorists would like trope to be used for changes in meaning of one word only; for more than one word, figure. Quintilian, on the other hand, points out that change in meaning occurs on a larger scale than in single words, and that change in signification is the crucial issue.[129]

There is an analytic of difference for advancing this scholarly dialectic,[130] which can set up a critical vocabulary for tracing the play between identity and alterity in the many public practices of remembrance. Through this critical lens, detailed accounts of the subjection strategies of public memory can be understood. Such an analytic of difference can illuminate the formation,

---

of persuasion) and public controversies over collective memories of past events. See B Vivian, 'Review of the book *Politics for Everybody: Reading Hannah Arendt in Uncertain Times, by Ned O'Gorman*,' *Quarterly Journal of Speech*, vol. 107, no. 1, 2021, pp. 136-139.

126 Bradford Vivian, '"A Timeless Now": Memory and Repetition,' in Kendall Phillips (ed.), *Framing Public Memory*, pp. 187–211, University of Alabama Press, Tuscaloosa, 2004.

127 Bradford Vivian 'Jefferson's Other,' *Quarterly Journal of Speech*, vol. 88, no. 3, 2002, pp. 284–302, p. 185.

128 G. Mitchell Reyes, 'Memory and Alterity: The Case for an Analytic of Difference,' *Philosophy & Rhetoric*, vol. 43, no. 3, 2010, pp. 222-252, p. 224.

129 Richard A Lanham, *A Handlist of Rhetorical Terms*, University of California Press, Berkeley, 1991, pp. 154-155.

130 The term "analytic" marks a rejection of the scholarly impulse to theorize or conceptualize difference. Michel Foucault, *The History of Sexuality*, Pantheon, New York, 1978, p. 82.

maintenance, then destruction, of public identities, even while doing what Jeff Nealon called "alterity politics."[131]

5. Reciprocity and Alterity in Lévy-Strauss

5.1. The Semantic Field of Alterity

The well-known last lines of *The Elementary Structures of Kinship*[132] of Lévy-Strauss[133] state as follows:

> To this very day, mankind has always dreamed of seizing and fixing that fleeting moment when it was permissible to believe that the law of exchange could be evaded, that one could gain without losing, joy without sharing. At either end of the earth and at both extremes of time, the Sumerian myth of the golden age and the Andaman of the future life correspond, the former placing the end of primitive happiness at a time when the confusion of languages made words common property, the latter describing the bliss of the hereafter a heaven where women will no longer be exchanged, i.e., removing to an equally unattainable past or future the joys, eternally to social man, of a world in which one might keep to oneself [*vivre entre soi*].[134]

Such words end a book whose aim was to demonstrate that human groups have resisted the temptation of living in isolation in order to live with others. Essentially, what Lévy-Strauss is considering here are the social forms of reproduction, such the sexual relationships between men and women, uncontainable within the group and therefore involving external relationships. Thus, life must come from outside the group. The establishment of these relationships is the purpose of kinship systems, so that Lévy-Strauss could

[131] Jeffrey Nealon, *Alterity Politics: Ethics and Performative Subjectivity*, Duke University Press, Durham, 1998; G Mitchell Reyes, 'Memory and Alterity: The Case for an Analytic of Difference,' *Philosophy & Rhetoric*, vol. 43, no. 3, 2010, pp. 222-252, p. 225.

[132] Claude Lévy-Strauss, *The Elementary Structures of Kinship*, Beacon Press, Boston, 1969.

[133] Claude Lévy-Strauss, (1908 –2009), was an ethnologist and anthropologist who developed theories of structuralism and structural anthropology. He held the Collège de France chair of Social Anthropology from 1959 to 1982, was elected in 1973 as member of the Académie française and was a member of the School for Advanced Studies in the Social Sciences, Paris. Rachel Briggs & Janelle Meyer, *"Structuralism," Anthropological Theories: A Guide Prepared by Students for Students*, University of Alabama, Mobile, 2015.

[134] Claude Lévy-Strauss, *The Elementary Structures of Kinship*, Beacon Press, Boston, 1969, pp. 496-497.

reduce this necessity of going outside the consanguineous group to a single formulation, namely, the prohibition against incest,[135] as the very genesis of institutions.[136] This prohibition is a fundamental expression of a continuing demand for reciprocity among human groups. Like exogamy, which is its converse, the prohibition of incest is such a rule of reciprocity. Those women, whom one may not take, are for that reason offered up. She is offered, sometimes to a group circumscribed by institutions, and other times to an indeterminate collective, limited only by excluding near relatives, such as operates in our society.[137] The primary objective of this prohibition is to make the consanguineous group exogamic. This means forcing this group to seek out another group to reproduce as a group. Thus, a human group exists only by defining itself by the alliance of marriage. The marriage alliance is a bringing together of other and other, for agreement between the one and the other. This permits better understanding of Lévy-Strauss's aphorism: "we must not seek to discover the social origin of symbolism, but rather to understand the symbolic origin of society."[138] Thus, the marriage alliance is sealed in mutual exchanges of wives, as ceremonial gifts, such as Marcel Mauss described them in his work *The Gift: The Form and Reason for Exchange in Archaic Societies [Essai sur le don, 1924].*[139]

Lévy-Strauss acknowledges that Mauss's essay was his main inspiration for his scholarship on kinship. Of all the kinds Mauss explored, the matrimonial alliance is the most decisive, because it involves the group's life and generational survival. Lévy-Strauss remarked "it would be false to say that one exchanges or gives gifts at the same time that one exchanges or gives women. For the woman herself is nothing other than one of these gifts, supreme gift among those that can only be obtained in the form of reciprocal gifts."[140] In the last pages of his book, he added that the prohibition is "the

---

135 Marcel Hénaff & Robert Doran, 'Living with Others: Reciprocity and Alterity in Lévy-Strauss,' *Yale French Studies*, no. 123, 2013, pp. 63-82, p. 64.

136 Marcel Hénaff, *Lévy-Strauss and the Making of Structural Anthropology*, Mary Baker (trans.), University of Minnesota Press, Minneapolis, 1998, Chs. 2, 3.

137 Claude Lévy-Strauss, *The Elementary Structures of Kinship*, Beacon Press, Boston, 1969, p. 51.

138 "Mauss still thinks it possible to develop a sociological theory of symbolism, whereas it is obvious that what is needed is a symbolic origin of society". Claude Lévy-Strauss, *Introduction to the Work of Marcel Mauss*, Routledge & Kegan Paul, New York, 1987, p. 21.

139 Marcel Mauss, *The Gift: The Form and Reason for Exchange in Archaic Societies*, Routledge, London, 2002; Marcel Hénaff & Robert Doran, 'Living with Others: Reciprocity and Alterity in Lévy-Strauss,' *Yale French Studies*, no. 123, 2013, pp. 63-82, p. 65.

140 Claude Lévy-Strauss, *Introduction to the Work of Marcel Mauss*, Routledge & Kegan Paul, New York, 1987, p. 65.

supreme rule of the gift."[141] It is central to know that for this exchange, there must be the element of alterity, as manifested in the sexual instinct, which Lévy-Strauss said was "man's only instinct requiring the stimulation of another person."[142] This is illustrated in Elkin's[143] study of marriagc rclations within Australian tribes,[144] emphasizing the doxical group status of women.[145] Lévy-Strauss commented:

> The sole reason is that she is same whereas she must (and therefore can) become other. Once she becomes other (by her allocation to men of the opposite moiety), she therefore becomes liable to play the same role, vis-à-vis the men of her own moiety, as she originally played to the men of the opposite moiety. In feasts, the same presents can be exchanged; in the custom of kopara, the same women that were originally offered can be exchanged in return. All that is necessary on either side is the sign of otherness, which is the outcome of a certain position in a structure and not of any innate characteristic.[146]

This characterological alterity, a required element of the prohibition against incest, propagates in situations, behaviors and relationships. Lévy-Strauss vividly demonstrates this in cases where a person either ignores the other person's alterity, by denying him any response, or when abusing the means of communication and exchange.[147] From this, Lévy-Strauss's conclusion was:

---

[141] ibid., p. 481.

[142] "It is a question of "overcoming the contradiction by which the same woman was seen under two incompatible aspects: on the one hand, as the object of personal desire, thus exciting sexual and proprietorial instincts; and on the other, as the subject of the desire of others, and seen as such, i.e., as the means of binding others through alliance with them" Claude Lévy-Strauss, *Introduction to the Work of Marcel Mauss*, Routledge & Kegan Paul, New York, 1987, p. 496.

[143] Adolphus Peter Elkin, (1891 –1979), was a member of Anglican clergy, an Australian anthropologist during the mid 20th century and a proponent of the proposed assimilation of Indigenous Australians. EJ Telfer, *Amongst Australian Aborigines: forty years of missionary work: the story of the United Aborigines Mission*, EJ Telfer, Sydney, 1939, pp. 188, 227.

[144] AP Elkin, 'Studies in Australian Totemism: The Nature of Australian Totemism,' *Oceania*, vol. 4, no. 2, 1933, pp. 113-131.

[145] Marcel Hénaff & Robert Doran, 'Living with Others: Reciprocity and Alterity in Lévy-Strauss,' *Yale French Studies*, no. 123, 2013, pp. 63-82, p. 66.

[146] Claude Lévy-Strauss, *Introduction to the Work of Marcel Mauss*, Routledge & Kegan Paul, New York, 1987, p, 114.

[147] Marcel Hénaff & Robert Doran, 'Living with Others: Reciprocity and Alterity in Lévy-Strauss,' *Yale French Studies*, no. 123, 2013, pp. 63-82, p. 67.

> These prohibitions are all thus reduced to a single common denominator: they all constitute a misuse of language, and on this ground they are grouped together with the incest prohibition, or with acts evocative of incest. What does this mean, except that women themselves are treated as signs, which are misused when not put to the use reserved to signs, which is to be communicated?[148]

Women therefore are signifiers for both alterity and matrimonial alliance pledges. In the result, speaking, marrying and relating to other humans or animals, always means a relationship is only worthy, if it is both reciprocal and recognizes the alterity of all others. Lévy-Strauss gives other examples of this logic, writing that:

> ... during Polynesian ceremonial exchanges it is required that goods be exchanged within the group of near paternal relatives, but must as far as possible go to other groups and into other villages. To fail in this duty is called soritana, 'eating from one's basket.'[149]

This was what Lévy-Strauss called "a sort of social incest."[150] From all this, the formula is: "Incest in the broadest sense of the word consists in obtaining by oneself, and for oneself, instead of by another, and for another."[151]

6. The Strangeness of Alterity

6.1. Stranger, Other and Alterity

In respect of defining the border separating the familiar and the unfamiliar, strangeness and ownness, Levinas stated that there was no common border separating "me" and "the Other," because any boundary both unites and separates. The alterity of the other person is unique such that beyond this border, or even without any border, it is still in relation. Levinas wrote: "Other with an alterity that does not limit the same, for in limiting the same, the other

[148] Claude Lévy-Strauss, *Introduction to the Work of Marcel Mauss*, Routledge & Kegan Paul, New York, 1987, pp. 495-496.
[149] Claude Lévy-Strauss, *Introduction to the Work of Marcel Mauss*, Routledge & Kegan Paul, New York, 1987, pp. 57-58.
[150] ibid., p, 58.
[151] ibid., p. 489.

would not be rigorously other: by virtue of the common frontier the other, within the system, would yet be the same."[152] The other and the self have nothing in common, that could facilitate the assimilation of the one to the other. The strangeness of the Other remains foreign, even with no country border for separation. Although Levinas observed that the stranger is not entirely in my location, and could never be there, there could still be a "twilight zone,"[153] or a "threshold."[154] Thus, Levinas extrapolates an "infinite distance," between me and the Other.[155] In respect of radical alterity, the image of the stranger returns, as Levinas articulated the "infinite distance of the stranger."[156] Despite the fact that Levinas used the same word for the foreigner, the stranger and the absolute stranger, the difference between them is clear, with the linking directly to alterity as the Other who is different like the foreigner. This alterity is also alien because other creates moral obligations of the highest order. The "I," having no common conception with the stranger, is just like him, as the two both have no genus.[157]

Since the Other is essentially alien, strange and foreign, this link had led Waldenfels to acknowledge that for Levinas "the experience of the alien as alien resists every form of totalizing and universalizing. This is closely tied to an irrevocable asymmetry of my relation to others."[158] This facet of strangeness in the Other implies an unbridgeable distance between the "I" and the Other. Levinas understood alterity as functioning like a transcendental disposition of the peculiar, strange, foreign and weird, with the transcendence being ethical rather than epistemological.[159] From this, we can posit that a power group can operate under the tenets of different ethical deliberations to those of a subaltern group.

---

[152] E Lévinas, *Totality and Infinity: An Essay on Exteriority*, Duquesne University Press, Pittsburgh, 1969, §39.

[153] Bernhard Waldenfels, *Phenomenology of the Alien: Basic Concepts*, Northwestern University Press, Evanston, 2011.

[154] Richard Kearney, *Strangers, Gods, and Monsters: Interpreting Otherness*, Routledge, New York, 2003.

[155] Jolanta Saldukaitytė, 'The Strangeness of Alterity,' *Levinas Studies*, vol. 11, 2016, pp. 95-120, p. 109.

[156] E Lévinas, *Totality and Infinity: An Essay on Exteriority*, Duquesne University Press, Pittsburgh, 1969, §50.

[157] E Lévinas, *Totality and Infinity: An Essay on Exteriority*, Duquesne University Press, Pittsburgh, 1969, §39.

[158] Bernhard Waldenfels & Anthony J Steinbock, 'Experience of the Alien in Husserl's Phenomenology,' *Research in Phenomenology*, vol. 20, no. 1, 1990, pp. 19-33, pp. 29–30.

[159] Jolanta Saldukaitytė, 'The Strangeness of Alterity,' *Levinas Studies*, vol. 11, 2016, pp. 95-120, p. 111.

Thus, these two kinds of strangeness have unavoidable ambiguity, as there is awareness that the other person is unfamiliar, so that Kant would say that this unfamiliar other therefore had dignity.[160] Levinas focused on the alterity of the other in its form as moral obligation, being someone who was elevated, and thus coming first. "The absolutely foreign alone can instruct us. And it is only man who could be absolutely foreign to me."[161] This suggests a subaltern group is somehow morally obliged to the commanding social group.

Levinas speaks about breaking univocal discourse, so that for him "it is between strangers that the encounter takes place; otherwise, it would be kinship."[162] The ethical relation of responsibility unites two different persons while securing their distance, which Levinas named "proximity,"[163] and which cannot be measured in geometrical space. Similarly, Levinas used the spatial terms "distance" and "exteriority" non-spatially. These terms suggest that, while real encounters occur between strangers, the other person always remains unfamiliar, and is therefore a stranger. "In that relation to the other, there is no fusion: the relation to the other is envisioned as alterity. The other is alterity."[164]

The other is both different and essentially strange. This other comes from ethical transcendence, and therefore from moral altitude, as the source of his own meaning, outside any possible shared context.[165] Levinas argues, "The other is not other because he would have other attributes, or would have been born elsewhere or at another moment, or because he would be of a different race. . . . It is not difference which makes alterity: alterity makes difference."[166] Thus, the alterity had existed prior to the commanding group cognizing its own moral superiority. This alterity cannot be eliminated, even in erotic embraces. Levinas articulated it as follows:

---

[160] Kant's main themes were that all persons, regardless of social class or rank, had an intrinsic equal worth, or, dignity. Human dignity was innate status or worth, unearned and not susceptible to forfeiture. I Kant, *Groundwork for the Metaphysics of Morals*, TE Hill, Jr. & A Zweig (eds.), Oxford University Press, Oxford, 2002.

[161] E Lévinas, *Totality and Infinity: An Essay on Exteriority*, Duquesne University Press, Pittsburgh, 1969, §73.

[162] Georges Bénézé, *Allure du transcendental*, Vrin, Paris, 1936, p. 97.

[163] "Proximity appears as the relationship with the other, who cannot be resolved into 'images' or be exposed in a theme." Emmanuel Levinas, *Otherwise than Being, or Beyond Essence*, Alphonso Lingis (trans.), Duquesne University Press, Pittsburgh, 2008, p. 100.

[164] Georges Bénézé, *Allure du transcendental*, Vrin, Paris, 1936, p. 103.

[165] Jolanta Saldukaitytė, 'The Strangeness of Alterity,' *Levinas Studies*, vol. 11, 2016, pp. 95-120, p. 112.

[166] E Lévinas, 'L'inspiration religieuse de l'Alliance,' *Paix et Droit*, vol. 15, no. 8, 1935, §106.

> The absolutely foreign alone can instruct us. And it is only man who could be absolutely foreign to me — refractory to every typology, to every genus, to every characterology, to every classification — and consequently the term of a 'knowledge' finally penetrating beyond the object. The strangeness of the Other, his very freedom! Free beings alone can be strangers to one another.[167]

The other is always different with differing characteristics, but the alterity of the other is other in an absolute sense.[168]

Conclusion

The research question asked how the alterity, that is inherent in the "fit and proper test," might generate the subaltern groups of fit and proper professions, clients and others. Argument has sought to sustain the view that the fit and proper professions are priestly enterprises of manipulated public memory, by commanding descending chains of the meanings of technical terms, so that the subaltern groups of clients and the general public are somehow morally obliged, inferring a duty, to the institutions of the professions.

Argument has identified five facets of this subaltern project, those of religion, psychology, language, hierarchy and anthropology. Dealing first with religion, the very conception of any kind of origin of religion can be understood in both phenomenological and historical senses. In this way, an origin of religion can be linked to the historical blocs that created the subaltern public acquiescence in hegemony. Alterity may be understood as the phenomenological genesis of religion, by which people are constrained within a large social group, to the exclusion of those who do not profess such a religion. Binding notions of the numinous, developed by Rudolf Otto, mean arousing spiritual or religious emotion, mysterious, or awe-inspiring. Also, the associated *mysterium tremendum*, which means a great or profound mystery, clearly provides an open opportunity for public manipulation of reality.

Dealing second with psychology, La Barre's psychoanalytic argument, beginning from neoteny, was a way to ground alterity, as the state of being "other" or "different," in the human body, and to incorporate the otherness of

---

[167] E Lévinas, *Totality and Infinity: An Essay on Exteriority*, Duquesne University Press, Pittsburgh, 1969, §73.

[168] Jolanta Saldukaitytė, 'The Strangeness of Alterity,' *Levinas Studies*, vol. 11, 2016, pp. 95-120, p. 113.

religion to the other of the father, thereby attaching the authority of the father to the power of the priesthood. This inferred a non-priestly subaltern mass of assumed religious adherents. Hannah Arendt thought that public practices of remembrance were the lifeblood of the city form of state. It appeared that without remembrance, collective identity and historical responsibility essentially disappeared, raising the question of whether such collectivity was nothing more than the legislated remembering of what the person had never experienced, this kind of false memory being a catastrophic move to subaltern status. Alterity becomes obliterated in those discourses of memory that appropriate personal views, suggesting that subalterity might only be maintained by memories the person has never had. In the light of alterity, public memory transforms from a governance method for creating collective identities, to an arena in which identity and alterity can interact, so that identity can be introjected into the collective as that which its members are not. In tracing the various others into Jefferson's official image, Vivian shifts from the either/or binary logic of remembering and forgetting, to an "either/or, or, or" logic of alterity, raising the issue of whether public identities are subalterities created by metonymic chains of signifiers. Accordingly, the other and the self have nothing in common that could facilitate the assimilation of the one to the other. Alterity is thus alien, because an other creates moral obligations of the highest order. The "I," having no common conception with the stranger, is just like the stranger, inasmuch as the two both have no genus. They are Platonic forms. The other is not other because he would have other attributes, or would have been born elsewhere or at another moment, or because he would be of a different race. It is not difference the makes alterity, rather, alterity makes difference. Thus, the alterity had existed prior to the commanding group's cognizing its own moral superiority.

Dealing third with language, Rappaport posited that at the human fall from grace, the consequent evolution of language caused the splitting of parts of the psyche. This emergence of language therefore implied some preceptual rupture, which itself constituted a deep alterity, characterized by both coexisting otherness and fallen otherness. If emerging language placed alterity into a structure of existence, then there must have been a second level of alterity, where the one level forever corrected the other, with the first other imagining it had a right from birth to correct the second "fallen" other. Language has ever more powerfully reached out from the species in which it emerged to reorder, by making meanings, and subordinating the natural systems in which populations of that species participate. This unveils alterity within language, as a human other many steps above a natural other. The

process of making meaning could be a distorting, inadequate and inhuman apolitical tool that reworks experience so that it conforms to the demands of power, implying that a personal perception of experience could be distorted by external power, such that a person's experience could simply be ignored. In Wittgensteins's *Tractatus*, he attempted to explain the relationship between the three realms of language, thought and reality, up to that time thought to be merely parallel. After all, without knowing a word's meaning, one could not use that word to exploit reality. Wittgenstein thus issued a veiled warning that language and thought could manipulate reality by seizing power over canonized meanings of words.

Dealing fourth with hierarchy, Otto is telling us that it is possible to experience apart from the schema of categories, that is, to have experience of reality as *a priori*, not yet structured for the human project, making reality itself very simply other. Alterity is a fundamental aspect of being human, a plain structure of existence, and misunderstanding this has caused both misery and creativity in the life of humanity, when hierarchical groupings purport to control by power the human project itself. By way of example, Martin Luther warned Erasmus to turn one's mind more to the compassionate and preached will of God, as demanded by the gospels, as written by canonized authors, rather than to the veiled and aweful will of the deity. This demonstrated Luther's use of gospels to replace, and alter at will, the deity itself, suggesting a chain of meanings moving down between the deity and the gospels. Thus, the deconstructions of Derrida are premised on permitting differance its voice, where "différance" is the endless deferring of any final meaning of a sentence or word, because of the likely infinite series of other and equally uncertain signs or words. Any such infinite series thus may be turned into a power hierarchy, turning alterity into subalterity, constructed from subaltern groups. Aquinas stated that, concerning God, we could not grasp what he is, but only what he is not, and how other beings stand in relation to him. Putting the two parts of this dictum together, Aquinas permitted the human project to cognize the deity through a chain of subaltern groupings, each subaltern level absolutely not being the next level up. Similarly Levinas understood alterity as functioning like a transcendental disposition of the peculiar, strange, foreign and weird, with the transcendence being ethical rather than epistemological. From this, we can posit that a commanding power group could operate under

the tenets of different ethical deliberations to those of a subaltern group. This leads to Levinas' focus on the alterity of the other in its form as moral obligation, being someone who was elevated, and thus coming first, with only the absolutely foreign able to instruct us. This suggests a subaltern group is somehow morally obliged to the commanding social group.

Dealing fifth with anthropology, the prohibition against incest is the supreme rule of the gift. It is central to know that for this exchange, namely the gifting of women, there must be the element of alterity, as manifested in the sexual instinct, which Lévy-Strauss said was man's only instinct requiring the stimulation of another person. This emphasizes the doxical group status of women, which can be changed by power changes in doxa. Such characterological alterity, a required element of the prohibition against incest, propagates downwards in situations, behaviors and relationships. This takes place in cases where a person either ignores the other person's alterity, by denying him or her any response, or when abusing the means of communication and exchange. Women therefore are unifying signifiers to bind together both alterity and the confected controlling institution of matrimony.

Extending these syntheses, the *mysterium tremendum*, which means a great or profound mystery, clearly provides an open opportunity for public manipulation of reality. There is an inferred non-priestly subaltern mass of assumed religious adherents, whose reality is controlled by public practices of forced remembrance, but with operative alterity really having existed prior to the commanding group's cognizing its own apparent moral superiority. If emerging language placed alterity into a structure of existence, then there must have been a second level of alterity, where the one level forever corrected the other, with the first other imagining it had a right from birth to correct the second "fallen" other by canonizing the meaning of words. In this way, Luther had used gospels to replace, and alter at will, the deity itself, suggesting a descending chain of meanings between the deity and the gospels. This implies a subaltern group is somehow morally obliged to the commanding social group. To achieve this, women are structured as unifying signifiers, subject at any time to command alteration of the doxa within their significations, to bind together both alterity and the confected religious institution version of the ancient custom of matrimony, in order to command the entire human project of propriety.

References

Adler, Joseph, *Rudolf Otto's Concept of the Numinous*, Kenyon College, Gambier, 2016.

Agamben, Giorgio, *Homo sacer: Sovereign power and bare life*, Stanford University Press, Stanford, 1995.

Allen, Charlotte, 'Is nothing sacred?,' *Lingua Franca*, November, 1996, pp. 30–40.

Allen, Wayne F, 'Hannah Arendt: existential phenomenology and political freedom,' *Philosophy & Social Criticism*, vol. 9, no. 2, 1982, pp. 170–190.

Anderson, Benedict, *Imagined Communities: Reflections on the Origin and Spread of Nationalism,* Verso, New York, 1991.

Angier, Carole, *The Double Bond: Primo Levi: A Biography,* Penguin, London, 2002.

Arendt, Hannah, *The Origins of Totalitarianism*, Harcourt, Brace, New York, 1968.

Assmann, Jan, 'Collective Memory and Cultural Identity,' *New German Critique*, vol. 65, 1995, pp. 125–33.

Augustine, 'The Confessions III,' in John E. Rotelle (ed.), *The Works of St. Augustine: A Translation for the 21st Century*, Maria Boulding (trans.), vol. 1/1, New City Press, New York, 1997.

Bass, Alan (trans.), 'Différance,' in *Margins of Philosophy*, Chicago University Press, Chicago, 1982.

Beard, Mary, 'Frazer, Leach, and Virgil: The Popularity (and Unpopularity) of the Golden Bough,' *Comparative Studies in Society and History*, vol. 34, no. 2, 1992, pp. 203–224.

Beloe, William (transl.), *The History of Herodotus*, Leigh and Sotheby, London, 1741.

Bénézé, Georges, *Allure du transcendental*, Vrin, Paris, 1936.

Bergo, Bettina, 'Emmanuel Levinas, in Edward N Zalta (ed.), *The Stanford Encyclopedia of Philosophy*, Stanford University, Palo Alto, 2015.

Blake, William, *The Marriage of Heaven and Hell*, Oxford University Press, Oxford, 1988.

Bodnar, John, *Remaking America: Public Memory, Commemoration, and Patriotism in the Twentieth Century*, Princeton University Press, Princeton, 1992.

Bradford, Vivian, '"A Timeless Now": Memory and Repetition,' in Kendall Phillips (ed.), *Framing Public Memory*, pp. 187–211, University of Alabama Press, Tuscaloosa, 2004.

Briggs, Rachel, & Janelle Meyer, *"Structuralism," Anthropological Theories: A Guide Prepared by Students for Students*, University of Alabama, Mobile, 2015.

Buber, Martin, *I and Thou*, Charles Scribner's Sons, New York, 1970.

Caputo, John D, 'God Is Wholly Other - Almost: Différance and the Hyperbolic Alterity of God,' in Orrin F Summerell (ed.), *The Otherness of God*, University Press of Virginia, Charlottesville, 1998.

Casey, Edward E, *Remembering: A Phenomenological Study*, Indiana University Press, Bloomington, 2000.

Catechism of the Catholic Church, Our Sunday Visitor, Publishing Division, United States, 2000.

Charles Scott, *The Time of Memory*, State University of New York Press, Albany, 1999.

Chisholm, Hugh (ed.), 'Tylor, Edward Burnett,' *Encyclopædia Britannica*, vol. 27, Cambridge University Press, Cambridge, 1911.

Csordas, Thomas J, 'Asymptote of the Ineffable: Embodiment, Alterity, and the Theory of Religion,' *Current Anthropology*, vol. 45, no. 2, 2004, pp. 163-185.

D'Angelo, Frank J, *Composition in the Classical Tradition*, University of Arizona Press, Tucson, 2000.

Das, Veena, & Deborah Poole (eds.), *Anthropology in the Margins: Comparative Ethnographies*, SAR Press, Santa Fe, 2004.

Davis, Diana, 'Addressing Alterity: Rhetoric, Hermeneutics, and the Nonappropriative Relation,' *Philosophy and Rhetoric*, vol. 38, no. 3, 2005, pp. 191–212.

de la Durantaye, Leland, *Giorgio Agamben: A Critical Introduction*, Stanford University Press, Stanford, 2009.

Deleuze, Gilles, *Difference and Repetition*, Columbia University Press, New York, 1994.

Delvecchio Good, MJ, & BJ Good, 'Culture, medicine and psychiatry: Twenty years and more,' *Culture, Medicine and Psychiatry*, vol. 20, no. 1, 1996, pp. vii–xi.

Derrida, Jacques, 'Faith and Knowledge,' in *Religion*, Samuel Weber (trans.), Stanford University Press, Stanford, 1996, pp. 1-78.

Derrida, Jacques, 'How to Avoid Speaking,' in Harold Coward & Toby Foshay (eds.), *Derrida and Negative Theology*, Ken Frieden (trans.), SUNY Press, Albany, 1992.

Derrida, Jacques, 'Sauf le nom,' in Thomas Dutoit (ed.), *On the Name*, John P. Leavey Jr. (trans.), Stanford University Press, Stanford, 1995.

Derrida, Jacques, *Limited Inc*., Northwestern University Press, Evanston, 1988.

Descartes, René, 'Meditations on First Philosophy with Selections from the Objections and Replies,' in Karl Ameriks (ed.), *Cambridge Texts in the History of Philosophy*, John Cottingham (trans.), Cambridge University Press, Cambridge, 1996.

Descartes, René, *Meditations on First Philosophy*, J Cottingham (trans.), Cambridge University Press, Cambridge, 1996.

Dickinson, Greg, 'Memories for Sale: Nostalgia and the Construction of Identity in Old Pasadena,' *Quarterly Journal of Speech*, vol. 83, no. 1, 1997, pp. 1–27.

Eliade, Mircea, *Shamanism: Archaic Techniques of Ecstasy*, Princeton University Press, Princeton, 2004.

Elkin, AP, 'Studies in Australian Totemism: The Nature of Australian Totemism,' *Oceania*, vol. 4, no. 2, 1933, pp. 113-131.

Fardon, Richard, 'Immortality yet? Or, the permanence of Mary Douglas,' *Anthropology Today*, vol. 34, no. 4, 2018, pp. 23–26.

Foucault, Michel, *The History of Sexuality*, Pantheon, New York, 1978.

Frye, Northrop, & Robert D Denham, *Collected Works of Northrop Frye*, University of Toronto Press, Toronto, 2006.

Fynes, RCC, 'Müller, Friedrich Max (1823–1900),' in *Oxford Dictionary of National Biography*, Oxford University Press, Oxford, 2004.

Geertz, Clifford, 'The pinch of destiny: Religion as experience, meaning, identity, power,' in *Available light: Anthropological reflections on philosophical topics*, University Press, Princeton, 2000.

Gillis John R (ed.), *Commemorations: The Politics of National Identity*, Princeton University Press, Princeton, 1994.

Gramsci, Antonio, *Quaderni di Carcere* [*Prison notebooks*], Valentino Gerratana (ed.), Einaudi, Torino, 1977.

Green, Linda, 'Reviewed work: Social Suffering, Arthur Kleinman, Veena Das, Margaret Lock,' *Medical Anthropology Quarterly*, vol. 13, no. 3, 1999, pp. 375–377.

Haggbloom, Steven J, Renee Warnick, Jason E Warnick, Vinessa K Jones, Gary L Yarbrough, Tenea M Russell, Chris M Borecky, Reagan McGahhey, John L Powell, Jamie Beavers, Emmanuelle Monte, 'The 100 Most Eminent Psychologists of the 20th Century,' *Review of General Psychology*, vol. 6, no. 2, 2002, pp. 139–152.

Halbwachs, Maurice, *On Collective Memory,* University of Chicago Press, Chicago, 1992.

Hansson, Klas, 'Nathan Söderblom's ecumenical cope: A visualization of a theological and ecumenical concept,' *Studia Theologica – Nordic Journal of Theology*, vol. 66, no. 1, 2012, pp. 62-79.

Hariman, Robert, & John Lucaites, 'Performing Civic Identity: The Iconic Photograph of the Flag Raising on Iwo Jima,' *Quarterly Journal of Speech*, vol. 88, no. 4, 2002, pp. 363–392.

Hénaff, Marcel, & Robert Doran, 'Living with Others: Reciprocity and Alterity in Lévy-Strauss,' *Yale French Studies*, no. 123, 2013, pp. 63-82.

Hénaff, Marcel, *Lévy-Strauss and the Making of Structural Anthropology*, Mary Baker (trans.), University of Minnesota Press, Minneapolis, 1998.

Hurst, Charles E, *Social Inequality: Forms, Causes, and Consequences*, Allyn and Bacon, Boston, 2007.

James, William, *The varieties of religious experience*, Collier Books, New York, 1961.

Kammen, Michael, *Mystic Chords of Memory: The Transformation of Tradition in American Culture*, Knopf, New York, 1991.

Kant, I, *Groundwork for the Metaphysics of Morals*, TE Hill, Jr. & A Zweig (eds.), Oxford University Press, Oxford, 2002.

Kattago, Siobhan, *Ambiguous Memory: The Nazi Past and German National Identity*, Praeger, Westport, 2001.

Kearney, Richard, *Strangers, Gods, and Monsters: Interpreting Otherness*, Routledge, New York, 2003.

Klein, Terrance W, 'Adventures In Alterity: Wittgenstein, Aliens, Anselm and Aquinas,' *New Blackfriars*, vol. 88, no. 1013, 2007, pp. 73-86.

Kleinman, Arthur, 'Everything that really matters: Social suffering, subjectivity, and the remaking of human experience in a disordering world,' *Harvard Theological Review,* vol. 90, 1997, pp. 315–335.

La Barre, Weston, *The Ghost Dance: The origins of religion*, Dell, New York, 1970.

Lacan, Jacques, 'The Mirror Stage As Formative of the Function of the I As Revealed in Psychoanalytic Experience,' in Jacques Lacan, *Écrits: A Selection*, Alan Sheridan (trans.), WW Norton and Company, New York, 1977.

Lane, Jessica, 'The Poetics of Legal Interpretation,' *Columbia Law Review*, vol. 87, no. 1, 1987, pp. 197-216.

Lanham, Richard A, *A Handlist of Rhetorical Terms*, University of California Press, Berkeley, 1991.

Lasker, Gabriel Ward, 'The Human Animal. Weston la Barre,' *American Anthropologist,* vol. 57, no. 2, 1955, pp. 377–378.

Lawler, Lillian B, 'Proteus Is a Dancer,' *The Classical Weekly*, vol. 36, no. 10, 1943), pp. 116-117.

Leitch, Vincent B, *Postmodernism: Local Effects, Global Flows*, State University of New York Press, Albany, 1996.

Lévy-Strauss, Claude, *Introduction to the Work of Marcel Mauss*, Routledge & Kegan Paul, New York, 1987.

Lévy-Strauss, Claude, *The Elementary Structures of Kinship*, Beacon Press, Boston, 1969, pp. 496-497.

Lévinas, Emmanuel, 'L'inspiration religieuse de l'Alliance [The religious inspiration of the Alliance],' *Paix et Droit*, vol. 15, no. 8, 1935.

Lévinas, Emmanuel, 'The Old and the New,' in *Time and the Other*, Duquesne University Press, Pittsburgh, 1987.

Lévinas, Emmanuel, *Otherwise than Being, or Beyond Esse*nce, Alphonso Lingis (trans.), Duquesne University Press, Pittsburgh, 2008.

Lévinas, Emmanuel, *Totality and Infinity: An Essay on Exteriority*, Duquesne University Press, Pittsburgh, 1969.

Long, Charles, 'The oppressive elements in religion and the religions of the oppressed,' *Harvard Theological Review*, vol. 59, 1976, pp. 397–412.

Luther, Martin, 'The Bondage of the Will,' in Helmut T. Lehmann (ed.), *Luther's Works*, Philip S Watson & Benjamin Drewery (trans.), vol. 33, Fortress Press, Philadelphia, 1972.

Luther, Martin, Lectures on Genesis: Chapters 45–50, Jaroslav Jan Pelikan, Hilton C Oswald, and Helmut T Lehmann (eds.), vol. 8, *Luther's Works*, Concordia Publishing House, Saint Louis, 1999.

Mauss, Marcel, *The Gift: The Form and Reason for Exchange in Archaic Societies*, Routledge, London, 2002.

McCarthy, Joseph M, 'Fustel de Coulanges, Numa,' in Kelly Boyd (ed.), *Encyclopedia of historians and historical writing* (1999), Taylor & Francis, London, 1999.

Moore, Jerry D, *Victor Turner: Symbols, Pilgrims, and Drama: Visions of Culture*, Alta Mira Press, Lanham, 2012.

Nealon, Jeffrey, *Alterity Politics: Ethics and Performative Subjectivity*, Duke University Press, Durham, 1998.

Novick, Peter, *The Holocaust in American Life,* Houghton Mifflin, Boston, 1999.

O'Nolan, K, 'The Proteus Legend,' *Hermes*, vol. 88, no. 2, 1960, pp. 129-138.

Olick, Jeffrey K, *The Politics of Regret: On Collective Memory and Historical Responsibility*, Routledge, New York, 2007.

Otto, Rudolf, *The idea of the holy*, Oxford University Press, Oxford, 1923.

Perry, Ralph Barton, *The Thought and Character of William James*, vol. 1, Vanderbilt University Press, Nashville, 1996.

Peters, FE, *Greek Philosophical Terms*, New York University Press, New York, 1967.

Rappaport, Roy A, 'Logos, liturgy, and the evolution of humanity,' in Astrid Beck, Andrew Bartlet, Paul Raabe & Chris Franke (eds.), *Fortunate the eyes that see: Essays in honor of David Noel Freedman*, pp. 601–32, WD Eerdmans, Grand Rapids, 1995.

Rappaport, Roy A, 'Ritual Regulation of Environmental Relations among a New Guinea People,' *Ethnology*, vol. 6, no. 1, 1967, pp. 17–30.

Rappaport, Roy A, *Ecology, meaning, and religion*, North Atlantic Books, Richmond, 1979.

Rappaport, Roy A, *Ritual and religion in the making of humanity*, Cambridge University Press, Cambridge, 1999.

Reid, Jennifer, & David Carrasco (eds.), *With This Root about My Person: Charles H. Long and New Directions in the Study of Religion*, University of New Mexico Press, Santa Fe, 2020.

Reyes, G Mitchell, 'Memory and Alterity: The Case for an Analytic of Difference,' *Philosophy & Rhetoric*, vol. 43, no. 3, 2010, pp. 222-252.

Saldukaitytė, Jolanta, 'The Strangeness of Alterity,' *Levinas Studies*, vol. 11, 2016, pp. 95-120.

Scott, Charles, 'Th e Appearance of Public Memory,' in *Framing Public Memory*, Kendall Phillips (ed.), pp. 147–56, University of Alabama Press, Tuscaloosa, 2004.

Sharpe, Matthew, 'On Reading Heidegger—After the "Heidegger Case"?,' *Critical Horizons*, vol. 19, no. 4, 2018, pp. 334–360.

Shweder, Richard A, & Byron Good (eds.), *Clifford Geertz by His Colleagues*, University of Chicago Press, Chicago, 2005.

Sotiris, Panagiotis, 'Gramsci and the Challenges for the Left: The Historical Bloc as a Strategic Concept,' *Science & Society*, vol. 82, no. 1, 2018, pp. 94–119.

Taylor, Diana, *The Archive and the Repertoire: Performing Cultural Memory in the Americas*, Duke University Press, Durham, 2003.

Taylor, Mark C, *Erring: A Postmodern A/theology*, University of Chicago Press, Chicago, 2013.

Taylor, Mark, 'Postmodern Times,' in Orrin F Summerell (ed.), *The Otherness of God*, University Press of Virginia, Charlottesville, 1998.

Telfer, EJ, *Amongst Australian Aborigines: forty years of missionary work: the story of the United Aborigines Mission*, EJ Telfer, Sydney, 1939.

Thomson, Ian, *Primo Levi*, Picador, London, 2019.

Turner, Edith, 'The Literary Roots of Victor Turner's Anthropology,' in Kathleen M Ashley (ed.), *Victor Turner and the Construction of Cultural Criticism*, Indiana University Press, Indianapolis, 1990.

van der Leeuw, Gerardus, *Einführung in die Phänomenologie der Religion* [*Introduction to the phenomenology of religion*], Ernst Reinhardt, München, 1925.

van der Leeuw, Gerardus, *Religion in essence and manifestation (1938)*, Princeton University Press, Princeton, 1986.

Venturinha, Nuno, *The Textual Genesis of Wittgenstein's Philosophical Investigations*, Routledge, 2013.

Vivian, B, 'Review of the book Politics for Everybody: Reading Hannah Arendt in Uncertain Times, by Ned O'Gorman,' *Quarterly Journal of Speech*, vol. 107, no. 1, 2021, pp. 136-139.

Vivian, Bradford, 'Jefferson's Other,' *Quarterly Journal of Speech*, vol. 88, no. 3, 2002, pp. 284–302.

Vredeveld, Harry, 'The Ages of Erasmus and the Year of his Birth,' *Renaissance Quarterly*, vol. 46, no. 4, 1993, pp. 754–809.

Waldenfels, Bernhard, & Anthony J Steinbock, 'Experience of the Alien in Husserl's Phenomenology,' *Research in Phenomenology*, vol. 20, no. 1, 1990, pp. 19-33.

Waldenfels, Bernhard, *Phenomenology of the Alien: Basic Concepts*, Northwestern University Press, Evanston, 2011.

Watt, Donald, (ed.), *Aldous Huxley*, Routledge, London, 1975.

Wertsch, James V, *Voices of Collective Remembering*, Cambridge University Press, Cambridge, 2002.

Wiebe, Donald, *The politics of religious studies*, Palgrave, New York, 1999.

Wiebe, Donald, *The Science of Religion: A Defence, Essays by Donald Wiebe*, Brill, Leiden, 2019.

Wilson, Mona, *The Life of William Blake*, The Nonesuch Press, Nonesuch Press, London, 1927.

Wittgenstein, Ludwig, *Tractatus Logico-Philosohicus*, DF Pears & BF McGuinness (trans.), Routledge, London, 1961.

Young-Bruehl, Elisabeth, *Hannah Arendt: For Love of the World*, Yale University Press, 2004.

Zelizer, Barbie, 'The Voice of the Visual in Memory,' in Kendall Phillips (ed.), *Framing Public Memory*, pp. 157–86, University of Alabama Press, Tuscaloosa, 2004.

Chapter 5

Délation of Character

Gary I. Lilienthal[1,*], PhD
and Muhamad Hassan bin Ahmad[2], PhD
[1]Carrington Rand, Hong Kong SAR, Peoples Republic of China
[2]Ahmad Ibrahim Kulliyyah of Laws, International Islamic University, Kuala Lumpur, Malaysia

Abstract

The Metropolitan Opera of New York, in the United States, has now banned Internationally famous Russian soprano Anna Netrebko for two years because she is Russian. In the light of the obvious contradiction, and absence of reasoned elaboration, of this determination of Netrebko's fitness and propriety, identifying the significance of denunciation in hegemonic groups' control of skilled work, the objective of this research is to examine critically the relevant aspects of public denunciation. Today's publicly announced purpose of licensure is "protection of the public through assurance of minimum level of competence", and appears to have had the effect of continually recreating the medieval monopolies, for the stated avowed purposes of public good. The commonplace oratory could access people's hatred for non-criminal errors, when stated in the public domain as maxims. When embedded within a judicial denunciation, commonplace served as a criminal judgment without a crime. Although it is said to be unnecessary to make an account of an acknowledged crime or error, commonplace had instead a goal of amplifying only what has been already acknowledged, such as for example a folk maxim. As such, it can assume guilt regardless of the overwhelming circumstances to the contrary. The research question asks

* Corresponding Author's E-mail: carrington.rand@icloud.com.

In: Regulation of the Professions in East Asia
Editors: Gary I. Lilienthal and Muhamad Hassan bin Ahmad
ISBN: 979-8-88697-409-6

whether a negative finding of fitness and propriety constitutes commonplace denunciation, through a judicial failure of sufficient reasoned elaboration. Argument seeks to demonstrate the proposition that fitness and propriety is nothing more than inadequately defended commonplace denunciation. Lord Coleridge had failed to elaborate the conception of being protean, and therefore the conception of the public interest was not elaborated in reason. Without this, nobody could be unfit and improper. The conception of the public interest therefore fell to the implied lessons of general and folk maxims, forcing Lord Coleridge's final judgment into the form of a commonplace denunciation. Lord Coleridge had decided to avoid the contradictions of commonplace and reach the same judgment in another way. Since there was a maritime custom in operation, the egregious act was not a crime. Therefore, a crime must be found in another way. A speaker could always construct an illusory enthymeme and present it as a delight to the audience. Commonplace attacks the target person's past life events. It sets out to amplify only what the public mind has already acknowledged and hated. It allows the assumption of a mere indicium of hypothesis of guilt, regardless of overwhelming evidence to the contrary. This had allowed délation to rise to the rank of high sacred duty, filling the land with spies, rendering every man an object of suspicion by hegemonic groups. Consequent denunciation, in outline, was to reveal the hidden, to collate small pieces of knowledge gleaned from individuals into a general corpus of understanding, and last, therefore, to protect the state from its opponents. This was a mass exercise in weak inductive reasoning, but persuasive to public opinion. It allowed public debate to convert a paramount duty to save the state into an individual duty and derived right of denunciation. The Jacobins tried to resolve contradictory locus of the "sovereign people", as it validated all folk maxims, by grounding the Terror in the expulsion of its opposition. Now, they could peer into the darkness of a newly voiceless imagined opposition personality or character, to make this imaginary secret public. This suggested the genesis in removal of political opposition of declaring a person not fit and proper.

Keywords: reasoned elaboration, fitness and propriety, commonplace denunciation, folk maxims, délation, character

1. Introduction

The Metropolitan Opera of New York, in the United States, has now banned Internationally famous Russian soprano Anna Netrebko for two years.

Metropolitan Opera General Manager Peter Gelb banned Netrebko because of the Ukraine war and the US-NATO response to it. Gelb said "It is a great artistic loss for the Met and for opera … Anna is one of the greatest singers in Met history, but with Putin killing innocent victims in Ukraine there was no way forward". Gelb added, "It's hard to imagine a scenario in which she will return to the Met".[1] Thus, Netrebko has been denounced as unsuitable to sing there, even although the denouncers agree she is one of the greatest singers in the history of the Metropolitan Opera in New York. In effect, she is not fit and proper to sing there. In the light of the obvious contradiction, and absence of reasoned elaboration, of this determination of Netrebko's fitness and propriety, identifying the significance of denunciation in hegemonic groups' control of skilled work, the objective of this research is to examine critically the relevant aspects of public denunciation.

The licensing of members of the professions had originated in the gilds of the middle ages. Admission to a gild was the equivalent of modern professional licensure and was the gild's specific monopoly granted by the monarch. The phases and terminologies of modern professional education still follow much of the organizational skeleton of the medieval gilds and professions. Today's publicly announced purpose of licensure is "protection of the public through assurance of minimum level of competence", and appears to have had the effect of continually recreating the medieval monopolies, for the stated avowed purposes of binding members to the public good,[2] suggesting the operation in this of the public mind.

The commonplace oratory could access people's hatred for non-criminal errors, when stated in the public domain as maxims. When embedded within a judicial denunciation, commonplace served as a criminal judgment without a crime. Although it is said to be unnecessary to make an account of an acknowledged crime or error, commonplace had instead a goal of amplifying only what has been already acknowledged, such as for example a folk maxim. As such, it assumes guilt regardless of the possibility of overwhelming, but ignored, circumstances to the contrary.[3]

---

[1] Fred Mazelis, 'Metropolitan Opera announces the banning of soprano Anna Netrebko', *World Socialist Website*, 5th March 2022.

[2] G Lester Anderson & Merton W Ertell, 'Extra-institutional forces affecting professional education', in *Education for the Professions*, National Society for the Study of Education, Chicago, 1962, p. 236.

[3] George A Kennedy, *Progymnasmata: Greek Textbooks of Prose Composition and Rhetoric*, Society of Biblical Literature, Atlanta, 2003, pp. 202, p. 203.

In the 2002 case of *Frugtniet v Board of Examiners*, Pagone J stated that it was not the Court's task to find affirmatively that Frugtniet was 'not a fit and proper person for admission to practice',[4] but while based on the materials before the Court, Frugtniet could not satisfy the Court he was fit and proper for admission.[5] Thus, the Court was not satisfied, but did not hold he was not "fit and proper", suggesting commonplace denunciation. Frugtniet had been publicly denounced for life, for failing to disclose his omissions, implying an egregious instance of commonplace denunciation.

In the 2009 Supreme Court of Victoria Court of Appeal case of *Medical Practitioners Board of Victoria v Lal*,[6] the Court held as follows.

> The public interest is a protean concept. What is relevant to the public interest depends on the statutory context in which the concept is used. Its content cannot be confined by reference to any predetermined generic criteria. Sound registration practices also confer an indirect form of public protection, through the establishment and the maintenance of public confidence in the medical profession. If the public at large have confidence in doctors, they are more likely to seek medical advice and treatment when the need arises. This is conducive to the general health of the community.[7]

With this entire dictum apparently protean in structure, especially including the court's reasoning about the public interest, no reasoned argument could yet proceed beyond this point without developing an incisive understanding of the term "protean", while to the contrary, the court had failed to elaborate this point.

Herbert Wechsler proposed, in his oration of the 1959 Holmes Lectures,[8] that matters relating to an established set of precepts must be decided by what he called "neutral principles",[9] requiring judges to support their choices by reasoned explanations,[10] reached by that kind of analysis and reasoning that

---

[4] *Frugtniet v Board of Examiners* [2002] VSC 140, [15].

[5] Nathalie Ng, 'Fitness and Propriety, Spent Convictions and Technology: Lessons from ASIC Investigations', *Australian Institute of Administrative Law Forum*, vol. 92, 2018, pp. 1-112, p. 69.

[6] *Medical Practitioners Board of Victoria v Lal* [2009] VSCA 109.

[7] ibid., [56].

[8] The three-part Holmes Lecture series are the most prestigious talks at Harvard Law School. They were named after former Supreme Court Justice Oliver Wendell Holmes Jr., with the lecture series occurring every three years.

[9] Herbert Wechsler, 'Toward Neutral Principles of Constitutional Law', *Harvard Law Review*, vol. 73, no. 1, 1959, pp. 1-35.

[10] ibid., p. 15.

rises above the present result. He identified this process as "reasoned elaboration", stating "It is a more serious charge that a court (or a judge) is acting illegitimately than that it is mistaken; [the absence of] reasoned elaboration makes the latter critique more likely than the former".[11] Thus, the question arises as to whether a negative finding of fitness and propriety constitutes commonplace denunciation, when through a judicial failure of sufficient reasoned elaboration. Argument seeks to demonstrate the proposition that a negative assessment of fitness and propriety is nothing more than inadequately defended commonplace denunciation.

This chapter's research paradigm is historiographic, and thus, its research methodology is doctrinal, arguing a stated thesis by bringing the relevant library-based evidence, arranged as a legal narrative. This allows the building of new argument on top of evidence already accepted by the international scholarly community, through new Aristotelian syntheses. Argument begins with a main section on Commonplace, comprising the two subsections of Judicial Denunciation, and, Commonplace Denunciation. The second main section is entitled Introduction to the Practices of Denunciation in Modern European History, which includes the two subsections of Denunciation in Comparative Perspective: An Overview, and, Discourses of Denunciation. The third major section is entitled The Theory and Practice of Denunciation in the French Revolution. It covers the following five sub-sections: Denunciation and the Enemy Other; The Pre-legal Ethics of Denunciation; The Pious Denouncer and Patriotism; The Jacobins and the Terror; and finally, Suspicion, Jealousy and the Mask.

The likely research outcome will be as follows. Lord Coleridge had failed to elaborate the conception of being protean, and therefore the conception of the public interest was not elaborated in reason. Without this elaboration, nobody could be unfit and improper. The conception of the public interest therefore fell to the implied lessons of general and folk maxims, forcing Lord Coleridge's final judgment into the form of a commonplace denunciation. Lord Coleridge had decided to avoid the contradictions of commonplace and reach the same judgment in another way. Since there was a maritime custom in operation, the egregious act was not a crime. Therefore, a crime must be found in another way. A speaker could always construct an illusory enthymeme and present it as a delight to the audience. Commonplace attacks the target person's past life events. It sets out to amplify only what the public

---

[11] Daniel A Farber & Suzanna Sherry, *Judgment Calls: Principle and Politics in Constitutional Law*, Oxford University Press, Oxford 2009, p. 45.

mind has already acknowledged and hated. It allows the assumption of a mere indicium of hypothesis of guilt, regardless of overwhelming evidence to the contrary. This had allowed délation to rise to the rank of high sacred duty, filling the land with spies, rendering every man an object of suspicion by the hegemonic groups. Consequent denunciation, in outline, was to reveal the hidden, to collate small pieces of knowledge gleaned from individuals into a general corpus of understanding, and last, therefore, to protect the state from its opponents. This was a mass exercise in weak inductive reasoning, but nevertheless persuasive to the public mind's opinion. It allowed public debate to convert a paramount duty to save the state into an individual duty and derived right of denunciation. The Jacobins tried to solve the riddle over the contradictory locus of the so-called sovereign people, as it validated all folk maxims, by grounding the Terror in the expulsion of its opposition. Now, they could peer into the darkness of a newly voiceless imagined opposition personality, or character, to make this imaginary secret public. This suggested the genesis, in removal of political opposition, of declaring a person not fit and proper.

2. Commonplace

2.1. Judicial Denunciation

The fact pattern of the 1884 English case of *R v Dudley and Stephens*[12] merits a brief background examination, as an example of denunciation, with key omissions and failures of elaboration in the court's records. In the case of *R v Dudley and Stephens*,[13] the official law record is very short on possibly highly relevant background facts. Professor Simpson's research, at the University of Chicago, on the case background, greatly clarifies much of this significant lawsuit.[14] First, we learn from Simpson that Dudley was in fact the captain and was engaged to sail a specified yacht from the United Kingdom to Sydney, Australia. This was a long and dangerous voyage to attempt. The men were shipwrecked and stranded at sea. Edwin Stephens was the mate, although he possessed a master mariner's certificate. Dudley held no master mariner's

[12] *R* v *Dudley and Stephens* (1884) 14 QBD 273.
[13] ibid.
[14] Alfred William Brian Simpson, 'Cannibals at Common Law', *The Law School Record*, vol. 27, 1981, pp. 3-10.

certificate. The boy they cannibalized, Richard Parker, was an orphan who was only 17 years of age.[15]

It was Captain Dudley who killed the orphan Richard Parker, a fact omitted in the official court report. Thus, the ship's captain killed his cabin boy. In the face of this, Lord Coleridge read the only example of a late 19th century court decision whose elements of argument had pretensions to literature. The large moral aspect of the case, in this murder case, appeared to call for great literary grandeur as a rhetorical device for denunciation of the ancient maritime custom of cannibalism, when stranded, a custom still widespread and operational in the 19th century.[16]

In this 1884 English case of *R v Dudley and Stephens*,[17] Lord Coleridge expressly precluded using the oratorical device of "commonplace" to denounce the appellants. He argued that, if he used this kind of rhetoric, it would have been too easy for him to succeed with a mere denunciation of the appellants, while they were acting out of the necessity arising from overwhelming thirst, hunger and the need for their own survival. As a relevant aside, denunciation had been divided into two kinds, during the French Revolution. Dénonciation was the word used for the good and public-spirited form of denunciation, whereas délation meant the bad, treacherous, self-interested, form of denunciation,[18] suggesting that the court publicly stated that it wanted to avoid the easily available and appealable délation.

With the use of rhetoric, the speaker can create a generally accepted premise, defined as that which is accepted by everyone or by the majority or by the philosophers, that is, by all, or by the majority, or by the most notable and illustrious of them. On such a premise, the speaker can proceed to further construct an illusory enthymeme and present it as a delight to the audience.[19] This enthymeme was termed by Aristotle as a syllogism, but a syllogism of denunciation by probability, example, proof or indication.[20] It is this style of enthymeme the court said it wanted to avoid and which we now examine.

---

[15] ibid.

[16] ibid.

[17] *R* v *Dudley and Stephens* (1884) 14 QBD 273.

[18] Denis Diderot & Jean le Rond d'Alembert, . (). *Encyclopédie, ou Dictionnaire raisonné des sciences, des arts et des métiers*. Sociétés typographiques, Bern and Lausanne, 1779.

[19] Ch Perelman, *The Realm of Rhetoric*, University of Notre Dame Press, Notre Dame, 1982.

[20] HC Lawson-Tancred, *Aristotle The Art of Rhetoric*, Penguin Books, London, 1991; Richard A Lanham, *A Handlist of Rhetorical Terms*, University of California Press, Berkeley, 1991.

2.2. Commonplace Denunciation

The ancient Greek progymnasmata's standard exercises in rhetorical production can be traced back to the fifth century BCE Greek sophists and the textbooks of their times and of the subsequent century. The key development in the progymnasmata tradition probably occurred during the Hellenistic era of the 3rd to 1st centuries BCE, when a sequence of a dozen or so exercises emerged as a standard curriculum in writing and speaking instruction, occupying that vital middle ground between the young child's grammatical work and the older student's themes and declamations. By the beginnings of the first century BCE, virtually all Greek and Roman rhetoric students were working their way through this more-or-less standard cycle of exercises.[21]

Commonplace is an oratorical exercise from this ancient Greek progymnasmata. It is used to elaborate on a state of affairs, where states of affairs are entities that are situational conditions,[22] in terms of the public's perceptions of justice.[23] Elaboration has been characterized as the proportion of subordinate to superordinate ideas contained within a passage.[24] The concept of subordination allows measurement of the degree to which writers have integrated and unduly embellished their ideas within hierarchical relationships.[25] Commonplace had been used in this way since early antiquity for effective public denunciation. Commonplace is based on *topos*, which is a text amplifying something already considered to be an act either of bravery or of a fault.[26] Thus, a *topos* is an easy place to start the elaboration when seeking to find new arguments, formulated against a person not admitting they were wrong. *Topos* denounces a person, after the speaker first assumes his or her guilt.[27] The structure of the commonplace argument's elaboration begins with the target's moral choice, the extent of the evil, how much suffering was

---

[21] J David Fleming, 'The Very Idea of a "Progymnasmata"', *Rhetoric Review*, vol. 22, no. 2, 2003, pp. 105-120.

[22] Ernest Sosa, *Cambridge Dictionary of Philosophy*, Cambridge University Press, Cambridge, 1999.

[23] George A Kennedy, *A New History of Classical Rhetoric*, Princeton University Press, Princeton, 1994, pp. 3 *et seq.*

[24] RE Johnson, 'Recall of Prose as a Function of the structural importance of the Linguistic Units', *Journal of Verbal Learning and Verbal Behavior*, vol. 9, 1970, pp. 12-20.

[25] Stephen L Benton & Paul J Blohm, (1988). Elaboration of Ideas in Prose Production. *The Journal of Experimental Education*, vol. 56, no. 2, 1988, pp. 1960-1966.

[26] George A Kennedy, *Progymnasmata: Greek Textbooks of Prose Composition and Rhetoric*, Society of Biblical Literature, Atlanta, 2003, p. 42.

[27] ibid., p. 43.

caused to others, and, from how the actor profits from the exercise.[28] In this way, *topos* can be built onto any mundane event, and where the term "common" carries a technical meaning, known in the old Greek rhetoric as *koinos*, meaning "common, shared, unclean or ritually defiled. It refers to the spiritual desecration of treating what is sacred as ordinary".[29]

Hermogenes, who was an ancient Athenian philosopher, in or around 400 BCE, and was a close friend of Socrates, had stated that *topos* could be altered by this Greek concept of *koinos*, to manufacture what is then known as commonplace. Commonplace is thus an exercise in which the speaker amplifies something that has already been assumed and agreed. It is as if the argument demonstrations were already completed before the proposition was uttered. The speaker constructs commonplace by first investigating the opposite and then formulating a statement of the subject action. Then the speaker makes a comparison and applies an apparently relevant maxim. According to Noy's maxim, *consuetudinem est alter lex*,[30] customs are a second or alternate law.[31] Maxims are general customs, as distinguished from all those particular customs used in specific counties, cities, towns, or lordships. Every maxim is its own thoroughly sufficient authority, whose status as a maxim, according to Noy, could only be determined by the judges.[32] Commonplace continues by attacking the target person's past life events, but with new conjectures based apparently on the common wisdom present-time maxims. Then, the speaker argues for a rejection of pity for the target, by using the so-called "final headings" of the just, the legal, the possible, the beneficial and the appropriate. This further elaboration allows the audience to perceive a more colorful outline of the subject bad action.[33]

Aphthonius the Sophist, a 4th century BCE writer of a textbook on the elements of rhetoric, thought that commonplace was language that amplified whatever evils were said to be attached to something. Thus, it could fit all those people in common, who had taken part in a specific deed to be denounced. For example, any speech directed against an alleged traitor could

---

[28] ibid., p. 44.

[29] James Strong, *Strong's Exhaustive Concordance of the Bible*, Hendrickson, Peabody, 2007, p. G2843.

[30] Custom is an alternative law.

[31] William Noy, *The Sounds and Maxims and also an Analysis of The English Laws*, Riley, Middletown, 1808, p. 39.

[32] ibid.

[33] George A Kennedy, *Progymnasmata: Greek Textbooks of Prose Composition and Rhetoric*, Society of Biblical Literature, Atlanta, 2003, p. 80.

be applied to all those in common who shared in the traitorous act.[34] This is called "making an example of someone", which is thus an indicium of commonplace denunciation.

Nicolaus the Sophist, one of the four 5th century BCE writers of textbooks on the progymnasmata,[35] suggested commonplace ought to be positioned after the oratorical exercises refutation and confirmation, within the gradated exercises of the progymnasmata. For Nicolaus the Sophist, commonplace could be used to amplify either acknowledged evil or human goodness. It could be either as denunciation or praise. It was not used for targeting any particular person, but always used against an identified class of people to make an example of them. It set up a starting point for argument, from which subsequent attacks could be made against the specific categories of person.[36]

John of Sardis explained four facets of a complete hypothesis, used here in a formal logic sense, to denote the antecedent of a proposition. They were: "prooemion, narration, proofs, epilogue".[37] He suggested that fable and narration served as prooemion and narration. The chreia, the maxim and the refutation served as proofs in the hypothesis. From this, he taught that commonplace is placed logically as an epilogue in a completed hypothesis,[38] implying an available defense of characterizing a commonplace denunciation as merely suggestive of a hypothesis.

Sopatros, who wrote a collection of 81 declamation themes, around 320 CE, inserted in the discussion that commonplace was used judicially in courts to sharpen the court's targeting for punishing either a crime or a mere error. In as much as a crime had a definitely stated punishment set by law, and involved a widely unacceptable act by some person committed towards another person, a mere error carried no such penalty described in law. Despite this, everyone still hated the commission of an error. Such errors could include drunkenness, wastefulness, sloth, fornication, and similar acts. This allowed the orator of commonplace to access people's heavy dislike for non-criminal errors, when articulated in the public domain as based in common or general maxims. Whenever it was embedded inside a judicial denunciation, commonplace served in the public mind as a kind of criminal judgment without a crime. Although it is unnecessary to narrate a detailed account of any acknowledged crime or error, commonplace sets out to amplify only what the public mind

[34] ibid., p. 105.
[35] ibid.
[36] ibid., p. 148.
[37] ibid., p. 201.
[38] ibid.

has already acknowledged and hated.[39] In this way, commonplace allows the assumption of an indicium of hypothesis of guilt regardless of overwhelming evidence to the contrary.

3. Introduction to the Practices of Denunciation in Modern European History

3.1. Denunciation in Comparative Perspective: An Overview

Denunciation takes place to some extent in all established societies, in all times, dependent upon cultural and political traditions, and the extent to which the state offers its encouragement. The Venetian Republic had long time traditions of denunciations, where the jaws of the Lion of St. Mark's[40] were always open for the receiving of citizens' denunciations. In Russia, during the Muscovite and Petrine periods, there was a state-imposed "duty to denounce" on citizens. In other kinds of states, such as Britain, tradition holds a skepticism of state power, as well as a fear of its abuse, and there is a tendency to discourage denunciation. State laws or religious decrees may place a demand on citizens to denounce some kinds of crimes against the state or the church.[41] Thus, in France, the *Napoleonic Penal Code* of 1810[42] provided for severe penalties for failing to denounce crimes against state security. These penalties were abolished in 1832, but again established just before World War II.[43]

Failure to denounce crimes has also been a crime under many other national criminal codes.[44] In the Roman Empire at the beginning of the Christian era, there were financial rewards for denouncers, as in the semi-mythical narrative example of Judas Iscariot. In the English Restoration

---

[39] ibid., pp. 202, 203.

[40] In heraldry, the "Lion of St. Mark" refers to all winged lions. The true Lion of St. Mark was one used only within religious badges to signify the saint, with a halo. Arthur Fox-Davies, *A Complete Guide to Heraldry*, TC & EC Jack, London, 1909, pp. 185-186.

[41] Sheila Fitzpatrick and Robert Gellately, 'Introduction to the Practices of Denunciation in Modern European History', *The Journal of Modern History*, vol. 68, no. 4, 1996, pp. 747-767, p. 759.

[42] The Penal Code of 1810 was a French code of criminal laws created under Napoleon, replacing the French Penal Code of 1791. Carla Hesse, 'The Law of the Terror', *MLN*, vol. 114, no. 4, 1999, pp. 702-718, p. 704.

[43] Larousse (Firm), *Grand Larousse encyclopédique*, Librairie Larousse, Paris, 1960, vol. 3.

[44] For example, the Imperial Russian criminal code; see Entsiklopedicheskii slovar' 'Granat', 7th ed., vol. 18 (Moscow, n.d. [ca. 1914]), p. 623.

period,[45] there were many denunciations of dissenters, because they derived a share in the fine levied by the state against those denounced. An English Act of 1692 established bounties, as parliamentary rewards, for anyone providing information which led to successful prosecution of highwaymcn. Similarly styled rewards were established for proving authorities with information on other commissioned offenses, such as burglary, followed soon after.

> ... in case any Dispute shall happen to arise between the persons so apprehending any the said Thieves and Robbers touching their right and title to the said Reward that then the said Judge or Justices so respectively certifying as aforesaid shall in and by their said Certificate direct and appoint the said Reward to be paid unto and amongst the Parties claimeing the same in such share and proportions as to the said Judge or Justices shall seem just and reasonable.[46]

As a result, there arose a class of people who made their living by prosecuting apparent offenders.[47] There is also a nexus between denunciation and the police, whose duties also include reporting to superiors any dangerous opinions and moods within the populace. This has been a characteristic of the early modem European absolutist states.[48] All police organizations develop a network of informants among the criminal classes, as well as receiving spontaneous denunciations from members of the public. A late 19th-century edition of Larousse noted that even today "the most precious discoveries of the police are due not to overt or secret agents but to anonymous denunciations (délations) which arrive every day at Rue de Jerusalem, products of the vengeance of betrayed women and friends or jealous parents."[49] This

[45] The Restoration of the English King Charles II, in 1600, restored not only the Stuart dynasty, but also the Anglican Church, with the king agreeing first to certain issues of "religious tolerance", in return for allowing him to back to the throne from his exile in Europe. Clyde L. Grose, 'The Religion of Restoration England', *Church History*, vol. 6, no. 3, 1937, pp. 223-232, p. 223.

[46] John Raithby (ed.), William and Mary, 1692, 'An Act for encouraging the apprehending of Highway Men', in *Statutes of the Realm*, vol. 6, 1685-1694, pp. 390-391.

[47] JJ Tobias, *Crime and Police in England*, 1700-1900, St. Martin's Press, New York, 1979, pp. 119-20.

[48] Arlette Farge, *Subversive Words: Public Opinion in Eighteenth-Century France*, Rosemary Morris (trans.), Penn State University Press, University Park, 1994.

[49] *Larousse grande dictionnaire universel du XIXe siècle*, vol. 6, Administration du Grand Dictionnaire Universel, Paris, 1870.

continued to be true, even a century and more later.[50] A political form of police force, with its own network of informants, is however, not a requirement for a practice of denunciation. Any properly constituted authority, either ecclesiastical or secular, can receive denunciations. In 18th-century France, *lettres de cachet* conveyed to the king were instruments of denunciation, where people could petition the state to imprison their delinquent spouses or children.[51] In the 20th century, newspapers have been major recipients of denunciation,[52] written by those perceiving themselves to be targets of bureaucratic persecution or injustice,[53] or who desire to disclose the wrongs by large corporations and government departments.[54]

In late medieval and early modern times, denunciation was closely connected with the expunging of witchcraft and heresy. In places of active Inquisition, denunciation flourished as well.[55] As Kamen wrote, "There was no need to rely on a secret police system, because the population as a whole was encouraged to recognize the enemy within the gates .... The majority of denunciations were made ... by ordinary people, neighbors, acquaintances, in response to appeals made in the edicts of faith or simply as a result of personal conflicts."[56] Denunciations for cases of moral lapse, and for backsliding, were promoted and practiced in Christian Protestant "communities of saints", such as in Calvin's Geneva.[57] The practice of denunciation continued within the

---

50 Jean-Paul Brunet, *La police de l'ombre: Indicateurs et provocateurs dans la France contemporaine*, Paris, 1990; Nicole Czechowski & Jacques Hassoun (eds.), *La delation: Un archaisme, une technique*, Autrement, Paris, 1992, pp. 59-68.

51 Arlette Farge & Michel Foucault, *Le desordre des familles: Lettres de cachet des Archives de la Bastille*, Gallimard, Paris, 1982.

52 Sheila Fitzpatrick and Robert Gellately, 'Introduction to the Practices of Denunciation in Modern European History', *The Journal of Modern History*, vol. 68, no. 4, 1996, pp. 747-767, p. 760.

53 For an analysis of denunciations sent to the French newspaper Le monde in the 1980s, Luc Boltanski, *L'amour et la justice comme competences*, Métailié, Paris, 1990, and Luc Boltanski, Yann Darré & Marie-Ange Schiltz, 'La dénonciation', *Actes de la Recherche en Sciences Sociales*, vol. 51, 1984, pp. 3–40. Letters to Soviet newspapers are discussed in Sheila Fitzpatrick, 'Signals from Below: Soviet Letters of Denunciation of the 1930s', *The Journal of Modern History*, 1996, vol. 68, no. 4, pp. 831-866.

54 Alan F Westin (ed.), *Whistle Blowing! Loyalty and Dissent in the Corporation*, McGrawHill, New York, 1981.

55 Carlo Ginzburg's miller, Menocchio, was called in by the Roman Inquisition in 1583 after a denunciation to the Holy Office that evidently came from a local priest. Carlo Ginzburg, *The Cheese and the Worms: The Cosmos of a Sixteenth-Century Miller*, John Tedeschi & Anne Tedeschi (trans.), Penguin Books, Harmondsworth, 1986, pp. 2, 4.

56 Henry Kamen, *Inquisition and Society in Spain in the 16th and 17th Centuries*, Indiana University Press, Bloomington, 1985, p. 143.

57 In supporting for Calvin's reform proposals, the council of Geneva enacted the *Ordonnances ecclésiastiques*, (Ecclesiastical Ordinances), 20th November 1541. They provided for four

Catholic Church into the late 19th and early 20th centuries. Police states, revolutionary states, theocracies, and 20th century totalitarian countries have urged their citizens or members to submit written denunciations, against each other, to maintain social control through ideological purity. The hunt for heretics or counter revolutionaries often reaches a fever pitch when tides of denunciation for absurd offenses overwhelm the authorities. For example, consider the 17th century Salem witch obsession, the 1794 Jacobin Terror of France,[58] the Stalinist purges in the 1930s, and the American anti-Communist fervor of the 1950s.[59]

War and foreign power occupations have provided fertile grounds for flourishing denunciations in the 20th century. During World Wars I and II, total mobilization of society in the various belligerent countries produced new and widespread denunciations, even in England, of saboteurs, spies, Germans, and more, with states insisting that patriotism and allegiance to the nation-state should override all other loyalty. Nevertheless, this raised level of patriotism did not fully explain the tides of denunciations that French people sent in to the German occupiers during World War II.[60] Neither did it explain the denunciations that Vichy zone residents made against socialists, communists and Jews.[61] Nor did it explain the denunciations of neighbors that

---

orders of ministry: (1) pastors to preach and to administer the sacraments; (2) doctors to instruct believers in the faith; (3) elders to provide discipline; and (4) deacons to care for the poor and needy. Alexandre Ganoczy, 'Calvin's life', in Donald K McKim (ed.), *The Cambridge Companion to John Calvin*, Cambridge University Press, Cambridge, 2004, pp. 15–17; E William Monter, *Enforcing Morality in Early Modern Europe*, E William Monter Books, London, 1987.

[58] A Jacobin was a member of the Jacobin Club, which was a revolutionary political movement, and was the most famous political club of the French Revolution, of 1789–1799. Tony Judt, *Marxism and the French Left: Studies on Labour and Politics in France, 1830–1981*, New York University Press, New York & London, 2011, p. 108

[59] Sheila Fitzpatrick and Robert Gellately, 'Introduction to the Practices of Denunciation in Modern European History', *The Journal of Modern History*, vol. 68, no. 4, 1996, pp. 747-767, p. 761.

[60] André Halimi, *La Délation sous l'Occupation*, Editions Alain Moreau, Paris, 1983; 'Une certaine France sous l'Occupation', in Nicole Czechowski & Jacques Hassoun (eds.), La delation: Un archaisme, une technique, Autrement, Paris, 1992, pp. 138-45. During the Occupation in France, the French wrote between 3 and 5 million letters of denunciation, most of them signed. They were sent to French authorities like the Commissariat G6neral aux Affaires Juives as well as the Gestapo. Radio-Paris had a program called Repetez-le that "consisted only of letters from listeners denouncing their neighbor, their rival in love or in business, even their own families" (André Halimi, 'Une certaine France sous l'Occupation', in Nicole Czechowski & Jacques Hassoun (eds.), *La délation. Un archaïsme, une technique, un mode de gouvernement*, Autrement,Paris, 1992, p. 139).

[61] Marc Ferro, *Pétain*, Feyard, Paris, 1987, pp. 149-52, 235-41.

Polish peasants sent in 1941 to the Soviet occupying authorities of Eastern Poland.[62]

Late 20th-century America gave the impression that denunciation continued to play a role in everyday life. Regular "whistle-blowing" is reported in the United States press, as are strong public exhortations to inform and report to the authorities a wide range of minor delinquencies.[63] Thus, in the 1980s and 1990s, the United States experienced a kind of witch craze, whereby many parents, priests and day-care workers were accused of child abuse and incest.[64]

Denunciation has many marks, such as pre-demonized enemies of the people, alleged cases of witchcraft, religious heretics, communists, counter-revolutionaries, commissions of child abuse, or even terrorists. It may target people newly defined as outsiders or pariahs, like the social aliens in the former USSR. Examples were gypsies, Jews, religious dissenters, homosexuals, foreigners, stigmatized social groups such as the aristocrats and priests during the French Revolution, or capitalists during the Russian Revolution.[65] Speakers denounce both major and minor criminals. People of public spirit, malicious persons, or those who desire to become regular police informants make such denunciations. Denunciations may target powerful people by those of lesser power who seek to exercise what Boltanski designated as "the competence of justice."[66] But many denunciations in most societies are directed against ordinary people, such as neighbors or colleagues where an everyday grievance is at work. In these cases, denouncers might not even first stigmatize targets as, for example, witches or child abusers.[67]

---

62 Jan T Gross, *Revolution from Abroad: The Soviet Conquest of Poland 's Western Ukraine and Western Belorussia*, Princeton University Press, Princeton, 1988, pp. 145-146.

63 For example, speeding on the highways, violations of zoning laws, tax evasion, illegal immigrants, and so on. *Chicago Tribune*, October 16, 1994, sec. 8, p. 1; October 21, 1994, pp. 1, 21.

64 According to the *New York Times* (October 31, 1994), thousands of court cases involving child molestation and sensational press accounts of adults who "rediscovered" hidden memories of incestuous abuse under psychotherapy "have led many people to believe that there is a nationwide network of satanic groups preying upon the young." Out of more than twelve thousand accusations of "group cult sexual abuse based on satanic ritual" investigated in a 1994 survey, not one had been substantiated.

65 Sheila Fitzpatrick and Robert Gellately, 'Introduction to the Practices of Denunciation in Modern European History', *The Journal of Modern History*, vol. 68, no. 4, 1996, pp. 747-767, pp. 762, 763.

66 Luc Boltanski, *Love and Justice as Competencies: Three Essays on the Sociology of Action*, Polity Press, Paris, 1990, pp. 36-45.

67 Sheila Fitzpatrick and Robert Gellately, 'Introduction to the Practices of Denunciation in Modern European History', *The Journal of Modern History*, vol. 68, no. 4, 1996, pp. 747-767, p. 763.

3.2. Discourses of Denunciation

That of the denouncer is one role of a citizen, when invoking the state, or some other kind of greater authority, to commence disciplinary action against some other citizen. The investigating of this singularity of denunciation is an exploration of the essence of citizens' dedication of loyalty to the state, such as for example by members of the three bourgeoisie elements of entrepreneurs, managers and government accredited professionals, as an incompatible commitment to solidarity with fellow citizens. The practice of denunciation puts to the test the relative powers of these fundamental commitments. As Colin Lucas had put it, denunciation lies along the interface between those both in tension with the state and with their own identity within the conception of the state. This kind of state is divided between one that is "externalized" and one that is "internalized" by its citizens. In that in many differing societies denunciation has constituted two opposite discourses, one promoting it as a personal duty to the state, with the other condemning it as treachery to one's fellow human beings, very little about denunciations is more significant than the abrupt contradictions in how it is represented. These contradictions are so sharp that, in French, and even earlier in English, no single word could encompass them. In the light of this, dénonciation is the word for the good and public-spirited form of denunciation, whereas délation means the bad, treacherous, self-interested, form of denunciation.[68]

The problem of the dénonciation-délation continuum was explored intensely during the French Revolution. But the dichotomy, identified as above was never resolved satisfactorily, despite various Jacobin attempts to void the pejorative implications of délation.[69] In the dénonciation discourse, denunciation of wrongs is an act of civic goodness, or a religious duty involving the denouncer's personal risk or sacrifice or risk. Zola's famous "J'Accuse!", in the form of an 1898 public letter to President Felix Faure,[70] denouncing those who arranged and conducted the trial of Dreyfus and his

---

[68] With its separate entries for dénonciation and délation, Denis Diderot & Jean le Rond d'Alembert, *Encyclopédie, ou Dictionnaire raisonné des sciences, des arts et des métiers*, Sociétés typographiques, Bern and Lausanne, 1778-1779, vol. 10, set a pattern that has been followed by virtually all French encyclopedias since.

[69] Sheila Fitzpatrick and Robert Gellately, 'Introduction to the Practices of Denunciation in Modern European History', *The Journal of Modern History*, vol. 68, no. 4, 1996, pp. 747-767, p. 763.

[70] Félix François Faure, (1841 – 1899), was President of France from 1895 until his death. Hugh Chisholm (ed.), *Encyclopædia Britannica*, Cambridge University Press, Cambridge, 1911.

pre-arranged conviction,[71] was a timeless example. Zola wrote that the treatment of Dreyfus was outrageous and unjust that had besmirched France. Zola went on to say that Dreyfus only had in mind the interests of truth and justice, had neither malice nor hatred toward his denouncers, and acted only "in the name of humanity". His intervention was "only a revolutionary means for hastening the explosion of truth and justice?"[72]

Similarly emotional rhetoric was articulated during the French Revolution to defend the necessity of denunciation for the protection of the transparency and purity of the revolution.[73] In the McCarthy period in the United States,[74] the 1954 film *On the Waterfront*, directed by Elia Kazan, had disclosed the names of former Communists to the House Un-American Activities Committee. It justified this informing with its narrative of a character struggling with his conscience, fearing ostracism, before informing against the gang controlling the dock, "achiev[ing] heroic stature as he single-handedly takes on the mob at the risk of his life."[75] Some 10 years earlier, the Soviet director Sergei Eisenstein had filmed a similar encomium to denunciation in the film *Bezhin Meadow*, based on the story of Pavlik Morozov.[76] In the western world, more recently, "whistle-blowers" have risked their lives and their careers to expose corruption and graft. In the opposite discourse of délation, a denunciation means betrayal, the denunciation corrupting rather than protecting public morals. The denouncers are treated as beyond contempt, cowards, motivated maliciously. This specific denunciatory discourse arises

---

[71] Alfred Dreyfus was a French artillery officer, of Jewish ancestry, whose defective denuncian, trial and conviction for treason, in 1894, became a politically polarizing issue in modern France. Piers Paul Read, *The Dreyfus Affair*, Bloomsbury Publishing, London, 2013, p. 83.

[72] Emile Zola, *J'Accuse!*, Bay Side Press, Soquel, 1992, pp. 15, 28.

[73] See the essay by Colin Lucas ("The Theory and Practice of Denunciation in the French Revolution") in this issue.

[74] McCarthyism was the political practice of publicly denouncing people for subversion and treason, especially in relation to socialism and communism. The term referred to the public practices of United Staes Senator Joseph McCarthy, in the period of the "Second Red Scare", from the 1940s through the 1950s. Ellen Schrecker, *Age of McCarthyism: A Brief History with Documents*, Bedford, Boston, 1994, p. 3

[75] Victor S Navasky, *Naming Names*, Penguin, Harmondsworth, 1981, p. 209. For more on McCarthy-period exhortations to denounce Communists to the FBI and popular approval of this practice, Stephen J Whitfield, *The Culture of the Cold War*, Johns Hopkins University Press, Baltimore, 1991, pp. 102, 136-40; David Caute, *The Great Fear: The Anti-Communist Purge under Truman and Eisenhower*, Simon and Schuster, New York, 1978, p. 121.

[76] The film was criticized for "formalism" and never released. Jay Leyda, *Kino: A History of the Russian and Soviet Film*, George Allen & Unwin, London, 1973, pp. 327-34, 338-39.

in Anglo-Saxon Protestant indictments during the Inquisition in Rome.[77] Henry Charles Lea wrote of the Spanish Inquisition, as follows.

> No more ingenious device has been invented to subjugate a whole population, to paralyze its intellect and to reduce it to blind obedience .... It elevated délation to the rank of high religious duty, it filled the land with spies and it rendered every man an object of suspicion, not only to his neighbor but to the members of his own family and to the stranger whom he might chance to meet. Continued through generations, this could not fail to leave its impress on the national character.[78]

The way American and English authors impeached totalitarian regimes during the 20th century strongly resembled this older rhetoric against the former Inquisition. In the 1950s United States, American leftists like Arthur Miller attacked McCarthyism in similar terms. Miller was a member of the blacklisted "Hollywood Ten". His 1953 play *The Crucible* discussed baseless denunciations of an innocent couple in the times of the Salem witch craze, drawing an analogy between witch hunting in 17th century Massachusetts and the anti-Communist frenzy of his own era. In his 1955 play *A View from the Bridge*, Miller argued denunciation as betrayal, in the play's story of a waterfront worker informing authorities that his own nephew was an illegal immigrant."[79]

The discursive duality of dénonciation and délation is not universal. In involuted institutions such as boarding schools and prisons, a unitary délation discourse seems to be normalized. Dénonciation, often called "squealing", "ratting" or "tale-telling", is encouraged in such contexts, while at the same time incurring especial revulsion. Sykes observed, thus.

---

[77] The Inquisition was a group of institutions inside the Catholic Church, with the aim of combatting heresy and conducting trials of denounced heretics. The majority of sentences consisted of mere penances, but cases of repeat heresy were given to the secular courts, generally resulting in either execution or imprisonment for life. Henry Charles Lea, 'The Inquisition Founded', in Henry Charles Lea, A History of the Inquisition In The Middle Ages, Rarebooksclub, online, 2013, vol. 1, ch 7; Sheila Fitzpatrick and Robert Gellately, 'Introduction to the Practices of Denunciation in Modern European History', *The Journal of Modern History*, vol. 68, no. 4, 1996, pp. 747-767, p. 764.

[78] Henry Charles Lea, *A History of the Inquisition of Spain in Four Volumes*, Macmillan, London, 1906, 2:91.

[79] Victor S Navasky, *Naming Names*, Penguin, Harmondsworth, 1981, pp. 200-222; Michel Ciment, 'Les aveux les plus durs', in Nicole Czechowski & Jacques Hassoun (eds.), *La délation. Un archaïsme, une technique*, Autrement, Paris, 1992, pp. 128-37, pp. 128-37. A View from the Bridge was, of course, also a rebuttal of the film On the Waterfront, directed by Miller's former friend and colleague, Elia Kazan (see above).

> In the prison the word rat or squealer carries an emotional significance far greater than that usually encountered in the free community .... It represents the most serious accusation that one inmate can level against another, for it implies a betrayal that transcends the specific act of disclosure. The rat is a man who has betrayed not just one inmate or several; he has betrayed inmates in general by denying the cohesion of prisoners as a dominant value when confronting the world of officialdom.[80]

However, this insight is not limited to closed kinds of institutions. The discourse of délation is always based on the assumption of a community of subalterns, as for example prisoners, to which group an individual owes loyalty.[81] This could conflict with any obligation of loyalty to the state, recognized simultaneously. From this comes the dénonciation/délation dichotomy.

Nevertheless, prisoners do not accept obligations of loyalty to their form of state, the prison administration, because they became its constituents without their own free consent. Here, there is no conflict in loyalty, with the prisoner's only obligation being to the prisoner community. In the light of this, underlying dénonciation and délation are the major philosophical conceptions of citizenship and loyalty. The English novelist E. M. Forster famously said, as follows, "If I had to choose between betraying my country and betraying my friend, I hope I should have the guts to betray my country"?[82] However, the American moral philosopher Judith Shklar rebuked Forster for irresponsibility and frivolity.[83] In Shklar's view, Forster failed to distinguish between so-called good countries, those having a decent legal system, like Britain or the United States, where denouncing wrongdoing is fitting, and so-called bad countries like the former Soviet Union, where denunciation was shameful. This infers that evaluating any specific acts of denunciation is an ideological issue. If a regime is opposed, or even a church, or party, people regard its interests as separate from and opposite to the citizens' interests. In such cases, people condemn any citizen who freely offers to the authorities information about another citizen. They will characterize this action as betrayal or collaboration. Contrariwise, if people approve of their regime, they

---

[80] Gresham M Sykes, The Society of Captives: A Study of a Maximum Security Prison, Princeton University Press, Princeton, 1958, p. 87.

[81] Sheila Fitzpatrick and Robert Gellately, 'Introduction to the Practices of Denunciation in Modern European History', *The Journal of Modern History*, vol. 68, no. 4, 1996, pp. 747-767, p. 765.

[82] EM Forster, *Two Cheers for Democracy*, Harcourt, Brace, New York, 1951, pp. 68-69.

[83] Judith N Shklar, *Ordinary Vices*, Harvard University Press, Cambridge, 1984, p. 156.

will tend to minimize any perceived distinction between the interests of the state and the citizens.[84]

4. The Theory and Practice of Denunciation in the French Revolution

4.1. Denunciation and the Enemy Other

Denunciation was long neglected as a facet of the history of the French Revolution. In recent times, the three historians Lucien Jaume,[85] A. de Baecque[86] and J. Guilhaumou,[87] have turned their minds to it.

> Denounce the crimes, denounce the criminals, a double reward awaits you: the voice of your conscience, for denunciation is a virtue; and a legitimate reward, for the National Convention is just and desires that each virtuous act should be a means by which the sansculotte may improve his lot .... Friends, nothing can, nothing should constrain your ardor here: former servants must not forget that the Motherland is their sole mistress; nor relatives forget that it alone is their mother; nor citizens forget that they owe themselves utterly to this Motherland which rewards their zeal so effectively, but which would sanction without pity their negligence and punish their criminal silence.[88]

---

[84] The judgmental qualities of the main discourses of denunciation since the French Revolution have sometimes found their way into the scholarship (such as it is) relating to practices of denunciation. See, e.g., the curious postwar essay by two French psychologists who, no doubt reacting to the waves of denunciation that swept France during the German occupation in World War II and after liberation, treat the practices of denunciation as a childish behavior that well-adjusted adults ought to have outgrown: LJH Colaneri & G Gérente, *La Dénonciation et les Dénonciateurs*, Bibliothèque de Philosophie contemporaine, Paris, 1948. Anthropologists have been more successful in escaping the judgmental trap in their studies of one type of denunciation, witchcraft accusations: Mary Douglas (ed.), *Witchcraft Confessions and Accusations*, Tavistock Publications, London, 1970; Max Marwick, *Witchcraft and Sorcery: Selected Readings*, Penguin Books, Harmondsworth, 1982; Sheila Fitzpatrick & Robert Gellately, 'Introduction to the Practices of Denunciation in Modern European History', *The Journal of Modern History*, vol. 68, no. 4, 1996, pp. 747-767, p. 766.

[85] Lucien Jaume, *Le discours Jacobin et la démocratie*, Fayard, Paris, 1989, pp. 192-215.

[86] A de Baecque, *Le corps de l'histoire*, Calmann Lévy, Paris, 1993, pp. 257-302.

[87] J Guilhaumou, 'Fragments of a Discourse on Denunciation (1789-94)', in KM Baker (ed.), *The Terror*, Pergamon Press, Oxford, 1994, pp. 139-55.

[88] *La Commission Temporaire a tous les vrais sans culottes*, Commune-affranchie, Lyon, 1793.

This proclamation was promulgated in 1793 by the Commission Temporaire,[89] which was an ad hoc revolutionary authority, established in Lyon after the Federalist revolt,[90] and is a fairly routine instance of the public rhetoric used during the radical Terror.[91] Underlying its serious claims of civic bad behavior, was the objective of discovering precious objects secreted by the insurrectionists. One twentieth of their value was promised to all denouncers. Nevertheless, the proclamation evoked the major themes of French revolutionary denunciation. These themes were: (a) the principles of citizen and civic action; (b) the idea of critical hazard for the Revolution; (c) profiling the denounced as criminals; (d) the relationships between private and public; a subsisting Classical Roman reference; (e) tension between defending liberty and the threat to liberty by this defense; and, (f) how denunciation ought to be done so that it could destroy threats to the Revolution.[92]

Studying denunciation creates an understanding of the process of the French Revolution as well as how revolutionaries tried to think through the changes from the Old Regime through to the new society. Because these were divisive issues, and denunciation was similarly divisive, the revolutionaries wanted to define it for themselves. Thus, the Jacobins' version of denunciation, such a close match to the Terror, was rooted in dilemmas, which arose from the beginning of the Revolution. The main arguments of this issue were set in 1789-1790, with the necessity and function of denunciation based on the revolution's fragility, due to its many dangerous enemies, so that the

---

[89] The *Commission Temporaire* of Lyon was responsible for widespread judicial repression of Lyon and its environs. Paul Friedland, *Political Actors, Representative Bodies and Theatricality in the Age of the French Revolution*, Cornell University Press, New York, 2002, p. 174.

[90] A widespread revolt against the French National Convention, in 1793, in the several months after the fall of the French monarchy, after leading Girondins were expelled from the Convention. Paul R Hanson, *Jacobin Republic Under Fire: The Federalist Revolt in the French Revolution*, Pennsylvania State University Press, University Park, 2010, p. 3.

[91] The Reign of Terror, usually called The Terror, was a period in the times of the French Revolution when a series of massacres and public executions took place in reaction to revolutionary fervour, sentiment against clerics, and allegations of treason by the Committee of Public Safety. The Terror began either in 1793, or possibly in 1789, when the first revolutionary killing took place. Jean-Clément Martin, *La Terreur, part maudite de la Révolution*, Découvertes/Gallimard, 2010, pp. 14-15; Michel Biard et Hervé Leuwers, 'Visages de la Terreur', dans Michel Biard et Hervé Leuwers (dir.), *Visages de la Terreur. L'exception politique de l'an II*, Armand Colin, Paris, 2014, pp. 5-14.

[92] Colin Lucas, 'The Theory and Practice of Denunciation in the French Revolution', *The Journal of Modern History*, vol. 68, no. 4, 1996, pp. 768-785, p. 768.

justification for denunciation was the real and imminent threat to the Revolution.[93]

Historians have discussed the role of the enemy "Other" in revolutionary symbolism, arguing that a revolutionary sovereign Nation with a general will necessarily implied a Hegelian dialectic,[94] specifying opposition and dissent as an antithetical and criminal Other. From this, the revolutionaries imagined a pervasive enemy in a death struggle with them, and whose imagined power did not accord with the available evidence. Such available evidence inferred only disparate dissent varying from militancy to mere grumbling. This kind of radical Manichaeism appeared in the Jacobin spirit of the Terror.[95] Revolutionaries had both a property owners' desire for order, in the form of public peace, and also, by an Enlightenment[96] view that they were making a new social harmony for France grounded in nature's universal principles. Therefore, they understood opposition as criminal, unnatural, corrupt and selfish. They connected popular protests with the grasp of corrupt and selfish predators over the uninformed poor.[97]

Since the earliest times of the Revolution, there was verifiable evidence of resistance, plots, and disorder, beginning with the resistance of the privileged membership of the Estates General,[98] and the events of 14th July

---

[93] ibid., p. 769.

[94] Hegelian dialectic, usually presented in a threefold manner, was stated as comprising three dialectical stages of development: a thesis, giving rise to its reaction; an antithesis, which contradicts or negates the thesis; and the tension between the two being resolved by means of a synthesis. Michael Allen Fox, *The Accessible Hegel*, Prometheus Books, New York, 2005, p. 43; A. V. Miller (trans.), *Phenomenology of Spirit*, Clarendon Press, Oxford, 1977, ss. 50, 51, pp. 29, 30.

[95] Manichaeism was a major religion founded in the 3rd century CE by the Parthian prophet Mani, (216–274 CE). Manichaeism taught a dualistic cosmology telling of the struggle between a good spiritual world of light and an evil material world of darkness. R van den Broek & Wouter J Hanegraaff, *Gnosis and Hermeticism from Antiquity to Modern Times*, SUNY Press, Albany, 1998, p. 37; Ehsan Yarshater, *The Cambridge History of Iran, The Seleucid, Parthian and Sasanian Periods*, Cambridge University Press, Cambridge, 1983, vol. 3 no. 2.

[96] The Age of Enlightenment was a 17th and 18th century European intellectual and philosophical movement. It comprised a variety of ideas about (1) the value of human happiness, (2) the pursuit of knowledge obtained by means of reason and the evidence of the senses, and (3) ideals such as liberty, progress, toleration, fraternity, constitutional government, and separation of church and state. Dorinda Outram, Panorama of the Enlightenment, Getty Publications, Los Angeles, 2006, p. 29; Milan Zafirovski, The Enlightenment and Its Effects on Modern Society, Springer, New York, 2010, p. 144.

[97] Colin Lucas, 'The Theory and Practice of Denunciation in the French Revolution', *The Journal of Modern History*, vol. 68, no. 4, 1996, pp. 768-785, p. 769.

[98] The Estates-General was a meeting of the three estates within French society. It comprised the clergy, nobility and peasant classes. Members of the Roman Catholic clergy, numbering

1789, when the Bastille was attacked by an angry and aggressive mob.[99] Both moderate and radical revolutionaries viewed each other as the organizers of selfish and corrupt counter revolutionary acts, with radical factions profiling each other in the same way. Thus, the preeminence of Jacobinism in the Terror and the rise of denunciation as a systemic element of government did not change the revolutionary discourse against its enemies. On 28th July 1789, Adrien Duport proposed the establishment of a Comité des Recherches,[100] in the National Assembly. He stated to members, with hardly a whisper of dissent, as follows.

> ... plots are being mounted against the well-being of public affairs [la chose publique], we can be in no doubt of that. There can be no question of deferring this to the law courts .... We must acquire ghastly and indispensable knowledge .... We will learn terrible but necessary truths .... Let our vigilant eye be turned in every direction.[101]

This proposed committee was formed only to inspect appropriated correspondence, but it became enmeshed in debates over the inviolability of the mails. This opened the door to the search for "terrible truths", through the method of denunciation, as was clear in October of 1789 when the Commune of Paris[102] established its own Comité des Recherches, expressly to receive denunciations. It called upon all "good citizens" to disclose to it all information and knowledge they possessed on conspiracies against the public good. They said "One of the obstacles to restoring good order and public peace

---

about 100,000, made up the first estate. The second estate was the French nobility, numbering some 400,000. All others, merchants, lawyers, poor laborers, and ordinary peasants some 97% of the population comprised the third estate. Ruth F. Necheles, 'The Curés in the Estates General of 1789', *The Journal of Modern History*, vol. 46, no. 3, 1974, pp. 425-444, pp. 425-426.

99 Colin Lucas, 'The Theory and Practice of Denunciation in the French Revolution', *The Journal of Modern History*, vol. 68, no. 4, 1996, pp. 768-785, p. 769.

100 The national Comité des Recherches and its municipal counterpart, the Comité de Recherche, were formed from a widespread suspicion of secrets. The committees, however, began to work in secret, becoming powerful committees of rigged justice during the Terror. Barry M Shapiro, 'Revolutionary Justice in 1789-1790: The Comité des Recherches, the Châtelet, and the Fayettist Coalition', *French Historical Studies*, vol. 17, no. 3, 1992, pp. 656-669, p. 656.

101 Laurent Mavidal, *Archives parlementaires de 1787 à 1860*, vol. 8, Librairie Administrative de Paul Dupont, Paris, 1869, 8:293.

102 *The Paris Commune was a radical, populist-led government ruling Paris from 18th March to 28th May 1871. It formed after France's defeat in the Franco-German war, with the dissolution of* the *Second Empire of Napoleon III, (1852–1870).* Samuel Bernstein, 'The Paris Commune', *Science & Society*, vol. 5, no. 2, 1941, pp. 117-147, p. 117.

is the mystery with which the authors of plots surround themselves," and "the safety of the State depends upon their discovery."[103]

This government perspective was further particularized, in November 1791, when the new Legislative Assembly set up a Comité des Recherches to gather all facts known to citizens. Basire announced publicly, thus.

> We are introducing the measure, surrounded by conspirators; everywhere plots are under way and you are continually receiving denunciations of individual facts, which are all connected with the great conspiracy, about whose existence none of us can have any doubt. These facts are all separate and, if they were all put together, they would offer a general body of crime which would finally throw a great light on the intentions of our enemies.[104]

These texts clarify the lasting purpose of denunciation, in outline: to reveal the hidden; to collate small pieces of knowledge from individuals into a general corpus of understanding; and, therefore, to protect the Revolution from its opponents.[105]

4.2. The Pre-Legal Ethics of Denunciation

In these attempts at definition, denunciation was a limited phenomenon, it being addressed only to the National Assembly or to the Paris Commune. It was likely limited to great conspiracies against the new state. It was also conceived as an initial step in the process of determining where trouble might be hiding, leading to an inquiry and a consequent corpus of evidence to be referred to the courts, or else purpose-built tribunals, for trial. In the French legal system, it was a new and additional part of the procedure of instruction, this function confirmed by the 1789 order of the Paris Commune establishing its Comité des Recherches.[106]

---

[103] S Lacroix (ed.), *Actes de la Commune de Paris pendant la Revolution*, Société de l'Histoire de la Révolution Française, Paris, 1895, 2:366 (October 21).

[104] Laurent Mavidal, *Archives parlementaires de 1787 à 1860*, vol. 35, Librairie Administrative de Paul Dupont, Paris, 1869, 35:361.

[105] Colin Lucas, 'The Theory and Practice of Denunciation in the French Revolution', *The Journal of Modern History*, vol. 68, no. 4, 1996, pp. 768-785, p. 770.

[106] S Lacroix (ed.), *Actes de la Commune de Paris pendant la Revolution*, Société de l'Histoire de la Révolution Française, Paris, 1895, 2:366 (October 21).

Additionally, the Paris Commune distinguished between evidence and denunciations, authorizing its committee to take "dénonciations et depositions", depositions being the term for that kind of evidence handed to inquiring magistrates. This distinction was obvious. The term "deposition" was part of a formal legal procedure, one that could be made mandatory whenever it was not given voluntarily. Thus, it was a written public declaration of something already agreed and known. However, the term "dénonciation" was spontaneous, a communication conveyed voluntarily about a possibly unknown but suspected thing, even when not fully understood. In this way, denunciation was a separate class of action, separated from proof or probative evidence. Denunciation was controversial in the extreme. It was accorded different meanings and senses by some radical revolutionaries. The Paris Commune Comité des Recherches authorized its sub-committee to arrest and question denounced people, while putting together their body of instruction. This authority permitted a conflation of procedures, while ostensibly maintaining a continuing semantic separation of them. The somewhat restrained journalist Loustalot articulated the obvious dangers. He said that this had established a "civil inquisition", as "a means to destroy morals, to destroy all confidence between citizens and all security; this is a means to provoke calumny and to favor informing [délation].... It resembles dictatorship, it is the best shield for tyranny".[107] With this, Loustalot was only exposing publicly a debate that had begun in the National Assembly around July 1789, and which would continue around the Comité des Recherches of both the National Assembly and the Paris Commune into 1790.[108]

An ongoing debate, of how to prevent the defense of liberty from destroying liberty, remained in the form of a dilemma over the difference between dénonciation and délation, the practices of denouncing and informing. This debate was never resolved, and the Revolution never escaped such contradictions. The elites of the Revolution were guided by the history of Rome, as a result of their early-life education of those Roman authors hostile to both the Roman Empire and to the disintegrating Roman Republic. These sources looked back in time to a pure and mythical era of a Republic grounded in virtue. These perceptions, reproduced in 18th century philosophical texts, educated the public debate on denunciation. Classical Rome offered this kind of model, as it was without any formal state structure

---

107 S Lacroix (ed.), Révolutions de Paris, no. 8 (November 14, 1789).

108 Colin Lucas, 'The Theory and Practice of Denunciation in the French Revolution', *The Journal of Modern History*, vol. 68, no. 4, 1996, pp. 768-785, p. 771.

for prosecution, its courts depending upon individual denouncers initiating cases by the laying of informations against the denounced. Those individuals who filed informations, in this way, were named as "delatores". However, the revolutionaries in France knew about the Roman imperial record of delatores, as those who informed the Emperor in secret, their information rewarded, whenever it led to a senator being convicted. This reward included the victim's estate and his rank as a senator. These French revolutionaries knew that Tacitus had condemned this practice as being responsible for the Empire's disintegration.[109]

There was also the Classical model of the two censores, who supervised the citizens' morality.[110] These were a constituent part of the Roman Republic, as they vanished under the Empire, only to return when emperors occasionally took these powers. This was a welcomed model, as the censores were mostly preoccupied with extravagance and luxury, as also were those of enlightened opinion during the latter periods of the Old Regime. In 1790, Pierre Manuel began his aggressive description of the Old Regime's policing arrangements for Paris by proposing that, rather than a police force, each town ought to have an official who informed the town administrators of their errors and to teach citizens respect for the administrators.[111] Jean-Paul Marat was also in favor of republican censors, suggesting they act as denouncers to a revolutionary tribunal. This was a much more deadly project than the original model of censors, who could only award administrative black marks.[112]

The Roman classical model was inadequate in France, because it was the delatores that better fitted the Revolution's requirement for voluntary information from the people. Although these delatores were tarnished in the records of history, the censores remained untarnished. In the model offered was scrutiny by two magistrates who imposed "hardly more than a blush" on

---

[109] Publius Cornelius Tacitus, (circa 56 - circa 118 CE), was a Roman historian. His most famous works were *Histories* and *Annals*, covering the history of the Roman Empire from the times of the Julio-Claudians to the reign of Domitian, (regnant 81-96 CE). He also had a long career in public service, s a quaestor in 81 CE, a praetor in 88 CE, a consul in 97 CE, and proconsul of Asia from 112-113 CE. JS Reid, 'Tacitus as a Historian', *The Journal of Roman Studies*, vol. 11, 1921, pp. 191-199.

[110] AE Austin, 'Regimen Morum', *Journal of Roman Studies*, vol. 78, 1988, pp. 14-34; Colin Lucas, 'The Theory and Practice of Denunciation in the French Revolution', *The Journal of Modern History*, vol. 68, no. 4, 1996, pp. 768-785, p. 772.

[111] Pierre Manuel, *La police de Paris devoile*, Paris, 1790, 1:ix-x.

[112] JP Marat, 'Appel à la Nation', in A Vermorel (ed.), *Oeuvres de JP Marat*, Décembre-Alonnier, Paris, 1869; Colin Lucas, 'The Theory and Practice of Denunciation in the French Revolution', *The Journal of Modern History*, vol. 68, no. 4, 1996, pp. 768-785, p. 772.

the people they named, as Cicero had put it.[113] Nevertheless, as usual during the Revolution, the imperfect Classical model influenced how revolutionaries thought through their problems. This was evident in the debates over délation, which was in the nature of informing, in the period 1789-1790. For the conservative Stanislas de Clermont-Tonnerre, when a constitutional and free society states the general will was the law, then it prevented itself from spying, informing or violence. The general and popular will could only be pure while opinions were free, with truth to be found in the diversity of opinion and error not feared. M. de Clermont-Tonnerre articulated the view that a love of liberty in society guaranteed the failure of the enemy.[114]

Those with more radical and patriotic opinions naturally tried to incorporate suitable meanings of the word "liberty" into the new revolutionary vocabulary to meet their perceived needs. Pierre-Jean Agier wrote a report on the activities of the Paris Commune's committee.[115] Noting the reluctance of thinking people about denunciation, even where the state was at stake, he stated that the time had arrived to get rid of such prejudices, fit only for slaves, and unworthy of a newly free people. It had been correct to spurn the informer in times of the Old Regime, as he delivered innocent people to an arbitrary state authority and its biased, cruel and secret justice system. Now, the new purpose was the denunciation of plots that threatened the state. In this new system, the accused would come before his peers immediately, for examination, to be either exonerated or sent for justice, but in any event "to a humane, public, impartial justice, which can be terrible only to wrongdoers" .... "as far as informing is concerned, silence is a virtue under Despotism; it is a crime, yes indeed, a crime under the rule of Liberty."[116]

Agier was far from being alone in his views, with similar reports having emerged. Mirabeau said "in the perils which surround us, informing ... must be seen as the most important of our new virtues". Desmoulins said "I am trying to rehabilitate the word 'informing.' . . . In our present circumstances, we need to see the word honored". Mercier said that denunciation was one of

113 "The censor's verdict inflicted hardly more than a blush of shame. That is why, just as this way of judging only concerns reputation, the penalty with which it strikes is called *ignominia*, loss of reputation". Cicero, *La République*, E Breguet (trans.), Gallimard, Paris, 1994, IV, 7, fragment 5, p. 119.

114 Stanislas de Clermont-Tonnerre, *Nouvelles observations sur les comites de recherches*, Chez Desenne Libraire au Palais-Royale, Paris, nd.

115 P-J Agier, *Compte-rendu a l'Assemblee generale des representants de la Commune, au nom du Comite de Recherches, le 30 novembre 1789*, Paris, nd.

116 ibid.

the "heroic virtues".[117] With an explicit reference to Rome, Mirabeau cited the age-old Senatorial maxim *Caveant Consules ne respublica quid detrimenti capiat*, meaning that the Consuls shall take care that the state shall suffer no harm. Des Moulins cited Cicero's phrasc *Accusatores multos esse in civitate utile est*, meaning it was useful to have many accusers among us. Mirabeau concluded with a dictum of Cicero to the effect that half-proof would be enough to initiate speech, because during the night all the faithful dogs could bark at people passing by, because of the likelihood of thieves.[118]

4.3. The Pious Denouncer and Patriotism

The widespread belief in a need for such strong mechanisms arose clearly from the early attitudes of so-called patriots, with their struggle using the word délation reflecting their difficulty in incorporating it into their new society. Informants were still too closely identified with the hated police spy system of the Old Regime. A widely held perception that informing was just the corrupt settling of private disputes was too closely connected with the tyranny of the Old Regime government, along with a strong and residual Classical Roman heritage attaching to the word délation.[119]

Pierre Manuel's close analysis of Old Regime policing began with the point that it was the swarm of petty police agents that had reduced the population into a species of slavery.[120] Revolutionary conceptions therefore moved to the use of a different word, namely dénonciation, newly defined as a uniquely revolutionary practice. Despite this, anyone reading the Encyclopédie[121] would already have viewed the weakness in such an undertaking. The Encyclopédie had attempted to separate contemporary notions from Classical ones, having sought specifically to distinguish between

---

[117] A de Baecque, *Le corps de l'histoire*, Calmann Lévy, Paris, 1993, p. 272; C Labrosse and P Rétat, *Naissance de journal revolutionnaire: 1789*, Presses universitaires de Lyon, Lyon, 1989, pp. 201-202.

[118] ibid.

[119] On the hatred of police spies and its significance in the early Revolution, see David Andress, 'Social Prejudice and Political Fears in the Policing of Paris', *French History*, vol. 9, 1995, pp. 202-226.

[120] Pierre Manuel, *La police de Paris devoile*, Paris, 1790.

[121] *Encyclopédie, ou dictionnaire raisonné des sciences, des arts et des métiers*, (Encyclopedia, or a Systematic Dictionary of the Sciences, Arts, and Crafts), was better known as the Encyclopédie, was a general encyclopedia published in France, (1751 – 1772), with subsequent revised editions. Ian Buchanan, *A Dictionary of Critical Theory*, Oxford University Press, Oxford, 2010, p. 151.

informing and denouncing. It still had to agree that "the condition of being an informer and that of being a denouncer are at root the same",[122] inferring that commonplace denunciation could be grounded in either dénonciation or délation.

There were two fundamental elements in the revolutionary statements that separated virtue and publicity as the two attributes constituting the key difference between informing and revolutionary denunciation. The notion that denunciation was a civic act remained central all the way through to the Terror. In the conceptions of the more radical, denunciation was the critical action of citizenship, as a simple update of that old Classical conception of civic virtue that informed a necessary public concern in public affairs for the *res publica*.[123]

Denunciation was the citizen's civic duty, in expressing a citizen's vigilance and care for public affairs, as it was his individual duty to defend the Revolution and to maintain its transition from tyranny to liberty and equality.[124] As counter-revolutionary threats and radical suspicions took the Revolution into the Terror, debate of this early definition of denunciation increased, so that denunciation turned into a new virtuous imperative, with the idea of affect-free virtue related to how disinterested the denouncer was. The Jacobins phrased this disinterested stance as the denouncer's "purity", implying its opposite was indeed ritual defilement. Thus, in the public political mind, this virtue insured against any misuse of denunciation, which might have allowed it to slip down to mere informing. Jean-Paul Marat led this view, all Jacobins following him, while proclaiming his purity of intention and his devotion to the People's cause. With this fresh public persona in place, Marat used his mask to convert denunciation from a duty to a right. He delivered this mutating argument by declaring that the state's salvation was the supreme law, so therefore its defense was the paramount duty of the citizenry. He declared "the denunciation to the Motherland as traitors of all those who attack the people's rights and threaten public liberty is . . . the right of every

122 Denis Diderot & Jean le Rond d'Alembert, *Encyclopédie, ou Dictionnaire raisonné des sciences, des arts et des métiers*, Sociétés typographiques, Bern and Lausanne, 1778-1779, 4:777.

123 A Latin phrase meaning "public affair"; Colin Lucas, 'The Theory and Practice of Denunciation in the French Revolution', *The Journal of Modern History*, vol. 68, no. 4, 1996, pp. 768-785, p. 774.

124 Colin Lucas, 'The Theory and Practice of Denunciation in the French Revolution', *The Journal of Modern History*, vol. 68, no. 4, 1996, pp. 768-785, p. 774.

individual".[125] Thus, a paramount duty to save the state became an individual right of denunciation.

This position of Marat generated two separate and new notions. The first was that denunciation was a supreme act of sovereignty, made by a member of the corpus of sovereign people, addressed to these sovereign people. It was an involuted discourse, binding those outside the discourse. The second was publicity, with all those debating the issue of denunciation before 1793 insisting on publicity as being centrally important. Denunciation constituted a public act, so that denouncers must sign their denunciations. There were many Roman prescriptions cited against making false denunciations. It was intended that the names of false denouncers were to be posted beside public lists of the enemies of the People. This publicity was regarded as the juxtapositional guarantee against defamation and the public settling of any private score.[126]

Despite these arrangements, the idea of publicity necessarily included the notion that it evoked public opinion as arbiter. Baker argued the significance of the role of public opinion in the pre-Revolutionary absolute monarchy.[127] During the Revolution, this key notion of public opinion was a locus for debate between moderates and radicals about how the sovereign people might be characterized and how it articulated its views. They had posited a sovereign people without first identifying them. Thus, Marat's view was that denunciation exposed the weakness of confining sovereignty to the National Assembly.[128]

Publicity raised the issue of who purported to denounce whom. This conception of publicity included soliciting the people as a "tribunal of public opinion". It invoked this version of the public as the ultimate voice of the sovereign people, impartial and paramount dispensers of justice. Jean-Pierre Brissot stated a folk maxim, during his pre-Girondin phase, "Publicity can never harm innocence … sooner or later, innocence will triumph because the public is an impartial judge."[129] Such acts of definition suited the radicals who wanted to subvert the National Assembly's power by fixing on another arena

---

[125] 'Le Publiciste Parisien', *Journal politique, libre et impartial*, no. 5, 12th - 15th September Paris, 1789.

[126] J.-P. Brissot, *Lettres a Monsieur le Chevalier de Pange sur sa brochure*, Paris, 1790: "The means of removing the danger of délations is to force their conversion into public accusations".

[127] KM Baker, *Inventing the French Revolution*, Cambridge University Press, Cambridge, 1990, pp. 167-99.

[128] Colin Lucas, 'The Theory and Practice of Denunciation in the French Revolution', *The Journal of Modern History*, vol. 68, no. 4, 1996, pp. 768-785, p. 775.

[129] J-P Brissot, *Réplique de J-P Brissot à Stanislas Tonnerre*, Paris, 1790.

of politics external to it. In reality, the explosion of the press during the revolutionary crisis produced a strong invasion of the public space by a storm of commentary in print, half information and half exhortation. The radical press expressed itself as the People's vigilant eye, denouncing to the People its enemies' dangerous and secret maneuvers. The titles of pamphlets and newspapers demonstrated this phenomenon: "Sentinelle, Observateur, Spectateur, Vrites, Secrets dévoilés, Wridique, Amis, Censeur, Dénonciateur".[130]

In key ways, the press became public opinion itself, as a new forum where denunciation and its defense were litigated. The revolutionary mind, full of fear and suspicion of undisclosed enemies, could be exercised there. Marat and Hebert did so, even more violently. While press denunciation could be represented as a trigger for legal proceedings, the truth was that its justice was a summary popular justice. Marat's *Ami du peuple*,[131] each edition of which was a new denunciation, was such an example. These matters of denunciation circumscribed the revolution's debate about press freedom.[132]

Defenders of press freedom regarded journalists as the vigilant proxies of the People. To those who opposed press freedom, public opinion could never formulate comprehensive judgments of complex issues. It was too easily moved by rhetoric. Journalists were, to them, just delateurs, reporters of calumny, and therefore, generators of public discord.[133] The debate ended with the matter of press freedom resolved by the Jacobins designating all rival presses as counter-revolutionary. They were closed by force in 1793, while the Jacobin press continued this kind of denunciation unabated. The victory of radicalism after the king fell in 1792, combined with the 1793 victory of Jacobinism led to some changes of degree. The crises in the economy, with many military defeats, the Vendée peasant rebellion[134] and the anti-Jacobin

---

[130] C Labrosse and P Rétat, *Naissance de journal revolutionnaire: 1789*, Presses universitaires de Lyon, Lyon, 1989, pp. 193-197; J Guilhaumou, 'Fragments of a Discourse on Denunciation (1789-94)', in KM Baker (ed.), *The Terror*, Pergamon Press, Oxford, 1994, pp. 139-155.

[131] *L'Ami du peuple*, (The Friend of the People), was a newspaper run by Jean-Paul Marat, during the French Revolution. Robert Darnton & Daniel Roche (eds.), *Revolution in Print: the Press in France, 1775-1800*, University of California Press, Berkeley, 1989, p. 162.

[132] Colin Lucas, 'The Theory and Practice of Denunciation in the French Revolution', *The Journal of Modern History*, vol. 68, no. 4, 1996, pp. 768-785, p. 776.

[133] Chevalier de Pange, *Réflexions sur la délation et sur le* comité des recherches, Chez Barrois l'aîné, Paris, 1790.

[134] In Spring 1793, peasants and farmers of the Vendée region in western France revolted against the National Convention. They disliked the revolutionary government's treatment of the king and church. The Vendée uprising was the largest counter-revolutionary movement during the French Revolution, enjoying some successes but eventually government troops

urban rebellion intensified the public sense of betrayal and danger, with commensurate intensification and broadening of the practices of denunciation. Felix Lepeletier's funeral speech, of July 1793, for the murdered Marat, loudly stated that "Denunciation is the mother of virtues just as vigilance is the surest safeguard of the people and of liberty."[135]

4.4. The Jacobins and the Terror

The Terror saw three transformations in the practices of denunciation. To begin with, denunciations of enemies in the Jacobin press continued, great oratorical denunciations of factional competitors as counter revolutionaries continued inside the Convention, but individual denunciations became gradually more secretive. Etienne Barry presented his ideas on political denunciation on 25th July 1793,[136] coinciding with an exhortation in the Parisian Jacobin Club to expand denunciation into a general procedure throughout France. Barry made three new claims about the character of generalized denunciation. His first was that individual denunciation was a collective act by a member of the collective of sovereign people on behalf of the sovereign people. His second claim was that denunciation could be anonymous without any responsibility apportioned to the denouncer. Third, denunciation was an act of citizenship to discipline those who spurned integral membership of the collective. His view was that denunciation was disciplinary, didactic and a protective measure against treason,[137] this juxtaposition thus punishing treason without it being committed.

Barry's views point to the phenomenon of the growing secrecy of individual denunciations as part of the Terror. Denunciations were newly made to the vigilance committees of the comites de surveillance, established by decree in March 1793, because of, and symbiotic with, the intensifying emergency. Still, denunciations had to be in writing and signed, even although they were now delivered to a small group of people to consider them in seclusion. This was a major change from the publicity of the early Revolution that separated denunciation from mere informing. Publicity confirmed the fact

---

put it down later in 1793. Harvey Mitchell, 'The Vendee and Counterrevolution: A Review Essay', *French Historical Studies*, vol. 5, no. 4, 1968, pp. 405-429, p. 405.

[135] Lucien Jaume, *Le discours Jacobin et la démocratie*, Fayard, Paris, 1989, p. 204.

[136] ibid., p. 203.

[137] Colin Lucas, 'The Theory and Practice of Denunciation in the French Revolution', *The Journal of Modern History*, vol. 68, no. 4, 1996, pp. 768-785, p. 777.

that the denouncer addressed the public and revealed knowledge the People must have for their defense of liberty. Therefore, denunciation had been a component of revolutionary democracy, which itself was an unstable idea, as radical revolutionaries' dilemmas with the conception of the sovereign people. After all, popular agitation was both capable of triggering insurrection against the enemies of liberty, and riotous attacks on people and their property.[138]

The Jacobins used "public opinion" to express the notion of the sovereign people, while recognizing the unreliability of this opinion of people easily misled, thus making publicity a potential danger. Pierre-Gaspard Chaumette spoke in October 1793 about the Girondins trial just before he himself was swept up in a factional purge. He said "The men now before the Revolutionary Tribunal have a plan; the sessions are held in public, and ten thousand people can attest to this fact: they have tried to justify themselves to the people and to pass as innocent, at the very least in the eyes of posterity. They have relied upon their eloquence".[139] The Terror government adopted a well-adapted solution to this problem. It began with silencing Georges Danton by his 1794 trial. It culminated in the Law of 22 Prairial Year II of 10th June 1794, which deprived all accused of lawyers to defend them, on the stated premise of a folk maxim that innocence needed no defender and crime deserved none.[140]

The Jacobins tried to solve the riddle over the locus of the sovereign people by grounding the Terror in the expulsion of the Girondins, so that the Convention would now stand purified of traitors. Therefore, according to its form of logic, it spoke as the sovereign people. In this way, denunciation was now an instrument of the state's power. This was the second of the three major changes referred to above. These vigilance committees made up of local patriots were exactly as Loustalot[141] had characterized as tyrannical in the Paris Commune's Comité des Recherches. They had necessary *a priori* powers

---

[138] C Lucas, 'Revolutionary Violence, the People and the Terror', in KM Baker (ed.), *The Terror: The French Revolution and the creation of modern political culture*, Emerald, Bingley, 1994, pp. 57-79.

[139] F-A Aulard, *La société des Jacobins*, Librairie Jouaust, Librairie Nobelet, Paris, 1889-97, 5:482. As evidence of the uncertainty of Jacobin discourse in this domain, see how in the same debate Hebert states that "public opinion has already made up its mind about the crimes of this atrocious faction" and that the trial should therefore be hurried to its conclusion.

[140] Colin Lucas, 'The Theory and Practice of Denunciation in the French Revolution', *The Journal of Modern History*, vol. 68, no. 4, 1996, pp. 768-785, p. 778.

[141] Elysée Loustallot, (1761 – 1790), was a French lawyer and journalist. He was a republican editor of the *Revolutions of Paris* during the French Revolution. Marcellin Pellet, *Élysée Loustallot et les Révolutions de Paris (juillet 1789-septembre 1790)*, A le Chevalier, Paris, 1872.

of arrest, by this basic repression leading up to prison, then up to the revolutionary tribunals, and finally, up to the guillotine itself.

As a coercive and combative government during extreme emergency, the Terror regime made systemic the suspicion of the revolutionary years into the new *Law of Suspects* of 17th September 1793.[142] This law required summary arrest of any person who was a suspect. Denunciation was thus parallel to the *Law of Suspects*, because denunciation was the articulation of suspicion in the absence of proof. State Terror could now be understood as the three elements of vigilance committee, denunciation and arrest. The bloody inquisitorial times of the Venetian Republic had been reinstated, and the Roman Imperial delatores had been revived.[143] In the anti-Jacobin violence of the Thermidorian Reaction of 1795,[144] the denouncer was the most despised.[145]

The third major path to the Terror could be found in the form of the denunciatory text. Denunciation had two objects in the early times of the Revolution.[146] The Revolution's losers formed one kind of denunciation. They were such as princes of the blood, former ministers, parlementaires, aristocrats and nonjuror priests. The other kind was denunciation of government, where journalists functioned as a category of censuring intervention. With the crisis

---

[142] The *Law of Suspects* was a decree passed by the French National Convention on 17th September 1793, arguably beginning the so-called Reign of Terror. The law provided for the arrest of all enemies and suspected enemies of the Revolution, especially aimed at nonsubmissive former nobles, émigrés, officials removed from office, officers under suspicion of treason, and hoarders of goods. Later, the decree was expanded with implementation of the law and its arrests entrusted to oversight committees. The decree introduced the maxim that subjects must prove their innocence, later extended by the *Law of 22 Prairial of 10th June 1794*. Jean Tulard, Jean-François Fayard & Alfred Fierro, *Histoire et Dictionnaire de la Révolution française*, C Bouquins (ed.), Robert Laffont, Parus, 1997; Augé, P Larousse (ed.), *Encyclopédie Larousse du XXe siècle*, Union générale d'éditions, Paris, 1975; Lee Baker & Gregory Fremont-Barnes (eds.), Encyclopedia of the Age of Political Revolutions and New Ideologies, 1760-1815, Greenwood Publishing Group, Westport, 2007, p. 397.

[143] Under the Roman Principate, (27 BCE to 284 CE), during the prosecution by the delator, Mamercus Scaurus of C. Silanus, who had previously been a consul in 10 CE, Silanus was prosecuted for violating the "godhead of Augustus" and "spurning the majesty of Tiberius". WW Flint, 'The Delatores in the Reign of Tiberius, as Described by Tacitus', *The Classical Journal*, vol. 8, no. 1, 1912, pp. 37-42.

[144] The Thermidorian Reaction, during the French Revolution, was the parliamentary revolt on 9th Thermidor, year II, 27th July 1794, precipitating the fall of Maximilien Robespierre, the collapse of revolutionary fervour, and collapse of the French Reign of Terror. Howard G Brown, 'Echoes of the Terror', *Historical Reflections/Réflexions Historiques*, vol. 29, no. 3, 2003, pp. 529-558, p. 529.

[145] C Lucas, 'Themes in Southern Violence after 9 Thermidor', in G Lewis & C Lucas (eds.), *Beyond the Terror*, Cambridge University Press, Cambridge, 1973, pp. 152-94.

[146] Colin Lucas, 'The Theory and Practice of Denunciation in the French Revolution', *The Journal of Modern History*, vol. 68, no. 4, 1996, pp. 768-785, p. 779.

of 1792,[147] this narrowness could not be sustained. The arrival of the Terror in 1793 shifted the objects of denunciation, with denunciation becoming less a censuring watch on the government, although in high politics denunciation continued to be a weapon among Jacobin factions. Therefore, denunciation continued to operate among suspect government officials.

For example, the trials of Danton and his associates were based on their denunciation by Saint-Just, in the Convention on 11 Germinal Year II of 31st March 1794. Saint-Just began with a theoretical exegesis on the inevitability of subversion, subsisting conspiratorial factions, machinations of foreign powers, plans for a new Orleanist monarchy, carefully juxtaposed with a freshly-presented list of previously agreed traitors. From this web, he emphasized one thread that, through allegations and juxtapositions, damned Danton as an integral part of everything that had gone before. His speech ascended to several accusatory heights: "Danton, you have served tyranny"; "Could you really be that blind to the general interest?"; "Danton, you were thus the accomplice of Mirabeau, d'Orleans, Dumouriez, Brissot"; "Bad citizen, you are a conspirator."[148]

In the smaller towns, denunciations reflected problems in food supply, seigneurial exaction, nonresident landlords, and similar. Also, genuine concern about commitment to the revolutionary cause was visible, such as in the denunciations of nonjuror priests and clandestine Catholic rites.[149] Only in larger towns were there real cases of polemical denunciation along with criminal behavior. The most serious case was the revolutionary committee and the "Compagnie Marat" of Nantes. They brutalized prisoners, stole their property, and drowned some of them in the River Loire.[150] Denunciation was integral with suspicion, and "Suspicion," said Robespierre,[151] "is the guardian

---

147 In April of 1792, France declared war on Austria. After the war went badly for France, king Louis XVI was accused of treason, subsequently stripped of his titles and then imprisoned. In September 1792, the new National Convention declared France a republic, the monarchy abolished. Eugene Nelson White, 'The French Revolution and the Politics of Government Finance, 1770-1815', *The Journal of Economic History*, vol. 55, no. 2, 1995, pp. 227-255, p. 228.

148 *Œuvres complètes de Saint-Just*, Éditions de la Cité universelle, Paris, 1946, pp. 221-236; Colin Lucas, 'The Theory and Practice of Denunciation in the French Revolution', *The Journal of Modern History*, vol. 68, no. 4, 1996, pp. 768-785, p. 780.

149 In French history, non-jurors, or refractory clergy, were those members of clergy, declining to swear any oath of allegiance to the state. David P French, 'Swift, the Non-Jurors, and Jacobitism', *Modern Language Notes*, vol. 72, no. 4, 1957, pp. 258-264, p. 259.

150 RC Cobb, *Les armées révolutionnaires*, Paris, 1961-63, 1:576-87.

151 Maximilien François Marie Isidore de Robespierre, (1758 –1794), was a French lawyer and statesman of the French Revolution. While serving as a member of both the Constituent Assembly and the Jacobin Club, he campaigned for universal manhood suffrage, abolition

of the rights of the People; it is to the profound feeling for liberty what jealousy is to love."[152] But denunciation was more than a mere articulation of suspicion, akin to jealousy. It was a procedure for externally attributing meaning to gestures, behavior and mere appearances.[153] When Huard was pressured in the Paris Jacobin Club, the most persuasive denouncer was he who invited people to note: "how he has listened to the discussion. Just by looking at him, I would pronounce him guilty."[154]

4.5. Suspicion, Jealousy and the Mask

Early in the Revolution, revolutionary denunciations were rarely clear announcements of a counterrevolutionary act. Denunciations were always descriptive, with an interpretation of the description either by juxtaposition with external considerations or by attributing a meaning to the description based on general truths or maxims. Consider the following several instances of typological suspicion. A man's journey to another town might be suspect if he was a noble. A slamming door at night could be suspect if it was at a bakery. A woman with a large basket at a late hour could be suspicious if she were a rich person's servant. A wealthy merchant would be considered more hostile to the Revolution than would a shopkeeper. Prostitutes were more likely to miss the Old Regime than unmarried pregnant servant girls. The 1793 denunciation by Louis-Pierre Dufourny of Francois Chabot, within Jacobin Club confines, triggering Chabot's inexorable path to the guillotine, was a prototypical instance of denunciation structured with the weaving of facts with mere implications and assertions.[155]

Dufourny commenced his remarks by alleging that Chabot had said there should be an opposition within the Convention. Dufourny advised that debating the public good was necessary, but France was not like England, where since there was a ministerial party of the regime, that therefore there

---

of clergy celibacy and the abolition of slavery. In 1791, he was elected as "public accuser". His stated goals were forequality before the law, the abolition of prerogatives and direct democracy. David P Jordan, 'Robespierre', *The Journal of Modern History*, vol. 49, no. 2, 1977, pp. 282-291.

[152] *Oeuvres de Maximilien Robespierre*, Société des études robespierristes, Paris, 1961, 8:76.

[153] Colin Lucas, 'The Theory and Practice of Denunciation in the French Revolution', *The Journal of Modern History*, vol. 68, no. 4, 1996, pp. 768-785, p. 781.

[154] F-A Aulard, *La société des Jacobins*, Librairie Jouaust, Librairie Nobelet, Paris, 1889-97, 5:489.

[155] ibid., 5:518.

must be a party of the people to serve as its opposition. He asked whether there was an opposition right wing party in the Jacobin Club, thereby putting him in opposition to the Jacobin Club. Dufourny proceeded with Chabot's recent marriage to the sister of the Frey brothers, who were wealthy Austrian Jewish bankers. This wife apparently had a large dowry, but Dufourny added that a deputy ought not seek wealth, implying this was Chabot's primary motive in the marriage. Dufourny wondered out loud as to the exact time this marriage to an Austrian took place, informing the Club that it was at the very time when the Austrian woman Marie-Antoinette was appearing at the Revolutionary Tribunal. He observed that this was when the nation was "at the height of its execration of foreigners", and "our brothers" at the frontiers were facing Austrian troops, and leaving widows and children for good people to sustain and console. Dufourny counseled that he ought to have enquired into his new wife's background. Also, he had had an affair with a French woman, giving birth to his baby, then he abandoned them to take a foreigner as a wife. Dufourny's denunciation juxtaposed political opinion with private life error in judgment. It tainted both notions by connecting them with the nation's war enemies. It distinguished the wealthy bride from the poor widows, victims of their husbands' great patriotism. The denunciation then proceeded to impute evil into Chabot's personal morality by delivering an unchecked assertion about some alleged previous liaison. Finally, it represented the end of the immoral liaison just as immoral as its beginning, and as well, unpatriotic.[156] The denunciation offered no argument of proof. It only presented observations arranged to infer proof. On top of this devastating beginning, accepted by the easily swayed Jacobin audience, much was later built.[157]

Fundamentally, suspicion and jealousy are alike, in that suspicion imagines the unprovable. In revolutionary imagination, subversion plots were always subterranean. That was the key to their danger and their imagined ramifications so endless. Therefore the function of denunciation was to discover what was hidden, to "discover" crime in the sense of being able to "uncover" it. The skill of denunciation was to remove a mask, so to penetrate this disguise, to peer into the darkness, to make this imaginary secret public. From this arose the revolutionary reasoning of coupling denunciation to vigilance. Denunciation was weaponized so that radicalism could pursue its

---

156 Colin Lucas, 'The Theory and Practice of Denunciation in the French Revolution', *The Journal of Modern History*, vol. 68, no. 4, 1996, pp. 768-785, p. 782.

157 N Hampson, 'François Chabot and His Plot', *Transactions of the Royal Historical Society*, vol. 26, 1976, pp. 1-14.

goal of individual and social transparency.[158] This made denunciation a semiotic art of reading signs, based on the specious premise that since appearances were deceiving, a person's looks, speech, clothes, relationships and habits must be scrutinized for artifacts of inner secrets of the real self. Because of this, denunciation carried a commensurate defensive discourse, that denounced the denouncer's hidden motives and presented a reframed description of the denouncee's patriotic record, a defensive interpretation framed to claim a more incisive degree of transparency than the denouncer's version.[159]

As the first denunciations against Danton began to develop, he stood before members of the Jacobin Club and asked them as follows.

> Have I, then, lost those features that mark the face of a free man? Am I no longer that same man who stood beside you in moments of crisis? Am I not he whom you have so often embraced as your friend and who shall die with you? Am I not the man who has been weighed down by persecution? I was one of Marat's most fearless defenders.... You will be astounded when I make known my private behavior.... I defy the malicious to provide any proof of crime against me.[160]

Therefore the structure of the defense against a denouncer was an Aristotelian demonstration that the denouncer had misunderstood reality for a mask.[161] However, this defense was not easy. François Chabot stood at the conclusion of Dufourny's speech and rejoined: "I deny categorically all these facts", approving unconsciously of Dufourny's brilliance at passing off mere inference for fact. He continued, "I call on all good citizens to help me to unmask the calumniators". Another Jacobin speciously said, destroying his defense, as follows. "That is the kind of thing conspirators always say".[162]

In this case, it was Chabot's mask that fell. Chabot, Danton and others thus discovered that a good record was not a good defense. For example, when Jacques-Alexis Thuriot stated a long list of the goodness of his revolutionary conduct, Jacques-Rene Hebert said, "What is proved by services rendered to

---

[158] A de Baecque, *Le corps de l'histoire*, Calmann Lévy, Paris, 1993, p. 272.

[159] Colin Lucas, 'The Theory and Practice of Denunciation in the French Revolution', *The Journal of Modern History*, vol. 68, no. 4, 1996, pp. 768-785, p. 783.

[160] F.-A. F-A Aulard, *La société des Jacobins*, Librairie Jouaust, Librairie Nobelet, Paris, 1889-97, 5:542.

[161] Sylvie Garnier, Les conduites politiques en l'an II, (doctoral dissertatiomn, Universite de Paris X - Nanterre, 1992.

[162] F-A Aulard, *La société des Jacobins*, Librairie Jouaust, Librairie Nobelet, Paris, 1889-97, 5:519.

the Revolution? Conspirators always adopt this method. In order to deceive the people, one has to have served it; one has to gain its confidence the better to abuse it".[163] Much more than evidence of patriotic behavior was needed to persuade people of an incorrect denunciation. Petit was lucky to have found a defense after his denunciation in the Jacobin Club.

> Roussel points out that Petit's son is crying in a corner of the hall. Young Petit, aged twelve, rushes forward to the rostrum and declares that his father is a good patriot and has raised him in the purest principles of the Revolution. The Society applauds this child with enthusiasm and the Chairman embraces him. The father is admitted to membership and the child is given an entry ticket to the Society's meetings.[164]

This display of the purity of childhood could not be surmounted as a defense. The triumph of Jacobinism was an evolution away from investigating likely denouncable categories, such as nonjuror priests and nobles, and instead noting apparently suspect conduct. This meant that counter revolutionary corruption could be hiding anywhere, with its corollary of a necessity for a minute study of conventional appearances.[165]

This Jacobin version of denunciation was designed to penetrate that most clandestine of all spaces, that of human intention.[166] This was initiated by Robespierre in 1792 when, while opposing the war demands of his Brissotin adversaries, he posed the question, "I ask myself who proposes it [the war], how, in what circumstances, and why?"[167] This was calculated to impute ill intention, extracted from interpretations of circumstantial evidence. When posed, this meant that virtue itself could be a mask that denunciation ought to penetrate. It was over this contradiction that the Jacobins ripped themselves apart during the Terror.

The pith of the problem of revolutionary denunciation was what one speaker cognized in the first Assembly debate on the subject of denunciation, in July 1789. This speaker said: "I ask you, what will be the limits on the powers that we shall exercise? Who will be able to judge us? Who will be able

---

163 ibid., 5:512.

164 ibid., 5:545.

165 This argument makes it evident that I disagree with Jaume's (n. 22 above) perception that Jacobin denunciation involved the deindividualization of the suspect (p. 205).

166 Colin Lucas, 'The Theory and Practice of Denunciation in the French Revolution', *The Journal of Modern History*, vol. 68, no. 4, 1996, pp. 768-785, p. 784.

167 *Oeuvres de Maximilien Robespierre*, Société des études robespierristes, Paris, 1961, 8:76.

to remind us of our principles?"[168] This invoked the Roman maxim *quis custodiet ipsos custodes*?, meaning if denunciation was to be the guardian of liberty, who might guard liberty against denouncers? Etienne Barry's view that the denouncer was just the expression of the sovereign People's vigilance, and was therefore just, was exposed as self-evident gibberish. Rather, the Jacobins agreed there was a guarantee in virtue, when it was in the virtue of the friends of the People. Thus, Marat's funeral monument had the inscription, "The virtues dear to patriots are probity, justice, and humanity", with justice being guaranteed by probity and humanity.[169] Therefore, it was the pure heart of the patriot denouncer that could guarantee the vigilance purpose within the denunciation.

However, if appearances were just a mask, and real virtue could only be verified by looking within the heart, there could not be any certainty that the denouncer's intentions were purer than the intentions perceived in the denounced, meaning that a precept of virtuous denunciation could not hold up. In the result, délation and dénonciation were indistinguishable, just as the great Encyclopedie had reasoned. This must be why one of the first acts of the Thermidorian Convention was to introduce into the revolutionary tribunal debate the question *intentionnelle*, which stated that counter revolutionary acts committed without any counter revolutionary intention could not be criminal.[170]

Conclusion

The research question asked whether a negative finding of fitness and propriety constituted commonplace denunciation, through a judicial failure of sufficient reasoned elaboration. Argument has sought to demonstrate the proposition that a negative assessment of fitness and propriety is nothing more than inadequately defended commonplace denunciation.

Fitness and propriety, as a component of the public interest, is arguably embedded in the public mind. However, the public interest is a protean

---

168 Laurent Mavidal, *Archives parlementaires de 1787 à 1860*, vol. 8, Librairie Administrative de Paul Dupont, Paris, 1869.

169 Emmanuelle Macaigne, *Musée de la Révolution française, Vizille guide des collections*, University of Illinois, Urbana-Champaign, 2019. In fact, the inscription was never completed and ends at "probity."

170 Colin Lucas, 'The Theory and Practice of Denunciation in the French Revolution', *The Journal of Modern History*, vol. 68, no. 4, 1996, pp. 768-785, p. 785.

concept. What is relevant to the public interest depends on the statutory context in which the concept is used. Its content cannot be confined by reference to any predetermined generic criteria. Sound professional registration practices confer a merely indirect form of public protection, through the stated establishment and the maintenance of public confidence in the profession. If the public at large have confidence in professionals, they are more likely to seek their advice and counsel when the need arises. This is said to be conducive to the general well being of the community. With this entire dictum apparently protean in structure, especially including the court's reasoning about the public interest, no valid argument could yet proceed beyond this point without developing an incisive understanding of the term "protean". The court failed to elaborate this point, and therefore the conception of the public interest was not elaborated in reason. The conception of the public interest therefore falls to the implied lessons of general and folk maxims. Denunciation is usually grounded in these kinds of maxims.

The fact pattern of the 1884 English case of *R v Dudley and Stephens* merits a brief background examination, as an example of denunciation, with key omissions and failures of elaboration in the court's records. The judge, Lord Coleridge, expressly precluded using the oratorical device of "commonplace" to denounce the appellants. He reasoned that, if he had used this kind of rhetoric, it would have been too easy for him to succeed with a mere denunciation of the appellants, while they were acting out of the necessity arising from overwhelming thirst, hunger and the need for their own survival. From this, we can deduce that, seeing the final judgment in the form of a commonplace denunciation, Lord Coleridge decided to avoid its contradictions and reach the same judgment in another way.

Thus, dénonciation was the word used for the good and public-spirited form of denunciation, whereas délation meant the bad, treacherous, self-interested, form of denunciation, suggesting that the court publicly stated that it wanted to avoid the easily available and appealable délation. This appeared like Lord Coleridge, sensing the délation character of his preliminary view of the case, and deciding that the maritime custom had to be voided in law, had instead determined to convert his judgment into dénonciation. The sense is assurably clear that Lord Coleridge was deciding whether the captain was "fit and proper" after his assumption of the customary procedure to kill the cabin boy, eat him and drink his blood, so that the others in the crew could survive. Since there was a maritime custom in operation, the act was not a crime. Therefore, a crime had to be found another way.

A speaker can always construct an illusory enthymeme and present it as a delight to the audience. Although this kind of enthymeme was termed by Aristotle as a syllogism, nevertheless it was a syllogism of denunciation by the inferences of probability, example, proof or indication. Commonplace is an oratorical exercise from the ancient Greek progymnasmata. It is used to elaborate on a state of affairs, where states of affairs are entities that are situational conditions, in terms of the public's perceptions of justice. The context of the cannibalism was thus a state of affairs. Commonplace had been used since early antiquity for effective public denunciation. Commonplace attacks the target person's past life events, but with new conjectures based apparently on the common wisdom of present-time maxims. Since the Captain's past life events were apparently creditable, the judge omitted them in his reasoning, instead opting to make an example of him as an indicium of commonplace denunciation. This set up a starting point for argument, from which subsequent attacks could be made against the specific categories of person.

However, the logical fault is that such a judgment is no more than a single component of a hypothesis. Commonplace was used judicially in courts to sharpen the court's targeting for punishing either a crime or a mere error. Whenever it was embedded inside a judicial denunciation, commonplace served in the public mind as a kind of criminal judgment without a crime. Lord Coleridge could, in this way, simply create the public appearance of the image of a crime – a protean outcome inferring fitness and propriety. Commonplace sets out to amplify only what the public mind has already acknowledged and hated. It allows the assumption of an indicium of hypothesis of guilt, regardless of overwhelming evidence to the contrary.

Denunciation takes place to some extent in all established societies, in all times, dependent upon cultural and political traditions, and the extent to which the state offers its encouragement. From this state encouragement, there arose a class of people who made their living by prosecuting apparent offenders. They became a component of bourgeoise hegemony by joining a newly erected profession.

They could make use of the most precious discoveries of the police, which were due not to overt or secret agents but to anonymous denunciations, délations, which would routinely which arrive every day in police offices. They were products of the vengeance of betrayed women, of friends or of jealous parents. In the absence of police participation, any properly constituted authority, either ecclesiastical or secular, such as statutory authorities, could receive these denunciations.

Denunciation has many marks, such as pre-demonized enemies of the people, alleged cases of witchcraft, religious heretics, communists, counter-revolutionaries, commissions of child abuse, terrorists, immigrants, people belonging to subaltern social groups, or more. Investigating this singularity of denunciation is the essence of citizens' dedication of loyalty to the state, such as for example by members of the three bourgeoisie elements of entrepreneurs, managers and government-accredited professionals. This could extend such investigations for years, the resultant oppression justified as a love of the state. The major contradiction of the problem of the dénonciation-délation continuum was explored intensely during the French Revolution. But this dichotomy, has never been resolved satisfactorily, to this day, despite various public French Revolution Jacobin attempts to void the pejorative implications of délation.

Henry Charles Lea had written of the Spanish Inquisition that no more ingenious device had ever been invented to subjugate the whole population, to paralyze its residual intellect and to reduce it to a slave-like blind obedience. Délation rose to the rank of high sacred duty, filling the land with spies, rendering every man an object of suspicion. Continued through generations, this must leave its permanent impression on the national character. From this, the national character could project this dissonance onto its decided subaltern enemies. By way of example, Shklar's view was that Forster had failed to distinguish between so-called good countries, those having a decent legal system, like Britain or the United States, where denouncing wrongdoing was fitting, and so-called bad countries like the former Soviet Union, where denunciation was shameful. The grounding of this view, in thought experiments of "good" and "bad" legal systems, implies that legally assessing any specific acts of denunciation is always an ideological issue.

In July 1789, Adrien Duport stated that there was no doubt that plots were being mounted against the well-being of public affairs. He counseled that such plots could not be dealt with in the law courts. He advised that there must be an acquisition of "ghastly and indispensable" knowledge, to learn necessary truths. Could this have been the genesis of the professions' statutory subpoena?

The Jacobins agreed that the lasting purpose of denunciation, in outline, was to reveal the hidden, to collate small pieces of knowledge from individuals into a general corpus of understanding and last, therefore, to protect the Revolution from its opponents. This was a mass exercise in weak inductive reasoning, based in folk maxims. It was mass commonplace.

Yet an ongoing debate, of how to prevent the defense of liberty from destroying liberty, remained in the form of a dilemma over the difference between dénonciation and délation, the practices of denouncing and informing. This debate was never resolved, and the Revolution never escaped such contradictions. In consequence of this, Jean-Paul Marat favored republican censors, suggesting they act as denouncers to a revolutionary tribunal. This was a deadly project than the original model of censors, who could only award administrative black marks. It would lead up to the guillotine itself. It was based in the folk maxim, still operating today, in the form of the trope "freedom and democracy", of M. de Clermont-Tonnerre's articulated view that a love of liberty in society guaranteed the failure of the enemy.

Such folk maxims were fortified with Classical references. With an explicit reference to Rome, Mirabeau cited the age-old Senatorial maxim *Caveant Consules ne respublica quid detrimenti capiat*, meaning that the Consuls should take care that the state shall suffer no harm. Des Moulins cited Cicero's phrase *Accusatores multos esse in civitate utile est*, meaning it was useful to have many accusers among us. Mirabeau concluded with a dictum of Cicero to the effect that half-proof would be enough to initiate speech, because during the night all the faithful dogs could bark at people passing by, because of the likelihood of thieves.

Denunciation was the citizen's civic duty, in expressing a citizen's vigilance and care for public affairs, The Jacobins phrased this disinterested stance as the denouncer's "purity", implying its opposite was indeed ritual defilement. This trope guaranteed the ritual purity of a denouncer practicing délation. It could destroy public perceptions of such as fitness and propriety, at the moment it was uttered. Marat even converted denunciation from a duty to a right. He delivered this mutating argument by declaring that the state's salvation was the supreme law, so therefore its defense was the paramount duty of the citizenry. He declared the denunciation to the Motherland as traitors of all those who attack the people's rights and threaten public liberty was therefore the right of every individual. Thus, a paramount duty to save the state became an individual right of denunciation. The names of false denouncers were to be posted beside public lists of the enemies of the People, apparently protecting the People from false publicity.

The onset of the Terror saw three transformations in the practices of denunciation. Individual denunciations became gradually more secretive, thus removing all protective publicity. Denunciation was characterized as disciplinary, didactic and a protective measure against treason, this juxtaposition thus punishing treason without it being committed. The publicity

protecting people from false denunciations had been converted into mass protection from treason. Any commonplace denunciation thus inferred treason as its inherent crime. To reinforce this development, the Jacobins used "public opinion" to express the notion of the sovereign people, while recognizing the unreliability of this opinion of people easily misled, thus making publicity a potential danger. Public opinion thus became a major contradiction of governance. The Jacobins tried to solve the riddle over the locus of the sovereign people by grounding the Terror in the expulsion of the opposition, so that the national Convention would now stand purified of traitors. Therefore, according to its form of logic, with the opposition eliminated and gone, the Convention naturally spoke as the sovereign people.

But denunciation was more than a mere articulation of suspicion, akin to jealousy. It was a procedure for externally attributing meaning to gestures, behavior and mere appearances. Such attribution would be easy simply by selecting the best folk maxim, implied in a public trope. Therefore, to facilitate this, denunciations were always descriptive, with an interpretation of the description either by juxtaposition with external considerations or by the speaker attributing a meaning to the description based on general truths or maxims.

Fundamentally, suspicion and jealousy are alike, in that suspicion imagines the unprovable. In revolutionary imagination, subversion plots were always subterranean. That was the key to their danger and their imagined ramifications so endless. Therefore the function of denunciation was to discover what was hidden, to "discover" crime in the sense of being able to "uncover" it. The skill of denunciation was to remove a mask, so to penetrate this disguise, to peer into the darkness of an imagined personality or character, to make this imaginary secret public. Could this have been the genesis of declaring a person not fit and proper, because of this kind of peering into an imagined character?

The structure of the defense against a denouncer was an Aristotelian demonstration that the denouncer had misunderstood reality for a mask. It meant that a good record was not a good defense. For example, Petit found a defense after his denunciation in the Jacobin Club by brining his 12-year-old child to declare that his father was a good patriot and had raised him in the purest principles of the Revolution. The Society Chairman embraced him, and the father was admitted to membership of the Jacobin Club. This display of the purity of childhood could not be surmounted as a defense. It meant that could be no commonplace denunciation in the presence of ritual purity, and

suggested why Lord Coleridge had decided against the ship's captain – because he killed a cabin boy.

Collating this conclusion into an extended synthesis, we read as follows. Lord Coleridge had failed to elaborate the conception of being protean, and therefore the conception of the public interest was not elaborated in reason. Without this, nobody could be unfit and improper. The conception of the public interest therefore fell to the implied lessons of general and folk maxims, forcing Lord Coleridge's final judgment into the form of a commonplace denunciation. Lord Coleridge had decided to avoid the contradictions of commonplace and reach the same judgment in another way. Since there was a maritime custom in operation, the egregious act was not a crime. Therefore, a crime must be found in another way. A speaker could always construct an illusory enthymeme and present it as a delight to the audience. Commonplace attacks the target person's past life events. It sets out to amplify only what the public mind has already acknowledged and hated. It allows the assumption of a mere indicium of hypothesis of guilt, regardless of overwhelming evidence to the contrary. This had allowed délation to rise to the rank of high sacred duty, filling the land with spies, rendering every man an object of suspicion by the hegemonic groups. Consequent denunciation, in outline, was to reveal the hidden, to collate small pieces of knowledge gleaned from individuals into a general corpus of understanding, and last, therefore, to protect the state from its opponents. This was a mass exercise in weak inductive reasoning, but persuasive to public opinion. It allowed public debate to convert a paramount duty to save the state into an individual duty and derived right of denunciation. The Jacobins tried to solve the riddle over the contradictory locus of the sovereign people, as it validated all folk maxims, by grounding the Terror in the expulsion of its opposition. Now, they could peer into the darkness of a newly voiceless imagined opposition personality, or character, to make this imaginary secret public. This suggested the genesis, in removal of political opposition, of declaring a person not fit and proper.

References

Agier, P-J, *Compte-rendu a l'Assemblee generale des representants de la Commune, au nom du Comite de Recherches, le 30 novembre 1789* [*Report to the General Assembly of representatives of the Commune, on behalf of the Research Committee, November 30, 1789*], Paris, nd.

Anderson, G Lester & Merton W Ertell, 'Extra-institutional forces affecting professional education', in *Education for the Professions*, National Society for the Study of Education, Chicago, 1962.

Andress, David, 'Social Prejudice and Political Fears in the Policing of Paris', *French History*, vol. 9, 1995, pp. 202-226.

Aulard, F-A, *La société des Jacobins* [*The Jacobins Society*], Librairie Jouaust, Librairie Nobelet, Paris, 1889-97.

Austin, AE, 'Regimen Morum', *Journal of Roman Studies*, vol. 78, 1988, pp. 14-34.

Baker, KM, *Inventing the French Revolution*, Cambridge University Press, Cambridge, 1990.

Baker, Lee & Gregory Fremont-Barnes (eds.), *Encyclopedia of the Age of Political Revolutions and New Ideologies, 1760-1815*, Greenwood Publishing Group, Westport, 2007.

Benton, Stephen L & Paul J Blohm, 'Elaboration of Ideas in Prose Production' *The Journal of Experimental Education*, vol. 56, no. 2, 1988, pp. 1960-1966.

Bernstein, Samuel, 'The Paris Commune', *Science & Society*, vol. 5, no. 2, 1941, pp. 117-147.

Biard, Michel & Hervé Leuwers, 'Visages de la Terreur' ['Faces of Terror'], dans Michel Biard et Hervé Leuwers (dir.), *Visages de la Terreur. L'exception politique de l'an II* [*Faces of Terror. The political exception of Year II*], Armand Colin, Paris, 2014.

Boltanski, Luc, *L'amour et la justice comme competences*, Métailié, Paris, 1990.

Boltanski, Luc, *Love and Justice as Competencies: Three Essays on the Sociology of Action*, Polity Press, Paris, 1990.

Boltanski, Luc, Yann Darré & Marie-Ange Schiltz, 'La dénonciation', *Actes de la Recherche en Sciences Sociales*, vol. 51, 1984, pp. 3–40.

Brissot, J-P, *Lettres a Monsieur le Chevalier de Pange sur sa brochure*, Paris, 1790.

Brissot, J-P, *Réplique de J-P Brissot à Stanislas Tonnerre*, Paris, 1790.

Brown, Howard G, 'Echoes of the Terror', *Historical Reflections/Réflexions Historiques*, vol. 29, no. 3, 2003, pp. 529-558.

Brunet, Jean-Paul, *La police de l'ombre: Indicateurs et provocateurs dans la France contemporaine*, Paris, 1990.

Buchanan, Ian, *A Dictionary of Critical Theory*, Oxford University Press, Oxford, 2010.

Caute, David, *The Great Fear: The Anti-Communist Purge under Truman and Eisenhower*, Simon and Schuster, New York, 1978.

Chicago Tribune, October 16, 1994, sec. 8, p. 1; October 21, 1994, pp. 1, 21.

Chisholm, Hugh (ed.), *Encyclopædia Britannica*, Cambridge University Press, Cambridge, 1911.

Cicero, *La République*, E Breguet (trans.), Gallimard, Paris.

Ciment, Michel, 'Les aveux les plus durs', in Nicole Czechowski & Jacques Hassoun (eds.), *La délation: Un archaïsme, une technique*, Autrement, Paris, 1992, pp. 128-37.

Cobb, RC, *Les armées révolutionnaires*, Paris, 1961-63.

Colaneri, LJH & G Gérente, *La Dénonciation et les Dénonciateurs*, Bibliothèque de Philosophie contemporaine, Paris, 1948.

Czechowski, Nicole & Jacques Hassoun (eds.), *La delation: Un archaisme, une technique*, Autrement, Paris, 1992.

Darnton, Robert & Daniel Roche (eds.), *Revolution in Print: the Press in France, 1775-1800*, University of California Press, Berkeley, 1989.

de Baecque, A, *Le corps de l'histoire*, CalmannLévy, Paris, 1993.

de Clermont-Tonnerre, Stanislas, *Nouvelles observations sur les comites de recherches*, Chez Desenne Libraire au Palais-Royale, Paris, nd.

de Pange, Chevalier, *Réflexions sur la délation et sur le* comité des recherches, Chez Barrois l'aîné, Paris, 1790.

Diderot, Denis & Jean le Rond d'Alembert, *Encyclopédie, ou Dictionnaire raisonné des sciences, des arts et des métiers*, Sociétés typographiques, Bern and Lausanne, 1778-1779.

Douglas, Mary (ed.), *Witchcraft Confessions and Accusations*, Tavistock Publications, London, 1970.

Farber, Daniel A & Suzanna Sherry, *Judgment Calls: Principle and Politics in Constitutional Law*, Oxford University Press, Oxford, 2009.

Farge, Arlette & Michel Foucault, *Le desordre des familles: Lettres de cachet des Archives de la Bastille*, Gallimard, Paris, 1982.

Farge, Arlette, *Subversive Words: Public Opinion in Eighteenth-Century France*, Rosemary Morris (trans.), Penn State University Press, University Park, 1994.

Ferro, Marc, *Pétain*, Feyard, Paris, 1987.

Fitzpatrick, Sheila & Robert Gellately, 'Introduction to the Practices of Denunciation in Modern European History', *The Journal of Modern History*, vol. 68, no. 4, 1996, pp. 747-767.

Fitzpatrick, Sheila, 'Signals from Below: Soviet Letters of Denunciation of the 1930s', *The Journal of Modern History*, 1996, vol. 68, no. 4, pp. 831-866.

Fleming, J David, 'The Very Idea of a "Progymnasmata"', *Rhetoric Review*, vol. 22, no. 2, 2003, pp. 105-120.

Flint, WW, 'The Delatores in the Reign of Tiberius, as Described by Tacitus', *The Classical Journal*, vol. 8, no. 1, 1912, pp. 37-42.

Forster, EM, *Two Cheers for Democracy*, Harcourt, Brace, New York, 1951.

Fox-Davies, Arthur, *A Complete Guide to Heraldry*, TC & EC Jack, London, 1909.

Fox, Michael Allen, *The Accessible Hegel*, Prometheus Books, New York, 2005.

French Penal Code, 1791.

French, David P, 'Swift, the Non-Jurors, and Jacobitism', *Modern Language Notes*, vol. 72, no. 4, 1957, pp. 258-264.

Friedland, Paul, *Political Actors, Representative Bodies and Theatricality in the Age of the French Revolution*, Cornell University Press, New York, 2002.

Frugtniet v Board of Examiners [2002] VSC 140.

Ganoczy, Alexandre, 'Calvin's life', in Donald K McKim (ed.), *The Cambridge Companion to John Calvin*, Cambridge University Press, Cambridge, 2004.

Garnier, Sylvie, *Les conduites politiques en l'an II*, (doctoral dissertatiomn, Universite de Paris X - Nanterre, 1992.

Ginzburg, Carlo, *The Cheese and the Worms: The Cosmos of a Sixteenth-Century Miller*, John Tedeschi & Anne Tedeschi (trans.), Penguin Books, Harmondsworth, 1986.

Grose, Clyde L, 'The Religion of Restoration England', *Church History*, vol. 6, no. 3, 1937, pp. 223-232.

Gross, Jan T, *Revolution from Abroad: The Soviet Conquest of Poland 's Western Ukraine and Western Belorussia*, Princeton University Press, Princeton, 1988.

Guilhaumou, J, 'Fragments of a Discourse on Denunciation (1789-94)', in KM Baker (ed.), *The Terror*, Pergamon Press, Oxford, 1994.

Halimi, André, 'Une certaine France sous l'Occupation', in Nicole Czechowski & Jacques Hassoun (eds.), *La délation. Un archaïsme, une technique, un mode de gouvernement* [*The denunciation. An archaism, a technique, a mode of government*], Autrement, Paris, 1992.

Halimi, André, *La Délation sous l'Occupation* [*The Denouncement under the Occupation*], Editions Alain Moreau, Paris, 1983.

Hampson, N, 'François Chabot and His Plot', *Transactions of the Royal Historical Society*, vol. 26, 1976, pp. 1-14.

Hanson, Paul R, *Jacobin Republic Under Fire: The Federalist Revolt in the French Revolution*, Pennsylvania State University Press, University Park, 2010.

Hesse, Carla, 'The Law of the Terror', *MLN*, vol. 114, no. 4, 1999, pp. 702-718.

Jaume, Lucien, *Le discours Jacobin et la démocratie* [The Jacobin discourse and democracy], Fayard, Paris, 1989.

Johnson, RE, 'Recall of Prose as a Function of the structural importance of the Linguistic Units', *Journal of Verbal Learning and Verbal Behavior*, vol. 9, 1970, pp. 12-20.

Jordan, David P, 'Robespierre', *The Journal of Modern History*, vol. 49, no. 2, 1977, pp. 282-291.

Judt, Tony, *Marxism and the French Left: Studies on Labour and Politics in France, 1830–1981*, New York University Press, New York & London, 2011.

Kamen, Henry, *Inquisition and Society in Spain in the 16th and 17th Centuries*, Indiana University Press, Bloomington, 1985.

Kennedy, George A, *A New History of Classical Rhetoric*, Princeton University Press, Princeton, 1994.

Kennedy, George A, *Progymnasmata: Greek Textbooks of Prose Composition and Rhetoric*. Society of Biblical Literature, Atlanta, 2003.

La Commission Temporaire a tous les vrais sans culottes [*The Temporary Commission has all the real no panties*], Commune-affranchie, Lyon, 1793.

Labrosse, C & P Rétat, *Naissance de journal revolutionnaire: 1789* [*Birth of revolutionary newspaper: 1789*], Presses universitaires de Lyon, Lyon, 1989.

Lacroix, S (ed.), *Actes de la Commune de Paris pendant la Revolution* [*Acts of the Paris Commune during the Revolution*], Société de l'Histoire de la Révolution Française, Paris, 1895.

Lacroix, S (ed.), *Révolutions de Paris* [*Paris Revolutions*], no. 8, (November 14, 1789).

Lanham, Richard A, *A Handlist of Rhetorical Terms*, University of California Press, Berkeley, 1991.

Larousse (Firm), *Grand Larousse encyclopédique* [*Great Encyclopedic Larousse*], Librairie Larousse, Paris, 1960.

Larousse grande dictionnaire universel du XIXe siècle [*Larousse large universal dictionary of the 19th century*], vol. 6, Administration du Grand Dictionnaire Universel, Paris, 1870.

Larousse, Augé (ed.), *Encyclopédie Larousse du XXe siècle* [*Larousse Encyclopedia of the 20th Century*], Union générale d'éditions, Paris, 1975.

Law of 22 Prairial of 10th June 1794.

Lawson-Tancred, HC, *Aristotle The Art of Rhetoric*, Penguin Books, London, 1991.

'Le Publiciste Parisien [The Parisian Publicist]', *Journal politique, libre et impartial*, no. 5, 12th - 15th September Paris, 1789.

Lea, Henry Charles, 'The Inquisition Founded', in Henry Charles Lea, *A History of the Inquisition In The Middle Ages*, Rarebooksclub, online, 2013.

Lea, Henry Charles, *A History of the Inquisition of Spain in Four Volumes*, Macmillan, London, 1906.

Leyda, Jay, *Kino: A History of the Russian and Soviet Film*, George Allen & Unwin, London, 1973.

Lucas, C, 'Revolutionary Violence, the People and the Terror', in KM Baker (ed.), *The Terror: The French Revolution and the creation of modern political culture*, Emerald, Bingley, 1994.

Lucas, C, 'Themes in Southern Violence after 9 Thermidor', in G Lewis & C Lucas (eds.), *Beyond the Terror*, Cambridge University Press, Cambridge, 1973.

Lucas, Colin, 'The Theory and Practice of Denunciation in the French Revolution', *The Journal of Modern History*, vol. 68, no. 4, 1996, pp. 768-785.

Macaigne, Emmanuelle, *Musée de la Révolution française, Vizille guide des collections* [*Museum of the French Revolution, Vizille collection guide*], University of Illinois, Urbana-Champaign, 2019.

Manuel, Pierre, *La police de Paris devoile* [*Paris police unveil*], Paris, 1790.

Marat, JP, 'Appel à la Nation', in A Vermorel (ed.), *Oeuvres de JP Marat* [*Works by JP Marat*], Décembre-Alonnier, Paris, 1869.

Martin, Jean-Clément, *La Terreur, part maudite de la Révolution* [*The Terror, cursed part of the Revolution*], Découvertes/Gallimard, 2010.

Marwick, Max, *Witchcraft and Sorcery: Selected Readings*, Penguin Books, Harmondsworth, 1982.

Mavidal, Laurent, *Archives parlementaires de 1787 à 1860* [*Parliamentary Archives from 1787 to 1860*], vol. 8, Librairie Administra-tive de Paul Dupont, Paris, 1869.

Mazelis, Fred, 'Metropolitan Opera announces the banning of soprano Anna Netrebko', *World Socialist Website*, 5th March 2022.

Medical Practitioners Board of Victoria v Lal [2009] VSCA 109.

Miller, AV (trans.), *Phenomenology of Spirit*, Clarendon Press, Oxford, 1977.

Mitchell, Harvey, 'The Vendee and Counterrevolution: A Review Essay', *French Historical Studies*, vol. 5, no. 4, 1968, pp. 405-429.

Monter, E William, *Enforcing Morality in Early Modern Europe*, E William Monter Books, London, 1987.

Navasky, Victor S, *Naming Names*, Penguin, Harmondsworth, 1981.

Necheles, Ruth F, 'The Curés in the Estates General of 1789', *The Journal of Modern History*, vol. 46, no. 3, 1974, pp. 425-444, pp. 425-426.

Ng, Nathalie, 'Fitness and Propriety, Spent Convictions and Technology: Lessons from ASIC Investigations', *Australian Institute of Administrative Law Forum*, vol. 92, 2018, pp. 1-112.

Noy, William, *The Sounds and Maxims and also an Analysis of The English Laws*, Riley, Middletown, 1808.

Œuvres complètes de Saint-Just [*Complete Works of Saint-Just*], Éditions de la Cité universelle, Paris, 1946.

Oeuvres de Maximilien Robespierre [*Works by Maximilien Robespierre*], Société des études robespierristes, Paris, 1961.

Ordonnances ecclésiastiques, (*Ecclesiastical Ordinances*), 20th November 1541.

Outram, Dorinda, *Panorama of the Enlightenment*, Getty Publications, Los Angeles, 2006.

Pellet, Marcellin, *Élysée Loustallot et les Révolutions de Paris (juillet 1789-septembre 1790)* [*Élysée Loustallot and the Revolutions of Paris (July 1789-September 1790)*], A le Chevalier, Paris, 1872.

Perelman, Ch, *The Realm of Rhetoric*, University of Notre Dame Press, Notre Dame, 1982.

R v Dudley and Stephens (1884) 14 QBD 273.

Raithby, John (ed.), William and Mary, 1692, 'An Act for encourageing the apprehending of Highway Men', in *Statutes of the Realm*, vol. 6, 1685-1694.

Read, Piers Paul, *The Dreyfus Affair*, Bloomsbury Publishing, London, 2013.

Reid, JS, 'Tacitus as a Historian', *The Journal of Roman Studies*, vol. 11, 1921, pp. 191-199.

Russian criminal code Entsiklopedicheskii slovar' 'Granat', vol. 18, Moscow, n.d. [ca. 1914]).

Schrecker, Ellen, *Age of McCarthyism: A Brief History with Documents*, Bedford, Boston, 1994.

Shapiro, Barry M, 'Revolutionary Justice in 1789-1790: The Comité des Recherches, the Châtelet, and the Fayettist Coalition', *French Historical Studies*, vol. 17, no. 3, 1992, pp. 656-669.

Shklar, Judith N, *Ordinary Vices*, Harvard University Press, Cambridge, 1984.

Simpson, Alfred William Brian, 'Cannibals at Common Law', *The Law School Record*, vol. 27, 1981, pp. 3-10.

Sosa, Ernest, *Cambridge Dictionary of Philosophy*, Cambridge University Press, Cambridge, 1999.

Strong, James, *Strong's Exhaustive Concordance of the Bible*, Hendrickson, Peabody, 2007.

Sykes, Gresham M, *The Society of Captives: A Study of a Maximum Security Prison*, Princeton University Press, Princeton, 1958.

The Law of Suspects, 1793.

The Penal Code of 1810.

Tobias, JJ, *Crime and Police in England*, 1700-1900, New York, St. Martin's Press, 1979.

Tulard, Jean, Jean-François Fayard & Alfred Fierro, *Histoire et Dictionnaire de la Révolution française* [*History and Dictionary of the French Revolution*], C Bouquins (ed.), Robert Laffont, Parus, 1997.

van den Broek, R & Wouter J Hanegraaff, *Gnosis and Hermeticism from Antiquity to Modern Times*, SUNY Press, Albany, 1998.

Wechsler, Herbert, 'Toward Neutral Principles of Constitutional Law', *Harvard Law Review*, vol. 73, no. 1, 1959, pp. 1-35.

Westin, Alan F (ed.), *Whistle Blowing! Loyalty and Dissent in the Corporation*, McGraw Hill, New York, 1981.

White, Eugene Nelson, 'The French Revolution and the Politics of Government Finance, 1770-1815', *The Journal of Economic History*, vol. 55, no. 2, 1995, pp. 227-255.

Whitfield, Stephen J, *The Culture of the Cold War*, Johns Hopkins University Press, Baltimore, 1991.

Yarshater, Ehsan, *The Cambridge History of Iran, The Seleucid, Parthian and Sasanian Periods*, Cambridge University Press, Cambridge, 1983.

Zafirovski, Milan, *The Enlightenment and Its Effects on Modern Society*, Springer, New York, 2010.

Zola, Emile, *J'Accuse!* [I accuse!], Bay Side Press, Soquel, 1992.

Chapter 6

The Stasis of Disrepute

Gary I. Lilienthal[1,*], PhD
and Muhamad Hassan bin Ahmad[2], PhD
[1]Carrington Rand, Hong Kong SAR, Peoples Republic of China
[2]Ahmad Ibrahim Kulliyyah of Laws, International Islamic University, Kuala Lumpur, Malaysia

Abstract

In 2022, the broadcaster "Russia Today" had its United Kingdom license revoked, after British watchdog Ofcom ruled it was neither a "fit and proper" nor a "responsible" broadcaster. In the light of the significance of this apparently quasi-judicial characterization, the overall research objective of this research is to investigate critically the stasis of how decisions of fitness and propriety can be formulated. Early rhetoricians described the so-called 'moving apart' of opposing contentious assertions, by analogy to what the Sophists called "primary entities", those combining form with matter. Movement could only be predicated on these primary entities. Thus, when "movement" of the opposing components of a contentious matter came to rest, this was called "stasis." Stasis theory thus allowed the rhetorician to judge whether or not a conflict of wills really existed, and if so, in what ways. The research question asks whether there can be a stable stasis, between the applicant and the general public, with which the court can render its decision on whether or not the applicant is a "fit and proper" person. Argument seeks to demonstrate that prior denunciation of a fit and proper person is an attempt to make the person disreputable, destroying any chance of safe and stable judicial determination. The research is doctrinal, based on best available authoritative scholarship. In the result, the rhetor could

* Corresponding Author's Email: carrington.rand@icloud.com.

In: Regulation of the Professions in East Asia
Editors: Gary I. Lilienthal and Muhamad Hassan bin Ahmad
ISBN: 979-8-88697-409-6

denounce a person simply with a bare persuasive declamation and the situation's stasis would be one of 'conjecture,' by default, and all that would remain would be its effect in the public mind. A denunciation of a fit and proper person could have the same moving effect as the conception of murder *lingua vel facto*, before the matter arrived anywhere near a court of law. In the light of this, fit and proper administrative determinations were in the nature of an asystatic question, specifically the *asystatic* question of "disreputable", incapable of *stasis* because it did not have any issue. The subaltern groups, such as professionals have been constructed to receive less justice from their superior professional associations, while those inside the professional associations are protected as reputable by their own definition. To satisfy the axiom of modern stasis, accusing someone of violating either a legal or a moral norm must specify the violated norm, which must be neither unstable nor overly strict or absolute in liability, or else everyone breaches it.

Keywords: stasis, fitness and propriety, rhetorician, prior denunciation, disrepute, asystatic question

1. Introduction

In 2022, the broadcaster "Russia Today" had its United Kingdom license revoked, after British watchdog Ofcom ruled it was neither a "fit and proper" nor a "responsible" broadcaster. Ofcom said it took into account several factors, including the fact that the news channel was funded by the Russian state, which had recently invaded its neighboring country. Ofcom also cited recent changes to Russian law, on which it made its own judicial determination, saying that such laws "effectively" criminalized "independent journalism."[1] In the light of the significance of this apparently *ex parte* decision on unparticularized foreign norms, assessing fitness and propriety based on the news organizations' government policies, and a quasi-judicial characterization of recently enacted foreign laws, the overall research objective of this research is to investigate critically the stasis of how decisions of fitness and propriety can be formulated.

Early rhetoricians described the so-called 'moving apart' of opposing contentious assertions, by analogy to what the Sophists called "primary

---

[1] Sky News, 'Russia Today has UK broadcast licence revoked by Ofcom - but Kremlin calls decision "madness,"' *Sky News*, Friday 18th March 2022.

entities," those combining form with matter. Movement could only be predicated on these primary entities. Thus, when "movement" of the opposing components of a contentious matter came to rest, this was called "stasis."[2] Stasis theory thus allowed the rhetorician to judge whether or not a conflict of wills really existed, and if so, in what ways.

In the 2016 High Court of Hong Kong case of *Re "A"*,[3] the Applicant, "A", applied under s. 27 of the *Legal Practitioners Ordinance, Cap 159 (Ordinance)*, to be admitted as a barrister of the High Court of Hong Kong.[4] The issue was whether the Applicant was considered to be a "fit and proper person" to be admitted as a barrister, which was a requirement pursuant to s. 27(1) of the Ordinance.[5] The Court opined that the matter could best be put by citing Lam JA, in the 2013 Hong Kong Court of First Instance case of *Re Youh Alan Chuen Po*,[6] as follows.

> The "fit and proper person" criterion is an important one. It is a criterion which an applicant has to satisfy beyond meeting the academic and legal training requirements. There is a considerable degree of public trust and confidence placed upon a barrister. A person admitted as a barrister has the privilege of practicing as a member of one of the most respected professions in our society. Members of the public, the Judiciary and other members of the legal profession expect members of the Bar to have integrity, honour, high professional standard, reasonably sound judgment and competence in their practice. In Hong Kong, the Bar can say with justifiable pride that by and large such expectations are met. The conduct of a barrister in his or her professional practice often has immense ramifications for the life of a client beyond the immediate outcome of a case. Such ramifications can be financial, emotional, political or social. What happens in litigation could affect the physical, emotional or psychological well-being of a client or those close to him or her. It is therefore necessary for the law to place importance on the "fit and proper person" criterion. Given that we have an adversarial system, unless the court and members of the public can have confidence that those practicing at the Bar are fit and proper persons, the administration of justice under our system will be severely hampered and the rule of law, a core value in our society, will be tarnished ….[7]

---

2 Otto Alvin Loeb Dieter, 'Stasis', *Speech Monographs*, XVII, 1950, pp. 345-369.
3 HCMP2079/2016.
4 ibid., [1].
5 Ibid., [3].
6 [2013] 2 HKLRD 485.
7 [2013] 2 HKLRD 485, §§9-10, per Lam JA (as he then was); HCMP2079/2016 RE "A", [39].

This suggests an application of stasis theory to determine the actual nature of the matter between the Court, members of the public, and the applicant. According to this judicial construction, the following attributes appear to constitute the requirement for being "fit and proper": importance, public trust and confidence, privilege, respect, integrity, honour, high professional standard, reasonably sound judgment and competence, and, confidence. Interestingly, a very high level of sound competence is not required, suggesting that service to the public trust is not really a requirement. But of all these nine attributes, some six of them appear to rest entirely in the public mind, and therefore, cannot be assessed accurately by the court. This leaves only three: privilege, integrity and honor, to be assessed in the applicant, by the court. They are all three secondary entities, on which, alone, no movement can be predicated. Interestingly, a high professional standard can only mean a suitable giving up of personal rights in order to maintain a professional position. It is unlikely this waiving of rights can assist a client's cause.

In the 2018 Victorian Civil and Administrative Tribunal case of *Mr. Chooks Halal Chicken Pty Ltd v Primesafe (Review and Regulation)*,[8] the applicant was an operator of a business under the Meats Industry Act, 1993 (Vic). Wentworth (Senior Member) stated as follows.

> For the reasons, which follow, I have found that Mr. Taleb is not a fit and proper person for the purposes of the Act. I find that he lacks the necessary honesty, understanding, character and integrity to be a licensee or nominated operator in the meat industry. This is not to say that he is an inherently bad person or incapable of working in some other capacity in the meat industry.[9]

This articulation of judgment evinces an internal inconsistency, arguing for an assessment of a mask, and thus suggesting a defective prior determination of the matter's stasis. More recently, in the 2019 Victorian Civil and Administrative Tribunal case of *CJE v Medical Board of Australia*,[10] *the* Victorian Civil and Administrative Tribunal noted with approval the 2018 Victorian Civil and Administrative Tribunal case of *TGH v Secretary to the Department of Justice and Regulation (Review and Regulation)*,[11] in which the Tribunal had adopted the following propositions.

---

[8] [2018] VCAT 1932.

[9] ibid., [11].

[10] [2019] VCAT 1619, confirming the decision in the Supreme Court of Victoria Court of Appeal in *Medical Practitioners Board of Victoria v Lal* [2009] VSCA109.

[11] [2018] VCAT 110.

> Like the goodwill which attaches to a business, however, public confidence in the medical profession is not turned on and off like a switch. Public confidence is won – or lost – gradually, as the cumulative effect of the experiences of thousands of individuals in their dealings with medical practitioners over many years. The decision to register a particular person to practice medicine is unlikely, in our view, to have any material or lasting effect on the established reputation of the medical profession as a whole. It is not irrelevant that the standing of the medical profession in this community is very high.[12]

But see Lilienthal on defining goodwill, suggesting that goodwill might indeed be turned off like a switch, merely by exposing business nostrums, at which moment goodwill ceases to exist.[13] This suggests strongly an onus on the profession to prove its high standing in the community, as an inherent factor in making a "fit and proper" determination, in respect of the applicant, either to join or to continue in the profession, implying a defect in assessment of the matter's stasis. As explained by the High Court of Australia, in *Australian Broadcasting Tribunal v Bond*,[14] the expression "fit and proper" person, on its own, has no precise meaning.[15] It takes its meaning from its factual context,[16] thus suggesting the term is an argument based on facts, not law, triggering a requirement to examine critically the strength and character of the term 'fit and proper' as a contentious matter. Thus the question arises as to whether there can be a stable stasis, between the applicant and the general public, with which the court can render its decision on whether or not the applicant is a "fit and proper" person. Argument seeks to demonstrate that prior denunciation of a fit and proper person is an attempt to make the person disreputable, destroying any chance of safe and stable judicial determination.

The research is doctrinal, based on best available authoritative scholarship. The research is structured as follows. First, argument has a main section, entitled Decisions inferring Stasis Issues, followed by another main section, entitled Classical Stasis Theory. This main section covers the sub-

---

[12] ibid.

[13] "Goodwill is the value in the probability of the business continuing to maintain its connection with customers of good disposition to it, to induce local custom by means of its own nostrums and reputation, in the same way as in the past." G Lilienthal, 'Business Goodwill: Relationships of Production, Legal Superstructures and an Administrative Prerogative Act Developed in United Kingdom Ideology and Case Law', *Commonwealth Law Bulletin*, vol. 45, no. 1, 2019, pp. 92-114, p. 113.

[14] *Australian Broadcasting Tribunal v Bond* (1990) 170 CLR 321.

[15] ibid., [380].

[16] ibid.

section entitled Stasis and Murder *lingua vel facto*. Argument then proceeds to the main section A Modern Theory of Stasis, which covers The Ancient Heritage of Stasis Theory, The Burden of Proof in Accusation and Defense, The Dialectical Argument, The Harm Argument, The Danger Argument and The Justice Argument, concluding with a statement of The Axiom of Modern Stasis.

The research is likely to conclude that the rhetor could denounce a person simply with a bare persuasive declamation and the situation's stasis would be one of 'conjecture,' by default, and all that would remain would be its effect in the public mind. A denunciation of a fit and proper person could have the same moving effect as the conception of murder *lingua vel facto*, before the matter arrived anywhere near a court of law. In the light of this, fit and proper administrative determinations were in the nature of an asystatic question, specifically the *asystatic* question of "disreputable," incapable of *stasis* because it did not have any issue. The subaltern groups, such as professionals have been constructed to receive less justice from their superior professional associations, while those inside the professional associations are protected as reputable by their own definition. To satisfy the axiom of modern stasis, accusing someone of violating either a legal or a moral norm must specify the violated norm, which must be neither unstable nor overly strict or absolute in liability, or else everyone breaches it.

2. Decisions Inferring Stasis Issues

Analogies to ancient Greek concepts of motion gave classical rhetoricians an abstract framework for the analysis and conduct of rational argument.[17] The various 'grounds,' on which contrary motions came to a 'rest,' or, known as 'stasis,' were borrowed from the philosophic studies of kinesis, or, 'movements,' and *metabolai*, or, 'changes in Being.' First, Aristotle distinguished between two different ideas of the term *dunamis*. In the first and strictest sense, a *dunamis* was the *power* that a thing had to produce some kind of a change. A thing had a *dunamis*, in this first sense, when it had within it 'a starting-point of change in another thing or in itself insofar as it is other,'[18] raising the issue of movement arising from alterity. The exercise of such a power is called a *kinêsis*, which is a movement or process. Thus, by way of

[17] Otto Alvin Loeb Dieter, 'Stasis,' *Speech Monographs*, XVII, 1950, pp. 345-369.
[18] Aristotle, *Metaphysics*, Θ.1, 1046^{a}12; cf. Δ.12.

example, the craft of a house-builder is a kind of power, the exercise of which is the process of housebuilding. Second, a species is both real and separate, conceptually, from the specific individuals, which comprise it. However, in his *Categories*, Aristotle emphasized that it had no substantial existence apart from that of its material individuals. Thus, he reversed Plato's order of priority for the form of a species, to now merely being a mere 'secondary being.' The reality of a substantial individual, one which combined form with matter, was that of a 'primary being.'[19] These primary, individual subjects were the basic entities on which the insubstantial things, like qualities and changes, the *metabolai*, could be preconditioned.[20] *Metabolai* could not take place unless by an entity composed of both form and matter.

Using these ideas, rhetoricians described the 'moving apart' of opposing assertions, by analogy to primary entities. Stasis theory thus allowed the rhetorician to judge whether or not a conflict of wills really existed, and if so, in what ways. This paradigm allowed an anticipated central question to be resolved, which the Greeks called the *krinomenon*, the likely opposing accusatory and defense strategies, and consequently, how best to win the clash.[21] Quintilian said it thus:

> Respecting these matters, even Cicero is in some degree at variance with himself, for in his *Rhetorica*, as I said above, he has followed Hermagoras, and in his *Topica*, he expresses himself of opinion that κρινόμενον *(krinomenon)*, the "point of judgment," is the consideration arising from the *state,* and in addressing Trebatius, a lawyer of his time, he calls it "the point about which the discussion is" and terms the particulars in which that point is contained *continentia*, the "containing particulars" and the *firmamenta*, "supports," as it were, of the defense, without which there would be no defense at all. 19. But in his *Partitiones Oratoriae* he calls the *firmamentum* that which is opposed to the defense, because the *continens*, the "containing point," as it is the first thing, is advanced by the accuser, while the *ratio*, "mode of defense," proceeds from the defendant. From the opposition of the *ratio* and *firmamentum* arises the question for decision.[22]

---

[19] Aristotle, *Categories*, 2a11-14.

[20] Kelvin Knight, *Aristotelian Philosophy: Ethics and Politics from Aristotle to MacIntyre*, Polity Press, Cambridge, 2007, p. 5.

[21] David Goodwin, 'Controversiae Meta-Asystatae and the New Rhetoric,' *Rhetoric Society Quarterly*, vol. 19, no. 3, 1989, pp. 205-216, p. 205.

[22] Quintilian, *Institutes of Oratory*, Book 3, Chapter 11, Paragraph 18.

Thus, the two key issues are the *firmamentum*, the supports of the defense, and the *ratio* as the mode of the defense. The krinomenon rests entirely on the defense.

3. Classical Stasis Theory

Stasis theory of classical times dealt with such rhetorical matters as declamatory themes, real deliberative or forensic states of affairs.[23] Mendelson stated that classical pleaders structured their arguments as declamations. Practitioners of the declamation style would analyze either an historical or a legal problem and develop a pragmatic argument in response to the identified problem. They adapted their argument to a specific audience with a definite need to know.[24] Declamations were of two kinds, the *suasoria* or deliberative speech about history or politics, and the *controversia* or forensic speech on a specific legal case. Thus, the argument in a declamation was carefully cobbled together by an expert pleader trained in judicial rhetoric.[25] Mendelson added that in most of the Senecan *controversiae*, the declamation was structured beginning with a brief statement of the operative law, then a short narration of the facts and circumstances of the particular case, then arguments for and against, which were typically drawn from memory.[26]

Stasis theory pursues the classifications of these situations, consistent with each dispute's underlying structure.[27] Such classifications are of utility to the practicing rhetorician, as they may assist in identifying an appropriate strategy for argument. For example, they could discover a pattern of argument applicable to a factual question, such as 'did the defendant do what was alleged to have been done?' However, this question might have been irrelevant in a dispute requiring an evaluation, such as 'was the defendant justified in doing

[23] Aristotle describes the deliberative principle as manifesting itself in the actions of admonishment, rebuke and exhortation. Aristotle, *The Nichomachean Ethics*, Harvard University Press, Cambridge, 1999, p. 67.

[24] Michael Mendelson 'Declamation, Context, and Controversiality,' *Rhetoric Review*, vol. 13, no. 1, 1994, pp. 92-107, p. 92.

[25] ibid., p. 93.

[26] ibid., p. 104n.

[27] D Russell, *Greek Declamation*, Cambridge University Press, Cambridge, 1983, pp. 40-73; G Kennedy, *Greek Rhetoric under Christian Emperors*, Princeton University Press, Princeton, 1983, pp. 73-86; L Calboli Montefusco, *La dottrina degli status nella retorica greca e romana*, Hildesheim, New York, 1986.

what was alleged to have been done?'[28] Both cases derive their stasis from primary entities characterized by fact patterns.

The ancient rhetors could not always concur on classifying a problem. Consider the following case of an adulterer caught in the act, where the law provided that a husband might kill the adulterer discovered while in the middle of the act. Thus, the husband finds a eunuch lying in bed with his wife and immediately kills him. The husband is charged with having committed homicide. According to the reasoning of Hermogenes, the stasis of this matter is one of definition, because both the prosecutor and the defense agree on the facts, and the residual dispute is in categorizing the agreed facts.[29] The agreed facts of what the eunuch was doing did not constitute a completed example of adultery, as it lacked essential element(s) of the crime of adultery. If prosecutors classified this incomplete adultery as adultery, then the slaying would come under the law of adultery. Otherwise, it was either unlawful, or could be construed as a counterplea. Counterplea is the stasis of quality, where the defense pleads that the alleged act, the subject of the charge, is inherently lawful. Consider the following example. A rhetorician's encomium[30] on death is followed, in time, by a mass outbreak of suicides. The rhetorician is charged with having committed a crime against the public interest. The defense might argue that merely practicing his profession violated no law. Applying this counterplea analysis to the above case of the adulterous eunuch, and the husband's invocation of the law of adultery, to argue his admitted act was inherently lawful immediately determines the dispute's stasis as counterplea.[31] Thus, the facts may generate many possible constructions.

Disagreement among the ancient scholars, about how to classify a rhetorical dispute, required critical analysis of how stasis could generally be pinned down. Hermogenes' view was that it required an inspection of the 'krinomenon,' meaning 'that which - by the audience - is judged'.[32] If, after

---

[28] M Heath, 'The Substructure of Stasis-Theory from Hermagoras to Hermogenes,' *Classical Quarterly*, vol. 44, no. 1, 1994, pp. 114-129, p. 1.

[29] George A Kennedy (trans.), *Invention and Method: Two Rhetorical Treatises from the Hermogenic Corpus. The Greek Text, Edited by Hugo Rabe*, Society of Biblical Literature & Leiden, Brill, Atlanta, 2005, 60.19-61.3.

[30] Encomium is 'a composition expository of attendant excellencies.' Subjects include persons, things such as abstract ideas, times such as the seasons, places, animals, and growing things, either general or specific. William H Race, 'Pindaric Encomium and Isokrates' Evagoras,' *Transactions of the American Philological Association*, vol. 117, 1987, pp. 131-155.

[31] M Heath, 'The Substructure of Stasis-Theory from Hermagoras to Hermogenes,' *Classical Quarterly*, vol. 44, no. 1, 1994, pp. 114-129, p. 1.

[32] HE Butler (trans.), *The Institutio Oratoria of Quintilian*, 4 vols, Harvard University Press, Cambridge, 1920-1922 3, 6, 21.

such an inspection, it were still uncertain, then the situation's stasis would be one of 'conjecture,' by default.[33] If, in the alternative, it were clear but still incomplete, the stasis would be that of 'definition'.[34] If, after inspection, the krinomenon was complete, the stasis would be that of 'quality,'[35] which had its own many subdivisions. However, Hermogenes omitted any explanation or analysis of this idea of 'krinomenon,' or how to identify it.[36]

Thus, an uncertain conjectural dispute has three elements: the prosecutor's claim, such as for example 'You did this action,' followed by the defendant's response, as a counterclaim, such as for example 'I did not do that action.' Taken together, the claim and counter-claim infer a question for the trier of fact to resolve, namely, 'Did he do it?'[37] If the defendant denies the fact, the statement of defense will be 'I did not do it'. If the alleged fact pattern is conceded, the statement of defense will be 'I was justified in what I did.' This implies a stasis of quality. The complete krinomenon then will be 'Was he justified in doing what was alleged?'. This, in turn, requires further analysis, by answering the question 'on what grounds does the defense claim justification?'[38] Quintilian wrote, summarizing these situations, of four ways permissible to the defendant, as follows.[39]

In respect of the krinomenon, the following are the four ways possible of substantiating the defense. The four levels of stasis correspond to these, as follows: (a) the defense of denial leads to the first level of stasis, which Hermagoras called 'conjecture'; (b) the defense of redefinition, such as for example, 'not murder but manslaughter,' suggests the second level of stasis, which Hermagoras called 'definition'; (c) the defense of justification, or exoneration, suggests the third stasis of 'quality'; and, (d) the defense of procedural objection, such as for example an error in the law of procedure, or applying an incorrect jurisdiction, suggests the fourth stasis that Hermagoras

---

[33] George A Kennedy (trans.), *Invention and Method: Two Rhetorical Treatises from the Hermogenic Corpus. The Greek Text, Edited by Hugo Rabe*, Society of Biblical Literature & Leiden, Brill, Atlanta, 2005, 36.8-9.

[34] ibid., 37.1-2.

[35] ibid., 37.14-15.

[36] M Heath, 'The Substructure of Stasis-Theory from Hermagoras to Hermogenes,' *Classical Quarterly*, vol. 44, no. 1, 1994, pp. 114-129, p. 2.

[37] ibid.

[38] ibid., p. 4.

[39] HE Butler trans., *The Institutio Oratoria of Quintilian*, 4 vols, Harvard University Press, Cambridge, 1920-1922, 3, 6, 83.

called 'translation.'[40] It appears that only the stasis of definition might rest in a fit and proper matter, but it is less honorable.

Quintilian's view adds to that of Hermagoras by suggesting that each level of stasis is exclusive of each of the others. The Quintilian formulation also arranges the forms of stasis into levels of honour, with that of justification being the most honorable. Thus, stasis is a synthesis of both reason and a kind of honour that would exonerate the defendant.

3.1. Stasis and Murder *lingua vel facto*

In *R v Dudley and Stephens*,[41] Lord Coleridge's argument rejected the possibility in English Law of murder *lingua vel facto*, or, murder by words,[42] by his long reference to the ancient myth of Hero and Leander. By analogy, a denunciation of a fit and proper person could have the same effect as the conception of murder *lingua vel facto*, before the matter arrived anywhere near a court of law. Let us apply stasis theory to it.

Let us examine the fruits of Lord Coleridge's rejection, in the context of stasis theory. First, to understand the power of words, in Gorgias' *The Encomium to Helen*, Helen was the most notorious woman of Greece. She abandoned her husband Menelaus to run away with Paris, Prince of Troy. The encomium explained it was wrong to apportion blame to Helen. After epitomizing her birth and her marriage, it suggested four possible factual causes for why she went to Troy. They were: (a) mere chance by virtue of the gods; (b) excess of force; (c) persuasive oratory; or, (d) the exigencies of love. Gorgias showed that each of these was overpowering and irresistible. If she were subjected to any of them, she would be blameless with the stasis of quality. Rather than praise Helen expressly, the encomium succeeded in defending her from criticism. Gorgias demonstrated that speech was too powerful a sovereign.[43] His method, rather than the substance of his oratory, suggested the facts of such overwhelming force, the force of necessity, that the audience could only agree, by inference, that Helen was a mere pawn in

---

40 Antoine Braet, 'The Classical Doctrine of "Status" and the Rhetorical Theory of Argumentation,' *Philosophy & Rhetoric*, vol. 20, no. 2, 1987, pp. 79-93, p. 83.

41 (1884) 14 QBD 273.

42 Henry de Bracton, *De Legibus et Consuetudinibus Angliae, Libri Quinquw in Varios Tractatus Distincti*, vol. 2, Cambridge University Press, Cambridge, 2012, p. lviii.

43 DM MacDowell (ed.), *Gorgias, Encomium of Helen*, Bristol Classic Press, Bristol, 2005, p. 12.

the necessary events of her life. This inference could thus impinge on the public interest, as already discussed above, by creating an outbreak of crime. Ignoring this possibility in English law rests at the level of redefinition, even although the scholarship is cognizant of the possibility of an ensuing spate of crime. The definition of murder, at common law, was as "when a person, of sound memory and discretion, unlawfully kills any reasonable creature in being and under the king's peace, with malice aforethought, either express or implied."[44] Arguably, this formulation does not appear to exclude expressly murder *lingua vel facto.*

Thus, the woman Hero and the man Leander were lovers, with Hero seduced by the words of Leander. Hero's suicide was said to have followed inevitably from the death by misadventure of her lover Leander. The ancient myth of Hero and Leander tells of Leander's seduction of the virgin priestess Hero. It appeared in Ovid's Epistles,[45] and later, formed the subject matter of poems by Christopher Marlowe, published in 1598, and then later by Lord Byron published by John Murray in 1832.[46] Also, an apparently pre-Homeric poem by Musaeus included a version of the myth.

Hero was a beautiful young woman, who lived in an isolated tower, across dangerous waters, separating her tower from the mainland. The tower was a Temple of Aphrodite. The couple's seduction began with the attractive force of Leander's male gaze at her, and proceeded with his seductive words to Hero. After consummating their love affair, by the force of Leander's verbal persuasion, Leander made regular arrangements at night to swim the dangerous straits to visit Hero in her isolated lighthouse. She covenanted to light a lamp to guide his way through the often-treacherous waters. One evening, by misadventure, she failed to light the guiding lamp. The seas were unusually rough. Leander perished while swimming the straits. Hero decided to unite with Leander by throwing herself into the dangerous waters, to her inevitable death. Thus, it was said that she died by force of Leander's seductive words - *lingua vel facto.*

---

[44] Sir William Blackstone, *Commentaries on the Laws of England, Book the Fourth*, Chapter 14, Of Homicide, Strahan, London, 1791, p. 177.

[45] Publius Ovidius Naso, *The Epistles of Ovid, Translated into English Prose*, Davidson, London, 1746, epistle IX, pp. 245 et seq.

[46] TW Baldwin, 'Marlowe's Musaeus,' *Journal of Germanic and English Philology*, vol. 54, 1955, pp. 478–485.

Braden has suggested that Musaeus's *Hero and Leander* was the principal and direct source of Marlowe's poem.[47] The sophistical speeches of Leander were an important part of Marlowe's amplification of Musaeus, and indeed, most of Marlowe's strategy, in depicting Leander's seduction of Hero, was by way of verbal amplification.[48] This inferred that Leander was the accused.

When Hero chastised Leander for daring to approach her in her Temple, the more experienced Leander, of Musaeus, recognized that these threats actually indicated that this woman had been won over,[49] suggesting a stasis of quality. Later, Musaeus suggested that the woman's silence indicated acquiescence in the man's words inferring conjecture.[50] The Hero and Leander myth, as a secret courtship and consummation, was suggestive of, and analogous to, the widespread allure of the custom of clandestine marriage,[51] a controversial matter in Marlowe's time.[52] This was an instance of the state's practice of legislating against public reason. It interfered with the alluring contexts of the customs of young lovers, by designating a mere breach of sacred process as an immorality. In any event, it made the lovers' exchange of verbal promises inherently unlawful, if associated with marriage, in that instance suggesting the stasis of 'quality.' Thus, the unclear nature of the situation might finally let it rest at the stasis of 'conjecture,' and thus too uncertain to ground a safe judicial decision in a crime of murder.

---

[47] Gordon Braden, *The Classics and English Poetry: Three Case Studies*, Yale University Press, New Haven, 1978, p. 125; TW Baldwin, 'Marlowe's Musaeus,' *Journal of Germanic and English Philology*, vol. 54, 1955, pp. 478–485.

[48] William P Weaver, 'Marlowe's Fable: Hero and Leander and the Rudiments of Eloquence,' *Studies in Philology*, vol. 105, 2008, pp. 388-408, p. 401.

[49] Roma Gill (ed.), *The Complete Works of Christopher Marlowe*, 5 vols, Clarendon Press, Oxford, 1987, pp. 128-132.

[50] ibid., p. 165.

[51] A clandestine marriage was a marriage properly solemnized by ministers, but evading public exposure, through irregularities in public form: J Schellekens, 'Courtship, the Clandestine Marriage Act, and Illegitimate Fertility in England', *The Journal of Interdisciplinary History*, vol. 25, no. 3, 1995, pp. 433-444, p. 434. The Clandestine Marriage Act of 1754, 26 Geo II c 32, redefined marriage to exclude the custom of exchanges of verbal promises. This kind of marriage had been the preference of many people without property, for many centuries. Under the new Act, marriage had to be in a church, with its advent and details entered into the parish registry: J Schellekens, 'Courtship, the Clandestine Marriage Act, and Illegitimate Fertility in England,' *The Journal of Interdisciplinary History*, vol. 25, no. 3, 1995, pp. 433-444, p. 435.

[52] Katharine Cleland, '"Wanton loves, and yong desires": Clandestine Marriage in Marlowe's *Hero and Leander* and Chapman's Continuation,' *Studies in Philology*, vol. 108, 2011, pp. 215–37, p. 216.

4. A Modern Theory of Stasis

4.1. The Ancient Heritage of Stasis Theory

Stasis theory has been central to rhetorical theory since completion of its development by Hermagoras of Temnos, in the 2nd century BCE.[53] Hermagoras's original work had long been missing, however, its main components were reconstructed during the 20th century,[54] a reconstruction helped by its major role in nearly all rhetoric theory.[55] Stasis theory facilitates the identification of key issues in contentious matters of allegation and defense.[56] Hermagoras, the *Auctor ad Herennium*, and authors such as Quintilian, Cicero and Hermogenes of Tarsus, had created intricate models for breaking up the matter's main issue into hierarchically arranged sub-issues covering all possible and relevant questions.[57] While the hierarchy of Hermagoras had five levels, those of other authors presented differing, but equally complex schemas. Most of their classical stasis models gave a specific set of *topoi* for each of these issues, for guiding the accuser and the defendant in their searches for pertinent arguments.[58] Žagar cited the following as relevant.[59]

---

[53] There are earlier traces of stasis theory in Aristotle and the *Rhetorica ad Alexandrum* 1427a 24–28, 1443aa 15–28.

[54] Dieter Matthes, 'Hermagoras von Temno', PhD dissertation, University of Hamburg, 1955; Dieter Matthes, 'Hermagoras von Temnos,' *Lustrum*, vol. 3, 1958, pp. 58–214; Dieter Matthes, *Hermagoras "Temnitae testimonia et fragmenta"*, Teubner, Leipzig, 1962; Karl Barwick, 'Augustins Schrift "De Rhetorica" und Hermagoras von Temnos,' *Philologus*, vol. 105, 1961, pp. 97–110; Karl Barwick, 'Zur Erklärung und Geschichte der Staseislehre des Hermagoras von Temnos', *Philologus*, vol. 108, 1964, pp. 80–101; Karl Barwick, 'Zur Rekonstruktion der Rhetorik des Hermagoras von Temnos,' *Philologus*, vol. 109, 1965, pp. 186–218; Malcolm Heath, 'The Substructure of Stasis-Theory from Hermagoras to Hermogenes,' *Classical Quarterly*, vol. 44, 1994, pp. 114–29; Malcolm Heath, 'Hermagoras: Transmission and Attribution,' *Philologus*, vol. 146, 2002, pp. 287–98.

[55] Melanchton, *Elementa Rhetorics*, 1531; Vossius, *Commentariorum Rhetoricorum Oratoriarum Institutionum Libri VI*, 1606; Zachariä, *Anleitung zur gerichtlichen Beredsamkeit*, 1810; Ortloff, *Die gerichtliche Redekunst*, 1887.

[56] Cicero and Quintilian (among others) claimed that their stasis models could also be useful beyond the *genus iudiciale*, but both of them failed to substantiate this claim in the practical topics they attached to their models.

[57] Michael J Hoppmann, 'A Modern Theory of Stasis,' *Philosophy & Rhetoric*, vol. 47, no. 3, pp. 273-296, p. 273.

[58] Frans H Van Eemeren & Rob Grootendorst, *Argumentation, Communication, and Fallacies*, Lawrence Erlbaum, Hove, 1992, pp. 41–43; Frans H Van Eemeren & Rob Grootendorst, *A Systematic Theory of Argumentation*, Cambridge University Press, Cambridge, 2004, pp. 119–20, 140–41.

[59] Igor Žagar, '*Topoi* in Critical Discourse Analysis,' *Lodz Papers in Pragmatics*, vol. 6, no. 1, 2010, pp. 3-27, p. 5.

> ... topoi or loci can be described as parts of argumentation, which belong to the obligatory, either explicit or inferable premises. They are the content-related warrants or 'conclusion rules,' which connect the argument or arguments with the conclusion, the claim. As such, they justify the transition from the argument or arguments to the conclusion.[60]

Analyses of content-related argument schemes can be made using the extant list of *topoi*, in the following list:

> 1. Usefulness, advantage; 2. Uselessness, disadvantage; 3. Definition, name-interpretation; 4. Danger and threat; 5. Humanitarianism; 6. Justice; 7. Responsibility; 8. Burdening, weighting; 9. Finances; 10. Reality; 11. Numbers; 12. Law and right; 13. History; 14. Culture; and, 15. Abuse.[61]

It is clear that each of these topoi may be applied to denunciatory conclusions while re-framing the *topoi* as folk maxims. With classical rhetorical theory decaying and breaking up, stasis theory had effectively been removed from the corpus of rhetorical study by the latter part of the 19th century. Within the modern corpus of rhetoric, models of stasis are still routinely regarded as mere historical artifacts, and thus, are largely ignored in contemporary theory. The specialized discipline of modern legal studies has developed similar models, but only covering a part of what was covered in the classical models of stasis. Also, similar models have appeared in other genres of speech, such as that of academic debate. The English tradition on rhetoric has maintained a basic version of stasis theory, which divides the top-level divisions of stasis theory into: An sit? Quit sit? Quale sit?[62] However, it omits the complicated hierarchy at the lower levels, and drops the classical lists of *topoi*. In particular, it ignores the discussion of the *iudicatio/krinomenon*, which are the key points of conflict, and the list of *asystata*, which are the unsolvable issues.[63]

Before discussing the division of 'political questions' into *staseis*, Hermogenes had made some necessary clarifications. One division was that

---

60 Manfred Kienpointner, *Alltagslogik*, Frommann-holzboog, Stuttgart-Bad Cannstatt, 1992, p. 194.

61 Ruth Wodak & Michael Meyer (eds.), *Methods of Critical Discourse Analysis*, Sage, London, 2006, p. 74.

62 Edward PJ Corbett & Robert J Connors, *Classical Rhetoric for the Modern Student*, 4th edn, Oxford University Press, New York, 1999, pp. 28–29.

63 The first list of *asystata* is traditionally attributed to Hermagoras. Frédérique Woerther, 'Hermagoras et la doctrine des [asystata],' *Mnemosyne*, vol. 65, 2012, pp. 179–202, pp. 179–202.

of 'political questions' into *synestota*, which were those capable of *stasis*, in that they both had an issue and could be divided into heads. The second was *asystata*, that of asystatic questions, those incapable of *stasis* because they did not have any issue. Hermogenes also added a third group, namely, that of questions close to being *asystata*, or nearly *asystatic*, in that they were almost lacking any issue.[64] Hermogenes numbered the conditions a 'political question' had to satisfy to be capable of *stasis*. The conditions mentioned are the following: (i) The questions include person and act or one of them, (ii) There are persuasive arguments on both sides that (a) are different from those of the other party, and (b) have probative force, and (iii) the verdict (which is to be pronounced by the jury) is (a) not self evident, (b) not prejudiced, and (c) not unreachable.[65] This meant they had to be a likely subject of rhetorical investigation or declamation.[66]

Hermogenes numbered eight types of *asystatic* questions: one-sided, wholly equivalent, reversible, insoluble, implausible, impossible, disreputable, uncircumstantial,[67] suggesting that denunciation was asystatic, apart from its rhetorical persuasive effect. If modern reconstruction of Hermagoras' system was correct, then he had constructed four *asystatic* questions: deficient, one-sided, wholly equivalent, and insoluble.[68] Hermogenes' innovation changed the first part of the list of *asystatic* questions by annexing to it the *reversible* and taking away the *deficient*, which were one-sided, wholly equivalent, reversible, insoluble. To this he added the rest of *implausible*, *impossible*, *disreputable*, *uncircumstantial*, and absorbed the *deficient* into what he called *aperistaton*, *uncircumstantial*. The first half of this list included *asystatic* questions justified by lack of compliance with the prescribed conditions.[69] The four new types thus created some classification problems suggesting an unsatisfactory body of theory.[70]

Although this truncated approach makes stasis theory a generally applicable exploratory procedure that can be used in most matters, it loses much of stasis theory's guidance for analysis of accusation and defense. The

---

[64] Hermogenes, *On Staseis* 31, 19–34, 15.
[65] ibid.
[66] Malcolm Heath, *Hermogenes' On Issues: Strategies of Argument in Later Greek Rhetoric*. Clarendon Press, Oxford, 1995, pp. 66–70.
[67] Hermogenes, *On Staseis* 31, 19–34, 15.
[68] Ray Nadeau, 'Classical Systems of Stases in Greek: Hermagoras to Hermogenes,' *GRBS vol.* 2, 1959, pp. 52–71, pp. 66–71.
[69] Malcolm Heath, *Hermogenes' On Issues: Strategies of Argument in Later Greek Rhetoric*. Clarendon Press, Oxford, 1995, pp. 66–70.
[70] ibid., p. 67.

legal models are quite inaccessible to non–legal actors. They cover only a limited range of accusations and defenses. These are limited to those articulated before a court of law. Moreover, they are not articulated in the more widespread cases of social and moral accusations in society, such as commonplace denunciation. As the newer simplified models in the English tradition are inadequate for in-depth analysis of a contentious matter, today's rhetorical critique must still be grounded in classical stasis theory.

Nevertheless, the classical models are still incomplete in terms of today's needs. The Hermagoras cohort of scholars arranged for the practical cases of their time, but did not construct a completed and systematic theory for their genre. Although this would not have been a practical problem with the comparable social and legal and social exigencies,[71] an elision remained at the theoretical level.[72] Second, the classical models of stasis did not differentiate between key issues having the power to decide the case, and those issues of lesser significance, which were therefore not decisive. Rather, both vital and non-key issues were intermixed at random within their hierarchies, giving the defendant uncertainty of the task at hand, making the krinomenon chaotic. Last in this list, the various specialized *topoi* included in the models were similarly both incomplete and overwhelming in their opacity. Some of the individual components were more opaque than the larger models of stasis themselves.[73]

4.2. The Burden of Proof in Accusation and Defense

One of the main attributes that differentiates from others the rhetorical genre of accusation and defense, known as *genus iudiciale*, is the so-called "burden of proof" the protagonist accuser is said to carry. This protagonist's burden of proof, in dialogue, is largely determined by the defendant antagonist's presumptions.[74] The stronger the presumptions in favor of the antagonist, the more qualified is the protagonist's burden of proof. Where there is accusation and defense, the antagonist can use the strongest available of all presumptions,

---

[71] Michael J Hoppmann, 'A Modern Theory of Stasis', *Philosophy & Rhetoric*, vol. 47, no. 3, pp. 273-296, p. 274.

[72] Something that is needed or wanted.

[73] Michael J Hoppmann, 'A Modern Theory of Stasis', *Philosophy & Rhetoric*, vol. 47, no. 3, pp. 273-296, p. 275.

[74] Frans H Van Eemeren, Rob Grootendorst & Francisca Snoeck Henkemans, *Argumentation*, Lawrence Erlbaum, Mahwah, 2002, pp. 28–30.

namely, the presumption of innocence. Ever since the works of Whately,[75] the role of presumptions, more especially the presumption of innocence, has been acknowledged in all kinds of accusations, pursuant to all categories of norm, such as legal, religious, or moral.[76] When different reasons underlying the presumption of innocence become relevant under specific conditions, they must be fortified by other reasons, often weaker but still immune to contextual conditions.[77] The following sets out four of the chief arguments for the presumption of innocence: (1) dialectical; (2) harm; (3) danger; and, (4) justice.

4.2.1. The Dialectical Argument

When accusing someone of doing a bad act, or of breaching a norm, the accuser may choose from many likely norms and acts, limited only by the accuser's tactics and the evidence available. He or she might accuse the defendant of hitting another person, lying to another person, or violating an agreement, or more. The claim could allege that the deed was done at a named time, a named place, with a specified implement. The predatory ability to make such choices and to choose the peristaseis, the rhetorical circumstances, of the matter before even uttering the accusation places the accuser in a systemically better position within the dialectic. In order to balance this predatory benefit and for reasons of fairness in deciding the merits of the accusation, any reasonable society permits the defendant to undermine the accusation rather than to prove innocence. This dialectical category of argument implies only a weaker presumption of innocence. Yet it can apply to all accusations, with all kinds of underlying norms, creating a broad foundation.[78]

---

[75] Richard Whately, *Elements of Rhetoric*, Douglas Ehninger (ed.), Southern Illinois University Press, Carbondale, 1963.

[76] Michael J Hoppmann, 'A Modern Theory of Stasis,' *Philosophy & Rhetoric*, vol. 47, no. 3, pp. 273-296, p. 276.

[77] Joseph Wenzel, 'Arguers' Obligations: Another Perspective,' in Frans H van Eemeren (ed.), *Anyone Who Has a View*, Kluwer Academic, Dortrecht, 2003, pp. 227–236; Fred Kauffeld, 'The Ordinary Practice of Presuming and Presumption with Special Attention to Veracity and the Burden of Proof,' in Frans H van Eemeren (ed.), *Anyone Who Has a View*, et al., Kluwer Academic, Dortrecht, 2003, pp. 133–46; Michael Hoppmann, *Argumentative Verteidigung*, Weidler, Berlin, 2008.

[78] Takuzo Konishi, 'A Generalized Stasis Theory and Arguers' Dialectical Obligations', in Hans V Hansen, Christopher Tindale, J Anthony Blair, Ralph Johnstone & Robert Pinto (eds.), *Argumentation and Its Applications*, Meeting of the Ontario Society for the Study of Argumentation, Toronto, 2001; Jean Goodwin, 'Reply to Takuzo Konishi: A Generalized Stasis Theory and Arguers' Dialectical Obligations,' in Hans V Hansen, Christopher Tindale, J Anthony Blair, Ralph Johnstone & Robert Pinto (eds.), *Argumentation and Its Applications*, Meeting of the Ontario Society for the Study of Argumentation, Toronto,

4.2.2. The Harm Argument

Whenever an accusation is published as a denunciation, it might cause harm independently to the accused's reputation. If it remains unsubstantiated, the accusation is essentially unaltered as a mere denunciation, thereby violating the accused's personal rights. Any society interested in peaceful cooperation among its members installs a qualified burden of proof on any accuser, so to minimize any harm done by random and capricious accusations. Just as in the dialectical argument, this harm argument only requires a presumption of innocence of somewhat limited force. However, it is applicable universally to cases of accusation and defense, serving as a useful fundamental principle.[79]

4.2.3. The Danger Argument

The third argument, likely the strongest for the presumption of innocence is the argument of danger. Walton compared an accusation, taking place within the legal system, to a loaded firearm.[80] The accuser demands of society that it do severe damage to the liberty, property, and even the life of the accused, by way of punishment. Therefore, the accuser has a heightened duty of care while brandishing this loaded gun. While this is apparent and embedded in nearly all penal systems with a high burden of proof placed on the accuser, it is just as valid in social, moral and religious contexts, such as bare denunciation, where the penalty demanded is such as a socially completed denunciation, expulsion from a profession, loss of property, or more, could have grave effects on the accused.[81]

4.2.4. The Justice Argument

Arguably the most significant argument in favor of the presumption of innocence is the argument of justice. Perelman and Olbrechts-Tyteca had described acting justly as meaning "giving identical treatment to beings or situations of the same kind",[82] suggesting that subaltern groups such as

---

2001; Fred Kaufield, 'Pivotal Issues and Norms in Rhetorical Theories of Argumentation,' in Frans van Eemeren & Peter Houtlosser (eds.), *Dialectic and Rhetoric*, Kluwer Academic, Dortrecht, 2002, pp. 97–118, pp. 105–6.

[79] Fred Kauffeld, 'Presumptions and the Distribution of Argumentative Burdens in Acts of Proposing and Accusing,' *Argumentation*, vol. 12, 1998, pp. 245–66, pp. 245–66; Jean Goodwin, 'Designing Issues,' in Frans van Eemeren & Peter Houtlosser (ed.), *Dialectic and Rhetoric*, Kluwer Academic, Dortrecht, 2002, pp. 81–96.

[80] Douglas Walton, 'Burden of Proof,' *Argumentation*, vol. 2, 1998, pp. 233–54, p. 238.

[81] Michael J Hoppmann, 'A Modern Theory of Stasis,' *Philosophy & Rhetoric*, vol. 47, no. 3, pp. 273-296, p. 277.

[82] Chaim Perelman & Lucie Olbrechts-Tyteca, *The New Rhetoric*, trans. John Wilkinson and Purcell Weaver, University of Notre Dame Press, Notre Dame, 1969, §52; Chaim Perelman,

professionals are constructed to receive less justice from their professional associations. Thus, one must judge any accusation as if it were leveled against oneself. From the perspective of the defendant accused wrongly, the rule arises that it is preferable to allow a hundred guilty people to walk away free than to put one innocent person into prison. The much greater harm from wrongful punishment compared to the danger of unharmed wrongdoers over-balances the scales of social utility favoring a strong presumption of innocence, under normal conditions.[83] However, this argument, with very strong *ceteris paribus*,[84] fails under these two pre-conditions: (1) if the group of accused are largely different from the socially dominant group, for example female "witches," foreign "enemy combatants," the justice rule does not compel a consideration in the shoes of the accused; (2) if danger from unpunished wrongdoers threatens the fabric of society, for example such rhetorical devices as "witches," "terrorists," or McCarthyian "Communists", renegade lawyers or accountants, then there is a lessening of the comparative evil of punishing an innocent person. In these three cases, the utility scales tip towards the accuser and the other three arguments for the presumption of innocence are needed.

4.3. The Axiom of Modern Stasis

Five necessary elements apply to accusing someone of violating either a legal or a moral norm, and demanding punishment for that act or omission: (1) Any reasonable accusation must name the person accused; (2) It must specify the violated norm, which must be neither unstable nor overly strict or absolute in liability, or else everyone breaches it; (3) It must elaborate on the specific act or omission that violated the norm; (4) It must reason the connection between these three elements; and, (5) it should assume that the basic requirements for a reasonable and fair exchange have been fulfilled, with no special reasons against punishment in the event of guilt.[85] These elements constitute a self-

---

Über die Gerechtigkeit, trans. Ulrike Blüm and Ottmar Ballweg, Beck, Munich, 1967, p. 58.

[83] Douglas Walton, *Legal Argumentation and Evidence*, Pennsylvania State University Press, University Park, 2002, pp. 11–15.

[84] With other conditions remaining the same; other things being equal.

[85] HLA Hart, *Punishment and Responsibility*, Oxford University Press, Oxford, 1968, pp. 4, 5.

evident axiom for the deduction of a modern model of stasis for the genre of accusation and defense.[86]

Conclusion

The research question asked whether there could be a stable stasis, between the applicant and the general public, with which the court could render its decision on whether or not an applicant was a "fit and proper" person. Argument has sought to demonstrate that prior denunciation of a fit and proper person is an attempt to make the person disreputable, destroying any chance of safe and stable judicial determination.

Stasis theory allowed the rhetorician to judge whether or not a conflict of wills really existed, and if so, in what ways. This paradigm allowed an anticipated central question to be resolved, which the Greeks called the *krinomenon*, the likely opposing accusatory and defense strategies, and consequently, how best to win the clash. Stasis theory of classical times dealt with such rhetorical matters as declamatory themes, real deliberative or forensic states of affairs. Declamations were of two kinds, the *suasoria* or deliberative speech about history or politics, and the *controversia* or forensic speech on a specific legal case. In this way, the rhetor could denounce a person simply with a bare persuasive declamation. For example, a rhetorician's encomium on death is followed, in time, by a mass outbreak of suicides. The rhetorician is charged with having committed a crime against the public interest. The defense might argue that merely practicing his profession violated no law, and the rhetor would remain free, having denounced and killed.

Disagreement among the ancient scholars, about how to classify a rhetorical dispute, required critical analysis of how stasis could generally be pinned down. Hermogenes' view was that it required an inspection of the 'krinomenon,' meaning 'that which - by the audience - is judged,' reinforcing the view that the public mind is the ultimate arbiter of guilt, not conveniently stated rules said to have been breached. If, after such an inspection using stasis theory, the matter were still uncertain, then the situation's stasis would be one of 'conjecture,' by default, and all that would remain would be its effect in the public mind.

[86] Michael J Hoppmann, 'A Modern Theory of Stasis,' *Philosophy & Rhetoric*, vol. 47, no. 3, pp. 273-296, p. 279.

Quintilian's view adds to that of Hermagoras by suggesting that each level of stasis is exclusive of each of the others. Thus, stasis is a synthesis of both reason and a kind of honour that would exonerate the defendant, and more, if a persuasive declamation were merely persuasive in the public mind, other levels of stasis allowing a comprehensive defense would be nullified. Thus, for example, a denunciation of a fit and proper person could have the same effect as the conception of murder *lingua vel facto*, before the matter arrived anywhere near a court of law.

The Hero and Leander myth, as a secret courtship and consummation, was suggestive of, and analogous to, the widespread allure of the custom of clandestine marriage. However, the Parliament made clandestine marriage illegal. This legislation interfered with the alluring contexts of the customs of young lovers, by designating a mere breach of sacred process as an immorality. In any event, it made the lovers' exchange of verbal promises inherently unlawful, if associated with marriage, in that instance suggesting the stasis of 'quality,' merely on the basis of a political debate. Thus, the unclear nature of the situation might finally let it rest at the stasis of 'conjecture,' and thus too uncertain to ground a safe judicial decision. Nevertheless, charactering the young couple as having an illegal marriage would be a completed denunciation.

In stasis theory, topoi or loci could be described as parts of argumentation, which belonged to the obligatory, either explicit or inferable premises. They were the content-related warrants or 'conclusion rules.' It is clear that each of the topoi might be subverted and applied to denunciatory conclusions while re-framing these base *topoi* as mere folk maxims. This suggested that fit and proper administrative determinations were in the nature of asystatic questions, those incapable of *stasis* because they did not have any issue.

Hermogenes numbered eight types of *asystatic* questions: one-sided, wholly equivalent, reversible, insoluble, implausible, impossible, disreputable, uncircumstantial, suggesting that administrative denunciation of a fit and proper person was asystatic, apart from its rhetorical persuasive effect in the public mind.

The harm argument dealt with the presumption of innocence essential to stasis, a presumption gone after denunciation. Whenever an accusation is published as a denunciation, it might cause harm independently to the accused's reputation. If it remains unsubstantiated, the accusation is essentially unaltered as a mere denunciation, thereby violating the accused's personal rights. Arguably the most significant argument in favor of the presumption of innocence is the argument of justice. Perelman and Olbrechts-

Tyteca had described acting justly as meaning "giving identical treatment to beings or situations of the same kind," suggesting that subaltern groups such as professionals are constructed to receive less justice from their superior professional associations, and those inside the professional associations are protected.

Five necessary elements apply to accusing someone of violating either a legal or a moral norm, and demanding punishment for that act or omission: (1) Any reasonable accusation must name the person accused; (2) It must specify the violated norm, which must be neither unstable nor overly strict or absolute in liability, or else everyone breaches it; (3) It must elaborate on the specific act or omission that violated the norm; (4) It must reason the connection between these three elements; and, (5) it should assume that the basic requirements for a reasonable and fair exchange have been fulfilled, with no special reasons against punishment in the event of guilt.

In extended synthesis, the rhetor could denounce a person simply with a bare persuasive declamation and the situation's stasis would be one of 'conjecture,' by default, and all that would remain would be its effect in the public mind. A denunciation of a fit and proper person could have the same moving effect as the conception of murder *lingua vel facto*, before the matter arrived anywhere near a court of law. In the light of this, fit and proper administrative determinations were in the nature of an asystatic question, specifically the *asystatic* question of "disreputable," incapable of *stasis* because it did not have any issue. The subaltern groups, such as professionals have been constructed to receive less justice from their superior professional associations, while those inside the professional associations are protected as reputable by their own definition. To satisfy the axiom of modern stasis, accusing someone of violating either a legal or a moral norm must specify the violated norm, which must be neither unstable nor overly strict or absolute in liability, or else everyone breaches it.

References

Aristotle, *Categories*.

Aristotle, *Metaphysics*.

Aristotle, *The Nichomachean Ethics*, trans. H Rackham, Harvard University Press, Cambridge, 1999.

Australian Broadcasting Tribunal v Bond (1990) 170 CLR 321.

Baldwin, TW, 'Marlowe's Musaeus,' *Journal of Germanic and English Philology*, vol. 54, 1955, pp. 478–485.

Barwick, Karl, 'Augustins Schrift "De Rhetorica" und Hermagoras von Temnos [Augustine's writing "De Rhetorica" and Hermagoras of Temnos],' *Philologus*, vol. 105, 1961, pp. 97–110.

Barwick, Karl, 'Zur Erklärung und Geschichte der Staseislehre des Hermagoras von Temnos [On the explanation and history of the stasis doctrine of Hermagoras of Temnos],' *Philologus*, vol. 108, 1964, pp. 80–101.

Barwick, Karl, 'Zur Rekonstruktion der Rhetorik des Hermagoras von Temnos [On the reconstruction of the rhetoric of Hermagoras of Temnos],' *Philologus*, vol. 109, 1965, pp. 186–218.

Blackstone, Sir William, *Commentaries on the Laws of England, Book the Fourth*, Chapter 14, Of Homicide, Strahan, London, 1791.

Braden, Gordon, *The Classics and English Poetry: Three Case Studies*, Yale University Press, New Haven, 1978.

Braet, Antoine, 'The Classical Doctrine of "Status" and the Rhetorical Theory of Argumentation,' *Philosophy & Rhetoric*, vol. 20, no. 2, 1987, pp. 79-93.

Butler, HE (trans.), *The Institutio Oratoria of Quintilian* [The Institute of Oratory of Quintilian], 4 vols, Harvard University Press, Cambridge, 1920-1922.

CJE v Medical Board of Australia [2019] VCAT 1619.

Cleland, Katharine, '"Wanton loves, and yong desires": Clandestine Marriage in Marlowe's Hero and Leander and Chapman's Continuation,' *Studies in Philology*, vol. 108, 2011, pp. 215–237.

Corbett, Edward PJ & Robert J Connors, *Classical Rhetoric for the Modern Student*, 4th edn, Oxford University Press, New York, 1999.

de Bracton, Henry, *De Legibus et Consuetudinibus Angliae, Libri Quinquw in Varios Tractatus Distincti* [On the Laws and Customs of England, Five Books in Various Distinct Treatises], vol. 2, Cambridge University Press, Cambridge, 2012.

Dieter, Otto Alvin Loeb, 'Stasis,' *Speech Monographs*, XVII (November 1950), pp. 345-369.

Gill, Roma (ed.), *The Complete Works of Christopher Marlowe*, 5 vols, Clarendon Press, Oxford, 1987.

Goodwin, David, 'Controversiae Meta-Asystatae and the New Rhetoric [Meta-Assisted Controversies and the New Rhetoric],' *Rhetoric Society Quarterly*, vol. 19, no. 3, 1989, pp. 205-216.

Goodwin, Jean, 'Designing Issues,' in Frans van Eemeren and Peter Houtlosser (ed.), *Dialectic and Rhetoric*, Kluwer Academic, Dortrecht, 2002.

Goodwin, Jean, 'Reply to Takuzo Konishi: A Generalized Stasis Theory and Arguers' Dialectical Obligations,' in Hans V Hansen, Christopher Tindale, J Anthony Blair, Ralph Johnstone and Robert Pinto (eds.), *Argumentation and Its Applications*, Meeting of the Ontario Society for the Study of Argumentation, Toronto, 2001.

Hart, HLA, *Punishment and Responsibility*, Oxford University Press, Oxford, 1968.

Heath, M, 'The Substructure of Stasis-Theory from Hermagoras to Hermogenes,' *Classical Quarterly*, vol. 44, no. 1, 1994, pp. 114-129.

Heath, Malcolm, 'Hermagoras: Transmission and Attribution,' *Philologus*, vol. 146, 2002, pp. 287–98.
Heath, Malcolm, *Hermogenes' On Issues: Strategies of Argument in Later Greek Rhetoric*. Clarendon Press, Oxford, 1995.
Hermogenes, *On Staseis*.
Hoppmann, Michael J, 'A Modern Theory of Stasis,' *Philosophy & Rhetoric*, vol. 47, no. 3, pp. 273-296.
Hoppmann, Michael, *Argumentative Verteidigung* [Argumentative defense], Weidler, Berlin, 2008.
Kauffeld, Fred, 'Presumptions and the Distribution of Argumentative Burdens in Acts of Proposing and Accusing,' *Argumentation*, vol. 12, 1998, pp. 245–66.
Kauffeld, Fred, 'The Ordinary Practice of Presuming and Presumption with Special Attention to Veracity and the Burden of Proof,' in Frans H van Eemeren (ed.), *Anyone Who Has a View*, et al., Kluwer Academic, Dortrecht, 2003, pp. 133–46.
Kaufield, Fred, 'Pivotal Issues and Norms in Rhetorical Theories of Argumentation,' in Frans van Eemeren and Peter Houtlosser (eds.), *Dialectic and Rhetoric*, Kluwer Academic, Dortrecht, 2002, pp. 97–118, pp. 105–6.
Kennedy, G, *Greek Rhetoric under Christian Emperors*, Princeton University Press, Princeton, 1983.
Kennedy, George A (trans.), *Invention and Method: Two Rhetorical Treatises from the Hermogenic Corpus. The Greek Text, Edited by Hugo Rabe*, Society of Biblical Literature & Leiden, Brill, Atlanta, 2005.
Kienpointner, Manfred, *Alltagslogik* [*Everyday logic*], Frommann-holzboog, Stuttgart-Bad Cannstatt, 1992.
Knight, Kelvin, *Aristotelian Philosophy: Ethics and Politics from Aristotle to MacIntyre*, Polity Press, Cambridge, 2007.
Konishi, Takuzo, 'A Generalized Stasis Theory and Arguers' Dialectical Obligations,' in Hans V Hansen, Christopher Tindale, J Anthony Blair, Ralph Johnstone and Robert Pinto (eds.), *Argumentation and Its Applications*, Meeting of the Ontario Society for the Study of Argumentation, Toronto, 2001.
Lilienthal, G, 'Business Goodwill: Relationships of Production, Legal Superstructures and an Administrative Prerogative Act Developed in United Kingdom Ideology and Case Law,' *Commonwealth Law Bulletin*, vol. 45, no. 1, 2019, pp. 92-114.
MacDowell, DM (ed.), *Gorgias*, *Encomium of Helen*, Bristol Classic Press, Bristol, 2005.
Matthes, Dieter, 'Hermagoras von Temno [Hermagoras of Temnos],' PhD dissertation, University of Hamburg, 1955.
Matthes, Dieter, 'Hermagoras von Temnos [Hermagoras of Temnos],' *Lustrum*, vol. 3, 1958, pp. 58–214.
Matthes, Dieter, *Hermagoras "Temnitae testimonia et fragmenta,"* [*Hermagoras, "The Testimonies and Fragments of Temnita,"*] Teubner, Leipzig, 1962.
Medical Practitioners Board of Victoria v Lal [2009] VSCA109.
Melanchton, *Elementa Rhetorics*.
Mendelson Michael, 'Declamation, Context, and Controversiality,' *Rhetoric Review*, vol. 13, no. 1, 1994, pp. 92-107.

Montefusco, L Calboli, *La dottrina degli status nella retorica greca e romana* [*The doctrine of status in Greek and Roman rhetoric*], Hildesheim, New York, 1986.

Mr. Chooks Halal Chicken Pty Ltd v Primesafe (Review and Regulation) [2018] VCAT 1932.

Nadeau, Ray, 'Classical Systems of Stases in Greek: Hermagoras to Hermogenes,' *GRBS* vol. 2, 1959, pp. 52–71.

Naso, Publius Ovidius, *The Epistles of Ovid, Translated into English Prose*, Davidson, London, 1746, epistle IX.

Perelman, Chaim & Lucie Olbrechts-Tyteca, *The New Rhetoric*, trans. John Wilkinson and Purcell Weaver, University of Notre Dame Press, Notre Dame, 1969.

Perelman, Chaim, *Über die Gerechtigkeit* [*About Justice*], trans. Ulrike Blüm and Ottmar Ballweg, Beck, Munich, 1967.

Quintilian, *Institutes of Oratory*.

R v Dudley and Stephens (1884) 14 QBD 273.

Race, William H, 'Pindaric Encomium and Isokrates' Evagoras,' *Transactions of the American Philological Association*, vol. 117, 1987, pp. 131-155.

Re "A" HCMP2079/2016.

Re Youh Alan Chuen Po [2013] 2 HKLRD 485.

Rhetorica ad Alexandrum.

Russell, D, *Greek Declamation*, Cambridge University Press, Cambridge, 1983.

Schellekens, J, 'Courtship, the Clandestine Marriage Act, and Illegitimate Fertility in England,' *The Journal of Interdisciplinary History*, vol. 25, no. 3, 1995, pp. 433-444.

Sky News, 'Russia Today has UK broadcast licence revoked by Ofcom - but Kremlin calls decision "madness",' *Sky News*, Friday 18th March 2022.

TGH v Secretary to the Department of Justice and Regulation (Review and Regulation) [2018] VCAT 110.

The Clandestine Marriage Act, 1754, 26 Geo II c 32.

Van Eemeren, Frans H & Rob Grootendorst, *A Systematic Theory of Argumentation*, Cambridge University Press, Cambridge, 2004, pp. 119–20.

Van Eemeren, Frans H, Rob Grootendorst & Francisca Snoeck Henkemans, *Argumentation*, Lawrence Erlbaum, Mahwah, 2002.

Van Eemeren, H, Frans & Rob Grootendorst, *Argumentation, Communication, and Fallacies*, Lawrence Erlbaum, Hove, 1992.

Vossius, *Commentariorum Rhetoricorum Oratoriarum Institutionum Libri VI* [*Commentaries on Rhetorical Oratorical Institutions Book VI*], 1606.

Walton, Douglas, 'Burden of Proof,' *Argumentation*, vol. 2, 1998, pp. 233–54.

Walton, Douglas, *Legal Argumentation and Evidence*, Pennsylvania State University Press, University Park, 2002.

Weaver, William P, 'Marlowe's Fable: Hero and Leander and the Rudiments of Eloquence,' *Studies in Philology*, vol. 105, 2008, pp. 388-408.

Wenzel, Joseph, 'Arguers' Obligations: Another Perspective,' in Frans H van Eemeren (ed.), *Anyone Who Has a View*, Kluwer Academic, Dortrecht, 2003.

Whately, Richard, *Elements of Rhetoric*, Douglas Ehninger (ed.), Southern Illinois University Press, Carbondale, 1963.

Wodak, Ruth & Michael Meyer (eds.), *Methods of Critical Discourse Analysis*, Sage, London, 2006.

Woerther, Frédérique, 'Hermagoras et la doctrine des [asystata],' [Hermagoras and the doctrine of [asystata]] *Mnemosyne*, vol. 65, 2012, pp. 179–202.

Zachariä, *Anleitung zur gerichtlichen Beredsamkeit* [*Guide to judicial eloquence*], 1810; Ortloff, *Die gerichtliche Redekunst*, 1887.

Žagar, Igor, '*Topoi* in Critical Discourse Analysis,' *Lodz Papers in Pragmatics*, vol. 6, no. 1, 2010, pp. 3-27.

Chapter 7

Child Labor and the Subaltern Working Class

Salim Ibrahim Ali[1], PhD
and Gary I. Lilienthal[2,*], PhD
[1]School of Law, Alhadba College University, Mosul, Iraq
[2]Carrington Rand, Hong Kong SAR, Peoples Republic of China

Abstract

In Iraq, children account for a significant proportion of the population. The country has been faced with several major challenges, and risks to this demographic, in all its communities. Such challenges have posed threats and risks to the children's development by minimizing their access to education, and to the basic necessities of community development. As a result, child labor has become a significant factor in the national economy's regression. Therefore, in the light of this statement of significance, the overall research objective of this chapter is to examine critically the causes and drivers of child labor, and the worst forms of child labor in the context of Iraq. The research question is whether the excess of child labour in Iraq represents that kind of social engineering designed to create a long-term subaltern class of workers. Argument seeks to demonstrate that child labour becomes a hegemonic subaltern working class group. The research is doctrinal, based on the best literary evidence available. The research will arrive at the view that when the United States and its coalition forces invaded Iraq, it depleted families of their financial resources, making them completely vulnerable to economic shock. The natural consequences of this have been a national spread of child labour. Child labour refers to when children are working in any type of work that is dangerous and harmful to children's health, or, the work hinders their education. It is prevalent in the most vulnerable

* Corresponding Author's carrington.rand@icloud.com.

In: Regulation of the Professions in East Asia
Editors: Gary I. Lilienthal and Muhamad Hassan bin Ahmad
ISBN: 979-8-88697-409-6

of families, in that those that have low income, have little margin to take care of injury or illness of adults, or to handle disruptions stemming from abandonment or divorce. Since children are most easily managed and are not as aware of their rights, child labor significantly prevents the development of children. In Iraq, children's economic exploitation has now become the norm, preventing them from going to the schools and enjoying any opportunities for social integration. This suggests that the natural hegemonic consequences of the US invasion of Iraq created a long-term working class, unaware of its potential, through the restrictions on it to access to education and to achieve social integration.

Keywords: community development, child labor, hegemony, subaltern group

1. Introduction

In Iraq, children account for a significant proportion of the population. The country has been faced with several major challenges, and risks to this demographic, in all its communities. Such challenges have posed threats and risks to the children's development by minimizing their access to education, and to the basic necessities of community development.[1] As a result, child labor has become a significant factor in the national economy's regression.[2] Therefore, in the light of this statement of significance, the overall research objective of this chapter is to examine critically the causes and drivers of child labor, and the worst forms of child labor in the context of Iraq.

Throughout history, industries have exploited children for economic gain, by being subjugated to submit to employment by adults. Basically, this has prevented them from enjoying their childhood, health and education. The employment of children, as the common concept of child labor, has influenced millions of children all over the world. Employing children not only causes detrimental and dangerous consequences to children, but also, it prevents them from accessing various rights such as the need to obtain an education. According to the International Labor Organization (ILO) 2013,[3] around 168 million children are participating in child labor all over the world. with this

---

[1] Bureau of International Labor Affairs, *Child Labor and Forced Labor Reports - Iraq*, 2019.

[2] H Abdul Wahab, Z Amin Ayub & Salim Ibrahim Ali, 'Child Labor in its Worst Forms as Child Slavery', in G Lilienthal (ed.), *Human Capital and Development*, Nova Science Publishers, New York, 2021, p. 183.

[3] International Labour Organization, *Marking progress against child labour - Global estimates and trends 2000- 2012*, International Labour Office, Geneva, 2013.

constituting around 11% of the whole child population, the most significant proportion being in the Asia and Pacific regions. In fact, millions of children face the worst forms of child labor, which includes slavery and its practices of forced labor,[4] bonded labor,[5] child soldiering,[6] and the sexual exploitation of children. Some children are even employed by adults, in illicit activities, like the trafficking of drugs. Arguably, this can be seen through the lens of the hegemony theory of Gramsci.[7]

According to Gramsci, a dominant bourgeoisie class can achieve hegemony for itself by making arrangements for substantial coordination of its interests with the interests of the subordinate classes of workers. In order to effect this concrete coordination of the two classes of interests, the dominant class must never sacrifice the actual interests of the subordinate working classes, but rather, it must to some extent realize those interests of the subordinate working classes by sacrificing some of its own bourgeoise material interests. This may not mean that working classes have any rights attached to these interests. Therefore, in the absence of becoming the most dominant force in the world of production, the dominant bourgeois class cannot maintain the material base of the economic compromise it is in charge of constructing. This development of material forces of production provides the relative base for the establishment of hegemony of a dominant class, meaning that if the workers have no rights then the bourgeoise has established for itself an inexpensive hegemony over them. In order to reproduce this hegemony continuously, the dominant class should make every effort to reproduce the existing mode of production, suggesting a continuing removal of workers' rights. However, this compromise or the concession of the dominant class to the subordinate classes has to be be made within certain

[4] According to the ILO *Forced Labour Convention, 1930 (No. 29)*, forced labour is: 'all work or service which is exacted from any person under the threat of a penalty and for which the person has not offered himself or herself voluntarily.'

[5] 'Bonded labour is when a person is forced to work to pay off a debt. They often have no idea how much money they owe. Worse, enslavers often raise this amount arbitrarily., also known as debt bondage and peonage, which happens when people give themselves into slavery as security against a loan or when they inherit a debt from a relative.'; Krishna Upadhyaya, 'Bonded Labour in South Asia: India, Nepal and Pakistan', in Christien van den Anker (ed.), *The political economy of new slavery*, Palgrave Macmillan, London, 2004, pp. 118-136, p. 120.

[6] 'A child soldier is a human being less than 18 years old, recruited by an army or simply participating in an armed conflict'; Neil Boothby, Jennifer Crawford & Jason Halperin, 'Mozambique child soldier life outcome study: Lessons learned in rehabilitation and reintegration efforts', *Global Public Health*, vol. 1, no.1, 2006, pp. 87-107, p. 90.

[7] Antonio Gramsci, *Selections from the Prison Notebooks of Antonio Gramsci*, Lawrence & Wishart, London, 1971, p. 466.

limits. Thus, the dominant class can make concessions of the economic corporate interests to the subordinate classes limited by "such a compromise cannot touch the essential" economic order.[8] If the compromise "touched the essential", the dominant class could not reproduce the existing mode of production in the world of production and in the end could not maintain the dominant position in the world of production and would lose its material base of hegemony. This can be effected by removing most workers' rights, where workers are too young to realize what is happening. Thus a hegemonic class must be able to create and to maintain an equilibrium between its own fundamental paramount interests and those of subordinate working classes such that the dominant mode of production cannot be touched and at the same time that the subordinate classes are incapable of withdrawing their consent to the rule of the hegemonic class.[9] In this regard, in this chapter, the international conventions that combat and eradicate child labor problem are analyzed. These include the Convention of Child Rights 1989 or as is commonly referred to, the CRC created by the UN and the conventions of the ILO, an agency related to the UN, with all of the above working towards age determination of children and addressing the worst forms of child labor.

Thus, the research question arises as to whether the excess of child labour in Iraq represents that kind of social engineering designed to create a long-term subaltern class of workers. Argument seeks to demonstrate that child labour becomes a hegemonic subaltern working class group.

The research is doctrinal, based on the best literary evidence available. The chapter is structured first with the main section entitled The Relevant Historical Background. The second main section is entitled Definition of child labour. The third major section is entitled Main Contributing Factors to Child Labour, which includes subsections on Poverty, Lack of Access and Poor Quality of Education, Traditional, Social and Cultural Factors, Specific Vulnerabilities, and, Demand for Child Labor. The fourth major section is entitled Impact of Child Labor, followed by a major section on Child Labor in Iraq. The final major section is on the Legal Framework, which includes sub-sections on International Conventions, The Convention on the Rights of the Child (CRC) 1989 (Article 32), Optional Protocols to the CRC on Sex Trafficking, Armed Conflict, International Labor Organization Convention No. 182 & No. 138, The ILO Minimum Age Convention 1973 (No. 138),

---

[8] ibid., p. 161.

[9] ibid., p. 120.; Hyug Baeg Im, 'Hegemony and Counter-Hegemony in Gramsci', *Asian Perspective*, vol. 15, no. 1, 1991, pp. 123-156, p. 128.

National Legislation, The Constitution of Iraq 2005, The Iraqi Labor Law No. 37 of 2015, The Law of Compulsory Education (1976), and, The Iraqi Penal Code No. 111 of 1969.

The research will arrive at the view that when the United States and its coalition forces invaded Iraq, it depleted families of their financial resources, making them completely vulnerable to economic shock. The natural consequences of this have been a national spread of child labour. Child labour refers to when children are working in any type of work that is dangerous and harmful to children's health, or, the work hinders their education. It is prevalent in the most vulnerable of families, in that those that have low income, have little margin to take care of injury or illness of adults, or to handle disruptions stemming from abandonment or divorce. Since children are most easily managed and are not as aware of their rights, child labor significantly prevents the development of children. In Iraq, children's economic exploitation has now become the norm, preventing them from going to the schools and enjoying any opportunities for social integration, suggesting that the natural consequences of the US invasion of Iraq were a long-term working class, unaware of its potential through the restrictions placed on it, to access education and to achieve social integration.

2. The Relevant Historical Background

In the past, Iraq was a country considered to have a wealthy economy, rich culture, social resources and civilization. Iraq is in Mesopotamia, the cradle of ancient human civilization, extending along the Tigris and the Euphrates rivers.[10] Its location is to the north of the Arabian Gulf and south of the Taurus mountain range, which lies parallel to the Mediterranean Sea. Iraq used to be the centre of the Islamic Empire, stretching from Morocco to the Indian Subcontinent, with Baghdad being the political and cultural centre.[11] With the Mongols' invasion in the 13th century, the country was contained until Britain granted it independence in 1932.[12]

---

10 Susan Pedersen, 'Getting Out of Iraq—in 1932: The League of Nations and the Road to Normative Statehood', *The American Historical Review,* vol. 115, no. 4, 2010, pp. 975-1000, p. 987.

11 Sam T Roweis & Lawrence K Saul, 'Nonlinear dimensionality reduction by locally linear embedding', *Science,* vol. 290, no. 5500, 2000, pp. 2323-2326, p. 2324.

12 Douglas Porch, *The other gulf war: British intervention in Iraq, 1941*, Joint Force Quarterly, Seattle, 2004, p. 134.

The Republic of Iraq covers a land area of approximately 435,052 square kilometers and occupies an important position in the Middle East, with Iran to its east, Turkey to this north, Syria and Jordan to its west and Saudi Arabia and Kuwait to its south.[13] Iraq can be described as a federal parliamentary republic, comprising 19 governorates, with an estimated population of 38.6 million, the younger demographics dominating. In fact, the median age is 21.5 and more than 55% of the population is 25 years of age or below, 40% are 14 years of age or below, having an equal gender ratio. The ratio of youth dependency is estimated to be more than 69%.[14]

Iraq used to be the top country in the so-called MENA region,[15] when it came to child raising and protection, up until around 2003. From 1968 until 2003, Iraq entered a renaissance period in child protection and the Iraqi government was active in supporting Iraqi children as the future of the nation.[16] The government had also improved its stance and policies of taking care of orphaned children, living without a breadwinner, by establishing orphan shelters in every governorate and providing private buildings, social sciences researchers and the like to protect them. Iraq had also directed campaigns towards eradicating illiteracy and was granted the United Nations Educational Scientific and Cultural Organization (UNESCO) prize for literature[17] for its efforts in creating schools for every level and providing them for free throughout the country.[18]

However, Iraq's condition took a bad turn in March 2003, when the United States and its coalition forces invaded the country, after which it became the second most unstable country of the world, as evidenced by the annual index of failed states, and is now one of the world's top 10 vulnerable countries.[19] The chaotic events in the country resulting from the invasion have devastated the socio-economic situation and infrastructure of the country, and

---

[13] ibid.

[14] Saad Jawad, *The Iraqi constitution: structural flaws and political implications*, LSE Middle East Centre, London, 2013, p. 6.

[15] MENA is an English-language acronym referring to the Middle East and North Africa. The MENA acronym is often used in academia, military planning, disaster relief, media planning as a broadcast region, and business writing; Sahbi Hidri, *English language teaching research in the Middle East and North Africa*, Springer International Publishing, Berlin, 2019, p. 98.

[16] National Media Committee for Supporting Iraq in the Netherlands, *Facts and achievements under the rule of the Arab Socialist Ba'ath Party of Iraq*, 1988.

[17] Winners of the UNESCO International Literacy Prizes, *UNESCO King Sejong Literacy Prize*, Juvenile Education, 1989.

[18] Nadje Sadig Al-Ali & Nicola Christine Pratt, *What Kind of Liberation?: Women and the Occupation of Iraq*, University of California Press, California, 2009, p. 26.

[19] BBC, *Iraq Rises Up Failed States Index*, Global Policy Forum, New York, 2017.

negatively affected the welfare and lives of the Iraqi people. Regardless of the new constitution approved in 2005, and the parliamentary elections, and the development of a new government, due to continued insurgency and violence, national development still remains low, as a result of which the majority of its population was, as at 15th June, 2015, made up of internally displaced people numbering some 4 million. From this arises the need to protect health, food, education and the fundamental necessities, since families are depleted of financial resources and are completely vulnerable to economic shock.[20]

The more important issue brought about by the instability in the country is the negative effect of war on Iraqi children's health, with the mortality rate among children under 5 showing a great increase. Iraqi children generally suffer from mental trauma as evidenced by their stress, panic and fear of death precipitated by war,[21] and compounded by the negative experiences they face in their daily lives.[22]

3. Definition of Child Labour

According to Edmonds, the term child labour refers to when children are working in any type of work that is dangerous and harmful to children's health, or, the work hinders their education.[23] For Moyi, child labour refers to low wages, long hours, physical and sexual abuse.[24] According to Pavcnik child labour is viewed as a form of child labour abuse when children work in bad conditions and hazardous occupations.[25]

The meaning of the term of child labour also varies among organizations. The ILO argues that child labour is difficult to define, because it tends to depend on the kind of job, whether the worker's age is under 18 years of age,

---

20 A Weinstein, *Iraq's Election Aftermath Reveals a Failed State*, Global Policy Forum, New York, 2017, p. 65.

21 Berti Benedetta, *Power and Interest News Report (PINR)*, ALLAFRICA, Addis Ababa, 2006, p. 88.

22 Virgil Wiebe, 'Footprints of death: Cluster bombs as indiscriminate weapons under international humanitarian law', *The Michigan Journal of International Law,* vol. 22, 2000, pp. 85-104, p. 97.

23 Eric V Edmonds, 'Does child labour decline with improving economic status?', *Journal of Human Resources,* vol. 40, no. 1, 2005, pp. 77-99, p. 77.

24 Peter Moyi, 'Child labour and school attendance in Kenya', *Educational Research and Reviews,* vol. 6, no. 1, 2011, pp. 26-35, p. 26.

25 Sara Dillon, 'Child Labour and the Global Economy: Abolition or Acceptance?', *Nordic Journal of International Law*, vol. 84, no. 2, 2015, pp. 297-322, p. 312.

and, whether the work intervenes in the child's development and education.[26] A child, according to the United Nations Convention on the Rights of the Child (CRC) 1989 refers to a person under the age of eighteen.[27] The World Bank has posited that child labour could do serious harm to a country's long-term national investment.[28] Also, according to UNICEF, the problem of child labour can generate even more negative consequences than all the concerns of investment in its relation to economic activity.[29]

Bhat stated that child labour comprised three concepts, each of which he thought were hard to define: "child", "work" and "labour". He claims that the term "childhood" can be defined by age, but in some societies, people cease to be a child at different ages, as puberty occurs at different times for different children.[30] Therefore, in article 1 of the United Nations Convention on the Rights of the Child, and also, the ILO Convention on the Worst Forms of Child Labour, 1999 (No. 182), a child is a person under the age of 18 years.[31] The definition of child labour differs among societies. For example, in Africa and Asia, they do not consider the work of a fifteen year old person to be child labour, and they view child labour as a good task that teaches children valuable work-related skills. They make a distinction between child work and child labour, child work being part of the child's training for responsible adulthood, and, child labour being exploitative.[32]

Child labour comprises the following four elements: (i) Work was done by a child. According to international conventions, regional agreements and national laws, a child is a person below the age of 18 years. Usually, the age of employment is set at an age where children are expected to have completed their primary education. The age of employment can be below the age of 18 years, as long as the conditions of work are conducive to the growth and development of the child.[33] (ii) Hazardous. Work is considered harmful if it

---

[26] *International Labour Organization Report 2004, Global Employment Trends*, ILO, Geneva, 2004.

[27] *Convention on the Rights of the Child 1999.*

[28] World Bank, *Global Child Labour Program Update*, 2003.

[29] Edward Van Daalen, & Nicolas Mabillard, 'Human rights in translation: Bolivia's law 548, working children's movements, and the global child labour regime', *The International Journal of Human Rights,* vol. 23, no. 4, 2019, pp. 596-614, p. 604.

[30] Bilal Ahmad Bhat, 'Gender, education and child labour: A sociological perspective', *Educational Research and Reviews,* vol. 5, no. 6, 2010, pp. 323-328, p. 325.

[31] *Convention on the Worst Forms of Child Labour*, 1999.

[32] FO Omokhodion, SI Omokhodion & TO Odusote, 'Perceptions of child labour among working children in Ibadan, Nigeria', *Child: Care, Health and Development,* vol. 32, no. 3, 2006, pp. 281-286, p. 284.

[33] RH Kempe, 'Child survival, poverty, and labor in Africa', *Journal of Children and Poverty,* vol. 11, no. 1, 2005, pp. 19-42, p. 25.

causes harm to the development of the child, intellectually, psychologically, sexually, emotionally, physically and mentally. Hazards include elements of the workload, hours of work, working conditions, (working tools, etc.), and the age at which the child is employed.[34] (iii) Deprives the child an opportunity for education. A child works in circumstances that either limit or completely deny them access to education, that work being considered harmful. Education is promoted as a strategy for developing children's potential, by allowing them to learn so that they can eventually break the cycle of poverty. Education is emphasized in different forums.[35] (iv) It is illegal, as an offense punishable by the criminal law. Usually, governments will enact laws stipulating the minimum age for employment. The legislation will state the minimum age for employment, it will specify that kind of work considered hazardous, and it will provide a hazards list. All actors are expected to enforce the law by not engaging in such practices and also by setting strategies and mechanisms that will support the implementation of the laws.[36]

This does not mean that children ought not work. As part of the normal socialization process, children work, but preferably under conditions of close supervision, conditions that are neither hazardous nor damaging to the child, in non-exploitative circumstances and where they are allowed to attend school, play, socialize and develop.[37] Thus, child labour is defined as work depriving a child of childhood, opportunities for learning, growth, life potential and dignity. It is essentially harmful to the child's growth. It detracts from, and is distinguished from, helping parents at home, looking after siblings or working for pocket money after school hours and during holidays.[38]

4. Main Contributing Factors to Child Labour

Child labor refers to a developmental issue, embedded in complexity because of its disparate causes in poverty, lack of education, poor quality education, cultural and social norms, tradition and socio-economic and political instability. It relates to children being forced to work due to circumstances or

---

[34] ibid.

[35] OP Narayan, *Harnessing child development: Children and the right to education*, Gyan Publishing House, New Delhi, 2005, p. 34.

[36] ibid.

[37] Christine Ward Gailey, 'Rethinking child labor in an age of capitalist restructuring', *Critique of Anthropology*, vol. 19, no. 2, 1999, pp. 115-119, p. 116.

[38] Jyotsna Tiwari, *Child abuse and human rights*, Isha Books, Delhi, 2004, p. 76.

coercive tactics, which damage their psychological, physical and emotional being and prevents them from their childhood rights.[39] Child labor is detrimental to the child and endangers the child by violating his rights as stipulated by international law and national legislation. The worst forms of child labor encompass mental, physical or social activities that are morally harmful and dangerous to children. It prevents children from accessing the available education and requires them to carry the heavy burden of schooling and work at the same time.[40] Child labor can entail child slavery, separation from families, and immersion into poverty and deprivation.[41] Slavery may be characterized as the domestication of human beings, by a master's urge to control, which was just as strong as in the subjection of wild beasts.[42]

4.1. Poverty

Poverty is one of the factors underlying child labor, and ironically, child labor is one of the top outcomes of persistent poverty. In poor households, the contribution of children to the family income is around 20-25%. Because a large proportion of the family income is spent on food, the working children's contribution is necessary for the survival of the family. In Iraq, based on recent estimates, 35% of the population subsists below the poverty line, with persistent poverty rampant in rural areas and several governorates.[43]

4.2. Lack of Access and Poor Quality of Education

In the majority of countries, basic education is not offered for free and widely available to children, so that in most cases poor families are unable to cover the education costs appropriated for uniforms, school books and materials, transportation and food. As a result, families either keep their children from

---

[39] Ben White, 'Defining the Intolerable: Child Work, Global Standards and cultural relativism', *Childhood*, vol. 6, no. 1, 1999, pp. 133-144, p. 134.

[40] G Lilienthal & JG Valan Arasu, 'Human Progress Measured by the Human Development Index: The Capabilities Approach Advocating State Protection of Freedoms', in G Lilienthal (ed.), *Human Capital and Development*, Nova Science Publishers, New York, 2021, p. 64.

[41] *United Nations Development Assistance Framework (UNDAF) for Iraq*, 2015-2019.

[42] Karl Jacoby, 'Slaves by nature? Domestic animals and human slaves', *Slavery & Abolition*, vol. 15, 1994, pp. 89-99, p. 89.

[43] *Iraq Households Socio-Economic Survey II, 2012*, CSO-World Bank, 2012. The poverty threshold was set at IQD105, 500, around US$92, per month.

going to school, or only school a few of them instead of all, with girls usually the ones left behind. Schools' availability guarantees neither the provision of quality education nor relevant content for daily realities of the poor children and their families' existence. Evidence also indicates that children born to illiterate or poorly educated mothers are more likely not to go to school, but instead opt for work.[44] The rate of literacy in Iraq is still low, particularly when it comes to female children and youth, where low rates of enrollment for intermediate and secondary education remain an issue.[45]

4.3. Traditional, Social and Cultural Factors

In some instances, children may be forced to support their parents' work, such as in the fields, and in running the household, in which cases, children become responsible at an early age, and this is transmitted from one generation to the next, supporting the trend of practices that are harmful to society.[46]

4.4. Specific Vulnerabilities

Child labor is primarily prevalent in the most vulnerable of families, in that those that have low income, have little margin to take care of injury or illness of adults, or to handle disruptions stemming from abandonment or divorce.[47] Moreover, the crises, civil conflicts, instabilities, or the effects of natural disasters lead to the displacement of populations, exemplified in Iraq in the past several years. This can function as a causal factor for child labor, where children must earn for themselves and for their families.[48]

---

44 Patricia Kariger, Edward A Frongillo, Patrice Engle, Pia M Rebello Britto, Sara M Sywulka & Purnima Menon, 'Indicators of family care for development for use in multicountry surveys', *Journal of Health, Population, and Nutrition,* vol. 30, no. 4, 2012, pp. 472-486, p. 481.

45 UNICEF, MICS, *Multiple indicator cluster survey (MICS)*, 2015.

46 Roger A Hart, *Children's participation: The theory and practice of involving young citizens in community development and environmental care*, Routledge, London, 2013, p. 54.

47 FF Furstenberg & AJ Cherlin, *Divided families: What happens to children when parents part*, Harvard University Press, Cambridge, 1991, p. 65.

48 UNICEF, *Multiple indicator cluster survey (MICS)*, 2015.

4.5. Demand for Child Labor

A key reason for the popularity of child labor is the fact that children are easily managed and are not as aware of their rights. They are less argumentative and troublesome, they are more compliant, more trustworthy and not as likely to be absent from work.[49]

5. Impact of Child Labor

Children who are caught up in child labor are prevented from enjoying and availing themselves of an important part of their childhood, in that their work prevents them from developing physically, emotionally and socially. Children are different from adults in their physiological and psychological components and they are more vulnerable and more affected by particular hazards in the workplace.[50] Added to this, owing to their mental immaturity, they are not as aware of the potential risks prevalent at work, as a result of which they are more vulnerable. They suffer from poor physical health as their work exposes them to risks of injury and illness and these may have immediate or lifelong devastating consequences. The health hazards and risks faced by children are worsened by poor access to health facilities and education, poor residence and sanitation, poor personal hygiene and insufficiently nutritious diet.[51]

Further, the vulnerability of children to physical, emotional and sexual abuse and psychological damage is attributed to their living and working environment, within which constant denigration, humiliation and oppression and heaped onto them. Working children often work in environments that exploit them, expose them to danger, degrade them and isolate them, which often leads to their employer's ill-treatment, abuse and neglect of their welfare.[52] These frequently lead to the children's difficulty in forming attachments and feelings for others, interaction and cooperation problems and issues in having a real identity and sense of belonging. Theorists suggest that

---

[49] Christiaan Grootaert & Ravi Kanbur, 'Child labour: an economic perspective', *International Labour Review*, vol. 134, 1995, pp. 134-187, p. 181.

[50] Jo Boyden, 'Childhood and the policy makers: A comparative perspective on the globalization of childhood', in Martin D Ruck, Michael Freeman, Michele Peterson-Badal (eds.), *Constructing and reconstructing childhood*, Routledge, 2015, pp. 190-229, p. 195.

[51] ibid.

[52] Paul E Mullen, JL Martin, JC Anderson, SE Romans & GP Herbison, 'The long-term impact of the physical, emotional, and sexual abuse of children: A community study', *Child Abuse & Neglect*, vol. 20, no. 1, 1996, pp. 7-21, p. 9.

attachment and care-giving behavioral systems, such as family and schools, significantly increase our chances of survival. According to attachment theory,[53] attachment is the process through which the child seeks proximity to an attachment figure so that they will receive protection, care and nurturance. A secure parent-child bond should provide protection from various threats, a safe and secure environment in which the child can openly engage, and a source of soothing when distressed. According to Bowlby, for normal emotional and social development to unfold, children need a secure relationship with their caregivers. Therefore, attachment relationships are powerful physiological and psychological regulators.[54] Otherwise, children may lose confidence and suffer from low self-esteem, suggesting generation of a future subaltern status. Therefore, child labor significantly prevents the development of children and their potential to make something of themselves in their future lives.[55]

6. Child Labor in Iraq

In Iraq, war has led to the proliferation of poverty, violence and forced displacement and in increased child labor. Based on the UNICEF 2016 report, over half a million children are forced into child labor owing to non-existent family incomes, instances of violence and displacement. After the time of this report, the number of working children continued to rise to more than 575,000 from 1990. Additionally, when ISIS[56] took over the country's northern and western areas from 2014-2016, approximately 10% of Iraqi children and more than 4 million individuals were displaced by violence. As a result, 20% of the country's schools were shut down, leaving 3.5 million children without access to education.[57]

---

[53] J Bowlby, *Attachment and Loss*, Hogarth Press, London, 1969, p. 86.

[54] ibid., p. 87

[55] Paul E Mullen, JL Martin, JC Anderson, SE Romans & GP Herbison, 'The long-term impact of the physical, emotional, and sexual abuse of children: A community study', *Child Abuse & Neglect*, vol. 20, no. 1, 1996, pp. 7-21, p. 9.

[56] ISIS is the Islamic State in Iraq and Syria and is an extremist militant group that rules by Salafi law. In Arabic, the group is also known as Daesh. An example of ISIS is the terrorist group that is known for kidnapping western journalists and aid workers as part of their tactics; Graeme Wood, 'What ISIS really wants', *The Atlantic,* vol. 315, no. 2, 2015, pp. 78-94, p. 84.

[57] UNICEF, *Reaching children in Iraq, Children are especially at risk in Iraq crisis,* UNICEF, Iraq, 2017.

Towards the middle of 2016, around 10% of the population of Iraq, accounting for 3.4 million Iraqis, was displaced because of conflict-related economic decline, with consequent strain placed on the host societies and social systems. In this regard, the parties in conflict began breaching human rights, by engaging in numerous violations against children, the rate of which has been compounded throughout the years. The traditional view of a human right is that it is both universal and held by all.

> A human right by definition is a universal moral right, something which all men, everywhere, at all times ought to have, something of which no one may be deprived without a grave affront to justice, something which is owing to every human being simply because he is human.[58]

On the basis of the report by the Iraqi Observatory for Human Rights (IOHR),[59] there are innumerable instances of child labor, particularly when it comes to displaced children, as they are forced to work to obtain the basic needs of their families. This gives rise to the employers' exploitation of children and provision of minimal wages that all play on their requirement to earn a living for themselves and their families.[60] Child labor in Iraq represents the decline in humanitarian, moral and educational attributes of the country, regardless of the possible developments and extant resources the country still possesses. Nevertheless, it is not easy to resolve the issue of child labor by merely using such resources, as evidenced by the Iraqi daily lives. The scenario is such that child labor has been on an inclining trend in the country, with the sectarian system using quotas and ethnicities to form the Iraqi government and parliament.[61]

In relation to the above, the lack of specific legislation and laws for Iraqi child protection has led to lack of reports on the official statistics, coming from the Ministries of Planning, Labor, Social Affairs or Human Rights, concerning the actual number of Iraqi children working. Despite the adoption of article

---

[58] Marie-Benedicte Dembour, 'What are human rights?', in Thomas Cushman (ed.), *Handbook of Human Rights*, Taylor & Francis, Oxford, 2011, pp. 137-145, p. 141.

[59] The Iraqi Observatory for Human Rights publishes the annual report on situation of Human rights in Iraq which covers displaced, prisoners, minorities, and children's rights, women's rights, and freedom of expression; Ahmed Khalid Al-Rawi, 'Iraqi women journalists' challenges and predicaments', *Journal of Arab & Muslim Media Research,* vol.3, no. 3, 2010, pp. 223-236, p. 226.

[60] UNICEF. *Nowhere to Go: Children in Iraq trapped in cycles of violence and poverty as conflict reaches unprecedented levels,* UNICEF, Iraq, 2017.

[61] Tatyana P Soubbotina, *Beyond economic growth: An introduction to sustainable development*, World Bank Publications, Virginia, 2004, p. 47.

(29)(3) of the Constitution of Iraq, that prohibits economic exploitation of children of all forms, the state has yet to establish the required standards of protection.[62] As such, child labor continues to rise. This may be related to the failure of the government to set up economic and health protections for unemployed children and the necessity for economic, health and educational strategies in the short term. To date, child labor is still rampant throughout Iraqi governorates. It can be divided into different fields and forms, ranging from quarries and waste dumps, where children are called 'trash children', as their work is to sift through trash for the purpose of recycling cans, aluminum and other recyclable materials.[63]

Last, children are also employed in industrial factories that are not under the Iraqi Ministries of State's purview of Child Labor. This has spread throughout society, so much so that children's economic exploitation has become the norm, preventing them from going to the schools and enjoying any opportunities for social integration. The top danger originates from the ongoing political corruption of the ruling class, through which significant numbers of children are being prevented from accessing education, which serves to perpetuate the higher illiteracy rates in the country.[64]

7. Legal Framework

Iraq has ratified major international and regional instruments, when it comes to child labor and child rights. However, further legislative measures are called for in this matter, such as the need to update the Iraqi labor law in order to set up a legal environment combating child labor. Specifically, there is a need to emphasize the major International Conventions in Iraqi national legislation to combat child labor.

7.1. International Conventions

Children have long been exploited in agriculture, manufacturing and domestic services, as well as construction, fisheries, hawking and other street-based

[62] *Constitution of Iraq* (2005).

[63] W Masoudi, 'Rights of children and youth', *The Urban Dialogue*, vol. 22, 2013, pp. 1-22, p. 9.

[64] UNICEF, *Nowhere to Go: Children in Iraq trapped in cycles of violence and poverty as conflict reaches unprecedented levels*, UNICEF, Iraq, 2017.

activities.[65] The sexual exploitation of children, the worst form of child labour, also remains a problem in the world. Trafficking of children into various forms of exploitation has become widespread in the past decade and is inextricably linked to increased migratory flows, and in recent years, a regime of fear for national security that has seen controls on migration tightened.[66] The recruitment of children as soldiers, or in other roles allied to the militia, is also of concern, as armed conflict in some countries has either continued or re-emerged.[67]

In order to both eliminate and prevent child labor, the international legal framework of conventions and international treaties seeks to protect from child exploitation and abuse, and to guarantee their access to fundamental rights like education. The international community, particularly the United Nations' specialized agencies, largely work towards establishing a strategy mapping out protection and respect for child human rights. Such a map consists of extensive lists of conventions and treaties that with ratification by the member states, will work as both guide and support towards developing national legislation. These instruments will assist governments, social partners and civil society to facilitate a suitable environment that protects and respects human rights.[68] Several major instruments underpin the national efforts of preventing and eradicating child labor and they include the UN Convention on the Rights of the Child (1989), the ILO convention No. 138 on the Minimum Age of Employment (1973), and the ILO Convention No. 182 on the Worst Forms of Child Labor (1999). Any country that is inclined to adopt effective action against child labor has to ratify the above three mentioned instruments and has to have a sufficient national legal framework to support their application.[69]

---

[65] June Kane, 'What the economic crisis means for child labour', *Global Social Policy,* vol. 9, no. 1, 2009, pp. 175-196, p. 186.

[66] RH Kempe, 'Child survival, poverty, and labor in Africa', *Journal of Children and Poverty,* vol. 11, no. 1, 2005, pp. 19-42, p. 23.

[67] Krijn Peters, Paul Richards & Koen Vlassenroot, 'What Happens to Youth During and After Wars?', *RAWOO Working Papers*, 2003, pp. 1-55, p. 21.

[68] Assefa Bequele, 'Combating child labor: contrasting views and strategies for very poor countries', *Conditions of Work Digest,* vol. 10, no. 1, 1991, pp. 1-23, p. 9.

[69] Alexandra Xanthaki, 'Multiculturalism and international law: Discussing universal standards', *Human Rights Quarterly,* vol. 32, no. 1, 2010, pp. 21-33, p. 28.

7.1.1. The Convention on the Rights of the Child (CRC) 1989 (Article 32)

The CRC 1989, article 32, addresses child labor and protects children from being exploited and exposed to hazardous labor conditions, where the worst forms of child labor are promoted for total eradication. Child labor conditions are also enhanced to be consistent with the exigencies of working children. Based on article 32, it is an imperative that children be protected from working in certain proscribed occupations and with specified workforce hazards. This article advocates intervention in the face of child labor when it comes to protecting them from abuse and exploitation and providing them with the required services of healthcare and education. The article is in two major sub-sections, with the first laying emphasis on the child's right not to be exploited and exposed to hazardous labor, and the second calling for countries' proactivity in child labor prohibition. Specifically, article 32 (1) advocates the acknowledgement of the child's rights by the parties when it comes to protection from economic exploitation and hazardous work or exposure to harm that prevents the child's physical, mental, spiritual, moral and social development.[70] The article primarily aims to protect children from being employed in particular proscribed work occupations and to protect children who are unsuitable to be employed.[71]

Economic exploitation refers to forcing an individual to work, forsaking his health and welfare, and the development of the community.[72] Nevertheless, it is difficult to explain accurately the type of labor situations from article 32 that are circumscribed by the concept of economic exploitation.[73] This is due to the ambiguity of whether the child's health and social development are at risk in a workplace because of cause harm to the child's future life.[74]

The drafting process of article 32 required the states to sign a treaty in order to be cognizant of the child's right to be free from economic exploitation,[75] the main issue being that participating states were aware of the

---

[70] ibid.

[71] Thoko Kaime, 'The Normative Framework for Children's Rights in Refugee Situations', in M Rafiqul Islam & Md Jahid Hossain Bhuiyan (eds.), *An Introduction to International Refugee Law,* Leiden, Boston, 2013, pp. 401-426, p. 418.

[72] ibid., p. 414.

[73] Hillary V Kistenbroker, 'Implementing Article 32 of the Convention on the Rights of the Child as a domestic statute: protecting children from abusive labour practices', *Case Western Reserve Journal of International Law,* vol. 44, 2011, pp. 922-953, p. 932.

[74] ibid., p. 929.

[75] Audrey R Chapman & Benjamin Carbonetti, 'Human rights protections for vulnerable and disadvantaged groups: The contributions of the UN Committee on Economic, Social and Cultural Rights', *Human Rights Quarterly,* vol. 33, no. 3, 2011, pp. 682-732, p. 690.

types of work from which children had to be protected based on their rights.[76] The right of the child to be protected from economic exploitation in performing various labor types is thus recognized.[77]

In the Iraqi context, the government had ratified the CRC in 1994, which makes the state responsible for passing legislation on child workers protection and for establishing the required measures that prevent maltreatment, minimize the occurrence of maltreatment and prevent its recurrence.[78]

7.1.2. Optional Protocols to the CRC on Sex Trafficking, Armed Conflict

On 25th May 2000, the United Nations adopted two additional protocols to the CRC, the Optional Protocol to the CRC on the Sale of Children, Child Prostitution, and Child Pornography 2000 (Sex Trafficking Protocol) and the Optional Protocol to the Convention on the Rights of the Child on the Involvement of Children in Armed Conflict (Child Soldiers Protocol). The Sex Trafficking Protocol (STP) addressed the problem of sex trafficking, one among many purposes for which children are bought and sold, including, in addition, forced labour, adoption, and participation in armed conflicts, marriage, and trade in organs.[79] The Preamble refers to achieving "the purposes of the CRC" and to the need for States Parties to implement certain specific provisions. Among them are CRC articles 34 and 35 covering broad protections against child trafficking, sexual exploitation and abuse.[80] The

---

[76] The main linguistic changes centre around the exact wording of what children should be protected from. The first draft of Article 32 acknowledged the child's right to protection from 'all forms of neglect, cruelty, and exploitation.' The first revised version changed this language to 'all forms of discrimination, social exploitation, and degradation of his dignity.' The additional discussion finally led to the Working Group's adoption of the words 'economic exploitation', as it currently reads in article 32; Hillary V Kistenbroker, 'Implementing Article 32 of the Convention on the Rights of the Child as a domestic statute: protecting children from abusive labour practices', *Case Western Reserve Journal of International Law,* vol. 44, 2011, pp. 922-953, p. 923.

[77] Vanessa R Waldref, 'The Alien Tort Statute after Sosa: A Viable Tool in the Campaign to End Child Labour', *Berkeley Journal of Employment & Labour Law,* vol. 31, 2010, pp. 160-191, p. 169.

[78] Jason Hart & Anna Kvittingen, 'Rights without borders? Learning from the institutional response to Iraqi refugee children in Jordan', *Children's Geographies,* vol. 14, no. 2, 2016, pp. 217-231, p. 223.

[79] Cris R Revaz, 'The optional protocols to the UN Convention on the Rights of the Child on Sex Trafficking and Child Soldiers', *Human Rights Brief,* vol. 9, no. 1, 2001, pp. 13-16, p. 15.

[80] *United Nations Convention on the Rights of the Child 1989*, arts. 34, 35.

Preamble also foreshadows CRC language for protecting children from economic exploitation and from performance of harmful or hazardous work.[81]

In addition, it recognizes that a number of particularly vulnerable groups, including female children, are at greater risk of sexual exploitation and are disproportionately represented among the sexually exploited, and expresses concern over "the growing availability of child pornography on the Internet and other evolving technologies."[82] The Sex Trafficking Protocol defines and prohibits the sale of children, child prostitution, and child pornography. It obliges States Parties to punish certain proscribed acts under their criminal laws. It sets out grounds for States Parties' jurisdiction over actionable practices, and strengthens their authority to extradite offenders.[83] The STP also protects and assists victimized children throughout the many states' criminal justice procedures. It proclaims the best interests of the child as the guiding principle in the judicial treatment of children.[84] For purposes of prevention and redress of offenses, the victims must have access to procedures to seek compensation for damages from those legally responsible.[85] The Sex Trafficking Protocol also has provisions on strengthening international cooperation in regard to sex trafficking involving children and on reporting requirements for States Parties.[86]

7.1.3. International Labor Organization Convention No. 182 and No. 138

This is considered to be the pre-eminent major international convention addressing child protection from the worst forms of child labor. The convention states that working conditions can be enhanced and that only children of working age can be employed. Improving the environment at work encompasses the eradication of dangerous work elements. This convention places stress on the required interventions on employed children's lives,

---

[81] Silvia Scarpa, 'Child Trafficking: International Instruments to Protect the Most Vulnerable Victims', *Family Court Review,* vol. 44, no. 3, 2006, pp. 429-447, p. 433.

[82] Jonathan Todres, 'Taking prevention seriously: Developing a comprehensive response to child trafficking and sexual exploitation', *Vanderbilt Journal of Transnational Law,* vol. 43, 2010, pp. 1-56, p. 7.

[83] S Jackson & S Scott, 'Risk anxiety and the social construction of childhood', in D Lupton (ed.), *Risk and sociocultural theory: New directions and perspectives,* Cambridge University Press, Cambridge, 1999, pp. 86-107, p. 87.

[84] Anne Gallagher, 'Human Rights and the New UN Protocols on Trafficking and Migrant Smuggling: A Preliminary Analysis', *Human Rights Quarterly,* vol. 23, no. 4, 2001, pp. 976-1004, p. 982.

[85] *Optional Protocols to the CRC on Sex Trafficking, Armed Conflict*, art. 9(4).

[86] ibid., art. 12.

protecting them against work abuse and exploitation, and providing them with relevant services of healthcare and education.

Regarding the worst forms of child labor, Convention No. 182, Recommendation No. 190 states that dangerous work for a child below 18 years old involves work that is done underwater, underground or in confined spaces, or at extreme heights, work that involves the use of hazardous machinery, tools, or manual work, or heavy work, and work in unhealthy environments that exposes children to hazardous substances, agents or processes or extreme temperatures, hazardous noise levels or vibrations.[87]

The ILO adopted the Worst Forms of Child Labour Convention in 1999 as ILO Convention No. 182. In ratifying this Convention, States must take immediate action to eliminate and prohibit the worst forms of child labour. This Convention has enjoyed the speediest rate of ratification in ILO history.[88] Convention 182 calls for urgency of action to eliminate the worst forms of child labour without jeopardizing the associated goal of effective elimination of all child labour.[89] Consequently, Convention No. 182 neither revised nor replaced Convention No. 138. Rather, it complemented it. Convention 182, article 3, described the worst forms of child labour in the following terms:

(a) all forms of slavery or practices similar to slavery, such as sale and trafficking of children, bonded and forced labour and forced recruitment in armed conflict;
(b) Commercial sexual exploitation of children, including prostitution and pornography;
(c) Children used by adults in the commission of the crime and illicit activities, including the production and trafficking of drugs;
(d) Work likely to harm the health, safety or morals of children. [90]

Thus the Convention leaves it to national governments to determine the exact types of work to be prohibited as hazardous work under item (d). This

[87] International Labour Organization, *Worst Forms of Child Labour Convention*, 1999 (No. 182).
[88] Janice R Bellace, 'ILO Declaration of Fundamental Principles and Rights at Work, the', *International Journal of Comparative Labour Law and Indus,* vol. 17, no. 3, 2001, pp. 269-287, p. 279.
[89] Mary Gray Davidson, 'The International Labour Organization's Latest Campaign to End Child Labor: Will it Succeed Where Others Have Failed', *Transnational Law & Contemporary Problems,* vol. 11, 2001, pp. 203-224, p. 213.
[90] *Worst Forms of Child Labour Convention*, 1999 (No. 182), art. 3.

should be done after consultation with employers' and workers' organizations and taking into consideration relevant international standards.[91]

From this discussion, the worst forms of child labor can be divided into two categories, namely unconditional worst labor forms, which are child labor types that are intolerable under any circumstance, such as child prostitution, child soldiers, child engagement in illegal activities and forced labor. Such activities are often illegal *per se*.[92] The second category is legal by nature but the working conditions are rife with dangerous elements, contrary to the first category, in the second category, improvements can be made in working conditions and children of age can be employed. Dangerous work elements have to be eliminated and dangerous forms of child labor have to be pinpointed and mentioned in national laws, with conditions of clarification.[93]

Further, Convention No. 138, recommendation No. 148, lays down that it is required for the states to set up strategies and schemes to make sure that the convention is effectively enforced,[94] so that, a legal framework has to be set up by national governments to set up suitable and sufficient teaching systems.

7.1.4. The ILO Minimum Age Convention 1973 (No. 138)

The ILO Minimum Age Convention 1973 (No. 138) primarily aims to set up a general instrument to address the minimum employment age, with the objective of the complete abolition of child labor.[95] Each party state is mandated to pursue a national policy designed to ensure the effective abolition of child labor and to increase the minimum employment age to a level that is aligned with the maximal physical and mental development of children.[96] The minimum employment age has to specified by parties, subject to specific exceptions laid down by the MAC. The minimum may not be lower than the age of completion of compulsory schooling, less than 15 years of age, but may be set at 14 years if the economy of the state and the educational facilities in the state are underdeveloped.[97] Added to this, there are also exceptions to the

---

[91] Antonella Invernizzi & Brian Milne, 'Are children entitled to contribute to international policy making? A critical view of children's participation in the international campaign for the elimination of child labour', *The International Journal of Children's Rights,* vol. 10, no. 4, 2002, pp. 403-431, p. 408.

[92] MFC Bourdillon, D Levison, WE Myers & B White, *Rights and wrongs of children's work*, Rutgers University Press, Camden, 2010, p. 43.

[93] ibid.

[94] International Labour Organization, *Convention No. 138 on the minimum age for admission to employment and work.*

[95] *The ILO Minimum Age Convention*, 1973 (No.138), preamble.

[96] ibid., art. 1.

[97] ibid., art. 2.

age limit if the work is light or if the child is participating in an artistic performance.[98] On the other hand, the age is generally not to be lower than 18 years if the employment is hazardous to health, safety or the morality of the young person.[99]

It is evident from the Preamble to Convention No. 138 that it is based on the assumption of the requirement for a specific legislative provision that relates to children's employment, and that such provision should cover prescribed minimum age for employment. It is also evident from the same that the Convention intends to lay down the general application to throughout the aspects of economic activity and ultimately, child labor elimination is the objective.

On the above basis, Iraq had ratified the Child Rights Convention (CRC) in 1994 and ILO Conventions No. 138 in 1985 and No. 182 in 2001.[100] Article 29 of the Iraqi constitution states the right of children to be protected against exploitation and it ensures that the State will adopt the required steps for such protection. Added to this, several constitutional articles have been dedicated to the social protection of children, their free access to education and healthcare, and the right to socio-economic welfare and freedom. The State is apparently committed to the elimination of child illiteracy. Another article that is relevant to this is article 37 of the Iraqi Constitution that lays down the prohibition against forced labor, slavery, human trafficking and commercial sexual exploitation of all children and female citizens.[101]

7.2. National Legislation

In this study, the analysis and discussion of the various pieces of Iraqi legislation relevant to child labor are critically examined.

7.2.1. The Constitution of Iraq 2005

The present Iraqi constitution was enacted by referendum on 15th October, 2015, with the Constitution being drafted by the Iraqi Constituting Drafting

---

98 ibid., arts. 7, 8.

99 ibid., art. 3(1).

100 Jason Hart & Anna Kvittingen, 'Rights without borders? Learning from the institutional response to Iraqi refugee children in Jordan', *Children's Geographies,* vol. 14, no. 2, 2016, pp. 217-231, p. 223.

101 *The Constitution of Iraq*, 2005, arts. 29, 37.

Committee in order to replace the Law of Administration for the State of Iraq for the Transitional Period.[102]

With regard to child labor, Iraqi Constitution of 2005, article 29 lays down that; 1.A) the family is the basis of society and hence, the state preserves its existence as well as its religious, moral and national values, and ensures the protection of motherhood, childhood and aging. Article 30 of the same, lays down that; 1) the state ensures individual and family, particularly children and women, social and health insurance and the fundamental needs of life in a free and dignified manner, and provides sufficient income and suitable housing, 2) the state ensures social and health insurance to the citizens of Iraq in circumstances of aging, sickness, work inabilities, homelessness, orphanhood, or unemployment and it works towards the prevention of illiteracy, fear and poverty and establishing housing and special curriculum to qualify and provide care for them as regulated by the law. Article 37 III indicated the prohibition of forced labor, slavery and slave trafficking, particularly women, children trafficking and sex trafficking.[103] Further, on the basis of the articles 29 and 30 of the Iraqi Constitution, the family is considered to be the basis of society and as such, the state works towards preserving its existence and its religious, moral and national values. The state also works towards ensuring the protection of motherhood and childhood, staving off all types of violence and abuse in the family, school and the whole society. Article 37, III mentions the right of individuals to be protected from forced labor and slavery.

Therefore, evidence exists as to imply the government's responsibility to protect the family, with the child considered as an entity that deserves such protection. The constitution is the supreme law governing the state and thus, the mentioned text is representative of the legal basis and authority to legislate a new law for protecting Iraqi children against child labor in the country. Added to this, article 30 enumerated some of the State's responsibilities towards the individual and family, specifically towards women and children, but such provisions are not enough to protect the child. Hence, it is imperative to enact child protection law under the above articles of the Iraqi constitution. In this regard, the Iraqi authority has failed to legislate a law for protection of its children, while children are being faced with the worst cases of child labor, owing to poverty, government neglect, armed conflict and several other related factors.

---

[102] Zaid Al-Ali & Philipp Dann, 'Internationalized Pouvoir Constituant-Constitution-Making under External Influence in Iraq, Sudan and East Timor', *Max Planck YBUNL*, vol. 10, no. 1, 2006, pp. 423-463, p. 433.

[103] *The Constitution of Iraq*, 2005, arts. 29, 30, 37.

7.2.2. The Iraqi Labor Law No. 37 of 2015

Under the Iraqi Labor Law and the subsequent amendments made over the years, the issue of child labor has not been comprehensively addressed. The law sets the minimum age of employment at 15 years of age. Article 1, paragraph 21, states that a child is anyone that has not yet reached 15 years of age. Article 7 stipulates that the minimum labor age in the Republic of Iraq is 15 years old, while article 9 indicates that the law prohibits all forms of forced or compulsory labor.[104] In this regard, the Iraqi law explicitly states that 15 years of age is the minimum employment age. Despite the fact that the law also establishes the conditions and assurances for children and young workers from 15 to 18 years of age, the law is not enforced effectively. On this basis, Iraqi Labor Law does not effectively address child labor, with the exception of stipulating the age of child employment. The primary issue lies in the implementation of the law and punishing violators of the law, and until then, there is no strict law that prevents child abuse in the workplace.

7.2.3. The Law of Compulsory Education (1976)

Under the Law of Compulsory Education (1976), the national legislative framework addressing child labor is supported. In particular, the Law has made it the parents' and guardians' obligation to enroll the child in primary school from the age of 6 and to make sure that the child attends school regularly until the age of 15 or until completion of thew primary school level. Failing to do so will be met with fines or prison sentences.[105] Despite this law, it is still important that the Iraqi government seek to address child labor based on a robust and extensive legislative framework in order to promote consistency in all legislations that are related to the protection and promotion of children welfare to the Constitution of 2005. Hence, among the major future changes to be explored is to increase the age of compulsory education to be consistent with the minimum employment age because failure to do so would lead to a scenario within which children under 15 years of age may have completed compulsory primary education but have not reached the least required employment age. In this situation, especially for poor families, there is a high possibility that children will be forced to contribute to the ever-growing population of child laborers. Thus, the key to creating a solid platform to eradicate child labor is through policy, legislative coherence, and alignment of the two.

---

[104] *The Iraqi Labour Law*, (no. 37) of 2015, arts. 1, 7, 9.

[105] *The Law of Compulsory Education*, 1976, Iraq.

7.2.4. The Iraqi Penal Code No. 111 of 1969

The Iraqi Penal Code, articles 381-384 states several offenses relating to childhood, care of minors, and exposure of the young and the elderly to risks and family abandonment.[106] Nevertheless, owing to the prevailing corruption and internal conflicts, the Code has continued to fail in enforcing punishments against violators of child rights.

Finally, the national legislative framework appears to be limited in its protection of children against the worst forms of child labor, in that there is a lack in Iraqi legislation of child protection laws according to the authority of the Constitution of the country. Added to this, in the face of ongoing increases in child labor, coupled with the several socio-economic, political, and security challenges, in Iraq at present, it is not surprising that the legal provisions applications, enforcement and oversight are failing, with actual child labor statistics being under-reported.

Conclusion

The research question asked whether the excess of child labour in Iraq represented that kind of social engineering designed to create a long-term subaltern class of workers. Argument has sought to demonstrate that child labour becomes a hegemonic subaltern working class group.

In the past, Iraq had been a country considered to have a wealthy economy, rich culture, social resources and civilization. Iraq used to be the top country in the so-called MENA region, when it came to child raising and protection, up until around 2003. From 1968 until 2003, Iraq entered a renaissance period in child protection and the Iraqi government was active in supporting Iraqi children as the future of the nation. However, Iraq's condition took a bad turn in March 2003, when the United States and its coalition forces invaded the country, depleting families of their financial resources and making them completely vulnerable to economic shock.

The term child labour refers to when children are working in any type of work that is dangerous and harmful to children's health, or, the work hinders their education. Child labour comprised three concepts, each of which he thought were hard to define: "child", "work" and "labour". Thus, a child works in circumstances that either limit or completely deny them access to education, that work being considered harmful. Education is promoted as a strategy for

---

[106] *The Iraqi Penal Code,* (no. 111), 1969.

developing children's potential, by allowing them to learn so that they can eventually break the cycle of poverty. Child labor can entail child slavery, separation from families, and immersion into poverty and deprivation. Slavery may be characterized as the domestication of human beings, by a master's urge to control, which was just as strong as in the subjection of wild beasts. Child labor is primarily prevalent in the most vulnerable of families, in that those that have low income, have little margin to take care of injury or illness of adults, or to handle disruptions stemming from abandonment or divorce.

It is clear that children are most easily managed and are not as aware of their rights. Attachment relationships are powerful physiological and psychological regulators. Otherwise, without such attachment, children may lose confidence and suffer from low self-esteem, suggesting the generation of a future subaltern status. Therefore, child labor significantly prevents the development of children and their potential to make something of themselves in their future lives.

A human right by definition is a universal moral right, something which all men, everywhere, at all times ought to have, something of which no one may be deprived without a grave affront to justice, something which is owing to every human being simply because he is human. In this respect, child labor is still rampant throughout Iraqi governorates. It can be divided into different fields and forms, ranging from quarries and waste dumps, where children are called 'trash children', as their work is to sift through trash for the purpose of recycling cans, aluminum and other recyclable materials. Second, children are also employed in industrial factories that are not under the Iraqi Ministries of State's purview of Child Labor. This has spread throughout society, so much so that children's economic exploitation has become the norm, preventing them from going to the schools and enjoying any opportunities for social integration.

Convention 182, article 3, described the worst forms of child labour in the following terms: (a) all forms of slavery or practices similar to slavery, such as sale and trafficking of children, bonded and forced labour and forced recruitment in armed conflict; (b) Commercial sexual exploitation of children, including prostitution and pornography; (c) Children used by adults in the commission of the crime and illicit activities, including the production and trafficking of drugs; (d) Work likely to harm the health, safety or morals of children. Clearly, breach of this article constitutes grave violations of human rights. Adding to these human rights elisions, while the Iraqi Penal Code, articles 381-384 states several offenses relating to childhood, care of minors, and exposure of the young and the elderly to risks and family abandonment,

nevertheless, owing to the prevailing corruption and internal conflicts, the Code has continued to fail in enforcing punishments against violators of child rights.

In extended synthesis, the United States and its coalition forces invaded Iraq, depleting families of their financial resources and making them completely vulnerable to economic shock. The natural consequences of this have been a national spread of child labour. Child labour refers to when children are working in any type of work that is dangerous and harmful to children's health, or, the work hinders their education. It is prevalent in the most vulnerable of families, in that those that have low income, have little margin to take care of injury or illness of adults, or to handle disruptions stemming from abandonment or divorce. Since children are most easily managed and are not as aware of their rights, child labor significantly prevents the development of children. In Iraq, children's economic exploitation has now become the norm, preventing them from going to the schools and enjoying any opportunities for social integration, suggesting that the natural consequences of the US invasion of Iraq are constituted by the creation of a long term working class, unaware of its potential, through the restrictions to access to education and social integration.

References

Abdul Wahab, H, Z Amin Ayub & Salim Ibrahim Ali, 'Child Labor in its Worst Forms as Child Slavery', in G Lilienthal (ed.), *Human Capital and Development*, Nova Science Publishers, New York, 2021.

Al-Ali, Nadje Sadig & Nicola Christine Pratt, *What Kind of Liberation?: Women and the Occupation of Iraq*, University of California Press, California, 2009.

Al-Ali, Zaid & Philipp Dann, 'Internationalized Pouvoir Constituant-Constitution-Making under External Influence in Iraq, Sudan and East Timor', *Max Planck YBUNL*, vol. 10, no. 1, 2006, pp. 423-463.

Al-Rawi, Ahmed Khalid, 'Iraqi women journalists' challenges and predicaments', *Journal of Arab & Muslim Media Research*, vol. 3, no. 3, 2010, pp. 223-236.

Baeg Im, Hyug, 'Hegemony and Counter-Hegemony in Gramsci', *Asian Perspective*, vol. 15, no. 1, 1991, pp. 123-156.

BBC, Iraq Rises Up Failed States Index, *Global Policy Forum*, New York, 2017.

Bellace, Janice R, 'The ILO Declaration of Fundamental Principles and Rights at Work', *International Journal of Comparative Labour Law and Industrial Relations*, vol. 17, no. 3, 2001, pp. 269-287.

Benedetta, Berti, *Power and Interest News Report (PINR)*, ALLAFRICA, Addis Ababa, 2006.

Bequele, Assefa, 'Combating child labor: contrasting views and strategies for very poor countries', *Conditions of Work Digest*, vol. 10, no. 1, 1991, pp. 1-23.

Bhat, Bilal Ahmad, 'Gender, education and child labour: A sociological perspective', *Educational Research and Reviews*, vol. 5, no. 6, 2010, pp. 323-328.

Boothby, Neil, Jennifer Crawford & Jason Halperin, 'Mozambique child soldier life outcome study: Lessons learned in rehabilitation and reintegration efforts', *Global Public Health,* vol. 1, no.1, 2006, pp. 87-107.

Bourdillon, MFC, D Levison, WE Myers & B White, *Rights and wrongs of children's work*, Rutgers University Press, Camden, 2010.

Bowlby, J, *Attachment and Loss*, Hogarth Press, London, 1969.

Boyden, Jo, 'Childhood and the policy makers: A comparative perspective on the globalization of childhood', in Martin D Ruck, Michael Freeman, Michele Peterson-Badal (eds.), *Constructing and Reconstructing Childhood*, Routledge, 2015, pp. 190-229.

Bureau of International Labor Affairs, *Child Labor and Forced Labor Reports - Iraq*, 2019.

Chapman, Audrey R & Benjamin Carbonetti, 'Human rights protections for vulnerable and disadvantaged groups: The contributions of the UN Committee on Economic, Social and Cultural Rights', *Human Rights Quarterly*, vol. 33, no. 3, 2011, pp. 682-732.

Constitution of Iraq (2005).

Convention on the Rights of the Child 1999.

Convention on the Worst Forms of Child Labour, 1999.

Davidson, Mary Gray, 'The International Labour Organization's Latest Campaign to End Child Labor: Will it Succeed Where Others Have Failed', *Transnational Law & Contemporary Problems*, vol. 11, 2001, pp. 203-224.

Dembour, Marie-Benedicte, 'What are human rights?', in Thomas Cushman (ed.), *Handbook of Human Rights*, Taylor & Francis, Oxford, 2011, pp. 137-145.

Dillon, Sara, 'Child Labour and the Global Economy: Abolition or Acceptance?', *Nordic Journal of International Law*, vol. 84, no. 2, 2015, pp. 297-322.

Edmonds, Eric V, 'Does child labour decline with improving economic status?', *Journal of Human Resources*, vol. 40, no. 1, 2005, pp. 77-99.

Furstenberg, FF & AJ Cherlin, *Divided families: What happens to children when parents part*, Harvard University Press, Cambridge, 1991.

Gailey, Christine Ward, 'Rethinking child labor in an age of capitalist restructuring', *Critique of Anthropology*, vol. 19, no. 2, 1999, pp. 115-119.

Gallagher, Anne, 'Human Rights and the New UN Protocols on Trafficking and Migrant Smuggling: A Preliminary Analysis', *Human Rights Quarterly*, vol. 23, no. 4, 2001, pp. 976-1004.

Gramsci, Antonio, *Selections from the Prison Notebooks of Antonio Gramsci*, Lawrence & Wishart, London, 1971.

Grootaert, Christiaan & Ravi Kanbur, 'Child labour: an economic perspective', *International Labour Review*, vol. 134, 1995, pp. 134-187.

Hart, Jason & Anna Kvittingen, 'Rights without borders? Learning from the institutional response to Iraqi refugee children in Jordan', *Children's Geographies*, vol. 14, no. 2, 2016, pp. 217-231.

Hart, Roger A, *Children's participation: The theory and practice of involving young citizens in community development and environmental care*, Routledge, London, 2013.

Hidri, Sahbi, *English language teaching research in the Middle East and North Africa*, Springer International Publishing, Berlin, 2019.

International Labour Organization Report 2004, *Global Employment Trends*, ILO, Geneva, 2004.

International Labour Organization, *Marking progress against child labour - Global estimates and trends 2000- 2012*, International Labour Office, Geneva, 2013.

International Labour Organization, *Convention No. 138 on the minimum age for admission to employment and work.*

International Labour Organization, *Worst Forms of Child Labour Convention, 1999 (No. 182).*

Invernizzi, Antonella & Brian Milne, 'Are children entitled to contribute to international policy making? A critical view of children's participation in the international campaign for the elimination of child labour', *The International Journal of Children's Rights*, vol. 10, no. 4, 2002, pp. 403-431.

Iraq Households Socio-Economic Survey II, 2012, CSO-World Bank, 2012.

Jackson, S & Scott, S, 'Risk anxiety and the social construction of childhood', in D Lupton (ed.), *Risk and sociocultural theory: New directions and perspectives,* Cambridge University Press, Cambridge, 1999, pp. 86-107.

Jacoby, Karl, 'Slaves by nature? Domestic animals and human slaves', *Slavery & Abolition*, vol. 15, 1994, pp. 89-99.

Jawad, Saad, *The Iraqi constitution: structural flaws and political implications*, LSE Middle East Centre, London, 2013.

Kaime, Thoko, 'The Normative Framework for Children's Rights in Refugee Situations', in M Rafiqul Islam & Md Jahid Hossain Bhuiyan (eds.), *An Introduction to International Refugee Law,* Leiden, Boston, 2013, pp. 401-426.

Kane, June, 'What the economic crisis means for child labour', *Global Social Policy*, vol. 9, no. 1, 2009, pp. 175-196.

Kariger, Patricia, Edward A Frongillo, Patrice Engle, Pia M Rebello Britto, Sara M Sywulka & Purnima Menon, 'Indicators of family care for development for use in multicountry surveys', *Journal of Health, Population, and Nutrition,* vol. 30, no. 4, 2012, pp. 472-486.

Kempe, RH, 'Child survival, poverty, and labor in Africa', *Journal of Children and Poverty*, vol. 11, no. 1, 2005, pp. 19-42.

Kistenbroker, Hillary V, 'Implementing Article 32 of the Convention on the Rights of the Child as a domestic statute: protecting children from abusive labour practices', *Case Western Reserve Journal of International Law*, vol. 44, 2011, pp. 922-953.

Lilienthal, G & JG Valan Arasu, 'Human Progress Measured by the Human Development Index: The Capabilities Approach Advocating State Protection of Freedoms', in G Lilienthal (ed.), *Human Capital and Development*, Nova Science Publishers, New York, 2021.

Masoudi, W, 'Rights of children and youth', *The Urban Dialogue*, vol. 22, 2013, pp. 1-22.

Moyi, Peter, 'Child labour and school attendance in Kenya', *Educational Research and Reviews*, vol. 6, no. 1, 2011, pp. 26-35.

Mullen, Paul E, JL Martin, JC Anderson, SE Romans & GP Herbison, 'The long-term impact of the physical, emotional, and sexual abuse of children: A community study', *Child Abuse & Neglect* vol. 20, no. 1, 1996, pp. 7-21.

Narayan, OP, *Harnessing child development: Children and the right to education*, Gyan Publishing House, New Delhi, 2005.

National Media Committee for Supporting Iraq in the Netherlands, *Facts and achievements under the rule of the Arab Socialist Ba'ath Party of Iraq*, 1988.

Omokhodion, FO, SI Omokhodion & TO Odusote, 'Perceptions of child labour among working children in Ibadan, Nigeria', *Child: Care, Health and Development*, vol. 32, no. 3, 2006, pp. 281-286.

Optional Protocol to the Convention on the Rights of the Child on the involvement of children in armed conflict, adopted 25 May 2000, by General Assembly resolution A/RES/54/263.

Pedersen, Susan, 'Getting Out of Iraq—in 1932: The League of Nations and the Road to Normative Statehood', *The American Historical Review*, vol. 115, no. 4, 2010, pp. 975-1000.

Peters, Krijn, Paul Richards & Koen Vlassenroot, 'What Happens to Youth During and After Wars?', *RAWOO Working Papers*, 2003, pp. 1-55.

Porch, Douglas, 'The other gulf war: British intervention in Iraq, 1941', *Joint Force Quarterly*, Seattle, 2004.

Revaz, Cris R, 'The optional protocols to the UN Convention on the Rights of the Child on Sex Trafficking and Child Soldiers', *Human Rights Brief*, vol. 9, no. 1, 2001, pp. 13-16.

Roweis, Sam T & Lawrence K Saul, 'Nonlinear dimensionality reduction by locally linear embedding', *Science*, vol. 290, no. 5500, 2000, pp. 2323-2326.

Scarpa, Silvia, 'Child Trafficking: International Instruments to Protect the Most Vulnerable Victims', *Family Court Review*, vol. 44, no. 3, 2006, pp. 429-447.

Soubbotina, Tatyana P, *Beyond economic growth: An introduction to sustainable development*, World Bank Publications, Virginia, 2004.

The Constitution of Iraq, 2005.

The ILO Minimum Age Convention, 1973 (No.138).

The Iraqi Labour Law, (no. 37) of 2015.

The Iraqi Penal Code, (no. 111), 1969.

The Law of Compulsory Education, 1976 (Iraq).

Tiwari, Jyotsna, *Child abuse and human rights*, Isha Books, Delhi, 2004.

Todres, Jonathan, 'Taking prevention seriously: Developing a comprehensive response to child trafficking and sexual exploitation', *Vanderbilt Journal of Transnational Law*, vol. 43, 2010, pp. 1-56.

UNICEF, *Multiple indicator cluster survey (MICS)*, 2015.

UNICEF, *Nowhere to Go: Children in Iraq trapped in cycles of violence and poverty as conflict reaches unprecedented levels*, UNICEF, Iraq, 2017.

UNICEF, *Reaching children in Iraq, Children are especially at risk in Iraq crisis*, UNICEF, Iraq, 2017.

United Nations Convention on the Rights of the Child 1989.

United Nations Development Assistance Framework (UNDAF) for Iraq, 2015-2019.

Upadhyaya, Krishna, 'Bonded Labour in South Asia: India, Nepal and Pakistan', in Christien van den Anker (ed.), *The political economy of new slavery*, Palgrave Macmillan, London, 2004, pp. 118-136.

Van Daalen, Edward & Nicolas Mabillard, 'Human rights in translation: Bolivia's law 548, working children's movements, and the global child labour regime', *The International Journal of Human Rights*, vol. 23, no. 4, 2019, pp. 596-614.

Waldref, Vanessa R, 'The Alien Tort Statute after Sosa: A Viable Tool in the Campaign to End Child Labour', *Berkeley Journal of Employment & Labour Law*, vol. 31, 2010, pp. 160-191.

Weinstein, A, *Iraq's Election Aftermath Reveals a Failed State*, Global Policy Forum, New York, 2017.

White, Ben, 'Defining the Intolerable: Child Work, Global Standards and cultural relativism', *Childhood*, vol. 6, no. 1, 1999, pp.133-144.

Wiebe, Virgil, 'Footprints of death: Cluster bombs as indiscriminate weapons under international humanitarian law', *The Michigan Journal of International Law*, vol. 22, 2000, pp. 85-104.

Winners of the UNESCO International Literacy Prizes, UNESCO King Sejong Literacy Prize, Juvenile Education, 1989.

Wood, Graeme, 'What ISIS really wants', *The Atlantic*, vol. 315, no. 2, 2015, pp.78-94.

World Bank Global Child Labour Program Update, 2003.

Worst Forms of Child Labour Convention, 1999 (No. 182).

Xanthaki, Alexandra, 'Multiculturalism and international law: Discussing universal standards', *Human Rights Quarterly*, vol. 32, no. 1, 2010, pp. 21-33.

Chapter 8

Coercive Moral Hazard

Gary I. Lilienthal[1,*], PhD
and Muhamad Hassan bin Ahmad[2], PhD
[1]Carrington Rand, Hong Kong SAR, Peoples Republic of China
[2]Ahmad Ibrahim Kulliyyah of Laws, International Islamic University, Kuala Lumpur, Malaysia

Abstract

Trauma induced in the workplace may arise from bullying, racism, job insecurity or poor personal boundaries. Workers often conflate workplace trauma with the development of PTSD. Workers have reported long-term impacts on their careers, such as for example altering the form of their career decisions, how they observe and perceive workplace safety, and how they interact with managers. The objective of this chapter is to investigate critically how workplace trauma through the pressures of moral hazard might affect the employment tenure of a fit and proper person. The term "moral hazard" originally carried negative connotations, suggesting fraud or some immoral behavior, but when studied by economists during the 1960s, they ignored the research inputs of fraud and immoral behavior. Economists now use the term "moral hazard" to describe inefficiencies occurring when risks are either displaced or not fully evaluated. The expression 'fit and proper' person, on its own, has no precise meaning. 'Fit and proper' persons follow from an assessment of a person's personal qualities and conduct while discharging professional responsibilities, with the central characteristics being knowledge, honesty and ability: "honesty to execute truly without malice, affection or partiality; knowledge to know what one ought duly

* Corresponding Author's Email: carrington.rand@icloud.com.

In: Regulation of the Professions in East Asia
Editors: Gary I. Lilienthal and Muhamad Hassan bin Ahmad
ISBN: 979-8-88697-409-6

to do; and the ability to execute one's office diligently." The research question arises as to how a fit and proper person's capacity to execute truly without malice, affection or partiality, and maintain the ability to execute his or her office diligently, might be adversely affected in an employment environment of moral hazard. Argument seeks to sustain the view that moral hazard in the workplace is the deliberate and capricious exploitation by an employer, exercising a perceived disciplinary power abusively, *ultra vires* the contract of employment, placing the fit and proper person in a non-impartial position to execute his or her professional tasks faithfully and diligently. The research methodology is qualitative research, with the critical literature review allowing the identification of research gaps, research questions, and finally, interview questions, whose responses are duly analyzed through a narrative analysis. The research outcomes are that when principals misrepresent the terms of the employment contract, they will likely exploit their agents towards the end of the agent's employment, as employers typically had feared agent resignation in the early stages of the agreement. A fit and proper employee could be forced to remain in a state of moral hazard until the unfair employer released him or her from the contract of employment, this force based in duties arising from judicial policies of employee subordination. These are exemplified in coercive duties to endure employer disciplinary powers. An employed fit and proper person can, in theory, be in an ever-increasing state of moral hazard.

Keywords: fraud, disciplinary power, ultra vires coercion, inefficiencies, workplace trauma, immoral behavior, moral hazard

1. Introduction

Trauma induced in the workplace may arise from bullying, racism, job insecurity or poor personal boundaries. Dr Chi-Chi Obuaya, a London-based psychiatrist, notes that workers often conflate workplace trauma with the development of Post Traumatic Stress Disorder. Workers have reported long-term impacts on their careers, such as for example altering the form of their career decisions, how they observe and perceive workplace safety, and how they interact with managers.[1] In the light of this statement of significance, the objective of this chapter is to investigate critically how workplace trauma,

[1] Lexi McMenamin, 'Why long-term workplace trauma is a real phenomenon', BBC Worklife, 20th April 2021.

through the pressures of moral hazard, might affect the employment tenure of a fit and proper person.

English insurance companies used the term "moral hazard" in the late 19th century. The term carried negative connotations, suggesting fraud or some immoral behavior, usually by the insured. 18th Century mathematicians studying decision-making used the term "moral" to mean "subjective," clouding the full ethical significance of the term.[2] Economists began to study moral hazard during the 1960s,[3] beginning with economist Kenneth Arrow,[4] whose work ignored the research inputs of fraud and immoral behavior. Economists now use the term "moral hazard" to describe inefficiencies occurring when risks are either displaced onto others, or not fully evaluated. The economists ignore the term's facets of ethics or morals. Changes in economic thought, within the medieval theological literature, had suggested the normative conceptions of moral hazard from the insurance-industry literature were developing into these positive interpretations of the economic literature.[5]

The expression 'fit and proper' person, on its own, has no precise meaning.[6] It takes its meaning from its factual context,[7] thus suggesting the term is an argument based on facts, triggering a requirement to discuss stasis theory, to examine critically the strength and character of the term.[8] 'Fit and

---

2 Allard E Dembe and Leslie I Boden, 'Moral Hazard: A Question of Morality?', *Wayback Machine New Solutions*, vol. 10, no. 3, 2000, pp. 257–279.

3 Kenneth Arrow, 'Uncertainty and the Welfare Economics of Medical Care', *The American Economic Review, vol.* 53, no. 5, 1963, pp. 941–73; Mark V Pauly, 'The economics of moral hazard: comment', *The American Economic Review, vol.* 58, *no.* 3, 1968, pp. 531–37.

4 Amy Finkelstein, Kenneth J Arrow, Jonathan Gruber, Joseph P Newhouse, Joseph E. Stiglitz, 'Moral Hazard in Health Insurance', *Columbia University Press, 2015, doi:10.7312/fink16380.*

5 D Rowell, LB Connelly (2012) "A history of the term 'moral hazard'" Journal of Risk and Insurance 79 (4), 1051–75.

6 *Australian Broadcasting Tribunal v Bond* (1990) 170 CLR 321, [380].

7 ibid.

8 Ancient Greek concepts of motion gave classical rhetoricians an abstract framework for the analysis and conduct of rational argument. Otto Alvin Loeb Dieter, 'Stasis', Speech Monographs, XVII (November 1950), pp. 345-369. The various 'grounds', on which contrary motions came to a 'rest', (stasis) were borrowed from the philosophic studies of kinesis, or, 'movements', and *metabolai*, or, 'changes in Being'. Using these ideas, rhetoricians described the 'moving apart' of opposing assertions. Stasis theory thus allowed the rhetorician to judge whether or not a conflict of wills really existed, and if so, in what ways. This paradigm allowed an anticipation of the central question to be resolved, which the Greeks called the *krinomenon*, the likely opposing accusatory and defence strategies, and consequently, how best to win the clash. David Goodwin, 'Controversiae Meta-

proper' person follows from an assessment of a person's personal qualities and conduct while discharging professional responsibilities, with the central characteristics being knowledge, honesty and ability: "honesty to execute truly without malice, affection or partiality; knowledge to know what one ought duly to do; and the ability to execute one's office diligently."[9] The idea of a fit and proper person is the same across many vocations and fields.[10] In the 1965 case of *Maxwell v Dixon*,[11] Hale J observed:

> Clearly different qualifications are needed by e.g., lawyers, transport operators, hotel keepers and land agents ... [12]

These measures have been applied, among many others, for granting broadcasting licenses,[13] customs licensing for importing drugs,[14] Air Navigation Regulations licensing.[15] Thus, "fit and proper" can be considered to be a genus, rather than a specification, suggesting decisions based on enforced alterity.

In this way, the question arises as to how a fit and proper person's capacity to execute truly without malice, affection or partiality, and maintain the ability to execute his or her office diligently, might be adversely affected in an employment environment of moral hazard. Argument seeks to sustain the view that moral hazard in the workplace is the deliberate and capricious exploitation by an employer, exercising a perceived disciplinary power abusively, *ultra vires* the contract of employment, placing the fit and proper person in a non-impartial position to execute his or her professional tasks faithfully and diligently.

The critical literature review methodology is doctrinal, basing its syntheses on the available and most relevant evidence. The research methodology for the entire chapter, based as it is on the critical literature review, is qualitative research. The critical literature review allows the identification of research gaps, research questions, and finally, interview

---

Asystatae and the New Rhetoric', *Rhetoric Society Quarterly*, vol. 19, no. 3, 1989, pp. 205-216, p. 205.

[9] *Hughes and Vale Pty Ltd v State of NSW (No 2)* (1955) 93 CLR 127, [156].

[10] ibid.

[11] [1965] WAR 167, [169].

[12] *Maxwell v Dixon* [1965] WAR 167, [169]; Nathalie Ng, 'Fitness and Propriety, Spent Convictions and Technology: Lessons from ASIC Investigations', *Australian Institute of Administrative Law Forum*, vol. 92, 2018, pp. 1-112, p. 71.

[13] *Australian Broadcasting Tribunal v Bond* (1990) 170 CLR 321.

[14] *Re Dowling and Secretary to Department of Health* [1985] AATA 237; (1985) 8 ALD 171.

[15] *Re Taylor and Department of Transport* [1978] AATA 64; (1978) 1 ALD 312.

questions, whose responses are duly analyzed through a narrative analysis. Interviewees were selected for their serving functions either as human resources officers or fit and proper persons practicing consultations within the field.

The structure of the critical literature review has three body sections. The first is entitled 'Use and Abuse of Authority: A Behavioral Foundation of the Employment Relation', also covering: The Experiments of Bartling, Schmidt and Fehr; and, Coase and Marx. The second is entitled 'Uncertain Junctures between Employment and Contract Law'. The third is entitled 'The Elective and Automatic Theories of Termination in the Common Law of the Contract of Employment: Conundrum Resolved?', also covering: *Geys* in Context; and, Doctrinal Effect of *Geys*.

The research outcome will likely sustain the views that when principals misrepresent the terms of the employment contract, they will likely exploit their agents towards the end of the agent's employment, as employers typically had feared agent resignation in the early stages of the agreement. A fit and proper employee could be forced to remain in a state of moral hazard until the unfair employer released him or her from the contract of employment, this force based in duties arising from judicial policies of employee subordination. These are exemplified in duties to endure employer disciplinary powers, the coercive of which could affect employee diligence and faith. An employed fit and proper person can, in theory, be in an ever-increasing state of moral hazard.

2. Use and Abuse of Authority: A Behavioral Foundation of the Employment Relation

2.1. The Experiments of Bartling, Schmidt and Fehr

This initial discussion investigates the viability of employment contracts under the so-called employer moral hazard problem. A principal will typically decide to offer an agent either an employment contract or a sales contract. The sales contract determines the work the agent executes before the later uncertain state of its outcome. Although this assigned fixed task could be inefficient in the end, at least the agent can assess its exact cost when deciding whether he or she ought to accept the contract's offer, different tasks having different agent costs. However, the employment contract is more adaptable,

for the principal, giving the principal authority to make the task assignment when the entire state of affairs is already fully ascertained. Since the agent must decide whether or not to accept the contract, before knowing which task will be assigned, the employment contract affords the principal an opportunity to exploit the agent after acceptance, exploitation indicating moral hazard. The principal can demand the agent execute a most profitable task, even when it is very inefficient and expensive for the agent. This is in accordance with many countries' legal situation, where the employer has the right to tell employees what to do within the boundaries of local municipal labor law.[16]

The moral hazard investigation by Bartling et al. was conducted in two main treatments,[17] with a finite number of periods, one with fixed identification numbers and the other with random identification numbers. The random identification numbers treatment only allowed for one-time connections. The fixed identification numbers treatment allowed research subjects to develop long-term relationships, because they could identify each other across the various periods.[18] Thus, the agent can determine that the contract of employment came from a principal who had not abused power in a prior interaction regulated by such an employment contract,[19] implying that agents must determine the principal's bona fides before contract execution.

Were all the subjects both self-interested and rational, the employment contracts with random identification numbers would not be viable because these principals would always be exploitative. Rational agents would anticipate this outcome and only accept those employment contracts offering wages high enough to compensate for the exploitative task. However, this kind of task is inefficient, so that it is not worth it for principals to offer these wages.

---

[16] In Germany, for example, the employer's authority to give directives ("Weisungsrecht") is stipulated in §106 of the *German Industrial Code* ("Gewerbeordnung") : "The employer can determine the content, place, and time of job performance more precisely in equitable discretion unless the conditions of employment are determined by the labor contract, provisions of a company agreement, an applicable collective labor agreement, or legal provisions."

[17] Björn Bartling, Klaus M Schmidt and Ernst Fehr, 'Use and Abuse of Authority: A Behavioral Foundation of the Employment Relation', *Journal of the European Economic Association*, vol. 11, no. 4, 2013, pp. 711-742.

[18] ibid., p. 712.

[19] We call the imposition of the most profitable yet inefficient task in the employment contract an "abuse of power" or "exploitative" because the principals had to announce with their contract offer which task they intend to assign in each state of the world, but these announcements were not binding. The principals announced that they would not impose the most profitable yet very costly task on their agents in 98.2% of all employment contract offers. Thus, apart from imposing very high costs on the agents, the imposition of this task also represents the break of an announced intention in almost all cases.

Further, principals will not offer employment contracts for the fixed identification numbers treatment, because both parties can only interact for a small number of periods. Some models of social preferencing foresee that some principals remain fair-minded, refraining from exploiting the agents, even in the case of the treatment with random identification numbers.[20] The very subsistence of fair-minded principals suggests that even the self-interested principals, in the treatment with fixed identification numbers, had initially refrained from any abuses of power. This was to appear fair to establish a profitable long-lived relationship of employment. These specious principals will most usually begin exploiting their agents towards the end of the agent's tenure.[21]

The research outcomes found that power abuse in employment contracts is quite frequent in the treatment with random identification numbers. In this cohort, principals demanded their most profitable and least efficient task in about half the cases. However, employers treated agents fairly in the remaining half of the cases, demanding the efficient task from agents and sharing with them the benefits of efficiency of the employment contract. Both the self-interested and the fair principals had a large preference for deploying the employment contract. The selfish principals preferred it because they could make higher profits at the agent's cost, and fair principals preferred it because they benefitted from the more efficient task. Thus, the incidence of employment contracts was very high at the start, because agents were induced to trust the principals' pre-contractual representations. From the relatively high rate of abuse of power, agents experienced a high degree of uncertainty and earned far less than for engagements under sales contracts. Agents thus resisted engagement under employment contracts, eventually leading to a preponderance of sales contracts, with the ratio of employment contracts to sales contracts settling at around 40%.[22]

The reason why employment contracts did not completely vanish in the treatment with random identification numbers is that the percentage of fair principals was high enough to maintain viability. This proposition was the subject of a control treatment using random IDs, where employment contracts

---

20 Matthew Rabin, 'Incorporating Fairness into Game Theory and Economics', *American Economic Review*, vol. 83, 1993, pp. 1281-1302; Ernst Fehr and Klaus M Schmidt, 'A Theory of Fairness, Competition, and Cooperation', *Quarterly Journal of Economics*, vol. 114, 1999, pp. 817-868, p. 850.

21 Björn Bartling, Klaus M Schmidt and Ernst Fehr, 'Use and Abuse of Authority: A Behavioral Foundation of the Employment Relation', *Journal of the European Economic Association*, vol. 11, no. 4, 2013, pp. 711-742, p. 712.

22 ibid., p. 713.

were designed so that the principal was compelled to impose the most profitable but least efficient task on the agent, in 80% of instances. This treatment was called "unfair," because the agent knew he would mostly be treated unfairly if he accepted the employment contract. In this treatment, the proportion of employment contracts went down to very low levels.[23]

These facts diverge from the data pattern of the treatment with fixed identification numbers, where more than 80% executed contracts of employment, greater than in the treatment with random identification numbers. Just as in the treatment with random identification numbers, employers displayed a preference for employment contracts in the treatment with fixed identification numbers, with fewer principals abusing their power. These employers shared the returns with the agents, such that both principal and agent preferred the employment contract.[24]

The reason why principals abused their power less often in the treatment with fixed identification numbers was the agents' threat of terminating the employment. This disciplined the principals to perceive the likelihood of a large loss in the principal's future profits. Therefore, principals were interested in establishing a non-abusive relationship with agents, turning the employment contract into a long-term mutually beneficial relationship.[25]

2.2. Coase and Marx

Coase described the firm as a system within which power and subordination prevailed. In his 1937 work, he stated:

> If a workman moves from department Y to department X, he does not go because of a change in relative prices, but because he is ordered to do so.[26] [...] It is important to note the character of the contract into which a factor enters that is employed within a firm. The contract is one whereby the factor [...] agrees to obey the directions within certain limits. The essence of the contract is that it should only state the limits of the power of the entrepreneur. Within these limits, he can therefore direct the other factors of production.[27]

---

[23] ibid., p. 714.
[24] ibid.
[25] ibid.
[26] Ronald Coase, 'The Nature of the Firm', *Econometrica*, vol. 4, 1937, pp. 386-405, p. 387.
[27] ibid., p. 391.

Alchian and Demsetz questioned this perspective of the firm:

> It is common to see the firm characterized by the power to settle issues by fiat, by authority, or by disciplinary action superior to that available in the conventional market. This is delusion. [...] [The firm] has no power of fiat, no authority, no disciplinary action any different in the slightest degree from ordinary market contracting between any two people. [...] What then is the content of the presumed power to manage and assign workers to various tasks? Exactly the same as one little consumer's power to manage and assign his grocer to various tasks.[28]

Rather than substituting the price mechanism with a system of subordination and power, Alchian and Demsetz described the essential characteristic of usage of inputs and the centralized positioning of one party in an agreed contractual arrangement for all inputs.[29] Although there may be important roles for team production and a centralized observer in the firm, Alchian and Demsetz posited the argument that the firm's authority was no different from the small consumer's power to allot to his grocer various tasks. The employer is, in general, legally permitted to give binding instructions to workers, that must be followed, whereas the grocer rarely executes a contract obliging him or her to obey the small consumer's assignments of tasks, except of course in the case of the statutorily implied sale of goods contract,[30] or customers' collective product and service demands. The relationship between the small consumer and the grocer is grounded in a sales contract, importing all the warranties implied by hundreds of years of development of the law, so that a specific product is exchanged for an agreed price, in accordance with old sale of goods maxims.

> . . . the maxim, at law is, *caveat emptor*: let the buyer take care and inquire. If he is told falsehoods, then he has a right of action; but if he makes no inquiries, at law he has no remedy, though he may in equity. This is the distinction between fraud in the legal and equitable sense, though even in

---

28 Armen Alchian and Harold Demsetz, 'Production, Information Costs, and Economic Organization', *American Economic Review*, vol. 62, 1972, pp. 777-795, p. 777; Björn Bartling, Klaus M Schmidt and Ernst Fehr, 'Use and Abuse of Authority: A Behavioral Foundation of the Employment Relation', *Journal of the European Economic Association*, vol. 11, no. 4, 2013, pp. 711-742, p. 735.

29 Ronald Coase, 'The Nature of the Firm', *Economica*, vol. 4, 1937, pp. 386-405; Herbert Simon, 'A Formal Theory of the Employment Relationship', *Econometrica*, vol. 19, 1951, pp. 293-305.

30 Sale of Goods Acts in the various jurisdictions.

> equity there is no fraud in mere non-disclosure unless there is a duty to disclose, which there is not if the parties are in a position of equality in the transaction – that is, of equal knowledge and means of knowledge; and the doctrine of equitable fraud would only apply to matters in the knowledge only of the vendor, which he ought to disclose to the vendee.[31]

Thus, by way of further example of an ancient regulatory source, Fitzherbert's *Natura Brevium* referred to a the writ of deceit, as applicable, in the times of Henry VI and Elizabeth I, to the specific instance of sale of cloth, as follows.

> If a man sell cloths, and warrant them of a certain length, if they be not of such length, he who bought them shall have a writ of deceit against him upon his warranty, although the warranty be only by word. But if the warranty be made at another time after the bargain made, then it ought to be in writing, otherwise he shall not have an action upon that warranty, for he shall not have an action of deceit therefore, if the warranty be not made upon the bargain and at the time of the bargain.[32]

However, the relationship between the employer and the worker is grounded in a contract of employment that creates in the employer a right to assign tasks to the employee. Thus, the grocer faces no moral hazard, but rather, a public regulatory hazard, because the little consumer cannot assign to him or her an abusive task, whereas the agent in an employment contract does face this risk.

Due to the states of the world being unpredictable, legal norms and third party enforcement cannot resolve the inevitable moral hazard problems, although, it is always possible to discipline the employer during continuing exchanges. Some theoretical contributions,[33] as well as the evidence in other research,[34] suggest that enforcement of contracts, within the firm, where there

---

[31] WF Finlayson, *A Report of the Case of The Queen v Gurney and Others in the Court of Queens Bench: The Summing Up revised by the Lord Chief Justice with an Introduction Containing a History of the Case and an Examination of the Cases at Law and Equity applicable to it; or Illustrating the Doctrine of Commercial Fraud*, Stevens and Haynes, London, 1870.

[32] Anthony Fitzherbert, *The New Natura Brevium of the Most Reverend Judge Mr Anthony Fitz-Herbert*, Savoy, 6th edn., London, 1718, p. 217.

[33] W Bentley MacLeod and James M Malcomson, 'Implicit Contract, Incentive Compatibility, and Involuntary Unemployment', *Econometrica*, vol. 57, 1989, pp. 447-480; W Bentley MacLeod and James M Malcomson, 'Motivation and Markets', *American Economic Review*, vol. 88, 1989, pp. 388-402.

[34] Martin Brown, Armin Falk and Ernst Fehr, 'Relational Contracts and the Nature of Market Interactions', *Econometrica*, vol. 72, 2004, pp.747-780; Martin Brown, Armin Falk and

are moral hazard problems, infers a pervasive existence of rents. Therefore, breaking-up an employment relationship generally causes substantial costs for the parties, suggesting that both parties could have an interest in continuing their relationship.[35]

The experimental design and the data showed that the employment contract was the dominant and most efficient mode of governance, provided that reputation incentives disciplined employers and created long-term relationships. Considering the "Marxian" characterization of the firm,[36] the firm is a hierarchical system, under both Marxian and the Coasian views, where only the employers have the power to allocate resources within their firm. Whereas the Marxian view holds the firm's power and hierarchy to be a tool for exploiting workers, the Coasian view holds that these tools are deployed only for efficient allocations of resources within the firm. The Coasian view is that capricious decisions, based on power, is an allocation mechanism more efficient than price mechanisms, and is the raison-d'etre for firms' existence. The research confirms the Coasian view that lower transaction costs for an employment contract cause the viability of employment contracts. Thus, firms exist because they cause lower transaction costs. Despite this, the Marxian view that power is used for exploitation must be real, as many employees are abused in conditions where employers cannot or will not treat employees fairly. In such circumstances, employment contracts are used for exploitation. This employment contract tool only applies in the treatment with random identification numbers, because of the existence of fair-minded employers. Without such fair-minded employers, agents do not agree to employment contracts. Purely selfish employers always abuse the agents under employment contracts, causing workers to resist accepting employment contracts under such conditions. Therefore, reputational disciplinary mechanisms are not always enough to resolve the moral hazard problem.[37]

Ernst Fehr, 'Competition and Relational Contracts - The Role of Unemployment as a Disciplinary Device', *Journal of the European Economic Association*, vol. 10, 2012, pp. 887-907.

[35] Björn Bartling, Klaus M Schmidt and Ernst Fehr, 'Use and Abuse of Authority: A Behavioral Foundation of the Employment Relation', *Journal of the European Economic Association*, vol. 11, no. 4, 2013, pp. 711-742, p. 736.

[36] Stephen Alan Marglin, 'What Do Bosses Do?', *Review of Radical Political Economics*, vol. 6, 1974, pp. 60-112; Stephen Alan Marglin, 'What Do Bosses Do? Part II', *Review of Radical Political Economics*, vol. 7, 1975, pp. 20-37.

[37] It is tempting to relate the resistance against employment contracts in the treatment with random identification numbers to the historical evidence on workers' strong distaste to factory work during the early phase of the industrial revolution. Factory work during this

3. Uncertain Junctures between Employment and Contract Law

Although the common law of contract is a key basis for employment law, the irregular nature of the employment relationship makes this contract theory a discordant explanation for the employment relationship. In the 2012 case of *Geys v Societe Generale*,[38] (‘*Geys*’), the United Kingdom Supreme Court had to reconcile general contract principles with the rules of contracts of employment, by deciding whether the "automatic" or "elective" principles of termination of contract applied to employment contracts, resolving an old judicial dialectic in employment law.[39]

Geys[40] was an appeal by a former banker. He had been summarily dismissed by the Bank on 29th November 2007, the Bank having breached the terms of his contract of employment. Later, the Bank deposited a payment in lieu of notice into Geys's bank account, however it only notified him of the purpose of this payment in writing later, and received on 6th January 2008. If this summary dismissal was effective, Geys’s termination payment should have been approximately €5.5 million less than for a dismissal effective on 6th January 2008. The court held, with Lord Sumption in dissent, that Geys was indeed dismissed on 6th January 2008, allowing the appeal, and implying the higher termination payment.

The Supreme Court was tasked with dealing with these four questions:

> (1) whether repudiation of a contract of employment by an express and immediate dismissal automatically terminates the contract or whether the repudiation must be accepted by the other party before the contract is terminated ("the repudiation issue"); (2) when Mr. Geys's contract of employment was terminated ("the termination issue"); (3) whether there was any conflict between a contractual term allowing termination on three

time was characterized by unconstrained rights to determine working conditions, fines, and other disciplinary corporal punishment). Thus, "the very recruitment to the uncongenial work was difficult, worse by the deliberate or accidental modelling of many works on workhouses and known to the working population." Sidney Pollard, ‘Factory Discipline in the Industrial Revolution’, *The Economic History Review*, vol. 16, 1963, pp. 254-271, p. 254; Björn Bartling, Klaus M Schmidt and Ernst Fehr, ‘Use and Abuse of Authority: A Behavioral Foundation of the Employment Relation’, *Journal of the European Economic Association*, vol. 11, no. 4, 2013, pp. 711-742, p. 737.

[38] [2012] UKSC 63 (*Geys*).

[39] Alysia Blackham, ‘Uncertain Junctures between Employment and Contract Law’, *The Cambridge Law Journal*, vol. 72, no. 2, 2013, pp. 269-273, p. 269.

[40] [2012] UKSC 63 (*Geys*).

months' notice and an employee handbook provision allowing for immediate termination with a payment in lieu of notice (the majority of the court found there was not); and (4) whether Mr. Geys was entitled to maintain a claim for damages and breach of contract despite a contractual requirement for him to enter into a "termination agreement" waiving those rights (the majority found he was).[41]

For question (1), the court had to choose between the "automatic" and "elective" principles of contractual repudiation, as they might apply to employment contracts. In the automatic theory, contract repudiation caused automatic contract termination. In the elective theory, the repudiation would terminate the contract only when the other party elected to confirm the repudiation. Lord Wilson, speaking with the agreement of the majority of the court, spurned turning "basic principles of the law of contract upon their head," by adopting the principle of automatic termination within the employment relationship.[42] He preferred the elective theory. With this majority judgment, a repudiated contract of employment would only be terminated when the other party exercised an election to confirm the repudiation, implying that a fit and proper employee could remain in a state of moral hazard until the unfair employer released him or her from the contract of employment. It was on this point that Lord Sumption dissented. As Lord Carnwath had noted, Lords Sumption and Wilson had articulated the same judicial precedents to create equally persuasive, but diametrically opposed, historiographical analyses of the state of the law.[43] Lord Wilson opined that the elective theory better justified and explained prior judgments, and as well, was more fully consistent with entrenched precepts of contract and employment law.[44] However, Lord Sumption's view was that the automatic theory was a settled rule based on "the weight of [judicial] authority."[45] In Lord Hope's balancing view, "[the] fact has to be faced that there is still a degree of oscillation between the two theories," inferring that the court must make a decision grounded in whichever of the two theories was more "desirable."[46] Nevertheless, Lords Wilson and Sumption remained similarly divided on the merits of the automatic and

---

41 Alysia Blackham, 'Uncertain Junctures between Employment and Contract Law', *The Cambridge Law Journal*, vol. 72, no. 2, 2013, pp. 269-273, p. 270.
42 [2012] UKSC 63, at 66.
43 ibid., at 99.
44 Alysia Blackham, 'Uncertain Junctures between Employment and Contract Law', *The Cambridge Law Journal*, vol. 72, no. 2, 2013, pp. 269-273, p. 270.
45 [2012] UKSC 63, at 139.
46 ibid., at 17.

elective precepts. Lord Wilson held that the automatic theory would "reward the wrongful repudiator ... with a date of termination which he [sic] has chosen," most likely disadvantaging the innocent other party.[47] Lord Sumption articulated some practical issues surrounding the elective theory, such that an employment contract enduring without any obligation to work or pay wages, was "dead for all practical purposes," and could "[limp] on as a formal 'shell' or husk,'" for an indeterminate period.[48] This raised issues as to when the subsisting contract could finally be terminated. Nonetheless, as employment contracts could not endure wherever a party retained "no legitimate interest, financial or otherwise, in performing the contract rather than claiming damages,"[49] the elective theory would only permit employment contracts to subsist where some substantive contractual term remained to be enforced. This only ostensibly reduced Lord Sumption's view to minimal practical import, as a fit and proper employee might still be under a duty to advise the employer.

Also, Lords Wilson and Sumption appeared to disagree fundamentally on the law of repudiation. Lord Sumption cited the general contractual rule that an innocent party could not regard a repudiated contract as subsisting unless (i) they could execute remaining contractual obligations without the other party's cooperation; or (ii) they could force the other party's cooperation by an order in specific performance. Since employment contracts were generally not susceptible to orders in specific performance, it would be impossible for a party to treat the repudiated employment contract as subsisting, if it required the other party's cooperation, and thus, Lord Sumption's view was it would be without meaning for the other party to accept repudiation before the contract could be terminated. Lord Wilson characterized Lord Sumption's reasoning as a "jump from the absence of some remedies to the absence of all rights, heedless in particular of contractual rights other than to payment of wages or salary."[50] It is arguable, as a zero-sum argument, that Lord Sumption's reasoning failed to apportion sufficient weight to the contractual character of the relationship of employment, which still "remains at the core" of modern labour law, and instead, conceiving of employment in terms of status,[51]

---

47 ibid., at 66.
48 ibid., at 110.
49 *White and Carter (Councils) Ltd. v McGregor* [1962] A.C. 413, at 431, per Lord Reid.
50 [2012] UKSC 63, at 89; Alysia Blackham, 'Uncertain Junctures between Employment and Contract Law', *The Cambridge Law Journal*, vol. 72, no. 2, 2013, pp. 269-273, p. 271.
51 Simon F Deakin and Frank Wilkinson, *The Law of the Labour Market: Industrialization, Employment and Legal Evolution*, Oxford University Press, Oxford, 2005, at p. 108.

suggesting status-like employee duties based on their continuing subordination.

Despite this strong disagreement as between Lords Wilson and Sumption, the Supreme Court majority had now endorsed the elective theory as preferred in contracts of employment, even including in cases of wrongful dismissal. Despite this outcome, the Supreme Court had not adopted a workable form of the elective theory, as their decision would make it no easier to obtain any equitable remedy to maintain in operation a repudiated contract of employment.[52]

In relation to the court's question (2), which was the termination issue, Lady Hale, agreed with the majority of the court, and held that a term ought to be implied as a necessary incident to the relationship of employment that the parties should provide notice to each other, in "clear and unambiguous terms," when one party exercised a right to terminate the contract, and the party exercising its right should specify when and how the right was calculated to operate.[53] Although a "wise employer" would most often provide such written notice, it was unnecessary unless agreed in the contract itself.[54] In this way, the Bank's conduct was held to be "not good enough," as it failed to provide clear notice to Geys, until 6th January 2008, of its exercise of the right to terminate pursuant to the payment in lieu of notice provision.[55] The court's majority very readily created a new implied term into employment contracts in respect of the issue of termination. Lady Hale noted that her formulation reflected "general requirements applicable to notices of all kinds, and there is every reason why they should also be applicable to employment contracts."[56] Thus, the quick use of implied terms for instrumental ends may signal the likely character of the future development of employment law. Lord Sumption displayed little sympathy for Geys, calling him a "lucky man,"[57] who was to receive "a windfall amounting to several million euros" as a result of the Bank's failure to follow proper processes of termination.[58] The court's decision could also benefit other cohorts of employees, such as with final pensions,

---

[52] David Cabrelli and Rebecca Zahn, 'The Elective and Automatic Theories of Termination at Common Law: Resolving the Conundrum?', *Industrial Law Journal*, vol. 41, no. 3, 2012, pp. 346–357, p. 356.

[53] [2012] UKSC 63, at 57.

[54] ibid., at 60.

[55] ibid., at 59.

[56] ibid., at 57.

[57] ibid., at 108.

[58] ibid., at 110.

holiday pay, or a salary increases.[59] It is unclear whether employees of lower status may be beneficiaries of these legal developments.[60]

4. The Elective and Automatic Theories of Termination in the Common Law of the Contract of Employment: Conundrum Resolved?

4.1. *Geys* in Context

The Supreme Court's embrace of the elective theory in *Geys*[61] derived from a line of recent cases, which dealt with the common law of the employment contract. They were the 2010 case of *Gisda Cyf v Barratt*,[62] (*Gisda Cyf*), the 2011 case of *Autoclenz v Belcher*,[63] (Autoclenz) and the 2012 case of *Edwards v Chesteifield Royal Hospital NHS Trust*,[64] (*Edwards*). Taken together with *Geys*,[65] this caselaw could be analyzed on the bases of whether the Supreme Court: (i) embraced contractual orthodoxy; or, (ii) preferred labour community majority interests over the so-called minority managerial prerogatives.[66]

In *Geys*,[67] the Supreme Court applied contract law principles to contracts of employment, suggesting that the courts wanted to ensure that the employment contract was just the same as any other contract.[68] Thus, Lord Wilson remarked on the absurdity of suggesting that a gap should be opened in contract law, by adopting the automatic theory of termination in the common law contract of employment.[69] To the contrary, as Bogg had argued,[70]

---

[59] ibid., at 64.

[60] Alysia Blackham, 'Uncertain Junctures between Employment and Contract Law', *The Cambridge Law Journal*, vol. 72, no. 2, 2013, pp. 269-273, pp. 272, 273.

[61] [2012] UKSC 63.

[62] [2010] 4 All ER 851.

[63] [2011] 4 All ER 745.

[64] [2012] 2 AC 22.

[65] [2012] UKSC 63.

[66] G. Lilienthal, 'Business Goodwill: Relationships of Production, Legal Superstructures and an Administrative Prerogative Act Developed in United Kingdom Ideology and Case Law', *Commonwealth Law Bulletin*, vol. 45, no. 1, 2019, pp. 92-114; G Lilienthal, 'The Managerial Prerogative: A Meta-Legal Policy Analysis', *IBIMA*, vol. 28, no. 1, 2016.

[67] [2012] UKSC 63.

[68] David Cabrelli and Rebecca Zahn, 'The Elective and Automatic Theories of Termination in the Common Law of the Contract of Employment: Conundrum Resolved?', *The Modern Law Review*, vol. 76, no. 6, 2013, pp. 1106-1119, p. 1113.

[69] [2013] 2 WLR 50, 84F.

[70] A Bogg, 'Sham Self-Employment in the Supreme Court', *Industrial Law Journal*, vol. 41, 2012, pp. 331-332, p. 328.

a mere rationalizing of the court's mind-set as predominantly concerned with unity in contract law and denying any doctrinal autonomy in the common law of employment contracts would now be incorrect. In *Gisda Cyf*,[71] and in *Edwards*,[72] the Supreme Court diverged from orthodox contract law doctrine, in response to certain specifics of the employment relationship. In *Gisda Cyf*,[73] the Supreme Court held that, when an employer accepted an employee's repudiatory breach and then summarily dismissed the employee, the date of termination for purposes of statutory unfair dismissal provisions in Part X of the Employment Rights Act 1996 (ERA),[74] was only when the employee had read the notice, or else, had a reasonable opportunity to read it. This is unlike the general law of contract, where termination occurred when the employer had done everything reasonable to communicate the termination decision to confirm the employee's contract repudiation.[75]

Similarly, the *Edwards*[76] case concerned employee remedies available when management breached an express term of the contract of employment concerning disciplinary procedure.[77] The Supreme Court held that the employee could not recover damages for a breach of this term, as the matter concerned the manner of dismissal. Instead, the 'curious'[78] outcome was that injunction was the main remedy for enforcing a contractually agreed disciplinary procedure, suggesting that employer disciplinary powers were either pursuant to rights without remedies in the common law, or else were mere prerogatives without any basis in law. Thus, the court would create exceptions for the employment contract in some circumstances. Sometimes this has been done to reflect the character of the employment contract,[79] and in some other cases, it has been done to avoid undermining the employment

[71] [2010] 4 All ER 851,

[72] [2011] UKSC 58.

[73] [2010] 4 All ER 851.

[74] *Employment Rights Act 1996* (UK), part X.

[75] J Prassl, 'Interpreting Employment Protective Legislation: *Gisda Cyf v Barratt*', *Industrial Law Journal*, vol. 40, no. 1, 2011, pp. 103-107, p. 103.

[76] [2011] UKSC 58.

[77] H Collins, 'Compensation for Dismissal: In Search of Principle', *Industrial Law Journal*, vol. 41, no. 2, 2012, pp. 208-227; K Costello, '*Edwards v Chesterfield Royal Hospital* - Parliamentary Intention and Damages Caused by Maladministration of a Contractual Dismissal Procedure', *Modern Law Review*, vol. 76, no. 1, 2013, pp. 134-145.

[78] [2012] 2 AC 22, 71A, per Lord Kerr.

[79] *Autoclenz Ltd v Belcher* [2011] UKSC 41; *Edwards v Chesterfield Royal Hospital NHS Foundation Trust* [2011] UKSC 58.

protection legislation.[80] However, *Gisda Cyf*[81] and *Edwards*[82] could be contrasted with *Autoclenz*,[83] in which the Supreme Court adapted the common law 'sham' doctrine,[84] to approve the argument that the employer and employee relative bargaining power had to be considered to determine whether or not there really was contractual agreement.[85]

The question as to why courts often applied contractual principle, often modify them, and often abandon them, aligns with the larger consequences of the decisions in *Geys*[86] on employment law as a *sui generis* discipline. The current judicial recognition of employment, apparently transcending mere economic exchanges, in order to reflect an externally imposed social reality of subordination in the employment relationship,[87] implies powerful policy considerations, which force the court either to adhere to contractual orthodoxy or discard it. That legal doctrine and precedent must yield to policy in employment law,[88] in some circumstances, is unveiled in Lord Sumption's dissenting judgment in *Geys*:[89]

> Subject to the intervention of statute, contracts of employment are governed by the same principles as other contracts, except in those cases where their subject matter gives rise to compelling policy considerations calling for a different approach. The relationship of employer and employee is especially liable to give rise to policy considerations of this kind, because its incidents have significant social and economic implications. They affect a high proportion of the adult population and have profound impact both on their personal lives and on their relationships with others . . . the relationship of

[80] *Gisda Cyf v Barratt* [2010] UKSC 41; *Edwards v Chesterfield Royal Hospital NHS Foundation Trust* [2011] UKSC 58.

[81] *Gisda Cyf v Barratt* [2010] UKSC 41.

[82] [2011] UKSC 58.

[83] [2011] UKSC 41.

[84] *Snook v London and West Riding Investments Ltd* [1967] 1 All ER 518; David Cabrelli and Rebecca Zahn, 'The Elective and Automatic Theories of Termination in the Common Law of the Contract of Employment: Conundrum Resolved?', *The Modern Law Review*, vol. 76, no. 6, 2013, pp. 1106-1119, p. 1113.

[85] The persuasive analysis in A Bogg, 'Sham Self-Employment in the Supreme Court', *Industrial Law Journal*, vol. 41, 2012, pp. 331-332, pp. 328, 336-343; H Collins, 'Notes: Claim for Unfair Dismissal', *Industrial Law Journal*, vol. 30, no. 3, 2001, pp. 305-309. A Bogg, 'Sham Self-Employment in the Supreme Court', *Industrial Law Journal*, vol. 41, 2012, pp. 331-332, pp. 331-332.

[86] [2012] UKSC 63.

[87] H Collins, 'Notes: Claim for Unfair Dismissal', *Industrial Law Journal*, vol. 30, no. 3, 2001, pp. 305-309.

[88] A Bogg, 'Sham Self-Employment in the Supreme Court', *Industrial Law Journal*, vol. 41, 2012, pp. 331-332, pp. 331-332.

[89] [2012] UKSC 63.

employer and employee was traditionally regarded as a highly personal one. In an age of large corporate enterprises many of whose employees perform routine jobs, the personal character, which was once typical of employment relationships has lost much of its former importance. But employment is none the less a relationship based on mutual trust and confidence, a factor, which has assumed growing importance in the way that the law has developed over the past 30 years. . . . legal thinking in this area has always been influenced by a concern for the productive use of resources, including labour. This is evident in the development of common law relating, for example, to restrictive covenants and, at a more macro economic level, to the economic torts of interference with contractual relations procuring a breach of contract and aspects of the law of conspiracy. It is reflected in the abiding concern of the common law to ensure the terminability of contracts of employment, without prejudice to the subsequent regulation of the financial consequences by an award of damages. The harsher consequences of this approach for individuals have been mitigated in the last half century by a parallel scheme of statutory protection of employment, operating within defined limits and administered by specialized statutory tribunals with limited jurisdiction over purely contractual disputes.[90]

Policy objectives underlying various common law rules of the employment contract may well be modified by the courts and may recently have advanced progressively.[91] This has been by analogic process, such as for example the "equity of the statute,"[92] with the progression in statutory protection of employment,[93] responses to the unravelling of collectivization and unionization, "deregulation of the labour market, the privatization of public services, and the globalization of product and financial markets."[94] Thus, Lord Sumption had opined, in *Geys*[95] that the common law was not a

[90] [2013] 2 WLR 50, 90E-91D.

[91] L Barmes, 'The Continuing Conceptual Crisis in the Common Law of the Contract of Employment', *Modern Law Review*, vol. 67, no. 3, 2004, 435-464, p. 451.

[92] There appeared to be a principle that the courts, guided by the dictates of conscience and natural justice, could modify the rigor of a statute or apply its rules to cases not provided for, to avert hardship or injustice. WH Loyd, 'The Equity of a Statute', (1909) 58(2) *University of Pennsylvania Law Review and American Law Register*, vol. 58, no. 2, 1909, pp. 76-86, p. 82, citing Henry Campbell Black *Handbook on the construction and interpretation of the laws*, West Publishing Co, Minniapolis, 1911), p. 42.

[93] *Johnson v Unisys Ltd* [2003] 1 AC 518, 539C, per Lord Hoffinann; *Eastwood v Magtiox Electric PLC* [2005] 1 AC 503, 524, per Lord Nicholls; M Freedland, *The Personal Employment Contract*, Oxford University Press, Oxford, 2003, pp. 339-344.

[94] *Johnson v Unisys Ltd* [2003] 1 AC 518, 539D per Lord Steyn.

[95] [2012] UKSC 63.

primary source for worker-friendly workplace norms.[96] In *Edwards*,[97] the compelling policy issues were contrary to labour interests, whereas in *Autoclenz*,[98] *Gisda Cyf*[99] and *Geys*,[100] they were not. The ultimate issue is not one of law, but one of the balancing of competing interests. In *Geys*,[101] the Supreme Court emphasized justice and party autonomy as the normative grounds for its holdings for the employee. However, policy preferences grounded in certainty, practicability, or not frustrating parliamentary intention must also be recognized.[102]

4.2. Doctrinal Effect of *Geys*

Geys[103] clearly applies the elective theory in cases of wrongful resignations, inferring an affront to the principle of liberty said to be intrinsic to the common law's jurisprudence,[104] which implies a freedom to escape from moral hazard, since it appears to permit the employer to force the employee to continue work. However, common law rules designed to prevent a contracting party from forcing unwanted performance on the other party,[105] and then demanding payment, might be adapted to limit the oppressive facets of the elective theory.[106] Also, statutory modifications to the common law are in section 236 of the Trade Union and Labour Relations (Consolidation) Act 1992

---

[96] [2013] 2 WLR 50, 91D-91E.

[97] Which Collins describes as a case where the courts made 'a brute policy choice designed to subvert the contractual rights of employees': H Collins, 'Compensation for Dismissal: In Search of Principle', *Industrial Law Journal*, vol. 41, no. 2, 2012, pp. 208-227, p. 226.

[98] *Autoclenz Ltd v Belcher* [2011] UKSC 41.

[99] *Gisda Cyf v Barratt* [2010] UKSC 41.

[100] [2012] UKSC 63.

[101] ibid.

[102] A Bogg, 'Sham Self-Employment in the Supreme Court', *Industrial Law Journal*, vol. 41, 2012, pp. 331-332, p. 344; David Cabrelli and Rebecca Zahn, 'The Elective and Automatic Theories of Termination in the Common Law of the Contract of Employment: Conundrum Resolved?', *The Modern Law Review*, vol. 76, no. 6, 2013, pp. 1106-1119, p. 1116.

[103] [2012] UKSC 63.

[104] *Nokes v Doncaster Amalgamated Collieries Ltd* [1940] AC 1014, 1020, per Viscount Simon, and 1033, per Lord Atkin.

[105] The rules developed as exceptions to *White*, in *White and Carter (Councils) Ltd v McGregor* [1962] AC 413; *Photo Production Ltd v Securicor Transport Ltd* [1980] AC 827.

[106] *Attica Sea Carriers Corp v Ferrostaal etc.* [1976] 1 Lloyd's Rep 250; *The Alaskan Trader* [1984] All ER 129. For example, where the employer no longer has any legitimate interest in performance of the contract subsequent to the employee's wrongful resignation, the court has power to exercise its general equitable jurisdiction and refuse to permit the employer to insist its strict legal rights.

(TULR(C)A),[107] precluding the employer from injunctive or specific performance relief compelling the employee to work or attend for work. Thus, the employer could compel the employee to take garden leave for the remainder of the contractual notice period, which could give rise to judicial recognition of an implied term that employers may put employees on garden leave without an express term to the contrary.[108] During garden leave, the employee would still be bound by the implied terms of obligations of mutual trust and confidence.[109]

The elective theory has important implications in matters of summary dismissal, such as for example where the employer catches the employee stealing, and the employer dismisses the employee summarily, without prior notice, for gross misconduct. The employee's conduct would constitute a repudiatory breach. The employee might then refutes the employer's contention of gross misconduct, claiming that the summary dismissal was a repudiatory breach, then without any delay affirm the contract of employment. Thus, the issues quickly arise as to whether the employer must pay lost wages, now characterized as a debt, from the time of the employee's affirmation, and also contractual damages for failure to provide proper notice. Most probably this can only be resolved in litigation.

5. Critical Literature Review Conclusion

The research question arose as to how a fit and proper person's capacity to execute truly without malice, affection or partiality, and maintain the ability to execute his or her office diligently, might be adversely affected in an employment environment of moral hazard. Argument has sought to sustain the view that moral hazard in the workplace is the deliberate and capricious exploitation by an employer, exercising a perceived disciplinary power abusively, *ultra vires* the contract of employment, placing the fit and proper person in a non-impartial position to execute his or her professional tasks faithfully and diligently.

---

[107] *Trade Union and Labour Relations (Consolidation) Act 1992* (TULR(C)A) (UK).

[108] *William Hill Organisation Ltd v Tucker* [1999] ICR 291, 301F, per Lord Justice Morritt.

[109] Garden leave is where an employee takes paid leave after they have been given notice of termination or has resigned from a business. The employee is not required to perform their duties during this notice period. However, they must be available or contactable throughout the entire period.

Since the fit and proper agent must decide whether or not to accept the employment contract, before knowing which task will be assigned, the employment contract affords the principal an opportunity to exploit the fit and proper agent after contract acceptance, with likely exploitation indicating employee moral hazard. The research showed that principals demanded their most profitable and least efficient task in about half the cases. Thus, agents must determine the principal's bona fides before contract execution. This is made all the more difficult in that specious principals will most usually begin exploiting their agents towards the end of the agent's tenure.

The reason why, in some instances, principals abused their power less was the agents' threat of terminating the employment. This disciplined the principals to perceive the likelihood of a large loss in the principal's future profits. Thus, Coase described the firm as a system within which power and subordination prevailed. This subordination is reflected in the relationship between the employer and the worker, grounded in a contract of employment that creates in the employer a right to assign tasks to the employee. Thus, a grocer faces no moral hazard, but rather, a public regulatory hazard, because the little consumer cannot assign to him or her any abusive tasks, whereas the agent in an employment contract does face this risk. Enforcement of contracts, within the firm, where there are moral hazard problems, infers a pervasive existence of rents. Therefore, breaking-up an employment relationship generally causes substantial costs for the parties, suggesting that both parties could have an interest in continuing their relationship. This interest nevertheless may not balance employer propensity toward unfairness. The Coasian view is that the employer right of capricious decisions, based on power, is an allocation mechanism more efficient than price mechanisms, and is the very raison-d'etre for firms' existence. Thus, firms exist because they cause lower transaction costs, ensuring continuing employer unfairness.

Employer reputational disciplinary mechanisms are not always enough to resolve the moral hazard problem. The irregular nature of the employment relationship thus makes contract theory a discordant explanation for the employment relationship. In the automatic theory, contract repudiation caused automatic contract termination. In the elective theory, the repudiation would terminate the contract only when the other party elected to confirm the repudiation. A repudiated contract of employment would only be terminated when the other party exercised an election to confirm the repudiation, implying that a fit and proper employee could remain in a state of moral hazard until the unfair employer released him or her from the contract of employment.

The elective theory would only permit employment contracts to subsist where some substantive contractual term remained to be enforced. This only ostensibly reduced Lord Sumption's view to minimal practical import, as a fit and proper employee might still be under a duty to advise the employer. It is arguable, as a zero-sum argument, that Lord Sumption's reasoning failed to apportion sufficient weight to the contractual character of the relationship of employment, which still "remains at the core" of modern labour law, and instead, conceiving of employment in terms of status, suggesting status-like employee duties based on their continuing subordination.

Although a "wise employer" would most often provide written notice of termination, it was unnecessary unless agreed in the contract itself. That injunction was the main remedy for enforcing a contractually agreed disciplinary procedure suggested that employer disciplinary powers were either pursuant to rights without remedies in the common law, or else were mere prerogatives without any basis in law.

The court used the common law 'sham' doctrine, to approve the argument that the employer and employee relative bargaining power had to be considered to determine whether or not there really was contractual agreement. The current judicial recognition of employment, apparently transcending mere economic exchanges, in order to reflect an externally imposed social reality of subordination in the employment relationship, implies powerful policy considerations, mitigating against a finding of consensus *ad idem* agreement, as legal doctrine and precedent must yield to policy in employment law,

Policy objectives underlying various common law rules of the employment contract may well be modified by the courts and may recently have advanced progressively. This has been by analogic process, such as for example the "equity of the statute." *Geys* clearly applies the elective theory in cases of wrongful resignations, inferring an affront to the principle of liberty said to be intrinsic to the common law's jurisprudence, which implies a freedom to escape from moral hazard, since it appears to permit the employer to force the employee to continue to work.

Extending these syntheses, specious principals will most usually begin exploiting their agents towards the end of the agent's tenure. Principals fear the agent might terminate the agreement in the early stages of the agreement. That subordination causes moral hazard problems infers a pervasive existence of rents that mitigate against termination, suggesting a force for continuing moral hazard. A fit and proper employee could be forced to remain in a state of moral hazard until the unfair employer released him or her from the contract

of employment. Status-like employee duties are based on the social and judicial policy of subordination, which argues against the existence of any contractual agreement based on *consensus ad idem*. Employer disciplinary powers are likely based in this kind of judicial policy. In theory, a fit and proper person in a state of ever-increasing employment moral hazard can be forced to continue to work.

6. Research Gaps, Research Questions, Interview Questions

6.1. Research Gap 1

Specious principals will most usually begin exploiting their agents towards the end of the agent's tenure.

6.1.1. Research Question 1

At which times in the employment of a fit and proper person are they exploited?

6.1.2. Interview Question 1

Can you recall times during the tenure of a professional employee when he or she was exploited by management? At what stage(s) of his or her tenure of employment?

6.1.3. Interview Question 1.1

Does exploiting a professional employee reach the ears of regulatory authorities?

6.2. Research Gap 2

Principals fear the agent might terminate the agreement in the early stages of the agreement.

6.2.1. Research Question 2

What to principals think about their professional employees?

6.2.2. Interview Question 2

How to employers regard the status, authority and personality of professional employees? Are they in any way seen as difficult to manage?

6.3. Research Gap 3

That subordination causes moral hazard problems infers a pervasive existence of rents that mitigate against termination, suggesting a force for continuing moral hazard.

6.3.1. Research Question 3

Is subordination the cause of moral hazard?

6.3.2. Interview Question 3

Do managers assign inefficient and compromising tasks purely for reasons of exercising their authority over professional employees? Please give example(s).

6.4. Research Gap 4

A fit and proper employee could be forced to remain in a state of moral hazard until the unfair employer released him or her from the contract of employment.

6.4.1. Research Question 4

Do fit and proper employees tend to resign unexpectedly?

6.4.2. Interview Question 4

Can you categorize how and when professional employees tend to resign? Please give example(s).

6.4.3. Interview Question 4.1

When a professional employee resigns, how is the cost to the employer calculated?

6.5. Research Gap 5

Status-like employee duties are based on the social and judicial policy of subordination, which argues against the existence of any contractual agreement, based on *consensus ad idem.*

6.5.1. Research Question 5

Do employers routinely violate employment contracts?

6.5.2. Interview Question 5

In your view, do employers routinely get relevant legal advice, and heed this advice, before repudiating an employee's employment contract?

6.6. Research Gap 6

Employer disciplinary powers are likely based in judicial status-based policy.

6.6.1. Research Question 6

From where do employers source their disciplinary authority?

6.6.2. Interview Question 6

Can employers clearly articulate the source of their disciplinary authority?

6.6.3. Interview Question 6.1

What is the organizational cost of an employer not knowing the source of its disciplinary authority?

6.7. Research Gap 7

In theory, a fit and proper person in a state of ever-increasing employment moral hazard can be forced to continue to work.

6.7.1. Research Question 7

Do fit and proper persons find it difficult to resign?

6.7.2. Interview Question 7
Do professional employees find it difficult to resign? If so, for what reasons?

7. Discussion and Narrative Analysis Research Outcomes

The research gathered two cohorts of interviewees. The first cohort comprised human resources consultants who routinely placed fit and proper employees into business organizations. The second cohort comprised people who are fit and proper people by virtue of the professional nature of their work.

Interview Question 1: Can you recall times during the tenure of a professional employee when he or she was exploited by management? At what stage(s) of his or her tenure of employment?

The Cohort of HR Placements Officers who routinely placed "Fit and Proper" employees answered as follows: "I can recall one clear example of this. Often it would be covered up if possible and not publicized. After five years at COO level, set up for a financial fraud by the other senior executives. He was cornered as the fall guy."[110] The cohort of "Fit and Proper" interviewees answered as follows: "The management usually will start to exploit an employee like this almost immediately after he or she has accepted the job contract. An employer will explain a situation and then expect the employee to have his or her say or not about dealing with it."[111]

Interview Question 2: Does exploiting a professional employee reach the ears of regulatory authorities?

The Cohort of HR Placements Officers who routinely placed "Fit and Proper" employees answered as follows: "Not often. In this kind of case, only when the employer or employee is prosecuted. His being manipulated and being set up is generally not reported, as the shock and speed of the process sideswipes the employee. After several years, any sentence and court ruling could be overturned but the damage by then is already irreparable."[112] The

[110] Cohort of HR Placements Officers who Place "Fit and Proper" Employees, Interview by Author, Canberra, 1 February 2022.
[111] Cohort of "Fit and Proper" Interviewees, Interview by Author, Canberra, 1 February 2022.
[112] Cohort of HR Placements Officers who Place "Fit and Proper" Employees, Interview by Author, Canberra, 1 February 2022.

cohort of "Fit and Proper" interviewees answered as follows: "Usually it does not reach any regulatory authorities unless he or she loses the job under unlawful circumstances and wants to become a whistleblower, only when it is a serious matter."[113]

Interview Question 3: How do employers regard the status, authority and personality of professional employees? Are they in any way seen as difficult to manage?

The Cohort of HR Placements Officers who routinely placed "Fit and Proper" employees answered as follows:

> I cannot speak for all employers, as the range from owner with 3 employees to a large multi-national is quite different. I have also spent the last 10 years recruiting middle-level employees and not senior executives. In my prior experience, there is more concern around hiring senior executives who have more influence over the direction of the company and more complicated contracts are usually the result, with liabilities and responsibilities more evenly attributed to both parties.[114]

The cohort of "Fit and Proper" interviewees answered as follows: "Employers would usually regard professional employees as difficult to manage but might nevertheless somehow seek out and find a way to deal with them."[115]

Interview Question 4: Do managers assign inefficient and compromising tasks purely for reasons of exercising their authority over professional employees? Please give example(s).

The Cohort of HR Placements Officers who routinely placed "Fit and Proper" employees answered as follows:

> I cannot answer this question. I am sure it might happen but am not privy to enough managers' decisions to generalize. In my own experience, we were asked to come into the office to have a meeting each morning to explain what we were going to do each day and then have to leave the office and go and

[113] Cohort of "Fit and Proper" Interviewees, Interview by Author, Canberra, 1 February 2022.
[114] Cohort of HR Placements Officers who Place "Fit and Proper" Employees, Interview by Author, Canberra, 1 February 2022.
[115] Cohort of "Fit and Proper" Interviewees, Interview by Author, Canberra, 1 February 2022.

> do those things. It was pointed out to management that it would be more efficient to go straight to "work" and when finished, come back to the office to plan the next day. The culture of the company was clearly one of mistrust, and therefore illogical, inefficient requests were made solely for the purpose of reminding people daily they were not trusted.[116]

The cohort of "Fit and Proper" interviewees answered as follows:

> Yes managers usually do exercise their authority over professional employees, just to show who is the boss. For example, if you are an accountant and you show the manager that for this year your tax is approximately this amount and he or she insists that it should be made lower, and insists the accountant must do something about it.[117]

Interview Question 5: Can you categorize how and when professional employees tend to resign? Please give example(s).

The Cohort of HR Placements Officers who routinely placed "Fit and Proper" employees answered as follows: "Too broad a question for me. HR managers may have more insight."[118] The cohort of "Fit and Proper" interviewees answered as follows: "As per the above answer, this is the period where the principles of the professional employee collide with those of the employers, causing friction, and might end up with the employee's resignation."[119]

Interview Question 6: When a professional employee resigns, how is the cost to the employer calculated?

The Cohort of HR Placements Officers who routinely placed "Fit and Proper" employees answered as follows: "Depends on the contract. In addition, if a senior executive is not able to be replaced in a timely fashion, downtime in leadership or specific leadership function is an additional expense

---

[116] Cohort of HR Placements Officers who Place "Fit and Proper" Employees, Interview by Author, Canberra, 1 February 2022.
[117] Cohort of "Fit and Proper" Interviewees, Interview by Author, Canberra, 1 February 2022.
[118] Cohort of HR Placements Officers who Place "Fit and Proper" Employees, Interview by Author, Canberra, 1 February 2022.
[119] Cohort of "Fit and Proper" Interviewees, Interview by Author, Canberra, 1 February 2022.

to the company and hard to quantify."[120] The cohort of "Fit and Proper" interviewees answered as follows: "How the cost to the employer is calculated, when a professional employee resigns, differs by what complexity of jobs he or she is doing and how long he or she has been working for the company."[121]

Interview Question 7: In your view, do employers routinely get relevant legal advice, and heed this advice, before repudiating an employee's employment contract?

The Cohort of HR Placements Officers who routinely placed "Fit and Proper" employees answered as follows: "Yes. In my role as a Consulting Recruiter, I would also always advise a client to do so."[122] The cohort of "Fit and Proper" interviewees answered as follows: "Yes and no. Some employers do take advices in fear of the legal consequences. Some would ask for advice, but still act based on their emotion."[123]

Interview Question 8: Can employers clearly articulate the source of their disciplinary authority?

The Cohort of HR Placements Officers who routinely placed "Fit and Proper" employees answered as follows: "I would suggest not. Perhaps the problem lies in having a large bureaucratic structure where the line of authority is not always clear."[124] The cohort of "Fit and Proper" interviewees answered as follows: "In most jurisdictions, the source of their disciplinary authority is usually from the Labour Law."[125]

Interview Question 9: What is the organizational cost of an employer not knowing the source of its disciplinary authority?

The Cohort of HR Placements Officers who routinely placed "Fit and Proper" employees answered as follows: "To be discovered. Research such as

---

[120] Cohort of HR Placements Officers who Place "Fit and Proper" Employees, Interview by Author, Canberra, 1 February 2022.
[121] Cohort of "Fit and Proper" Interviewees, Interview by Author, Canberra, 1 February 2022.
[122] Cohort of HR Placements Officers who Place "Fit and Proper" Employees, Interview by Author, Canberra, 1 February 2022.
[123] Cohort of "Fit and Proper" Interviewees, Interview by Author, Canberra, 1 February 2022.
[124] Cohort of HR Placements Officers who Place "Fit and Proper" Employees, Interview by Author, Canberra, 1 February 2022.
[125] Cohort of "Fit and Proper" Interviewees, Interview by Author, Canberra, 1 February 2022.

this should help to ascertain the overall cost rather than incidences being seen as one-offs."[126] The cohort of "Fit and Proper" interviewees answered as follows: "It will end up with legal battle and payment of costs to the employees concerned, as well as unnecessary financial losses to the organization."[127]

Interview Question 10: Do professional employees find it difficult to resign? If so, for what reasons?

The Cohort of HR Placements Officers who routinely placed "Fit and Proper" employees answered as follows: "Yes. Usually in fear of missing out on bonuses, and this is all the more so in private enterprises."[128] The cohort of "Fit and Proper" interviewees answered as follows: "Professional employees who want to resign might have to serve prior notice for some months. If he or she finds it hard to resign, it is most likely for reasons of difficulties in finding other jobs carrying the same salary or higher."[129]

Conclusion: Interview Questions

Exploitation, cornering an employee into taking the blame for financial fraud, can be actively concealed by management. This can start almost immediately after execution of the contract, with apparent consultation with the employee. The sideswiping of the employee damages the employee's employability in the job market. Whistle blowing is the most likely way regulatory officials will hear about the exploitation problem. Managers tend to regard senior fit and proper employees as more difficult to manage, and thus, prefer to hire the less experienced. In all cases, managers seek out ways to manipulate fit and proper employees. Managers do tend to assign exploitative tasks to employees for the sole reason of demonstrating the manager's superior position in the workplace hierarchy. Fit and proper employees tend most often to resign when their principles are at odds with those of management. Employers calculating cost of fit and proper employees' resignations might prefer they resign after doing less complex tasks for a shorter period of time. It seems that employers

126 Cohort of HR Placements Officers who Place "Fit and Proper" Employees, Interview by Author, Canberra, 1 February 2022.
127 Cohort of "Fit and Proper" Interviewees, Interview by Author, Canberra, 1 February 2022.
128 Cohort of HR Placements Officers who Place "Fit and Proper" Employees, Interview by Author, Canberra, 1 February 2022.
129 Cohort of "Fit and Proper" Interviewees, Interview by Author, Canberra, 1 February 2022.

can regard professional legal advice as less compelling than organizational pressures or their own personal emotions. It is unclear whether or not employers know the proper source of their perceived disciplinary authority. Managers not knowing the proper source(s) of their perceived disciplinary authority is a cause of expensive legal battles. Therefore, fit and proper employees tend to consider the circumstances and timing of their resignation very carefully.

In summary, managers begin almost right away cornering an employee into taking the blame for the unlawful acts, either of other or forced onto them. Managers then actively conceal these conspiracies. This severely damages the employee's future employability, precipitating instances of whistle blowing. Thus, managers prefer to hire the less experienced, to make the cover-up easier. Employers can regard professional legal advice as less compelling than either organizational pressures or their own personal emotions. This may come from managers not understanding the proper source(s) of their disciplinary authority, but nevertheless still exercising an authority based solely on emotion. In the result, the fit and proper test is a serious failure of regulation as it might be sourced in public confidence in the profession and the professional's practical ability to perform the task with diligence and honor. The research outcomes confirm the extended syntheses of the above critical literature review.

References

Alchian, Armen, & Harold Demsetz, 'Production, Information Costs, and Economic Organization', *American Economic Review*, vol. 62, 1972, pp. 777-795.

Arrow, Kenneth, 'Uncertainty and the Welfare Economics of Medical Care', *The American Economic Review, vol.* 53, no. 5, 1963, pp. 941–73.

Attica Sea Carriers Corp v Ferrostaal etc. [1976] 1 Lloyd's Rep 250.

Australian Broadcasting Tribunal v Bond (1990) 170 CLR 321.

Autoclenz Ltd v Belcher [2011] UKSC 41.

Autoclenz v Belcher [2011] UKSC 41; [2011] 4 All ER 745.

Barmes, L, 'The Continuing Conceptual Crisis in the Common Law of the Contract of Employment', *Modern Law Review*, vol. 67, no. 3, 2004, 435-464.

Bartling, Björn, Klaus M. Schmidt & Ernst Fehr, 'Use and Abuse of Authority: A Behavioral Foundation of the Employment Relation', *Journal of the European Economic Association*, vol. 11, no. 4, 2013, pp. 711-742.

Black, Henry Campbell, *Handbook on the construction and interpretation of the laws*, West Publishing Co, Minneapolis, 1911.

Blackham, Alysia, 'Uncertain Junctures between Employment and Contract Law', *The Cambridge Law Journal*, vol. 72, no. 2, 2013, pp. 269-273.

Bogg, A, 'Sham Self-Employment in the Supreme Court', *Industrial Law Journal*, vol. 41, 2012, pp. 331-332.

Brown, Martin, Armin Falk & Ernst Fehr, 'Competition and Relational Contracts - The Role of Unemployment as a Disciplinary Device', *Journal of the European Economic Association*, vol. 10, 2012, pp. 887-907.

Brown, Martin, Armin Falk & Ernst Fehr, 'Relational Contracts and the Nature of Market Interactions', *Econometrica*, vol. 72, 2004, pp.747-780.

Cabrelli, David, & Rebecca Zahn, 'The Elective and Automatic Theories of Termination in the Common Law of the Contract of Employment: Conundrum Resolved?', *The Modern Law Review*, vol. 76, no. 6, 2013, pp. 1106-1119.

Coase, Ronald, 'The Nature of the Firm', *Economica*, vol. 4, 1937, pp. 386-405.

Collins, H, 'Compensation for Dismissal: In Search of Principle', *Industrial Law Journal*, vol. 41, no. 2, 2012, pp. 208-227.

Collins, H, 'Notes: Claim for Unfair Dismissal', *Industrial Law Journal*, vol. 30, no. 3, 2001, pp. 305-309.

Costello, K, '*Edwards v Chesterfield Royal Hospital* - Parliamentary Intention and Damages Caused by Maladministration of a Contractual Dismissal Procedure', *Modern Law Review*, vol. 76, no. 1, 2013, pp. 134-145.

Deakin, Simon F, & Frank Wilkinson, *The Law of the Labour Market: Industrialization, Employment and Legal Evolution*, Oxford University Press, Oxford, 2005.

Dembe, Allard E, & Leslie I Boden, 'Moral Hazard: A Question of Morality?', *Wayback Machine New Solutions*, vol. 10, no. 3, 2000, pp. 257–279.

Dieter, Otto Alvin Loeb, 'Stasis', *Speech Monographs*, vol. XVII, 1950, pp. 345-369.

Eastwood v Magtiox Electric PLC [2005] 1 AC 503.

Edwards v Chesterfield Royal Hospital NHS Foundation Trust [2011] UKSC 58; [2012] 2 AC 22.

Employment Rights Act 1996 (UK).

Fehr, Ernst, & Klaus M. Schmidt, 'A Theory of Fairness, Competition, and Cooperation', *Quarterly Journal of Economics*, vol. 114, 1999, pp. 817-868.

Finkelstein, Amy, Kenneth J Arrow, Jonathan Gruber, Joseph P Newhouse, & Joseph E. Stiglitz, '*Moral Hazard in Health Insurance*', Columbia University Press, 2015, doi:10.7312/fink16380.

Finlayson, WF, *A Report of the Case of The Queen v Gurney and Others in the Court of Queens Bench: The Summing Up revised by the Lord Chief Justice with an Introduction Containing a History of the Case and an Examination of the Cases at Law and Equity applicable to it; or Illustrating the Doctrine of Commercial Fraud*, Stevens and Haynes, London, 1870.

Fitzherbert, Anthony, *The New Natura Brevium of the Most Reverend Judge Mr. Anthony Fitz-Herbert*, Savoy, 6th edn., London, 1718.

Freedland, M, *The Personal Employment Contract*, Oxford University Press, Oxford, 2003, pp. 339-344.

German Industrial Code ("Gewerbeordnung").

Geys v Societe Generale [2012] UKSC 63; [2013] 2 WLR 50.

Gisda Cyf v Barratt [2010] UKSC 41; [2010] 4 All ER 851.
Goodwin, David, 'Controversiae Meta-Asystatae and the New Rhetoric', *Rhetoric Society Quarterly*, vol. 19, no. 3, 1989, pp. 205-216.
Hughes and Vale Pty Ltd v State of NSW (No 2) (1955) 93 CLR 127.
Johnson v Unisys Ltd [2003] 1 AC 518.
Loyd, WH, 'The Equity of a Statute', (1909) 58(2) *University of Pennsylvania Law Review and American Law Register*, vol. 58, no. 2, 1909, pp. 76-86.
MacLeod, W Bentley, & James M Malcomson, 'Implicit Contract, Incentive Compatibility, and Involuntary Unemployment', *Econometrica*, vol. 57, 1989, pp. 447-480.
Marglin, Stephen Alan, 'What Do Bosses Do? Part II', *Review of Radical Political Economics*, vol. 7, 1975, pp. 20-37.
Maxwell v Dixon [1965] WAR 167.
McMenamin, Lexi, 'Why long-term workplace trauma is a real phenomenon', *BBC Worklife*, 20th April 2021.
Ng, Nathalie, 'Fitness and Propriety, Spent Convictions and Technology: Lessons from ASIC Investigations', *Australian Institute of Administrative Law Forum*, vol. 92, 2018, pp. 1-112.
Nokes v Doncaster Amalgamated Collieries Ltd [1940] AC 1014.
Pauly, Mark V, 'The economics of moral hazard: comment', *The American Economic Review, vol.* 58, *no.* 3, 1968, pp. 531–37.
Photo Production Ltd v Securicor Transport Ltd [1980] AC 827.
Pollard, Sidney, 'Factory Discipline in the Industrial Revolution', *The Economic History Review*, vol. 16, 1963, pp. 254-271.
Prassl, J, 'Interpreting Employment Protective Legislation: *Gisda Cyf v Barratt*', *Industrial Law Journal*, vol. 40, no. 1, 2011, pp. 103-107.
Rabin, Matthew, 'Incorporating Fairness into Game Theory and Economics', *American Economic Review*, vol. 83, 1993, pp. 1281-1302.
Re Dowling and Secretary to Department of Health [1985] AATA 237; (1985) 8 ALD 171.
Re Taylor and Department of Transport [1978] AATA 64; (1978) 1 ALD 312.
Rowell, D, & LB Connelly, 'A history of the term 'moral hazard', *Journal of Risk and Insurance*, vol. 79, no. 4, 2012, pp. 1051–1075.
Sale of Goods Acts in the various jurisdictions.
Simon, Herbert, 'A Formal Theory of the Employment Relationship', *Econometrica*, vol. 19, 1951, pp. 293-305.
Snook v London and West Riding Investments Ltd [1967] 1 All ER 518.
The Alaskan Trader [1984] All ER 129.
Trade Union and Labour Relations (Consolidation) Act 1992 (TULR(C)A) (UK).
White and Carter (Councils) Ltd. v McGregor [1962] A.C. 413.
William Hill Organisation Ltd v Tucker [1999] ICR 291.

About the Editors

Dr. Gary I. Lilienthal holds a Sydney University law degree, a Sydney College of Law Graduate Diploma in Legal Practice, a Melbourne High Distinction Masters Degree in Freudian and Lacanian Psychoanalysis and a Perth Australia Doctorate in the history and development of the intellectual property tort of passing-off. He is widely published internationally, and functions privately as a Forensic Psychotherapist. Dr. Lilienthal was Senior Lecturer in Law at the Northern University of Malaysia, Associate Professor of Law and Scholar-in-Residence at Symbiosis University in India, and full Professor of Law at the University of Gondar in the Federal Democratic Republic of Ethiopia. He is now Professor of Law, by the Vice Chancellor's personal appointment, at NALSAR University of Law, Hyderabad, in India, and Professor of the University at Tashkent State University of Law. He is Visiting Professor at the BIHER School of Management and Commerce in Chennai, India, and sits on the Research Committee at St. Aloysius College in Jabalpur, India, where he conducted a 20-week program in scholarly writing techniques for 25 post-doctoral academic participants. In Malaysia, he convened the masters degree program in International Labour Organization Law, focusing on the laws of slavery, forced labour and child labour. In India, as Scholar-in-Residence, he was awarded the Silver Medal in National Security Law, after his presentation to military officials of the Indian National Security Council on the Chinese perception of international law. Also at Symbiosis Law School, he chaired a Committee supervising 75 research masters' degree students. In Ethiopia he formulated and implemented a new doctoral research preparation program for aspiring research students, and taught local academics in the fields of human rights law and academic research, focussing on the laws of torture, genocide and theories of rights. He now chairs the Carrington Rand collaboration of some 60 scholars from around the world. Carrington Rand develops published journal papers as pilot research projects, identifies their research gaps, for purposes of commercialised research with interested government clients. In 2018, he gave a keynote presentation on regulating foreign multinational corporations at a University conference at Shanghai Jiao Tong University in Shanghai. This paper is now published in the Peoples' Republic of China, in the form of a government book, by the Chinese Federal Ministry for Higher Education, in

Beijing. Dr. Lilienthal has more recently published a suite of 3 research pieces on the character and operation of Diplomatic Law, and is widely interviewed on world podcasts on the topic of Diplomacy and International Relations. He has published SCOPUS-indexed pilot research into the genesis of water rights. He is currently heading multinational research projects into Water Rights in the River Nile Basin. He has published a SCOPUS-indexed book entitled "Human Capital and Development", published by Nova Science Publishers in New York City, leading several professorial chapter authors. More recently he conducted a public lecture at UNUSA University in Surabaya Indonesia on the topic of post-doctoral academic writing, to some 190 attendees who were serving academics. He received the personal and public acclaim of the University's Rector for this presentation. Email: carrington.rand@icloud.com.

Dr. Muhamad Hassan bin Ahmad is an Assistant Professor at the Civil Law Department, Ahmad Ibrahim Kulliyyah of Laws, International Islamic University Malaysia (IIUM). He is also the 'External Examiner' for the 'Master of Laws (LLM) (International Business and Trade Law)' programme at the Taylor's Law School, where Taylor's University currently ranks as the Top Private University in Southeast Asia in the QS World University Rankings. He also served as the 'Adjunct Lecturer' for the 'Master of Laws (LLM) (International Law)' programme at the Faculty of Shariah and Law, Universiti Islam Sultan Sharif Ali (UNISSA), in Brunei. He graduated with the degrees of Bachelor of Laws (LLB), Master of Comparative Laws (MCL), and Doctor of Philosophy (PhD) from IIUM. He has special research interests in Public International Law, Private International Law, Alternative Dispute Resolution, Comparative Law, Jurisprudence, and Online Legal Education. He is the Editor-in-Chief of the 'Journal of Islamic Law Review' indexed in 'Index to Foreign Legal Periodicals (IFLP)', produced by the American Association of Law Libraries at University of California, Berkeley, School of Law, in the United States of America. He has published a number of research books, text books, and research articles in various academic journals; presented several research papers at numerous academic conferences as well as symposiums; and spoken in many public forums. Email: mdhassan@iium.edu.my.

Index

A

accusation, 183, 222, 232, 233, 234, 235, 236, 238, 239
agents, xi, 5, 14, 24, 27, 28, 29, 35, 37, 39, 108, 127, 176, 192, 206, 264, 278, 280, 281, 282, 283, 284, 287, 298, 299, 300
alterity, x, 19, 24, 33, 34, 35, 39, 123, 124, 127, 128, 129, 130, 131, 132, 133, 134, 139, 140, 142, 143, 144, 145, 146, 147, 148, 149, 150, 151, 152, 153, 154, 155, 156, 157, 158, 159, 160, 161, 162, 222, 280
analysis, ix, 2, 4, 7, 11, 12, 20, 23, 25, 36, 46, 64, 67, 124, 128, 130, 142, 168, 173, 177, 192, 215, 222, 225, 226, 230, 231, 232, 237, 243, 263, 266, 272, 278, 279, 281, 292, 294, 303
ancient heritage, 222, 230
argument, 7, 23, 32, 35, 43, 46, 64, 67, 80, 103, 112, 123, 126, 128, 131, 132, 133, 139, 140, 154, 166, 168, 169, 171, 172, 173, 174, 193, 201, 203, 204, 205, 206, 208, 217, 221, 222, 224, 227, 230, 231, 232, 233, 234, 235, 236, 237, 238, 240, 241, 242, 245, 248,269, 278, 279, 280, 285, 290, 294, 297, 299
asystatic question, xi, 218, 222, 232, 238, 239
authority, 9, 14, 27, 28, 33, 37, 38, 39, 54, 60, 78, 83, 85, 98, 99, 102, 103, 105, 132, 155, 173, 177, 180, 185, 189, 191, 206, 263, 267, 269, 281, 282, 283, 285, 287, 288, 289, 301, 302, 304, 305, 306, 308
automatic, 281, 288, 289, 291, 292, 294, 296, 298, 309
axiom, xi, 218, 222, 236, 237, 239

B

behavior, 4, 5, 6, 8, 9, 10, 11, 12, 13, 20, 28, 30, 36, 37, 38, 89, 102, 131, 133, 172, 184, 185, 199, 202, 203, 209, 213, 277, 279
bias, ix, 2, 5, 8, 13, 15, 33, 34, 35
burden, 222, 233, 234, 235, 241, 242, 254

C

capitalist, ix, 64, 67, 68, 69, 72, 73, 74, 75, 76, 77, 78, 79, 80, 114, 116, 253, 272
character(s), viii, xi, 4, 5, 6, 7, 8, 9, 11, 12, 13, 14, 15, 16, 17, 18, 20, 21, 22, 23, 25, 26, 29, 32, 33, 34, 35, 36, 37, 39, 41, 42, 47, 48, 49, 51, 52, 58, 61, 77, 85, 98, 106, 130, 131, 132, 135, 146, 161, 165, 166, 170, 181, 182, 196, 205, 207, 209, 210, 220, 221, 279, 284, 290, 291, 293, 295, 299, 312
child labor, viii, xi, 245, 246, 248, 249, 253, 254, 255, 256, 257, 258, 259, 260, 261, 263, 264, 265, 266, 267, 268, 269, 270, 271, 272
civil courts, 43, 44, 45
collapse, 67, 100, 198
commerce, 67, 88, 94, 115, 311
commonplace, x, xi, xii, 21, 26, 32, 35, 165, 166, 167, 168, 169, 170, 171, 172, 173, 174, 193, 204, 205, 206, 207, 209, 210, 233

commonplace denunciation, xii, 26, 32, 35, 166, 168, 169, 174, 193, 204, 205, 206, 209, 210, 233
community development, 245, 246, 255, 273
construct, 5, 20, 34, 64, 67, 72, 76, 81, 166, 169, 171, 206, 210, 233
contradictory, xi, 5, 21, 75, 136, 166, 170, 210
conveyancers, 5, 27, 30, 32, 36
credit, vii, 5, 27, 29, 30, 38
critique, 5, 20, 68, 143, 146, 158, 169, 233, 253, 272

D

danger, 194, 196, 197, 201, 209, 222, 231, 234, 235, 236, 256, 259
délation, viii, x, 165, 166, 170, 171, 178, 180, 181, 182, 183, 189, 191, 192, 193, 195, 204, 205, 207, 208, 210, 211, 212, 213
denouncer, 169, 180, 192, 193, 196, 197, 198, 200, 202, 204, 208, 209
denunciation, ix, x, 2, 5, 9, 13, 21, 25, 33, 34, 35, 165, 167, 168, 169, 170, 171, 172, 174, 175, 176, 177, 178, 179, 180, 181, 182, 183, 184, 185, 186, 187, 188, 189, 190, 191, 193, 194, 195, 196, 197, 198, 199, 200, 201, 202, 203, 204, 205, 206, 207, 208, 209, 210,212, 213, 214, 218, 222, 227, 232, 235, 238, 239
dialectical, 186, 222, 234, 235, 240, 241
disciplinary power, xi, 278, 280, 281, 293, 297, 299, 300, 302
discourse, 142, 144, 147, 153, 180, 181, 182, 183, 184, 187, 194, 195, 197, 202, 213, 230, 231, 243
disqualification, 5, 30, 31, 32
disrepute, viii, 49, 55, 217, 218

E

education, ix, xi, 8, 23, 33, 51, 52, 58, 60, 63, 64, 65, 66, 67, 72, 114, 117, 118, 167, 172, 189, 211, 245, 246, 248, 249, 250, 251, 252, 253, 254, 256, 257, 259, 260, 261, 264, 266, 268, 269, 271, 272, 274, 275, 311, 312
effect, 9, 19, 44, 47, 49, 66, 98, 107, 130, 165, 167, 192, 208, 218, 221, 222, 227, 232, 237, 238, 239, 247, 251, 281, 296
elective, 281, 288, 289, 291, 292, 294, 296, 297, 298, 299, 309
employment, xi, 51, 54, 55, 72, 80, 246, 252, 260, 262, 265, 266, 268, 273, 275, 277, 279, 280, 281, 282, 283, 284, 285, 286, 287, 288, 289, 290, 291, 292, 293, 294, 295, 296, 297, 298, 299, 300, 301, 302, 303, 306, 308, 309, 310
European, viii, 71, 126, 169, 175, 176, 177, 178, 179, 180, 182, 183, 184, 186, 212, 282, 283, 285, 287, 288, 308, 309
experiment(s), 9, 33, 207, 281

F

factors, 9, 22, 24, 38, 109, 218, 248, 253, 254, 255, 267, 284
fit and proper, viii, ix, xi, 1, 2, 3, 4, 5, 13, 14, 15, 16, 17, 18, 19, 20, 21, 22, 23, 24, 26, 27, 28, 29, 32, 34, 35, 36, 41, 42, 43, 44, 47, 48, 60, 123, 125, 127, 128, 154, 166, 167, 168, 170, 205, 209, 210, 217, 218, 219, 220, 221, 222, 227, 237, 238, 239, 277, 279, 280, 281, 289, 297, 298, 299, 300, 301, 302, 303, 304, 305, 306, 307, 308
fitness and propriety, viii, 5, 13, 17, 24, 26, 27, 28, 29, 31, 32, 38, 42, 123, 124, 125, 127, 165, 166, 167, 168, 169, 204, 206, 208, 215, 217, 218, 280, 310
folk maxims, xi, 166, 169, 205, 207, 208, 210, 231, 238
fraud, 1, 2, 47, 56, 93, 106, 277, 278, 279, 285, 286, 303, 307, 309
French Revolution, 80, 169, 171, 178, 179, 180, 181, 184, 185, 186, 187, 188, 189, 190, 193, 194, 195, 196, 197, 198, 199, 200, 201, 202, 203, 204, 207, 211, 212, 213, 214, 215, 216

G

geys, 281, 288, 291, 292, 294, 295, 296, 299, 309
gild, 63, 66, 67, 81, 88, 89, 93, 94, 95, 96, 97, 98, 99, 100, 107, 115, 167
good character test, ix, 2, 4, 32

H

hegemonic professions, x, 64
hegemony, ix, xi, 7, 64, 67, 68, 69, 70, 71, 72, 73, 74, 75, 76, 77, 78, 79, 80, 112, 113, 114, 116, 119, 120, 130, 154, 206, 246, 247, 248, 271
historical, ix, 5, 6, 21, 26, 33, 35, 64, 65, 67, 68, 71, 74, 75, 87, 92, 93, 94, 96, 97, 106, 112, 113, 116, 118, 119, 120, 130, 137, 145, 146, 154, 155, 161, 162, 187, 196, 198, 201, 211, 213, 214, 215, 224, 231, 248, 249, 274, 287
historical bloc, ix, 64, 67, 74, 75, 113, 116, 130, 154
honor, 3, 20, 41, 42, 61, 133, 134, 161, 220, 308

I

immoral behavior, 277, 278, 279
imperial legislation, ix, 1, 2, 4
inefficiencies, 277, 278, 279
integrity, 3, 8, 14, 17, 18, 27, 28, 29, 34, 41, 42, 46, 48, 54, 61, 219, 220

J

Jacobins, x, 166, 169, 170, 185, 193, 195, 196, 197, 200, 202, 203, 204, 207, 208, 209, 210, 211
jealousy, 169, 200, 201, 209
judicial, xi, 14, 15, 21, 25, 47, 50, 80, 81, 87, 99, 165, 167, 169, 170, 174, 185, 204, 206, 217, 218, 220, 221, 224, 229, 237, 238, 243, 263, 278, 281, 288, 289, 294, 297, 299, 300, 302
jurisdiction, 25, 43, 54, 57, 61, 65, 67, 84, 85, 86, 89, 104, 108, 111, 114, 127, 226, 263, 295, 296
justice, xi, 3, 10, 17, 19, 20, 26, 27, 35, 38, 39, 46, 48, 49, 87, 95, 96, 108, 109, 118, 168, 172, 177, 179, 181, 187, 191, 194, 195, 204, 206, 211, 215, 218, 219, 220, 222, 231, 234, 235, 238, 239, 242, 258, 263, 270, 286, 295, 296, 297, 309
justice argument, 222, 235

L

London, 6, 7, 12, 37, 38, 39, 63, 65, 66, 67, 69, 71, 73, 75, 78, 79, 81, 82, 84, 85, 86, 87, 88, 89, 90, 91, 92, 93, 95, 96, 97, 100, 101, 102, 103, 104, 105, 106, 107, 108, 109, 110, 111, 114, 115, 116, 118, 119, 120, 127, 129, 133, 136, 137, 144, 149, 158, 161, 162, 163, 171, 175, 178, 181, 182, 184, 212, 213, 214, 215, 228, 231, 240, 242, 243, 247, 250, 255, 257, 272, 273, 275, 278, 286, 294, 309, 310

M

Malaysia, viii, 1, 41, 42, 43, 44, 45, 46, 47, 48, 49, 50, 51, 52, 61, 62, 123, 165, 217, 277, 311, 312
mercantile gilds, ix, 64, 68, 97, 115, 117
moral character, 5, 6, 7, 9, 10, 11, 13, 20, 21, 23, 39
moral hazard, xi, 277, 278, 279, 280, 281, 282, 286, 287, 289, 296, 297, 298, 299, 301, 302, 310

O

otherness, 124, 125, 132, 133, 136, 137, 139, 140, 142, 143, 150, 152, 154, 155, 158, 160, 162

P

poverty, 16, 100, 248, 252, 253, 254, 257, 258, 259, 260, 267, 270, 273, 274

practice, 3, 4, 5, 6, 10, 14, 20, 23, 25, 26, 27, 30, 35, 37, 41, 42, 43, 44, 46, 47, 48, 49, 50, 51, 53, 54, 56, 57, 58, 59, 60, 61, 62, 65, 68, 78, 87, 93, 97, 106, 107, 168, 169, 177, 180, 181, 184, 185, 186, 187, 188, 189, 190, 192, 193, 194, 195, 196, 197, 198, 199, 200, 201, 202, 203, 204, 214, 219, 221, 229, 234, 241, 255, 273, 311
priestly enterprises, 123, 124, 128, 154
prior denunciation, 217, 218, 221, 237
professional advice, ix, 64, 67, 112, 116
professional qualifications, 41, 42, 61
protean deity, 124

Q

Quo Warranto, 67, 80, 83, 84, 120

R

reasoned elaboration, 165, 166, 167, 169, 204
religion, 43, 100, 128, 129, 130, 131, 132, 133, 134, 135, 136, 137, 138, 139, 140, 143, 154, 155, 159, 160, 161, 162, 163, 176, 186, 212
rhetorician, 23, 217, 218, 219, 223, 224, 225, 237, 279

S

Singapore, viii, 37, 38, 41, 42, 43, 45, 57, 58, 59, 60, 61, 62
stasis, viii, xi, 3, 17, 19, 23, 32, 34, 35, 36, 217, 218, 219, 220, 221, 222, 223, 224, 225, 226, 227, 229, 230, 231, 232, 233, 234, 235, 236, 237, 238, 239, 240, 241, 279, 309
stranger, 89, 94, 102, 115, 128, 151, 152, 153, 155, 182
subaltern group(s), viii, ix, x, xi, 112, 123, 124, 128, 129, 142, 143, 152, 153, 154, 156, 157, 218, 222, 235, 239, 246
subaltern masses, ix, 64, 67, 78, 79, 114, 116
Syariah courts, 43, 50

T

termination, 281, 288, 289, 291, 292, 294, 296, 297, 298, 299, 301, 309
theory(ies), viii, xii, 1, 3, 7, 9, 11, 13, 23, 32, 35, 36, 37, 69, 70, 73, 74, 76, 78, 81, 83, 84, 85, 113, 114, 118, 119, 120, 123, 124, 128, 129, 131, 132, 134, 137, 139, 140, 146, 148, 149, 158, 159, 169, 181, 184, 185, 186, 187, 188, 189, 190, 192, 193, 194, 195, 196, 197, 198, 199, 200, 201, 202, 203, 204, 211, 214, 217, 219, 220, 221, 223, 224, 225, 226, 227, 230, 231, 232, 233, 234, 235, 237, 238, 240, 241, 242, 247, 255, 257, 263, 273, 278, 279, 281, 283, 285, 288, 289, 291, 292, 294, 296, 297, 298, 299, 300, 302, 309, 310, 311
trades, x, 14, 64, 67, 68, 102, 103, 104, 106, 107, 108, 109, 110, 111, 116, 117
traditional, 16, 72, 248, 255, 258
trafficking, 247, 248, 260, 262, 263, 264, 266, 267, 270, 272, 274

U

ultra vires coercion, 278

W

workers, 10, 67, 72, 73, 77, 95, 101, 103, 110, 116, 179, 245, 247, 248, 257, 262, 265, 268, 269, 277, 278, 285, 287
working class, viii, ix, xi, 72, 245, 247, 248, 249, 269, 271
workplace trauma, 277, 278, 310